Essentials of WAIS®-IV Assessment

Essentials of Psychological Assessment Series
Series Editors, Alan S. Kaufman and Nadeen L. Kaufman

Essentials

of WAIS®-IV

Assessment

Elizabeth O. Lichtenberger
Alan S. Kaufman

John Wiley & Sons, Inc.

Library of Congress Cataloging-in-Publication Data:
Lichtenberger, Elizabeth O.
Essentials of WAIS-IV assessment / Elizabeth O. Lichtenberger, Alan S. Kaufman.
    p. cm. – (Essentials of psychological assessment series)
  Includes bibliographical references and index.
  ISBN 978-0-471-73846-6 (paper/cd-rom)
    1. Wechsler Adult Intelligence Scale. 2.   Intelligence tests. I.   Kaufman, Alan S., 1944–II. Title.
  BF432.5.W4L53 2009
  153.9'3–dc22

                                                                              2009015529
Printed in the United States of America

10 9 8 7 6 5 4 3

Romeo:

Oh wondrous and delightful life!

Oh all powerful charms!

Your sweet look enraptures me.

Your voice overwhelms me. . . .

I give you my soul;

It is yours, yours forever!

(Day breaks, the lark is heard)

Juliet:

Romeo, what are you doing?

Romeo (rising):

Ah, listen, Juliet! Dearest Juliet!

The lark that you hear is the herald of morn.

Juliet:

No! It is not yet daybreak.

No lark pierced your ear, love!

It is the sweet note of the nightingale,

the confidante of love.

Roméo:

O volupté de vivre!

O charmes tout puissants!

Ton doux regard m'enivre.

Ta voix ravit mes sens. . . .

Je t'ai donne mon âme;

À toi, toujours à toi!

(On entend chanter l'alouette)

Juliette:

Roméo, qu'as tu donc?

Roméo: (se levant):

Écoute, ô Juliette!

L'alouette déjà nous annonce le jour.

Juliette:

Non! Ce n'est pas le jour.

Ce n'est pas l'alouette dont cechant a frappé ton oreille inquìete!

C'est le doux rossignol,

Confident de l'amour.

Roméo et Juliette (1867)
Act IV, Scene 1
Music composed by Charles Gounod
Lyrics by Jules Barbier and Michel Carré
A. S. K.

CONTENTS

SERIES PREFACE

In the *Essentials of Psychological Assessment* series, we have attempted to provide the reader with books that will deliver key practical information in the most efficient and accessible style. The series features instruments in a variety of domains, such as cognition, personality, education, and neuropsychology. For the experienced clinician, books in the series offer a concise yet thorough way to master utilization of the continuously evolving supply of new and revised instruments, as well as a convenient method for keeping up to date on the tried-and-true measures. The novice will find here a prioritized assembly of all the information and techniques that must be at one's fingertips to begin the complicated process of individual psychological diagnosis.

Wherever feasible, visual shortcuts to highlight key points are utilized alongside systematic, step-by-step guidelines. Chapters are focused and succinct. Topics are targeted for an easy understanding of the essentials of administration, scoring, interpretation, and clinical application. Theory and research are continually woven into the fabric of each book, but always to enhance clinical inference, never to sidetrack or overwhelm. We have long been advocates of "intelligent" testing—the notion that a profile of test scores is meaningless unless it is brought to life by the clinical observations and astute detective work of knowledgeable examiners. Test profiles must be used to make a difference in the child's or adult's life, or why bother to test? We want this series to help our readers become the best intelligent testers they can be.

In *Essentials of WAIS-IV Assessment*, the authors present a state-of-the-art treatment of the recently published WAIS-IV, an exceptional instrument that reflects a thorough, theory-based, intelligent revision of its predecessor, the WAIS-III. This book includes content and approaches from the two previous books that Lichtenberger and Kaufman published on the WAIS-III—*Essentials of WAIS-III Assessment* and *Assessing Adolescent and Adult Intelligence*

(3rd ed.)—while offering dynamic new interpretive systems and research that are theory-based, clinically rich, and innovative. The interpretive approaches are based on the theory that Dr. Larry Weiss and colleagues at the Psychological Corporation used to develop the four-scale WAIS-IV (rooted in cognitive neuroscience research); on a five-factor model that derives primarily from Cattell-Horn-Carroll (CHC) theory and was validated by the results of a confirmatory factor analysis conducted by Dr. Tim Keith; on psychometric analyses of strengths and weaknesses conducted by Dr. Jack Naglieri; on an integrated approach to profile interpretation that has both normative and ipsative features, developed by Dr. Dawn Flanagan and colleagues; and on a clinical neuropsychological interpretive system that is carefully elucidated and illustrated by Dr. George McCloskey in his guest-written chapter. *Essentials of WAIS-IV Assessment* also presents the latest aging research on Wechsler's adult scales, thanks to unpublished data on the WAIS-IV that were kindly provided by Dr. J. J. Zhu and Pearson Assessments to Dr. Alan Kaufman. This new edition, fully equipped with a CD-ROM to automate Lichtenberger and Kaufman's thorough interpretive method and to present a variety of additional tables and interpretive aids, offers clinicians who routinely assess adolescents and adults of all ages a cutting-edge resource that will promote "intelligent testing" in today's rapidly changing society.

Alan S. Kaufman, PhD, and Nadeen L. Kaufman, EdD, Series Editors
Yale University School of Medicine

PREFACE

I nstead of a conventional preface, we have chosen to reprint an invited piece that Alan Kaufman wrote for *The School Psychologist* (Spring 1992, Vol. 46, No. 2). This paper, which is reprinted with the permission of Dr. Linda A. Reddy, Editor, and Dr. Michelle Athanasiou, Associate Editor, chronicles the special personal and professional relationship that Dr. Kaufman shared with Dr. David Wechsler.

DR. WECHSLER REMEMBERED

It is more than a decade since David Wechsler died in May 1981 at the age of 85, and I still miss him. More than any professor or older colleague, Dr. Wechsler was my mentor. I worked closely with him between late 1970 and early 1974 to help transform the WISC into a revised and restandardized battery—a test that was known as the WISC (Rev.) until a last-minute decision changed it to the WISC-R. The recent publication of the WISC-III represents a quiet burial for its predecessor, and for an important part of my past. But the changing of the guard has also rekindled a wealth of memories and feelings regarding the great man who had the courage to challenge Terman's Binet, and the vision to triumph.

I originally entitled this informal paper "David Wechsler Remembered" but realized immediately that I never called him by his first name. He was always *Dr.* Wechsler, and not just to me, then a kid in his mid-20s, a few months past his PhD. Even the gray-haired men who were my bosses— esteemed psychologists all, whose offices lined the east wall and overlooked the United Nations Building—called him Dr. Wechsler. Behind closed doors, they referred to him smugly as "David" and liked to joke that the manuals should say "Despite David Wechsler" instead of "By David Wechsler." But to his face, no one ever complained, and no one ever called him David—

unless it was after polishing off the second or third martini ("extra dry, straight up, with a twist of lemon") at the occasional, mandatory, ritualistic business lunches.

Dr. Wechsler possessed a rare blend of humility and grandeur. From the first day I met him, he treated me with kindness and with a respect I had not yet earned. He was soft-spoken, yet every word was carefully measured and carried authority. He was a man of unusual compassion and unflagging integrity. He lacked patience for the pomp and circumstance and protocol that permeated the first few corporate meetings that addressed the issue of a WISC revision. The meetings were tedious affairs, spiced with old recollections by Project Directors past, and an incredible amount of weasel wording and bush circling by distinguished executives who couldn't quite mouth the words, "Dr. Wechsler, there are a number of black psychologists who don't much care for the WISC, and there have been some serious complaints with a lot of specific items."

At the end of the third meeting, when once more nothing was accomplished, Dr. Wechsler ended the meeting by stating simply that this was the last group meeting; from now on, he said, "Alan will come alone to my apartment, and we'll hammer out the revised WISC." And that's exactly what happened. I'd take a taxi to his East Side Manhattan apartment, and for two or three hours, week after week, we'd engage in friendly battle. He insisted that I be totally honest and tell him every thought and concern. I couldn't do that at first, but I soon realized it was the most prudent course of action. After the first meeting, he told me to put down my pen. He then talked for about 20 minutes, recounting his version of what had just transpired; he revealed every one of my "secret" feelings and perceptions, unraveling in intricate detail my attitudes and emotions about every issue we discussed and each decision we had made. I just stared at him, probably looking like retarded Benny of *LA Law,* and said nothing; how could I argue, when we both knew he was on the mark with every comment? I had always prided myself on my poker face, but I was face to face with the master clinician— the best one I would ever meet.

From that point on, I never held back anything. He would usually respond calmly, but occasionally I'd strike a raw nerve, and his grandfatherly smile would evaporate. His temples would start to pulse, and his entire face and scalp would turn crimson. I'd unconsciously move my chair back in self-protection, the way I did when I tested hardcore prisoners on the old WAIS and had to ask the question, "Why should we keep away from bad company?" I struck that exposed nerve when I urged him to eliminate the

Comprehension item about walking away from a fight if someone much smaller starts to fight with you. The argument that you can't walk away from any fight in a black ghetto just added fuel to his rage. When I suggested, at a later meeting, that he just *had* to get rid of the item, "Why should women and children be saved first in a shipwreck?" or incur the wrath of the new wave of militant feminists, his response was instant. With red face and pulsing head, he stood up, leaned on his desk with extended arms, and said as if he were firing a semiautomatic, "Chivalry may be dying. Chivalry may be dead. *But it will not die on the WISC.*"

So I waited a couple of weeks before bringing up those two items again. That particular battle ended in a tie; the fight item stayed, the shipwreck item was mercifully dropped. Though it was a little like going one-on-one with Michael Jordan, I relished those meetings. He had a good sense of humor, but not when it came to eliminating items. Only once did he readily agree to dropping an item: "What should you do if you see a train approaching a broken track?" I mentioned that if a 6- or 7-year-old child sees a train coming near a broken track, waving a white flag is not the brightest thing in the world to do; a 3-point answer on a 2-1-0 scale is "Run like hell." He laughed.

One Saturday, I drove to Manhattan with my then 5-year-old daughter Jennie to deliver a manual chapter to Dr. Wechsler. For 15 minutes or so, he charmed her, played with her, and joked with her, all the while maintaining his keen clinician's eye. I still remember his nod of approval when she responded to his question "In what way are a mommy and a daddy alike?" by saying, "They're the same 'cause they're both parents—and both human beans too, y'know." He looked at me, smiled broadly, and said, "Jennie is *very* smart—y'know.'" I took Jennie's hand and walked to the elevator. The elevator operator, who knew me quite well by then, tried to engage me in conversation, but I didn't hear a word. In fact, I didn't need the elevator, I could have flown down the eight stories. *Wechsler had just told me my daughter was very smart!* I couldn't have been more elated if Freud had told me she had a nice personality or if Bert Parks had said she was beautiful.

Dr. Wechsler liked to test me too. Whenever I arrived for our meetings, his wife Ruth always greeted me and ushered me into his study. He had one of those lamps that turned on and off by touching it—common now, but not then. I was biding my time by turning it on and off, experimenting to see how light a touch would trigger the mechanism. Out of the corner of my eye, I saw Dr. Wechsler standing in the hallway studying me, smiling, enjoying himself. I wondered how long this consummate clinician had been there, and hoped I hadn't done anything really inappropriate.

I especially enjoyed Dr. Wechsler's warm, human side, which emerged in casual moments when he didn't have to be "on." The serious and sometimes gruff side came out in business meetings, and the occasional animal rage was reserved for anyone who challenged the perfection of nearly any of his hand-picked, time-tested items, especially one that had its roots in his original Wechsler-Bellevue scales. But he displayed unabashed boylike enthusiasm when he showed off materials for the new subtests he was constantly working on (at age 75!)—his favorite was a set of three Chinese dolls that had to be tapped in the right sequence—or when he sifted through a lifetime of comic strips that he saved for new Picture Arrangement items. And his eyes twinkled when he talked about his grandchildren; or reminisced about visiting Freud in Vienna; or spoke warmly about spending a week at the home of former Israeli Defense Minister Moshe Dayan and his wife; or boasted sheepishly about being greeted at the Bucharest airport by the King of Romania (his birthplace in 1896); or played for over an hour with our son James, then 7 months old and called Jamie, when he and Ruth visited my family in Athens, Georgia, in April 1975.

That visit was completely unexpected. I had called him to ask if he would speak by conference phone to my Intelligence Testing class the first year I was at the University of Georgia. I was crushed when he said he didn't want to do it; I had assured my class that my friend Dr. Wechsler would say yes (they already doubted that I had even met the man). A couple of days later, he sent me a letter saying that he didn't like talking to people unless he could see them. "I would prefer, and would suggest instead, a face-to-face session at the University," he wrote. "No fee for talk, but reimbursement for travel." My school psychology students enjoyed a private question-and-answer session with him. Later in the day, I experienced high anxiety introducing him to a standing-room-only auditorium crowd of students and faculty.

That evening, Nadeen and I had dinner with the Wechslers, and we were looking forward to a bit of quiet relaxation. It was not to be. Dr. Wechsler had two things that were heavy on his mind. One was the true meaning of being an intelligent adult (he started to doubt the WAIS's effectiveness for measuring adult IQ when he realized that he had trouble solving Block Design items quickly). His other concern was the Dan Rather IQ special that was to air for the first time that night, and he absolutely didn't want to miss seeing it in his hotel room. He kept asking Nadeen and me how one could tell if an adult was smart, and no matter what we answered, he probed and challenged us until we were limp, until he was satisfied that we had covered every aspect of the issue. He confided to us that he was starting to work on a test called the Wechsler Intelligence Scale for the Elderly; had he published it, the test would have had the best acronym ever—W.I.S.E. Though the meal wasn't as relaxed as we had hoped, he was quick to praise our ideas and took a few notes on his napkin. (Years later, we would think back to that discussion when we began developing the Kaufman Adolescent and Adult Intelligence Test, or KAIT.)

When Dr. Wechsler relented in his questioning of us, he revealed his almost desperate sadness about the Dan Rather special. Though he wouldn't see it until it aired that night, he had been tipped off by an acquaintance from the TV station that the program was blatantly anti-IQ testing. Dr. Wechsler and Ruth recalled how Rather had come to their apartment; charmed them during the interview and videotaping, and told them how much he personally valued the IQ concept and how important the Wechsler scales were to the world. Rather's demeanor led Dr. Wechsler to say things candidly and—in retrospect—a bit recklessly. He was chastising himself during the meal, but mostly he was furious at Rather's behavior. Dr. Wechsler was honest and straightforward and just couldn't fathom duplicity in someone else. The next morning, after the TV show had confirmed Dr. Wechsler's worst fears, we drove to the airport in almost total silence. When he did speak, it was clear that Dr. Wechsler's anger was under control, but he was deeply wounded by the dishonesty, the blatant abuse of trust. And he felt that the strong anti-IQ statements by "people who should know better" were a personal attack on his life's work.

The kindness that Dr. Wechsler showed me by traveling to Georgia to meet with my students was typical of how he treated me the whole time I knew him. He was aware of the steep status hierarchy that existed at The Psychological Corporation, and he made sure to praise me in the presence of the upper echelon. He consistently treated my ideas with respect and never dismissed them—even the stupid ones—without first thinking about them carefully (unless I was suggesting deleting an item). He trusted me in all aspects of test construction and deferred to my knowledge of psychometrics; when he questioned a statistical decision, he would usually give in, saying, "I'm just a clinician." It wasn't until the WISC-R was nearing publication that I found out from someone else that Dr. Wechsler had studied statistics under Charles Spearman and Karl Pearson in London after World War I.

One day, he decided that he wanted me to coauthor a book on children's intelligence with him, and he made the announcement in front of one of my bosses. It was the first I'd heard about it, and it was lucky I was sitting down when he said it. When I took the position at the University of Georgia, just after the WISC-R was published, we still planned on writing the book together. During his visit, he told me that he just didn't have the energy to participate too much in the writing of the book, and that he thought it would be hard to collaborate from a distance. But he made me promise to write a book devoted to the WISC-R, and I gave him my word. Those were the seeds for *Intelligent Testing with the WISC-R.*

The standardization of the WISC-R seemed to take forever to Dr. Wechsler, and he wanted the test to come out while he could still enjoy it. He would ask me in mock seriousness whether a standardization was even necessary. "After all," he'd say in a quiet voice while giving me a conspiratorial smile, *"we* know how well the children are going to perform on all those subtests, don't we? So why bother with all that standardization testing?" He was joking, but it was no joke that he believed firmly all he needed was 15 minutes or so of personal interview and a test item or two, and he could pinpoint a person's IQ within a few points and diagnose any pathology. He insisted that he could diagnose clinical patients by their answer to the question, "What is the population of the United States?" I never doubted that he could back up his boast. He didn't do too badly with his one-item, 15-minute assessment of my daughter Jennie's intelligence more than 20 years ago; she made Phi Beta Kappa in college, and has now almost completed her PhD in clinical psychology.

And how would Dr. Wechsler evaluate the WISC-III? Well, he'd like the artwork, but he'd insist that it wasn't necessary. The black-and-white pictures worked fine before, so why mess with them? And he'd be impressed by the immaculate standardization and supersophisticated psychometric treatment of the data, but he wouldn't admit it to anyone. Instead, he'd argue that his all–Coney Island standardization of the original Wechsler-Bellevue was pretty darned good; and he'd wonder aloud why you needed something called confirmatory factor analysis to tell the world what he knew axiomatically back in the early 1930s—that his scales primarily measured Verbal and Performance intelligence.

He wouldn't be too interested in the improved bottom and top for several subtests, most notably Arithmetic, which now gives bonus points for the six hardest items. He rejected most attempts that I made to add easy and hard items to the WISC-R, saying firmly, "My scales are meant for people with average or near-average intelligence, clinical patients who score between 70 and 130. They are *clinical* tests." When I reminded him that psychologists commonly use his scales for the extremes, and want to make distinctions within the "below 70" and "above 130" groups, he answered, "Then that is their misfortune. It's not what I tell them to do, and it's not what a good clinician ought to do. They should know better."

He wouldn't care much for the new Object Assembly item, the cut-up soccer ball. How do I know? Because when we were developing new items for the WISC-R tryout, I brought him a dozen envelopes, each with a cut-up puzzle I had made. I opened each envelope and assembled each puzzle, and he immediately said "Yes" or "No" to each one. He liked three, and hated nine. I couldn't figure out his decision rule, so he forced me to study the ones he liked and the ones he rejected, but every hypothesis I offered was wrong. Finally, with a touch of exasperation at my denseness, he said, "Don't you see. My Object Assembly items must have at least one puzzle piece that tells the person at once what the object is—like the horse's head or the front of the car. I don't want them fumbling around like one of Thorndike's cats or monkeys. I want them to know right away what they've got to put together." He also would not have permitted bonus points on the WPPSI-R for Block Design or the new Object Assembly subtest; as a clinician and grandfather he knew that even very bright young children often respond to puzzles like the fireman in the old Binet item who smoked a cigar before putting out the fire.

But the soccer ball and WPPSI-R time bonuses wouldn't have made Dr. Wechsler's temples start to pulse. That would have happened when he saw the Picture Arrangement items. He loved to expose examinees to emotion-laden situations, to watch how they solved the problems, to listen to their spontaneous comments, to study their reactions to danger, to conflict, to authority, to violence. "Where's the boxing match?" he would have stormed. "Replaced by a girl on a slide! And what happened to the burglar? And look what they did to the *fire* item! Instead of burning down his house, the kid's a damned hero!" And he would have been incensed at the emasculation of the *bench* item. In the old item, "Some poor sap gets hit by the bench and then gets clobbered in a fight. Great stuff! But now they just kiss and make up."

Dr. Wechsler also wouldn't have been too pleased with the elimination of *beer-wine* in Similarities or of *knife* and *gamble* in Vocabulary—all potent clinical stimuli. He never worried much about a person missing an item or two or three because of its clinical content. More than once, he'd chide me, until it finally sunk in, "First and foremost, the Wechsler scales are clinical tests—not psychometric tests but clinical tests." That was why he got so upset when someone complained about the unfairness of this or that item. What's a couple of items to a good clinician? He never could really accept the stupid way so many people interpreted his tests, with formulas, and cut-off points, and the like; it's not what he had ever planned for his clinical Wechsler scales.

When Nadeen and I started to develop the K-ABC back in 1978, the Wechsler influence was strong, although we differed from him in believing that tests such as Information and Vocabulary really measure achievement for schoolchildren, not IQ. (He didn't much care for my suggestion back in 1971 to pull out a few subtests from the Verbal Scale and offer the clinician a separate "Cultural Quotient.") Maybe it was because I felt a bit guilty at departing from his theory for our intelligence test, or maybe I just got too involved with too many things, but I stopped calling and writing Dr. Wechsler during the last years of his life. I didn't realize how much that hurt him until Ruth wrote to me, in response to our letter of sympathy, "I must tell you, Alan, he was very fond of you and admired you very much. I'm sorry you didn't write once in a while as he talked about you and what a pleasure it was to work with you on the WISC-R."

I can't undo it, though I wish I could, and her words still sting when I read them. But I try to focus instead on how much Dr. Wechsler taught me, both as a person and clinician. I was fortunate beyond words to have his life cross mine, to work so closely with this legend for several years, to have him as a mentor and friend. Those at The Psychological Corporation who did such a marvelous job of revising the WISC-R and assembling the WISC-III undoubtedly took for granted what I fervently wished for as a young Assistant Director two decades ago: the freedom to make objective item and subtest decisions without the interference and subjective whims of the author.

Little did I realize then that those battles with the Master would shape my own development as a test author and trainer of school psychologists, and would remain forever etched—fresh and vibrant and poignant—in my memory. The Project Directors of the "ISC-III" and the "PPSI-R" have no notion of their loss; they never knew the man behind the "W."

Alan S. Kaufman

ACKNOWLEDGMENTS

We would like to acknowledge several people for their special and extraordinary contributions. We wish to express our deepest appreciation to George McCloskey for providing a chapter on the neuropsychological interpretation of the WAIS-IV and assessment of learning disabilities; to Ron Dumont and John Willis for carefully evaluating the WAIS-IV in their chapter on strengths and weaknesses; to Clark Clipson and Shelley Lurie for providing outstanding case reports for inclusion in this book; to Darielle Greenberg, James C. Kaufman, and David Loomis for their research assistance; and to Tim Keith and Jack Naglieri for providing important data analyses for our interpretive chapter. We also appreciate the assistance and insights of numerous people at Pearson Assessment: Larry Weiss, Diane Coalson, J. J. Zhu, Susie Raiford, Jim Holdnack, Paul Williams, and Tom Cayton. Those who dedicated their time and clinical expertise to ensure that the automated *WAIS-IV DMIA* would be maximally useful to practitioners deserve special thanks as well: Ron Dumont, John Willis, Howell Gotlieb, Richard Schere, and Steven Migalski.

Finally, the contributions of Isabel Pratt and the rest of the staff at Wiley are gratefully acknowledged. Their expertise and pleasant and cooperative working style made this book an enjoyable and productive endeavor.

One

INTRODUCTION AND OVERVIEW

INTRODUCTION

The field of assessment, particularly intellectual assessment, has grown tremendously over the past couple of decades. New tests of cognitive abilities are being developed, and older tests of intelligence are being revised to meet the needs of the professionals utilizing them. There are several good sources for reviewing major measures of cognitive ability (e.g., Flanagan, Genshaft, & Harrison, 2005; Naglieri & Goldstein, 2009; Sattler, 2008); however, the new and revised measures multiply rapidly, and it is often difficult to keep track of new instruments, let alone know how to administer, score, and interpret them. One of the goals of this book is to provide an easy reference source for those who wish to learn essentials of the *Wechsler Adult Intelligence Scale—Fourth Edition* (WAIS-IV) in a direct, no-nonsense, systematic manner.

Essentials of WAIS-IV Assessment was developed with an easy-to-read format in mind. The topics covered in the book emphasize administration, scoring, interpretation, and application of the WAIS-IV. Each chapter includes several "Rapid Reference," "Caution," and "Don't Forget" boxes that highlight important points for easy reference. At the end of each chapter, questions are provided to help you solidify what you have read. The information provided in this book will help you to understand, in depth, the latest of the measures in the Wechsler family and will help you become a competent WAIS-IV examiner and clinician.

HISTORY AND DEVELOPMENT

The first assessment instrument developed by David Wechsler came on the scene in the 1939. However, the history of intelligence testing began several decades before that, in the late 19th century, and is largely an account of the measurement of the intelligence of children or retarded adults. Sir Francis Galton (1869, 1883) studied adults and was interested in giftedness when he developed what is often considered the first comprehensive individual test of intelligence, composed of sensory-motor tasks (Kaufman, 2000b). But despite Galton's role as the father of the testing movement (Shouksmith, 1970), he did not succeed in constructing a true intelligence test. His measures of simple reaction time, strength of squeeze, or keenness of sight proved to assess sensory and motor abilities, skills that relate poorly to mental ability and that are far removed from the type of tasks that constitute contemporary intelligence tests.

BINET-SIMON SCALES

Alfred Binet and his colleagues (Binet & Henri, 1895; Binet & Simon, 1905, 1908) developed the tasks that survive to the present day in most tests of intelligence for children and adults. Binet (1890a, 1890b) mainly studied children; beginning with systematic developmental observations of his two young daughters, Madeleine and Alice, he concluded that simple tasks such as those used by Galton did not discriminate between children and adults. In 1904, the minister of public instruction in Paris appointed Binet to a committee to find a way to distinguish normal from retarded children. Fifteen years of qualitative and quantitative investigation of individual differences in children—along with considerable theorizing about mental organization and the development of a specific set of complex, high-level tests to investigate these differences—preceded the "sudden" emergence of the landmark 1905 Binet-Simon intelligence scale (Murphy, 1968).

The 1908 scale was the first to include age levels, spanning the range from 3 to 13. This important modification stemmed from Binet and Simon's unexpected discovery that their 1905 scale was useful for much more than classifying a child at one of the three levels of retardation: moron, imbecile, idiot (Matarazzo, 1972). Assessment of older adolescents and adults, however, was not built into the Binet-Simon system until the 1911 revision. That scale was extended to age level 15 and included five ungraded adult tests (Kite, 1916). This extension was not conducted with the rigor that characterized the construction of tests for children, and the primary applications of the scale were for use with school-age children (Binet, 1911).

Measuring the intelligence of adults, except those known to be mentally retarded, was almost an afterthought. But Binet recognized the increased applicability of the Binet-Simon tests for various child assessment purposes just prior to his untimely death in 1911, when he "began to foresee numerous uses for his method in child development, in education, in medicine, and in longitudinal studies predicting different occupational histories for children of different intellectual potential" (Matarazzo, 1972, p. 42).

TERMAN'S STANFORD-BINET

Lewis Terman was one of several people in the United States who translated and adapted the Binet-Simon scale for use in the United States, publishing a "tentative" revision (Terman & Childs, 1912) 4 years before releasing his painstakingly developed and carefully standardized Stanford Revision and Extension of the Binet-Simon Intelligence Scale (Terman, 1916). This landmark test, soon known simply as the Stanford-Binet, squashed competing tests developed earlier by Goddard, Kuhlmann, Wallin, and Yerkes. Terman's success was undoubtedly due in part to heeding the advice of practitioners whose demand "for more and more accurate diagnoses . . . raised the whole question of the accurate placing of tests in the scale and the accurate evaluation of the responses made by the child" (Pintner & Paterson, 1925, p. 11). Terman (1916) saw intelligence tests useful primarily for the detection of mental deficiency or superiority in children and for the identification of "feeblemindedness" in adults. He cited numerous studies of delinquent adolescents and adult criminals, all of which pointed to the high percentage of mentally deficient juvenile delinquents, prisoners, or prostitutes, and concluded that "there is no investigator who denies the fearful role played by mental deficiency in the production of vice, crime, and delinquency" (p. 9). Terman also saw the potential for using intelligence tests with adults for determining "vocational fitness," but, again, he emphasized employing "a psychologist . . . to weed out the unfit" or to "determine the minimum 'intelligence quotient' necessary for success in each leading occupation" (p. 17).

Perhaps because of this emphasis on the assessment of children or concern with the lower end of the intelligence distribution, Terman (1916) did not use a rigorous methodology for constructing his adult-level tasks. Tests below the 14-year level were administered to a fairly representative sample of about 1,000 children and early adolescents. To extend the scale above that level, data were obtained from 30 businessmen, 50 high school students, 150 adolescent delinquents, and 150 migrating unemployed men. Based on a frequency distribution of the mental ages of a mere 62 adults (the 30 businessmen and 32 of the high school students above age 16), Terman partitioned the graph into the Mental Age (MA) categories: 13 to 15 (inferior adults), 15 to 17 (average adults), and above 17 (superior adults).

WORLD WAR I TESTS

The field of adult assessment grew rapidly with the onset of World War I, particularly after U.S. entry into the war in 1917 (Anastasi & Urbina, 1997; Vane & Motta, 1984). Psychologists saw with increasing clarity the applications of intelligence tests for selecting officers and placing enlisted men in different types of service, apart from their generation-old use for identifying the mentally unfit. Under the leadership of Robert Yerkes and the American Psychological Association, the most innovative psychologists of the day helped translate Binet's tests to a group format. Arthur Otis, Terman's student, was instrumental in leading the creative team that developed the Army Alpha, essentially a group-administered Stanford-Binet, and the Army Beta, a novel group test composed of nonverbal tasks.

Yerkes (1917) opposed Binet's age-scale approach and favored a point-scale methodology, one that advocates selection of tests of specified, important functions rather than a set of tasks that fluctuates greatly with age level and developmental stage. The Army group tests reflect a blend of Yerkes's point-scale approach and Binet's notions of the kind of skills that should be measured when assessing mental ability. The Army Alpha included the Binet-like tests of Directions or Commands, Practical Judgment, Arithmetical Problems, Synonym-Antonym, Dissarranged Sentences, Analogies, and Information. Even the Army Beta had subtests resembling Stanford-Binet tasks: Maze, Cube Analysis, Pictorial Completion, and Geometrical Construction. The Beta also included novel measures, such as Digit Symbol, Number Checking, and X-O Series (Yoakum & Yerkes, 1920). Never before or since have tests been normed and validated on samples so large; 1,726,966 men were tested (Vane & Motta, 1984).

Another intelligence scale was developed during the war, one that became an alternative for those who could not be tested validly by either the Alpha or Beta. This was the Army Performance Scale Examination, composed of tasks that would become the tools of the trade for clinical psychologists, school psychologists, and neuropsychologists into the 21st century: Picture Completion, Picture Arrangement, Digit Symbol, and Manikin and Feature Profile (Object Assembly). Except for Block Design (developed by Kohs in 1923), Army Performance Scale Examination was added to the Army battery "to prove conclusively that a man was weakminded and not merely indifferent or malingering" (Yoakum & Yerkes, 1920, p. 10).

WECHSLER'S CREATIVITY

In the mid-1930s, David Wechsler became a prominent player in the field of assessment by blending his strong clinical skills and statistical training (he studied under Charles Spearman and Karl Pearson in England) with his extensive experience in testing, gained as a World War I examiner. He assembled a test battery that comprised subtests developed primarily by Binet and World War I psychologists. His Verbal Scale was essentially a Yerkes point-scale adaptation of Stanford-Binet tasks; his Performance Scale, like other similar nonverbal batteries of the 1920s and 1930s (Cornell & Coxe, 1934; Pintner & Paterson, 1925), was a near replica of the tasks and items making up the individually administered Army Performance Scale Examination.

In essence, Wechsler took advantage of tasks developed by others for nonclinical purposes to develop a clinical test battery. He paired verbal tests that were fine-tuned to discriminate among children of different ages with nonverbal tests that were created for adult males who had flunked both the Alpha and Beta exams— nonverbal tests that were intended to distinguish between the nonmotivated and the hopelessly deficient. Like Terman, Wechsler had the same access to the available tests as did other psychologists; like Terman and Binet before him, Wechsler succeeded because he was a visionary, a man able to anticipate the needs of practitioners in the field.

While others hoped intelligence tests would be psychometric tools to subdivide retarded individuals into whatever number of categories was currently in vogue, Wechsler saw the tests as dynamic clinical instruments. While others looked concretely at intelligence tests as predictors of school success or guides to occupational choice, Wechsler looked abstractly at the tests as a mirror to the hidden personality. With the Great War over, many psychologists returned to a focus on IQ testing as a means of childhood assessment; Wechsler (1939), however, developed the first form of the Wechsler-Bellevue Intelligence Scale exclusively for adolescents and adults.

Most psychologists saw little need for nonverbal tests when assessing English-speaking individuals other than illiterates. How could it be worth 2 or 3 minutes to administer a single puzzle or block-design item when 10 or 15 verbal items could be given in the same time? Some test developers (e.g., Cornell & Coxe, 1934) felt that Performance scales might be useful for normal, English-speaking people to provide "more varied situations than are provided by verbal tests" (p. 9) and to "test the hypothesis that there is a group factor underlying general concrete ability, which is of importance in the concept of general intelligence" (p. 10).

Wechsler was less inclined to wait a generation for data to accumulate. He followed his clinical instincts and not only advocated the administration of a standard battery of nonverbal tests to everyone but placed the Performance Scale on an equal footing with the more respected Verbal Scale. Both scales would constitute a complete Wechsler-Bellevue battery, and each would contribute equally to the overall intelligence score.

Wechsler also had the courage to challenge the Stanford-Binet monopoly, a boldness not unlike Binet's when the French scientist created his own forum (the journal *L'Année Psychologique*) to challenge the preferred but simplistic Galton sensorimotor approach to intelligence (Kaufman, 2000b). Wechsler met the same type of resistance as Binet, who had had to wait until the French Ministry of Public Instruction "published" his Binet-Simon Scale. When Wechsler's initial efforts to find a publisher for his two-pronged intelligence test failed, he had no cabinet minister to turn to, so he took matters into his own hands. With a small team of colleagues, he standardized Form I of the Wechsler-Bellevue by himself. Realizing that stratification on socioeconomic background was more crucial than obtaining regional representation, he managed to secure a well-stratified sample from Brooklyn, New York.

The Psychological Corporation agreed to publish Wechsler's battery once it had been standardized, and the rest is history. Although an alternative form of the Wechsler-Bellevue Intelligence Scale (Wechsler, 1946) was no more successful than Terman and Merrill's (1937) ill-fated Form M, a subsequent downward extension of Form II of the Wechsler-Bellevue (to cover the age range 5 to 15 instead of 10 to 59) produced the wildly successful Wechsler Intelligence Scale for Children (WISC; Wechsler, 1949). Although the Wechsler scales did not initially surpass the Stanford-Binet in popularity, instead serving an apprenticeship to the master in the 1940s and 1950s, the WISC and the subsequent revision of the Wechsler-Bellevue, Form I (WAIS; Wechsler, 1955) triumphed in the 1960s. "With the increasing stress on the psychoeducational assessment of learning disabilities in the 1960s, and on neuropsychological evaluation in the 1970s, the Verbal-Performance (V-P) IQ discrepancies and subtest profiles yielded by Wechsler's scales were waiting and ready to overtake the one-score Binet" (Kaufman, 1983, p. 107).

Irony runs throughout the history of testing. Galton developed statistics to study relationships between variables—statistics that proved to be forerunners of the coefficient of correlation, later perfected by his friend Pearson (DuBois, 1970). The ultimate downfall of Galton's system of testing can be traced directly to coefficients of correlation, which were too low in some crucial (but, ironically, poorly designed) studies of the relationships among intellectual variables (Sharp, 1898–99; Wissler, 1901). Similarly, Terman succeeded with the Stanford-Binet while the Goddard-Binet (Goddard, 1911), the Herring-Binet (Herring, 1922), and other Binet-Simon adaptations failed because Terman was sensitive to practitioners' needs. He patiently withheld a final version of his Stanford revision until he was certain that each task was placed appropriately at an age level consistent with the typical functioning of representative samples of U.S. children.

Terman continued his careful test development and standardization techniques with the first revised version of the Stanford-Binet (Terman & Merrill, 1937). But 4 years after his death in 1956, his legacy was devalued when the next revision of the Stanford-Binet merged Forms L and M *without a standardization* of the newly formed battery (Terman & Merrill, 1960). The following version saw a restandardization of the instrument but without a revision of the placement of tasks at each age level (Terman & Merrill, 1973). Unfortunately for the Binet, the abilities of children and adolescents had changed fairly dramatically in the course of a generation, so the 5-year level of tasks (for example) was now passed by the average 4-year-old.

Terman's methods had been ignored by his successors. The ironic outcome was that Wechsler's approach to assessment triumphed, at least in part because the editions of the Stanford-Binet in the 1960s and 1970s were beset by the same type of flaws as those of Terman's competitors in the 1910s. The fourth edition of the Stanford-Binet (Thorndike, Hagen, & Sattler, 1986) attempted to correct these problems and even adopted Wechsler's multisubtest, multiscale format; the fifth edition (Roid, 2003) is theory-based and of exceptional psychometric quality. However, these improvements in the Binet were too little and too late to reclaim the throne it had shared for decades with Wechsler's scales.

WAIS-IV AND ITS PREDECESSORS

The first in the Wechsler series of tests was the Wechsler-Bellevue Intelligence Scale (Wechsler, 1939), so named because Wechsler was the chief psychologist at Bellevue Hospital in New York City (a position he held from 1932 to 1967). That first test, followed in 1946 by Form II of the Wechsler Bellevue, had as a key innovation the use of deviation IQs (standard scores), which were psychometrically superior to the mental age divided by chronological age (MA/CA) formula that Terman had used to compute IQ. The Don't Forget box on page 8 shows the history of Wechsler's scales. The WAIS-IV is the great-great-grandchild of the original 1939 Wechsler Bellevue Form I; it is also a cousin of the WISC-IV, which traces its lineage to Form II of the Wechsler Bellevue.

The development of Wechsler's tests was originally based on practical and clinical perspectives rather than on theory per se. (The origin of each of the WAIS-IV subtests is shown in Rapid Reference 1.1.) Wechsler's view of IQ tests was that they were a way to peer into an individual's personality. Years after the

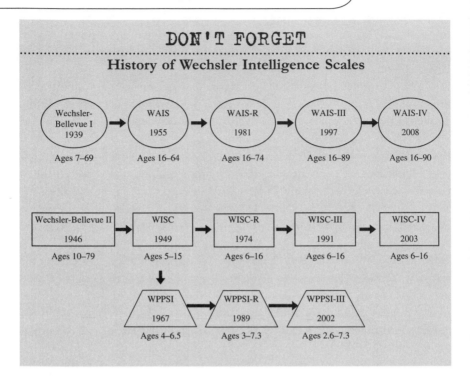

DON'T FORGET

History of Wechsler Intelligence Scales

development of the original Wechsler scales, extensive theoretical speculations have been made about the nature and meaning of these tests and their scores, and the newest WAIS-IV subtests were developed with specific theory in mind. However, the original Wechsler tasks were developed without regard to theory.

WECHSLER-BELLEVUE SUBTESTS THAT SURVIVE ON THE WAIS-IV

Wechsler selected tasks for the Wechsler-Bellevue from among the numerous tests available in the 1930s, many of which were developed to meet the assessment needs of World War I. Although Wechsler chose not to develop new subtests for his intelligence battery, his selection process incorporated a blend of clinical, practical, and empirical factors. His rationale for each of the nine well-known original Wechsler-Bellevue subtests that survive to the present day on the WAIS-IV is discussed in the sections that follow.[1] (Note: The WAIS-III

---

1. Wechsler's (1958) original quotes have been modified to avoid sexist language but are otherwise verbatim.

≡ Rapid Reference 1.1

Origin of WAIS-IV Subtests

Verbal Comprehension Subtest	Source of Subtest
Similarities	Stanford-Binet
Vocabulary	Stanford-Binet
Information	Army Alpha
Comprehension	Stanford-Binet/Army Alpha
Working Memory Subtest	
Digit Span	Stanford-Binet
Arithmetic	Stanford-Binet/Army Alpha
Letter-Number Sequencing	Gold, Carpenter, Randolph, Goldberg, & Weinberger (1997)
Perceptual Reasoning Subtest	
Block Design	Kohs (1923)
Matrix Reasoning	Raven's Progressive Matrices (1938)
Visual Puzzles	Paper Form Board tasks trace back to the late 1920s (Roszkowski, 2001)
Figure Weights	Novel task developed by Paul E. Williams, PsyD (2005; pers. comm.)
Picture Completion	Army Beta/Army Performance Scale Examination
Processing Speed Subtest	
Symbol Search	Shiffrin & Schneider (1977) and S. Sternberg (1966)
Coding	Army Beta/Army Performance Scale Examination
Cancellation	Diller et al. (1974); Moran & Mefford (1959), Talland & Schwab (1964)

contained three new subtests that were not part of the earlier Wechsler batteries: Letter-Number Sequencing, Symbol Search, and Matrix Reasoning. The WAIS-IV contains three additional new subtests: Visual Puzzles, Figure Weights, and Cancellation. Subtests that were not a part of the original Wechsler batteries are discussed in separate sections of this chapter and in later chapters.)

Similarities (Verbal Comprehension Index)

Wechsler (1958) noted that prior to the Wechsler-Bellevue (W-B), "similarities questions have been used very sparingly in the construction of previous scales . . . [despite being] one of the most reliable measures of intellectual ability" (p. 72). Wechsler felt that this omission was probably due to the belief that language and vocabulary were necessarily too crucial in determining successful performance. However, "while a certain degree of verbal comprehension is necessary for even minimal performance, sheer word knowledge need only be a minor factor. More important is the individual's ability to perceive the common elements of the terms he or she is asked to compare and, at higher levels, his or her ability to bring them under a single concept" (p. 73). A glance at the most difficult items on the W-B I, WAIS, WAIS-R, and WAIS-III Similarities subtests (fly-tree, praise-punishment), makes it evident that Wechsler was successful in his goal of increasing "the difficulty of test items without resorting to esoteric or unfamiliar words" (p. 73).

Wechsler (1958) saw several merits in the Similarities subtest: It is easy to administer, has an interest appeal for adults, has a high g loading, sheds light on the logical nature of the person's thinking processes, and provides other qualitative information as well. Regarding the latter point, he stressed the "obvious difference both as to maturity and as to level of thinking between the individual who says that a banana and an orange are alike because they both have a skin, and the individual who says that they are both fruit. . . . But it is remarkable how large a percentage of adults never get beyond the superficial type of response" (p. 73). Consequently, Wechsler considered his 0–1–2 scoring system to be an important innovation to allow simple discrimination between high-level and low-level responses to the same item. He also found his multipoint system helpful in providing insight into the evenness of a person's intellectual development. Whereas some individuals earn almost all 1s, others earn a mixture of 0, 1, and 2 scores. "The former are likely to bespeak individuals of consistent ability, but of a type from which no high grade of intellectual work may be expected; the latter, while erratic, have many more possibilities" (p. 74).

Vocabulary (Verbal Comprehension Index)

"Contrary to lay opinion, the size of a person's vocabulary is not only an index of schooling, but also an excellent measure of general intelligence. Its excellence as a test of intelligence may stem from the fact that the number of words a person knows is at once a measure of learning ability, fund of verbal information and of the general range of the person's ideas" (Wechsler, 1958, p. 84). The Vocabulary subtest formed an essential component of Binet's scales and the WAIS but, surprisingly, this task, which has become prototypical of Wechsler's definition of verbal intelligence, was not a regular W-B I subtest. In deference to the objection that word "knowledge" "is necessarily influenced by . . . educational and cultural opportunities" (p. 84), Wechsler included Vocabulary only as an alternative test during the early stages of W-B I standardization. Consequently, the W-B I was at first a 10-subtest battery, and Vocabulary was excluded from analyses of W-B I standardization data such as factor analyses and correlations between subtest score and total score. Based on Wechsler's (1944) reconsideration of the value of Vocabulary and concomitant urging of examiners to administer it routinely, Vocabulary soon became a regular W-B I component. When the W-B II was developed, 33 of the 42 W-B I words were included in that battery's Vocabulary subtest. Since many W-B I words were therefore included in the WISC when the W-B II was revised and restandardized to become the Wechsler children's scale in 1949, Wechsler (1955) decided to include an all-new Vocabulary subtest when the W-B I was converted to the WAIS.

This lack of overlap between the W-B I Vocabulary subtest and the task of the same name on the WAIS, WAIS-R, WAIS-III, and WAIS-IV is of some concern regarding the continuity of measurement from the W-B I to its successors. Wechsler himself (1958) noted: "The WAIS list contains a larger percentage of action words (verbs). The only thing that can be said so far about this difference is that while responses given to verbs are easier to score, those elicited by substantives are frequently more significant diagnostically" (pp. 84–85). This difference in diagnostic significance is potentially important because Wechsler found Vocabulary so valuable, in part because of its qualitative aspects: "The type of word on which a subject passes or fails is always of some significance" (p. 85), yielding information about reasoning ability, degree of abstraction, cultural milieu, educational background, coherence of thought processes, and the like.

Nonetheless, Wechsler was careful to ensure that the various qualitative aspects of Vocabulary performance had a minimal impact on quantitative score. "What counts is the number of words that a person knows. Any recognized meaning is acceptable, and there is no penalty for inelegance of language. So long as the subjects show that they know what a word means, they are credited with a passing score" (1958, p. 85).

Information (Verbal Comprehension Index)
Wechsler (1958) included a subtest designed to tap a person's range of general information, despite "the obvious objection that the amount of knowledge which a person possesses depends in no small degree upon his or her education and cultural opportunities" (p. 65). Wechsler had noted the surprising finding

that the fact-oriented information test in the Army Alpha group examination had among the highest correlations with various estimates of intelligence: "It correlated . . . much better with the total score than did the Arithmetical Reasoning, the test of Disarranged Sentences, and even the Analogies Test, all of which had generally been considered much better tests of intelligence. . . . The fact is, all objections considered, the range of a person's knowledge is generally a very good indication of his or her intellectual capacity" (p. 65). Wechsler was also struck by a variety of psychometric properties of the Army Alpha Information Test compared to other tasks (excellent distribution curve, small percentage of zero scores, lack of pile-up of maximum scores), and the long history of similar factual information tests being "the stock in trade of mental examinations, and . . . widely used by psychiatrists in estimating the intellectual level of patients" (p. 65).

Always the astute clinician, Wechsler (1958) was aware that the choice of items determined the value of the Information subtest as an effective measure of intelligence. Items must not be chosen whimsically or arbitrarily but must be developed with several important principles in mind, the most essential being that, generally, "the items should call for the sort of knowledge that average individuals with average opportunity may be able to acquire for themselves" (p. 65). Wechsler usually tried to avoid specialized and academic knowledge, historical dates, and names of famous individuals, "but there are many exceptions to the rule, and in the long run each item must be tried out separately" (p. 66). Thus, he preferred an item such as "What is the height of the average American woman?" to ones like "What is iambic tetrameter?" or "In what year was George Washington born?" but occasionally items of the latter type appeared in his Information subtest. Wechsler was especially impressed with the exceptional psychometric properties of the Army Alpha Information Test "in view of the fact that the individual items on [it] left much to be desired" (p. 65).

Although Wechsler (1958) agreed with the criticism that factual information tests depended heavily on educational and cultural opportunities, he felt that the problem "need not necessarily be a fatal or even a serious one" (p. 65). Similarly, he recognized that certain items would vary in difficulty in different locales or when administered to people of different nationalities: "Thus, 'What is the capital of Italy?' is passed almost universally by persons of Italian origin irrespective of their intellectual ability" (p. 66). Yet he was extremely fond of information, considering it "one of the most satisfactory in the battery" (p. 67).

Comprehension (Verbal Comprehension Index)

Measures of general comprehension were plentiful in tests prior to the W-B I, appearing in the original Binet scale and its revisions and in such group examinations as the Army Alpha and the National Intelligence Test. However, the test in multiple-choice format, though still valuable, does not approach the contribution of the task when individuals have to compose their own responses:

> [O]ne of the most gratifying things about the general comprehension test, when given orally, is the rich clinical data which it furnishes about the subject. It is frequently of value in diagnosing psychopathic personalities, sometimes suggests the presence of schizophrenic trends (as revealed by perverse and bizarre responses) and almost always tells us something about the subject's social and cultural background. (Wechsler, 1958, p. 67)

In selecting questions for the W-B I Comprehension subtest, Wechsler (1958) borrowed some material from the Army Alpha and the Army Memoirs (Yoakum & Yerkes, 1920) and included a few questions that were also on the old Stanford-Binet, "probably because they were borrowed from the same source" (p. 68). He was not bothered by overlap because of what he perceived to be a very small practice effect for Comprehension: "It is curious how frequently subjects persist in their original responses, even after other replies are suggested to them" (p. 68).

The WAIS Comprehension subtest was modified from its predecessor by adding two very easy items to prevent a pile-up of zero scores and by adding three proverb items "because of their reported effectiveness in eliciting paralogical and concretistic thinking" (Wechsler, 1958, p. 68). Wechsler found that the proverbs did not contribute to the subtest exactly what he had hoped; they were useful for mentally disturbed individuals "but 'poor' answers were also common in normal subjects . . . [and] even superior subjects found the proverbs difficult. A possible reason for this is that proverbs generally express ideas so concisely that any attempt to explain them further is more likely to subtract than add to their clarity" (p. 68). Despite the shortcomings of proverbs items, particularly the fact that they seem to measure skills that differ from prototypical general comprehension items (Kaufman, 1985), Wechsler (1981) retained the three proverbs items in the WAIS-R Comprehension subtest. Since these three items are relatively difficult (they are among the last five in the sequence), they are instrumental in distinguishing among the most superior adults regarding the abilities measured by WAIS-R Comprehension. Only two of the proverb items were retained on the WAIS-III, but the WAIS-IV includes four such items.

According to Wechsler (1958), Comprehension was termed a test of common sense on the Army Alpha, and successful performance "seemingly depends on the possession of a certain amount of practical information and a general ability to evaluate past experience. The questions included are of a sort that average adults may have had occasion to answer for themselves at some time, or heard discussed in one form or another. They are for the most part stereotypes with a broad common base" (pp. 68–69). Wechsler was also careful to include no questions with unusual words "so that individuals of even limited education generally have little difficulty in understanding their content" (p. 69). Comprehension scores are, however, dependent on the ability to express one's thoughts verbally.

Digit Span (Working Memory Index)

Memory Span for Digits (renamed Digit Span) combines in a single subtest two skills that subsequent research has shown to be distinct in many ways (Costa, 1975; Jensen & Figueroa, 1975): repetition of digits in the same order as they are spoken by the examiner and repetition of digits in the reverse order. Wechsler (1958) combined these two tasks for pragmatic reasons, however, not theoretical ones: Each task alone had too limited a range of possible raw scores, and treating each set of items as a separate subtest would have given short-term memory too much weight in determining a person's IQ— $^1/_6$ instead of $^1/_{11}$.

Wechsler was especially concerned about overweighing memory because Digit Span proved to be a relatively weak measure of general intelligence (g). He gave serious consideration to dropping the task altogether but decided to retain it for two reasons.

1. Digit Span is particularly useful at the lower ranges of intelligence; adults who cannot recall 5 digits forward and 3 backward are mentally retarded or emotionally disturbed "in 9 cases out of 10" (Wechsler, 1958, p. 71), except in cases of neurological impairment.
2. Poor performance on Digit Span is of unusual diagnostic significance, according to Wechsler, particularly for suspected brain dysfunction or concern about mental deterioration across the life span.

Digit Span also has several other advantages that may account for Wechsler's (1958) assertion that "perhaps no test has been so widely used in scales of intelligence as that of Memory Span for Digits" (p. 70): It is simple to administer and score, it measures a rather specific ability, and it is clinically valuable because of its unusual susceptibility to anxiety, inattention, distractibility, and lack of concentration. Wechsler noted that repetition of digits backward is especially impaired in individuals who have difficulty sustaining concentrated effort during problem solving. The test has been popularly "used for a long time by psychiatrists as a test of retentiveness and by psychologists in all sorts of psychological studies" (p. 70); because Wechsler retained Digit Span as a regularly administered subtest on the WAIS-R but treated it as supplementary on the WISC-R, it is evident that he saw its measurement as a more vital aspect of adult assessment than of child assessment.

Arithmetic (Working Memory Index)
Wechsler (1958) included a test of arithmetical reasoning in an adult intelligence battery because such tests correlate highly with general intelligence; are easily created and standardized; are deemed by most adults as "worthy of a grownup"; have been "used as a rough and ready measure of intelligence" prior to the advent of psychometrics; and have "long been recognized as a sign of mental alertness" (p. 69). Such tests are flawed by the impact on test scores of attention span, temporary emotional reactions, and of educational and occupational attainment. As Wechsler notes: "Clerks, engineers and businessmen usually do well on arithmetic tests, while housewives, day laborers, and illiterates are often penalized by them" (p. 69). However, he believed that the advantages of an arithmetical reasoning test far outweighed the negative aspects. He pointed out that adults "may be embarrassed by their inability to do certain problems, but they almost never look upon the questions as unfair or inconsequential" (p. 69). He took much care in developing the specific set of items for the W-B I and the WAIS and believed that his particular approach to constructing the Arithmetic subtest was instrumental in the task's appeal to adults. Wechsler constructed items dealing with everyday, practical situations such that the solutions generally require computational skills taught in grade school or acquired "in the course of day-to-day transactions" (p. 70), and the responses avoid "verbalization or reading difficulties" (p. 69). Whereas the WISC-R and W-B I involve the reading of a few problems by the subject, all items on the WAIS, WAIS-R, WAIS-III, and WAIS-IV are read aloud by the examiner. Bonus points for quick, perfect performance are not given to children on the WISC-R, but Wechsler considered the ability to respond rapidly to relatively difficult arithmetic problems to be a pertinent aspect of adult intelligence; bonus points are given to two items on the W-B I Arithmetic subtest, to four items on the WAIS task, to five items on WAIS-R Arithmetic, and to two items on WAIS-III Arithmetic. No bonus points are awarded on WAIS-IV Arithmetic, but only 30 seconds are allowed for each item.

Block Design (Perceptual Reasoning Index)

Kohs (1923) developed the Block Design test, which used blocks and designs that were red, white, blue, and yellow. His test was included in numerous other tests of intelligence and neuropsychological functioning before Wechsler adapted it for the W-B I. Wechsler (1958) shortened the test substantially; used designs having only two colors (although the W-B I blocks included all four colors, unlike the red and white WAIS and WAIS-III blocks); and altered the patterns that the examinee had to copy. Block Design has been shown to correlate well with various criterion measures, to be a good measure of *g*, and to be quite amenable to qualitative analysis (Wechsler, 1958). It intrigued Wechsler that those who do very well on this subtest are not necessarily the ones who treat the pattern as a gestalt; more often they are individuals who are able to break up the pattern into its component parts.

Wechsler (1958) believed that observation of individuals while they solve the problems, such as their following the entire pattern versus breaking it into small parts, provided qualitative, clinical information about their problem-solving approach, attitude, and emotional reaction that is potentially more valuable than the obtained scores. "One can often distinguish the hasty and impulsive individual from the deliberate and careful type, a subject who gives up easily or becomes disgusted, from the one who persists and keeps on working even after his time is up" (p. 80). He also felt that the Block Design subtest is most important diagnostically, particularly for persons with dementia or other types of neurological impairment. From Goldstein's (1948) perspective, those with brain damage perform poorly on Block Design because of loss of the "abstract approach," although Wechsler (1958) preferred to think that most "low scores on Block Design are due to difficulty in visual-motor organization" (p. 80).

Picture Completion (Perceptual Reasoning Index)

This subtest was commonly included in group-administered tests such as the Army Beta. A variant of this task known as Healy Picture Completion II, which involves placing a missing piece into an uncompleted picture, was given individually in various performance scales, including the Army Performance Scale Examination; however, individual administration of Picture Completion, though conducted with the Binet scale for an identical task named Mutilated Pictures, was less common. Wechsler (1958) was unimpressed with the group-administered versions of Picture Completion because the subject had to draw in (instead of name or point to) the missing part, too few items were used, unsatisfactory items were included, and items were chosen haphazardly (a typical set of items incorporated many that were much too easy and others that were unusually difficult).

Wechsler (1958) nonetheless believed that the test's "popularity is fully deserved" (p. 77); he tried to select an appropriate set of items while recognizing the difficulty of that task. "If one chooses familiar subjects, the test becomes much too easy; if one turns to unfamiliar ones, the test ceases to be a good measure of intelligence because one unavoidably calls upon specialized knowledge" (p. 77). He thought that the W-B I set of items was generally successful, although he had to increase the subtest length by 40% when developing WAIS Picture Completion to avoid a fairly restricted range of obtained scores. Although Wechsler was critical of the group-administered Picture Completion tasks, it is still noteworthy that four of the W-B I and WAIS items were taken directly from the Army Beta test, and an additional four items were clear adaptations of Beta items (using the same pictures, with a different part missing, or the same concept).

The subtest has several psychometric assets, according to Wechsler (1958), including brief administration time, minimal practice effect even after short intervals, and good ability to assess intelligence for low-functioning individuals. Two of these claims are true, but the inconsequential practice effect is refuted by data in the *WAIS-III Manual* (Psychological Corporation, 1997) and *WAIS-IV Technical Manual* (Psychological Corporation, 2008), which show test-retest gains for Picture Completion to average about 2 scaled-score points over intervals of a few weeks. Limitations of the task are that subjects must be familiar with the object in order to have a fair opportunity to detect what is missing and the susceptibility of specific items to sex differences. Wechsler (1958) notes that women did better in finding the missing eyebrow in the girl's profile and that men did better in detecting the missing thread on the electric light bulb. Similarly, on the WISC-R, about two-thirds of the boys but only about one-third of the girls across the entire 6–16 age range were able to find the missing "slit" in the screw; in contrast, many more girls than boys detected the sock missing from the girl who is running.

Because a person must first have the basic perceptual and conceptual abilities to recognize and be familiar with the object pictured in each item, Wechsler (1958) saw Picture Completion as measuring "the ability of the individual to differentiate essential from non-essential details" and "to appreciate that the missing part is in some way essential either to the form or to the function of the object or picture." But because of the total dependence of the assessment of this skill on the person's easy familiarity with the content of the item, "unfamiliar, specialized and esoteric subject matter must therefore be sedulously avoided when pictures are chosen for this test" (p. 78).

Coding (Processing Speed Index)

"The Digit Symbol [Coding on WAIS-IV] or Substitution Test is one of the oldest and best established of all psychological tests. It is to be found in a large variety of intelligence scales, and its wide popularity is fully merited" (Wechsler, 1958, p. 81). The W-B I Digit Symbol subtest was taken from the Army Beta, the only change being the reduction in response time from 2 minutes to 1½ minutes to avoid a pile-up of perfect scores. For the WAIS, the number of symbols to be copied was increased by about one-third, although the response time remained unchanged.

Wechsler's (1958) main concern regarding the use of Digit Symbol for assessing adult intelligence involved its potential dependency on visual acuity, motor coordination, and speed. He discounted the first two variables, except for people with specific visual or motor disabilities, but gave much consideration to the impact of speed on test performance. He was well aware that Digit Symbol performance drops dramatically with increasing age and is especially deficient for older individuals, who "do not write or handle objects as fast as younger persons, and what is perhaps equally important, they are not as easily motivated to do so. The problem, however, from the point of view of global functioning, is not merely whether the older persons are slower, but whether or not they are also 'slowed up'" (p. 81). Since correlations between Digit Symbol performance and total score remain high (or at least consistent) from age 16 through old age, Wechsler concluded that older people deserve the penalty for speed, "since resulting reduction in test performance is on the whole proportional to the subject's over-all capacity at the time he is tested" (p. 81). Although neurotic individuals also have been shown to perform relatively poorly on Digit Symbol, Wechsler attributed that decrement to difficulty in concentrating and applying persistent effort, that is, "a lessened mental efficiency rather than an impairment of intellectual ability" (p. 82).

Compared to earlier Digit Symbol or Substitution tests, Wechsler saw particular advantages to the task he borrowed from the Army Beta and included on his scales: It includes sample items to ensure that examinees understand the task, and it requires copying the unfamiliar symbols, not the numbers, lessening "the advantage which individuals having facility with numbers would otherwise have" (1958, p. 82).

Optional procedures were added to the WAIS-III Digit Symbol—Coding subtest, which were developed to help examiners assess what skills (or lack thereof) may be impacting examinees' performance on the subtest. These optional procedures involve recalling shapes from memory (Pairing and Free Recall) and perceptual and graphomotor speed (Digit Symbol—Copy). However, these optional procedures were removed on WAIS-IV Coding.

WECHSLER'S LEGACY

When put in historical perspective, Wechsler made some mighty contributions to the clinical and psychometric assessment of intelligence. His insistence that every person be assessed on both Verbal and Performance scales went against the conventional wisdom of his time. Yet discrepancies between Verbal and Performance IQs (and ultimately among the four Indexes that replaced the two IQs) would prove to have critical value for understanding brain functioning and theoretical distinctions between fluid and crystallized intelligence. Furthermore, Wechsler's stress on the clinical value of intelligence tests would alter the face of intellectual assessment forever, replacing the psychometric, statistical emphasis that accompanied the use and interpretation of the Stanford-Binet. And, finally, Wechsler's inclusion of a multiscore subtest profile (as well as three IQs instead of one) met the needs of the emerging field of learning disabilities assessment in the 1960s, to such an extent that his scales replaced the Stanford-Binet as king of IQ during that decade. It has maintained that niche ever since for children, adolescents, and adults (Alfonso, LaRocca, Oakland, & Spanakos, 2000; Archer, Buffington-Vollum, Stredny, & Handel, 2006; Archer & Newsom, 2000; Camara, Nathan, & Puente, 2000; Rabin, Barr, & Burton, 2005). The popularity of the adult Wechsler tests, starting with the WAIS and continuing with the WAIS-R and WAIS-III, is remarkable and pervasive. Wechsler's adult scales are by far the first choice for measuring intelligence among clinical neuropsychologists (Rabin et al., 2005), psychologists who conduct forensic assessments (Archer et al., 2006), clinical psychologists (Camara et al., 2000), psychologists who conduct evaluations in state correctional facilities (Gallagher, Somwaru, & Ben-Porath, 1999), psychology professors who train doctoral-level students (Belter & Piotrowski, 2001), and, indeed, psychologists who conduct assessments with adults for any other reason (Groth-Marnat, 2009; Kaufman & Lichtenberger, 2006). Harrison, Kaufman, Hickman, and Kaufman (1988) reported data from a survey of 402 clinical psychologists that showed 97% of these professionals utilized the WAIS or WAIS-R when administering an adult measure of intelligence. Even if the 97% figure is no longer exactly precise, it is axiomatic that the WAIS-IV will continue the Wechsler tradition as by far the most popular test of adult intelligence.

PURPOSES OF ASSESSING ADULTS AND ADOLESCENTS

As mentioned, historically, adults were assessed because of a need to place men into the appropriate level of the military service or to determine how mentally deficient a person was. Today, reasons for assessing adolescents and adults commonly include measuring cognitive potential or neurological dysfunction, obtaining clinical information, making educational or vocational placement decisions, and developing interventions for educational or vocational settings. Harrison et al. (1988) found that practitioners who assess adults most often report using intelligence tests to measure cognitive potential and to obtain clinically relevant information. About 77% of practitioners reported using intelligence tests for obtaining information about neurological functioning, and fewer than 50% reported using intelligence tests for making educational or vocational placements or interventions (Harrison et al., 1988). Camara and colleagues (2000) also reported that a large proportion of the assessment services of clinical psychologists and neuropsychologists are in the areas of intellectual/achievement assessment (20–34%) and neuropsychological assessment (13–26%).

FOUNDATIONS OF THE WAIS-IV: THEORY AND RESEARCH

Wechsler defined intelligence as "the capacity to act purposefully, to think rationally, and to deal effectively with his [or her] environment" (1944, p. 3). His concept of intelligence was that of a global entity which could also be categorized by the sum of many specific abilities. The most recent revision of Wechsler's adult intelligence scale, the WAIS-IV, has enhanced measures of more discrete domains of cognitive functioning, such as working memory and processing speed (Psychological Corporation, 2008) while continuing to provide a measure of global intelligence. Unlike the earliest Wechsler tests, the WAIS-IV also was developed with specific theoretical foundations in mind. In fact, revisions were made purposely to reflect the latest knowledge from literature in the areas of intelligence theory, adult cognitive development, and cognitive neuroscience. The theoretical constructs of fluid reasoning, working memory, and processing speed were of particular importance during the development of the WAIS-IV, just as they were in the development of the WISC-IV. Rapid Reference 1.2 defines these three theoretical constructs.

Wechsler's adult tests, from the Wechsler-Bellevue (1939) to the WAIS (1955) to the WAIS-R (1981), took the same basic form, with 6 subtests constituting the Verbal Scale, 5 making up the Performance Scale, and all 11 yielding the global entity of intelligence characterized by the Full Scale IQ. The WAIS-III departed slightly from the original form by offering four separate indexes (i.e., Verbal Comprehension Index, Perceptual Organization Index, Working Memory Index, and Processing Speed Index), in addition to the Verbal, Performance, and Full Scale IQs. The WAIS-IV, like the WISC-IV, departed dramatically from the

≡ *Rapid Reference 1.2*

Updated WAIS-IV Theoretical Foundations

Theoretical Construct	Fluid Reasoning	Working Memory	Processing Speed
Definition	Ability to process or manipulate abstractions, rules, generalizations, and logical relationships	Ability to actively maintain information in conscious awareness, perform some operation or manipulation with it, and produce a result	Ability to process information rapidly (which is dynamically related to one's ability to perform higher-order cognitive tasks)
References for the Construct	Carroll (1997) Cattell (1943, 1963) Cattell & Horn (1978) Sternberg (1995)	Beuhner, Krumm, Ziegler, & Pluecken (2006) Unsworth & Engle (2007)	Fry & Hale (1996) Kail (2000) Kail & Hall (1994) Kail & Salthouse (1994)

longtime Wechsler tradition by eliminating the Verbal and Performance IQs and, hence, the ever-popular V-P IQ discrepancy. The four indexes were retained in the WAIS-IV, alongside the Full Scale IQ, providing a more modern and conceptually clearer scale structure. The WAIS-IV and WISC-IV now offer the same four indexes: Verbal Comprehension (VCI), Perceptual Reasoning (PRI), Working Memory (WMI), and Processing Speed (PSI). (To achieve this synchrony, the WAIS-IV and WISC-IV Perceptual Organization Index was renamed the Perceptual Reasoning Index, and WISC-IV Freedom from Distractibility Index became the Working Memory Index.)

The focus on the four indexes in the WAIS-IV psychometric profile is a plus when it comes to understanding how to interpret individual profiles, from both a theoretical and a clinical perspective. However, this shift in focus also affects WAIS-IV Full Scale IQ (FSIQ), which is now computed from the sum of the 10 subtests that compose the four scales (3 VCI, 3PRI, 2 WMI, and 2 PSI). Traditionally, the WAIS FSIQ has been composed of 11 subtests, 6 Verbal and 5 Performance. The end result of these changes is a WAIS-IV FSIQ that differs substantially from WAIS-III FSIQ, as shown in Rapid Reference 1.3. Of the 11 WAIS-III Full Scale subtests, only 8 are retained on the WAIS-IV Full

≡ Rapid Reference 1.3

Comparison of the Subtest Composition of the WAIS-III and WAIS-IV Full Scales

WAIS-III Full Scale Subtests	WAIS-IV Full Scale Subtests
Verbal	
Vocabulary	Vocabulary (VCI)
Similarities	Similarities (VCI)
Information	Information (VCI)
Comprehension	
Arithmetic	Arithmetic (WMI)
Digit Span	Digit Span (WMI)
Performance	
Block Design	Block Design (PRI)
Matrix Reasoning	Matrix Reasoning (PRI)
	Visual Puzzles (PRI)
Picture Completion	
Picture Arrangement	
Digit Symbol—Coding	Coding (PSI)
	Symbol Search (PSI)

Scale. Although this shift is not as dramatic as the change from the WISC-III to the WISC-IV Full Scale (which share only 5 of 10 subtests), it is nonetheless notable.

Although two global scores were eliminated from the WAIS-IV (Verbal and Performance IQs), one new global score was added, the optional General Ability Index (GAI). The GAI is derived from the sum of scaled scores on the three Verbal Comprehension and three Perceptual Reasoning subtests, thereby eliminating the WMI and PSI from consideration and forming a global composite composed solely of the verbal and perceptual constructs. This new global score aids examiners in interpreting test profiles and is included in our step-by-step interpretive system (see chapter 5 in this volume), just as the WISC-IV GAI is incorporated into its interpretive system (Flanagan & Kaufman, 2009).

DON'T FORGET
New WAIS-IV Four-Factor Structure

Verbal	Performance
1. Verbal Comprehension	2. Perceptual Reasoning
3. Working Memory	4. Processing Speed

Note: The Perceptual Reasoning Index (PRI) was called the Perceptual Organization Index (POI) on the WAIS-III

Description of WAIS-IV

Several issues prompted the revision of the WAIS-IV; the Manual clearly details these issues and what changes were made (Psychological Corporation, 2008, pp. 7–23). Rapid Reference 1.4 lists key features that were adapted for the Fourth Edition.

WAIS-III examiners will recognize many of the core Wechsler subtests in the WAIS-IV, but there have been several notable changes with the addition of new subtests and modifications to the overall structure. (Rapid Reference 1.5 lists a description of all WAIS-IV subtests.) There are three new subtests:

1. **Visual Puzzles** (added to the Perceptual Reasoning Index, and is a visual variation of the Object Assembly subtest that was dropped in this revision)

Rapid Reference 1.4

WAIS-IV Key Revisions
- Updated theoretical foundations
- Updated norms
- Increased developmental appropriateness
- Increased user-friendliness
- Enhanced clinical utility
- Decreased reliance on timed performance
- Enhancement of fluid reasoning measurement by adding Figure Weights and Visual Puzzles subtests
- Strengthening the framework based on factor analysis
- Statistical linkage to other measures of cognitive functioning and achievement
- Extensive testing of reliability and validity

≡ Rapid Reference 1.5

....

WAIS-IV Subtest Abbreviations and Descriptions

Subtest	Abbreviation	Description
Verbal Comprehension Subtest		
Similarities	SI	The examinee is presented two words that represent common objects or concepts and describes how they are similar.
Vocabulary	VC	For picture items, the examinee names the object presented visually. For verbal items, the examinee defines words that are presented visually and orally.
Information	IN	The examinee answers questions that address a broad range of general knowledge topics.
Comprehension	CO	The examinee answers questions based on his or her understanding of general principles and social situations.
Perceptual Reasoning Subtest		
Block Design	BD	Working within a specified time limit, the examinee views a model and a picture or a picture only and uses red-and-white blocks to recreate the design.
Matrix Reasoning	MR	The examinee views an incomplete matrix or series and selects the response option that completes the matrix or series.
Visual Puzzles[a]	VP	Working within a specified time limit, the examinee views a completed puzzle and selects three response options that, when combined, reconstruct the puzzle.
Figure Weights[a]	FW	Working within a specified time limit, the examinee views a scale with missing weight(s) and selects the response option that keeps the scale balanced.
Picture Completion	PCm	Working within a specified time limit, the examinee views a picture with an important part missing and identifies the missing part.

Subtest	Abbreviation	Description
Working Memory Subtest		
Digit Span	DS	For Digit Span Forward, the examinee is read a sequence of numbers and recalls the numbers in the same order. For Digit Span Backward, the examinee is read a sequence of numbers and recalls the numbers in reverse order. For Digit Span Sequencing, the examinee is read a sequence of numbers and recalls the numbers in ascending order.
Arithmetic	AR	Working within a specified time limit, the examinee mentally solves a series of arithmetic problems.
Letter-Number Sequencing	LN	The examinee is read a sequence of numbers and letters and recalls the numbers in ascending order and the letters in alphabetical order.
Processing Speed Subtest		
Symbol Search	SS	Working within a specified time limit, the examinee scans a search group and indicates whether one of the symbols in the target group matches.
Coding	CD	Using a key, the examinee copies symbols that are paired with numbers within a specified time limit.
Cancellation[a]	CA	Working within a specified time limit, the examinee scans a structured arrangement of shapes and marks target shapes.

[a] New WAIS-IV subtest.

2. **Figure Weights** (added to the Performance Reasoning Index as a supplemental subtest)
3. **Cancellation** (added to the Processing Speed Index as a supplemental subtest)

How these new subtests were created gives interesting insight into the process of test development and revision. Professionals on the Research Development (RD) Team for the WAIS-IV shared how Figure Weights and Visual Puzzles were developed for the WAIS-IV (Cancellation was developed first for the WISC-IV). Dr. Susan Raiford (personal communication, November 25, 2008) revealed:

> Visual Puzzles was inspired by Object Assembly as an abstract nonmotor task that was similar. Jim Holdnack, one of the WMS-IV RDs, submitted the item type for consideration in April of 2005, and it was originally named "Puzzle Pieces. . . . As the subtest evolved we were aware of the similarities to the old Paper Form Board tests through reviews of Carroll's work and of existing measures (Quasha & Likert) published many years ago by Psychcorp. We found as we worked with the item type that difficulty could be controlled with complexity of cut and with internal cues (colors or lines), which is why the internal cues are there on the easier items and the complexity of piece cut gets greater as the items progress.

Dr. Holdnack (personal communication, November 25, 2008) continued:

> The subtest was inspired from the Object Assembly subtest and the Visual Puzzles and Geometric Puzzles on NEPSY-II, although, the make-up of this test varies considerably from those subtests. Mostly, I was shooting for the items to have elements of mental construction and rotation while limiting other confounding factors such as verbalization, processing speed, and fine-motor integration.

Paul Williams, a research director at the Psychological Corporation, submitted the original Figure Weights item in 2005 (Raiford, pers. comm.). Dr. Williams explained (personal communication, December 1, 2008):

> [T]he hard part was coming up with a way to create a relationship between the objects. I couldn't use symbols such as = +− because this would require prior knowledge. So the thought came to me that another way to symbolize > and < is by weight; which led to the idea of using a balance to create a rule or relationship between the figures. With this information a series of rules can be presented which has to be reasoned out by the examinee to balance the final scale. Susie then took it from there and did an amazing job building the items and doing the science necessary to develop the idea into a functional subtest.

Dr. Raiford (pers. comm.) continued:

> Paul told me at the time that he intended it to be a new item type for Matrix Reasoning, but we thought we could make a whole subtest out of it, and

wanted to because it seemed to be measuring quantitative reasoning, which we weren't measuring nonverbally yet. I switched the item type to a scale from the seesaws . . . because it seemed more intuitive. I also found we could get all the difficulty we needed with just two scales establishing relationships and a third scale with an empty tray.

In addition to these three new subtests, other modifications to the WAIS-III include the removal of two of Wechsler's original group of subtests from the revised test: Picture Arrangement and Object Assembly. The rationale for deleting these subtests was to lessen the motor demands of the test and to deemphasize time bonus points. When Object Assembly was originally developed, Wechsler (1958) "wanted at least one test which required putting things together into a familiar configuration" (pp. 82–83). He included Object Assembly, but only "after much hesitation" (p. 82), because of its known liabilities: relatively low reliability and predictive value, large practice effects, and low correlations with other subtests. In the development of Picture Arrangement, Wechsler selected items for his test based on "interest of content, probable appeal to subjects, ease of scoring and discriminating value" (p. 75). Yet he was never satisfied with the result, noting that "the final selection leaves much to be desired." He spent much time and statistical analysis trying to discern which alternative responses deserved credit and even called in a team of four judges, yet the final system for assigning credit for alternative arrangements "turned out to be more or less arbitrary" (p. 76). Although bonus points were included on earlier editions of the WAIS Picture Arrangement, Wechsler (1981) reversed this trend for the WAIS-R and deemphasized speed greatly by not allowing bonus points for any of the Picture Arrangement items. Thus, Wechsler's concerns about these two subtests are consistent with the Psychological Corporation's decision to eliminate them from the WAIS-IV (and from the WISC-IV). Nonetheless, had he been alive, Wechsler undoubtedly never would have agreed to eliminate these original subtests from any version of the WAIS or WISC. He would, however, have gained solace from the fact that both Object Assembly and Picture Arrangement are included in the Wechsler Nonverbal Scale of Ability (WNV; Wechsler & Naglieri, 2006).

Further deletions from the WAIS-III to the WAIS-IV included removal of the optional procedures: Digit Symbol—Incidental Learning and Digit Symbol—Copy. However, process scores were added to the WAIS-IV Block Design, Digit Span, and Letter-Number Sequencing subtests that allow examiners to analyze errors and qualitatively interpret test performance. For example, Block Design No Time Bonus is a process score that reflects a person's performance without additional time bonus for rapid completion of items. The Digit Span task offers three process scores that reflect an examinee's performance on the separate tasks of repeating digits forward, backward, and then sequencing digits. The addition of the Digit Span Sequencing task is consistent with the test publisher's theoretical emphasis on working memory. An additional process score is offered for another Working Memory subtest, which involves the calculation of the longest Letter-Number sequence recalled. A comparison of Digit Span Sequencing and Letter-Number Sequencing will provide an auditory analog of a comparison of Trail Making A and B. Rapid Reference 1.6 describes the subtests' process analyses.

≡ Rapid Reference 1.6

Subtests with Process Analysis

Subtest	Abbreviation	Process Score	Use
Block Design			
Block Design No Time Bonus	BDN	Score reflects performance on BD without additional time bonus for rapid completion.	Useful when physical limitations, problem-solving strategies, or personality charac-teristics affect performance on timed tasks.
Digit Span			
Digit Span Forward	DSF	Raw scores reflect the total number of DSF trials correctly completed before discontinuing.	May help to explain variable performance on Digit Span Tasks. DSF requires imme-diate auditory recall, whereas DSB and DSS place demands on working memory and attention.
Digit Span Backward	DSB	Raw scores reflect the total number of DSB trials correctly completed before discontinuing.	
Digit Span Sequencing	DSS	Raw scores reflect the total number of DSS trials correctly completed before discontinuing.	

Subtest	Abbreviation	Process Score	Use
Longest Digit Span Forward	LDSF	Raw scores reflect the number of forward digits recalled on the last trial scored 1 point.	May help to explain variable performance on DS tasks. Some examinees may arrive at their DS total raw score by inconsistently earning 1s and 0s across trials, whereas other examinees may show a pattern of consistently earning 1s until they discontinue the task.
Longest Digit Span Backward	LDSB	Raw scores reflect the number of backward digits recalled on the last trial scored 1 point.	
Longest Digit Span Sequencing	LDSS	Raw scores reflect the number of digits correctly sequenced on the last trial scored 1 point.	
Letter-Number Sequencing			
Longest Letter-Number Sequence	LLNS	Raw scores reflect the number of letters and numbers correctly sequenced on the last trial scored 1 point.	May help to explain variable performance on LN tasks. Some examinees may arrive at their LN total raw score by inconsistently earning 1s and 0s across trials, whereas other examinees may show a pattern of consistently earning 1s until they discontinue the task.

Validity of the WAIS-IV Model

With the addition of the 3 new subtests and removal of 2 subtests, the complete WAIS-IV comprises 15 subtests, although only 10 are core subtests needed to compute the 4 indexes and FSIQ. Like the WISC-IV structure, the WAIS-IV structure focuses users on the middle tier of scores—the Factor Indexes (see Figure 1.1). FSIQ and the indexes have a mean of 100 and a standard deviation of 15. Subtest scaled scores have a mean of 10 and standard deviation of 3.

Of the five supplemental subtests, three are normed only for ages 16 to 69: Letter-Number Sequencing (WMI), Figure Weights (PRI), and Cancellation

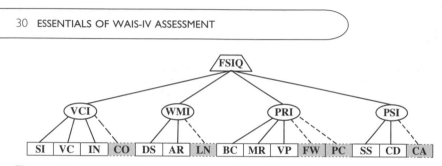

Figure 1.1. WAIS-IV Structure: Three-Tier Hierarchy

Note: Shaded subtests that are bordered with dashed lines and connected to indexes with dashed lines are supplemental and contribute to the calculation of the Index score only if they have substituted for one of the core subtests.

(PSI). Comprehension (VCI) and Picture Completion (PRI) are normed for the complete 16- to 90-year range. Supplemental subtests are not included in calculation of any of the Index scores.

The *WAIS-IV Technical and Interpretive Manual* (Psychological Corporation, 2008) reports the details of several confirmatory factor analysis studies that support the underlying four-factor structure of the WAIS-IV. For all ages, there is strong construct validity support for the four Indexes. However, at both ages 16–69 and ages 70–90, a model that allows Arithmetic to load on both the Working Memory Factor and the Verbal Comprehension Factor fits the data best. For ages 16–69, the Arithmetic subtest had a Factor loading of .75 on the Working Memory Factor and a small loading of .08 on the Verbal Comprehension Factor. For ages 70–90, the Arithmetic subtest had a loading of .48 on the Working Memory Factor and .33 on the Verbal Comprehension Factor. The Figure Weights subtest also had a split factor loading for ages 16–69, with factor loadings of .37 and .43 on the Working Memory Factor and Perceptual Reasoning Factor, respectively.

Preliminary findings from additional WAIS-IV confirmatory Factor analyses (CFA) have been conducted by Tim Keith (personal communication, January 30, 2009). He analyzed the averaged matrix for ages 16–90 shown in the *WAIS-IV Manual* (Psychological Corporation, 2008, p. 62) and used the technique of higher-order CFA. Keith's analyses compared various models, including the Four-Factor WAIS-IV model and a Five-Factor model that is in line with the Cattell-Horn-Carroll (CHC) theory. This CHC model included Matrix Reasoning and Figure Weights on the Fluid Reasoning (*Gf*) Factor, along with Arithmetic. The Visual Processing (*Gv*) Factor included Block Design, Visual Puzzles, and Picture Completion. The Crystallized Knowledge (*Gc*) Factor included Similarities, Vocabulary, Comprehension, and Information. Short-Term Memory (*Gsm*) included Digit Span and Letter-Number Sequencing, and Processing Speed (*Gs*) included Coding, Symbol Search, and Cancellation. Keith reported that the CHC model "fits better than the WAIS Scoring model." These comparisons suggest that a CHC model with separate *Gf* and *Gv* Factors fits the data especially well. Arithmetic, though included on the WMI, is associated with the *Gf* factor in Keith's analysis. The loadings are shown in Figure 1.2. Note that *Gf* is indistinguishable from the general factor (*g*). Also note that Figure Weights shows a high loading (.77) on a *Gf* Factor.

WAIS-IV Technical and Interpretive Manual (Psychological Corporation, 2008) also reported Model 5, in which it allowed a correlated error for Digit Span and

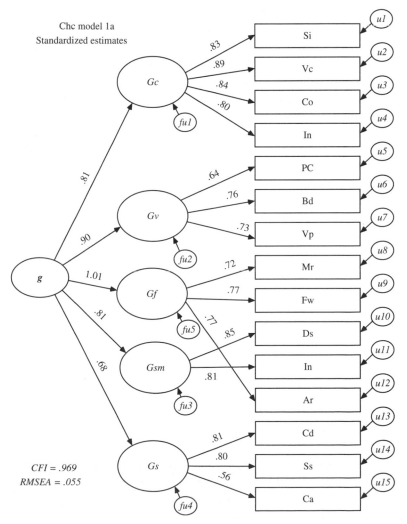

Figure 1.2. WAIS-IV CFA with CHC Model

Source: T. Keith, personal communication, January 30, 2009.

Letter-Number Sequencing and a cross-loading for Arithmetic on a Gc factor. In Keith's preliminary analyses, he found that these changes help the WAIS-IV scoring model considerably. With these changes, the scoring model fits better than the CHC model (Keith, pers. comm.).

However, Keith aptly points out that "relaxations are also reasonable for the CHC model." Arithmetic measures a complex mixture of skills. When he compared two CHC models—one that allowed Arithmetic to load on Gsm (in addition to Gf) and another that allowed Arithmetic to load on Gc and Gsm (in addition to Gf)—the second model was the best fitting of this series of CHC models. Interestingly, when Arithmetic is allowed to load on three Factors, it shows nearly equal loadings on Gf (.34) and Gsm (.31), and smaller on Gc (.19). Keith (pers. comm.) stated: "Arithmetic is obviously complex, requiring several abilities. I suspect that it is first a measure of g."

The final parts of Keith's preliminary confirmatory factor analyses examined three models that removed Arithmetic from the analyses. The WAIS-IV Four-Factor structure fits better than the CHC model when Arithmetic is excluded. If, however, a correlated error is allowed between Gf and Gv (equivalent to an intermediate factor between them and g, and something that has been found in previous research), this procedure provides an even better-fitting model (Keith, pers. comm.).

Keith concluded from his preliminary analyses that "a CHC-based interpretation of the WAIS-IV is, at minimum, worth considering. I would certainly consider that interpretation if there were inconsistencies among the Perceptual Reasoning tasks, or between Arithmetic versus the Working Memory tasks" (pers. comm.).

WAIS-IV's Relationship with the WAIS-III

The relationship between the WAIS-IV and its predecessor, the WAIS-III, was examined in a sample of 240 adults aged 16 to 88 (Psychological Corporation, 2008). Each test was administered in a counterbalanced order with a 1- to 23-week interval (mean = 5 weeks) between the testings. The overall correlation coefficients showed that the Full Scale IQs for the WAIS-III and WAIS-IV were the most highly related ($r = .94$) of the global scales, followed by the Verbal Comprehension Indexes ($r = .91$), Working Memory Indexes ($r = .87$), Processing Speed Indexes ($r = .86$), and the Perceptual Organization/Reasoning Indexes ($r = .84$). Thus, despite the substantial changes from the WAIS-III to the WAIS-IV in the composition of the Full Scale (see Rapid Reference 1.3), the extremely high coefficient of .94 indicates that the construct measured by Wechsler's Full Scale has not changed at all.

Table 1.1. Changes in Scores from the WAIS-III to the WAIS-IV

Scale	WAIS-III Mean[a]	SD	WAIS-IV Mean[a]	SD	WAIS-III— WAIS-IV Standard Score Difference	WAIS-III— WAIS-IV Correlation[b]
VCI	104.4	15.5	100.1	14.9	4.3	0.91
PRI or POI	103.7	15.3	100.3	15.5	3.4	0.84
WMI	100.0	14.5	99.3	13.7	0.7	0.78
PSI	100.8	17.2	100.1	14.9	0.7	0.86
FSIQ	102.9	15.0	100.0	15.2	2.9	0.94

[a]The values in the Mean columns are the average of the means of the two administration orders.

[b]The weighted average was obtained with Fisher's z transformation.

Source: Data are adapted from Table 5.5 of the *WAIS-IV Technical and Interpretive Manual* (Wechsler, 2008).

Note: Sample sizes ranged from 238 to 240. Correlations were computed separately for each order of administration in a counterbalanced design and corrected for the variability of the WAIS-III standardization sample (Guilford & Fruchter, 1978).

As shown in Table 1.1, the average WAIS-IV Full Scale IQ was 2.9 points lower than the WAIS-III Full Scale IQ, which is the same difference the WAIS-III FSIQ was from the WAIS-R FSIQ. The difference between the two instruments on both the Working Memory Index and the Processing Speed Index is negligible (0.7 points for both) but is more substantial for the Verbal Comprehension Index (4.3 points) and the Perceptual Organization/Reasoning Index (3.4 points). These differences are entirely consistent with the well-known Flynn Effect (Flynn, 1987, 2007; Flynn & Weiss, 2007) and indicate that a person's standard scores on an old test, with outdated norms (e.g., the WAIS-III), will tend to be spuriously high. The WAIS-IV will yield scores that are a little lower than the WAIS-III, especially on the FSIQ, VCI, and PRI, but these lower scores present a more accurate estimate of the person's intellectual abilities because they are derived from contemporary standards (i.e., the most recent norms groups).

Overall, the Flynn Effect has shown that, on average, American children and adults have increased their scores on intelligence tests at the rate of 3 points per decade between the 1930s and 1990s, with gains of 5 to 8 points per decade occurring for other developed nations, such as France, the Netherlands, and Japan (Flynn, 2007; Kaufman & Lichtenberger, 2006). The mean FSIQ difference in the WAIS-III/WAIS-IV study confirms the maintenance of the Flynn Effect in the United States into the first decade of the 21st century. However, post-2000 data from Norway and Denmark suggest that the Flynn Effect has stopped occurring in those countries and that there may even be a reverse Flynn Effect (i.e., decline in IQ) taking place, especially in Denmark (Singet, Barlaug, & Torjussen, 2004; Teasdale & Owen, 2005, 2008). Within the United States, Zhou and Zhu (2007) observed the Flynn Effect for individuals with IQs of 70 to 109 but observed a reverse Flynn Effect for children and adults with IQs of 110 and above (their analysis did not include the WAIS-IV). Consequently, it is conceivable that the Flynn Effect will slow down or reverse in the United States during the next decade and may have already reversed for those with above-average IQs.

STANDARDIZATION AND PSYCHOMETRIC PROPERTIES OF THE WAIS-IV

The standardization sample for the WAIS-IV (N = 2,200) was selected according to 2005 U.S. Census data and was stratified according to age, sex, race/ethnicity, geographic region, and education level. Thirteen age groups were created from large sample of adolescents and adults, with 100 to 200 subjects in each group between ages 16–17 and 85–90.

Reliability

The average split-half reliability for the FSIQ across the 13 age groups was strong, ranging from .97 to .98 (see Rapid Reference 1.7 for split-half and test-retest reliability for all scales and subtests). The Factor Indexes had average reliability coefficients ranging from .90 for Processing Speed to .96 for Verbal Comprehension. Individual subtest reliabilities ranged from an average of .94 on Vocabulary to .78 on Cancellation; median values were .89 for the 10 core subtests and .87 for the 5 supplemental subtests. A subset of the standardization sample (298 adults) provided test-retest data, with an average of 3 weeks between testings. The results of the test-retest study showed similar reliability coefficients for the four age-group subsamples (16–29, 30–54, 55–69, and 70–90 years). Average stability coefficients across all ages were .96 for the Full Scale IQ and Verbal Comprehension Index, .88 for the Working Memory Index, and .87 for

≡ Rapid Reference 1.7

Average WAIS-IV Reliability

Subtest/ Composite Score	Split-Half Reliability	Test-Retest Reliability
Block Design	.87	.80
Similarities	.87	.87
Digit Span	.93	.83
Matrix Reasoning	.90	.74
Vocabulary	.94	.89
Arithmetic	.88	.83
Symbol Search	.81	.81
Visual Puzzles	.89	.74
Information	.93	.90
Coding	.86	.86
Letter-Number Sequencing	.88	.80
Figure Weights	.90	.77
Comprehension	.87	.86
Cancellation	.78	.78
Picture Completion	.84	.77
Verbal Comprehension Index	.96	.96
Perceptual Reasoning Index	.95	.87
Working Memory Index	.94	.88
Processing Speed Index	.90	.87
Full Scale IQ	.98	.96

[a]For Coding and Symbol Search, and the composite of these two (Processing Speed), only test-retest coefficients are reported because of the timed nature of the subtests.

Source: Data are from Tables 4.1 and 4.5 of the WAIS-IV Technical and Interpretive Manual (Psychological Corporation, 2008).

both the Perceptual Reasoning and Processing Speed Index. The highest stability coefficient for the core subtests was .90 for Information, and the lowest was .74 for Matrix Reasoning and Visual Puzzles. Of the supplemental subtests, Comprehension had the highest stability coefficients, ranging from .86 for Comprehension to .77 for Figure Weights and Picture Completion.

Loadings on the General Factor

General intelligence or general mental ability (Spearman, 1927) is denoted by g The measurement of g may be done by several methods. Preliminary findings from Keith's WAIS-IV higher-order CFA (personal communications, January 30 and March 14, 2009), based on the average correlation matrix for ages 16 to 90 (Psychological Corporation, 2008, p. 62), provided the g-loadings reported here. These g loadings are the Factor loadings for each WAIS-IV subtest on the second-order general Factor that was obtained from the CFA. Factor loadings of .70 or greater are usually considered "good" measures of g; loadings of .50 to .69 are deemed "fair" g loadings; and loadings below .50 are considered poor. Rapid Reference 1.8 contains data on how well each subtest loads on the g factor.

Contrary to previous Wechsler scales on which measures of verbal comprehension and expression tended to yield the highest g loadings, the best measures

≡ Rapid Reference 1.8

WAIS-IV Subtests as Measures of General Ability (g)

	g loading	Strength as a measure of g
Arithmetic	.78	Good
Figure Weights	.77	Good
Matrix Reasoning	.73	Good
Vocabulary	.72	Good
Digit Span	.69	Fair
Block Design	.68	Fair
Comprehension	.68	Fair
Similarities	.68	Fair
Visual Puzzles	.66	Fair
Letter-Number Sequencing	.66	Fair
Information	.65	Fair
Picture Completion	.57	Fair
Coding	.55	Fair
Symbol Search	.54	Fair
Cancellation	.38	Poor

Source: T. Keith (personal communication, January 30, 2009).

of g on the WAIS-IV were Arithmetic and two Perceptual Reasoning tasks. Among the Verbal Comprehension subtests, only Vocabulary emerged as a good measure of g. The traditionally good measures, such as Comprehension, Information, and Similarities, were only fair measures, loading in the mid- to high .60s. Not surprisingly, the Processing Speed subtests were the weakest measures of g, but only Cancellation, with a dismal loading of .38, qualifies as a poor measure of g.

The concept of general intelligence is one whose usefulness has been debated in the intelligence literature. Interestingly, Horn (1989) and Carroll (1993) were at the opposite poles of this debate, despite the fact that their theories were merged to form CHC theory. Horn was a devout anti-g theorist, whereas Carroll had great respect for g and considered general ability to be Stratum III of his theory of intelligence. Because of their disagreements about the g construct, CHC theory focuses on Broad Abilities (Stratum II) and Narrow Abilities (Stratum I) and rarely addresses the role of g (McGrew, 2005).

From our perspective, g pertains to a practical, clinical construct that corresponds to FSIQ and, therefore, provides an overview of each person's diverse abilities. But we do not interpret it as a theoretical construct. Other theorists have argued otherwise (Carroll, 1993; Jensen, 1998; Spearman, 1904); even Wechsler[2] (1974) was a strong believer in g, maintaining that "[i]ntelligence is the overall capacity of individuals to understand and cope with the world around them" (p. 5). We believe that a subtest with a strong g loading should not be interpreted as one that is *the* representation of an individual's overall level of cognitive ability. Rather, as discussed in chapters 4 and 5 on interpretation, a cognitive test assesses diverse cognitive abilities, all of which need to be understood. The person's pattern of strengths and weaknesses on the four Indexes is far more important to interpret than FSIQ. The g loadings do represent how well psychometrically the subtests hang together as a whole but do not reflect a theoretical construct that underlies human intellect. The g loadings do offer aids to clinical interpretation by providing expectancies. For example, Arithmetic's high g loading and strong loading on the fluid reasoning Factor in Keith's CFA lead us to expect that a person will score about as well on the Arithmetic subtest as he or she scored on FSIQ and PRI. If, for example, the person scored much lower on Arithmetic than on FSIQ and PRI, that is contrary to expectations and we would seek an explanation, such as distractibility, anxiety, poor working memory, or poor ability to manipulate numbers. By contrast, an

---

2. Wechsler's (1974) quote has been modified to avoid sexist language but is otherwise verbatim.

extremely high or low score on Cancellation is anticipated and would not cause us to think twice about it.

COMPREHENSIVE REFERENCES ON TEST

The *WAIS-IV Administrative and Scoring Manual* (Wechsler, 2008) and the *WAIS-IV Technical and Interpretive Manual* (Psychological Corporation, 2008) currently provide the most detailed information about the WAIS-IV. These manuals review the development of the test, descriptions of each of the subtests and scales, standardization, reliability, and validity. *Assessing Adolescent and Adult Intelligence, Third Edition* (Kaufman & Lichtenberger, 2006) provides an excellent review of the research on the WAIS, WAIS-R, and WAIS-III, much of which is still pertinent for the WAIS-IV. Rapid Reference 1.9 provides basic information on the WAIS-IV and its publisher. The forthcoming books on the WAIS-IV by Sattler and Ryan (in press) and Weiss, Saklofske, Coalson, and Raiford (in press), along with

---

≡ Rapid Reference 1.9

Wechsler Adult Intelligence Scale—Fourth Edition

Author: David Wechsler

Publication Date: 2008

What the Test Measures: verbal comprehension, perceptual reasoning, working memory, processing speed, and general intelligence

Age Range: 16–90 years

Administration Time: 10 core subtests to obtain 4 indexes = 65–90 minutes; 15 core and supplemental subtests = 85–114 minutes

Qualification of Examiners: Graduate- or professional-level training in psychological assessment

Publisher: Pearson

19500 Bulverde Road

San Antonio, TX 78259

Customer Service: (800) 211–8378

http://pearsonassess.com

Price: WAIS-IV Basic Kit: Includes *Administration and Scoring Manual, Technical Manual,* 2 Stimulus Books, 25 Record Forms, 25 Response Booklet #1, 25 Response Booklet #2, Symbol Search Scoring Key, Coding Scoring Key, Cancellation Scoring Templates in a box. ISBN: 015-8980-808. $1,079.00 (in box); $1,139.00 (in hard- or soft-sided case).

Essentials of WAIS-IV Assessment, provide the most authoritative sources for administering, scoring, interpreting, and applying WAIS-IV test profiles.

📎 TEST YOURSELF 📎

1. Many of the tasks that David Wechsler used in his WAIS, WAIS-R, WAIS-III, and WAIS-IV were adapted from what sources?

2. Updating the WAIS-IV's theoretical foundations was achieved by considering the following theoretical constructs EXCEPT
   (a) Fluid reasoning
   (b) Working memory
   (c) Processing speed
   (d) Phonological processing

3. What was the major structural change implemented from the WAIS-III to the WAIS-IV?

4. Which of the following WAIS-IV subtests is a CORE subtest that is used to compute FSIQ?
   (a) Visual Puzzles
   (b) Letter-Number Sequencing
   (c) Picture Completion
   (d) Comprehension
   (e) Figure Weights

5. Which subtest is NOT new to the WAIS-IV?
   (a) Visual Puzzles
   (b) Figure Weights
   (c) Cancellation
   (d) Symbol Search

6. Which WAIS-IV subtest does NOT offer Process scores?
   (a) Digit Span
   (b) Visual Puzzles
   (c) Block Design
   (d) Letter-Number Sequencing

7. The results of confirmatory factor analysis that supported a Five-Factor CHC model showed three WAIS-IV subtests to load highly on the fluid reasoning (Gf) factor. These subtests are Figure Weights, Matrix Reasoning, and
   (a) Block Design
   (b) Picture Completion

(c) Letter-Number Sequencing

(d) Similarities

(e) Arithmetic

8. **Which index includes the subtests with the lowest loadings on the general (g) factor?**

(a) Verbal Comprehension

(b) Perceptual Reasoning

(c) Working Memory

(d) Processing Speed

Answers: 1. Army Alpha, Army Beta, Army Performance Scale Examination, and Stanford-Binet; 2. d; 3. Removal of the VIQ and PIQ; 4. a; 5. d; 6. b; 7. e; 8. d.

Two

HOW TO ADMINISTER THE WAIS-IV

One of the strengths of a standardized test, such as the WAIS-IV, is that it is able to provide scores that represent an individual's performance compared to other individuals of about the same age. However, to obtain results that are comparable to the national norms, examiners must be careful to adhere to the same administration and scoring procedures that were used during the standardization of the test. At the same time, examiners must not be rigid and unnatural in their manner of presentation. Thus, a delicate balancing act must take place to ensure the best possible administration.

APPROPRIATE TESTING CONDITIONS

Testing Environment

The physical surroundings in which the testing takes place may vary. Some examiners may test in a school, office, clinic, nursing home, or hospital, whereas others may find it necessary to test in a home. The most important features of the testing environment are that it is quiet, free of distractions and interruption, and comfortable for the examinee. The ideal situation would provide a room for only you, the examiner, and the examinee, as the presence of a third person can be disruptive.

A table is a necessity for testing. Since writing and drawing will be done, a smooth tabletop is ideal; however, a clipboard may provide a smooth writing surface if the table is rough. It is recommended that you sit opposite the examinee. This arrangement allows easy observation of test taking behaviors as well as easy manipulation of all test materials by the examiner.

Testing Materials

The WAIS-IV has become less cumbersome with its manipulatives than previous versions of the Wechsler tests. Because Object Assembly and Picture Arrangement were eliminated from the test battery, only Block Design requires any materials other than a stimulus book for the examiner to handle. There are still materials that need to be organized, such as the *WAIS-IV Administration and Scoring Manual*, Record Form, Stimulus Booklet, pencils, and stopwatch. However, experienced Wechsler test users will breathe a sigh of relief that they no longer have to try to hide Object Assembly pieces behind a shield while trying to pick up dropped pieces off the floor as they get them out of the box. Experienced examiners also will be able to stop sweating because they cannot find number two of the five Picture Arrangement cards. Generally, the WAIS-IV materials allow an efficient, user-friendly test administration, if examiners are well rehearsed.

During the testing, only the materials necessary for the task at hand should be on the table. Visible presence of other testing materials, such as the Block Design blocks or Symbol Search booklet, may be distracting or cause anxiety. Many examiners find it useful to place unused test materials on a chair close to them but out of the examinee's view.

Position the *Manual* so that it provides a shield behind which you can place the Record Form. This setup allows you to have easy access to all of the directions but makes the record of the examinee's scores less visible. However, you should avoid being secretive.

Almost everything needed to perform the assessment is included in the WAIS-IV kit. Necessary testing materials that do not come with the WAIS-IV kit include: stopwatch, extra #2 graphite pencils without erasers, clipboard, your own pen/pencil for recording responses, and extra paper for taking notes.

DON'T FORGET
....
Keys for Preparing to Administer the Test

- Quiet, distraction-free room
- Table large enough for two
- Smooth writing surface

Extra needed materials not in the WAIS-IV kit:
- Two #2 pencils without erasers
- Stopwatch
- Clipboard
- Extra paper and writing implement (just in case)

RAPPORT WITH EXAMINEE

Providing a comfortable interpersonal situation for the examinee is key to obtaining the best possible administration. Throughout the assessment session, it is important to facilitate a positive rapport. The tone of conversation should be natural, pleasant, and professional. To provide this natural and smooth interpersonal interaction, it is important to be completely familiar with all of the administration and scoring procedures of the test. If you are uncertain of how a task is to be administered or are fumbling with the testing materials, this indecision will likely cause awkward pauses and take away attention from the person who is being tested. Although it is not necessary to memorize the test manual, it will be extremely advantageous to be completely familiar with the details of the *Manual*, such as wording of the directions and when particular test materials should be used. Also, it is important to know exactly where to locate the needed information regarding start, stop, and timing rules.

Establishing Rapport

To facilitate building rapport at the beginning of the testing session, it is a good idea for you to provide a general introduction to the test, as was done during the collection of the standardization sample. Questions or concerns that the examinee may have should be addressed at this time too. As stated in the standard WAIS-IV instructions, some time should be spent explaining to the examinee that most test takers find some questions easy and some questions quite difficult, which helps to reassure them that it is okay if they do not know every answer. Elderly individuals may voice concern about their memory or ability to maneuver objects quickly. They should be reassured that they just need to do the best they can. They also may be told that the scores they earn are always based on the test performance of other adults about their age.

Maintaining Rapport

Once the testing has begun, care should be taken to adhere to the standardized language given in the *Manual*. However, small talk and reassuring statements are also needed throughout the testing to promote a comfortable testing environment. You must be vigilant in watching the examinee's level of fatigue, anxiety, and cooperation. Speeded tests or tests requiring fine motor coordination may be more taxing for older adults; thus, signs of fatigue should be considered, especially if testing an older person. If anything, such as loss of motivation, tiredness, or nervousness, appears to be impinging on the examinee's performance, you should try to insert more casual conversation between the subtests or provide more supportive statements. When providing supportive or encouraging statements, you should be careful not to give clues regarding the correctness of an examinee's answer. Indeed, it is important *not* to give encouraging comments and feedback *only* when an examinee is doing poorly or to praise only when correct. This type of selective feedback may inadvertently give cues to individuals that they are responding correctly or incorrectly to items, based on the examiner's verbalizations. Examinees should be praised for their level of effort ("You are really working hard"), or recognized for attempting items that were notably difficult ("Those were tough ones, but you're trying hard. Let's try another one.").

DON'T FORGET
....

Keys to Positive Examiner–Examinee Rapport during Assessment

1. Effectively introduce examinee to the testing activities by using the standardized introduction on page 63 of the *WAIS-IV Administration and Scoring Manual*; begin establishing rapport.

2. Interact comfortably with examinee. Don't be stilted.

3. Give eye contact. Don't bury your head in the *Manual*.

4. Make smooth transitions *between* subtests. Use some small talk.

5. Avoid small talk *during* a subtest.

6. Familiarize yourself ahead of time with test directions and test materials.

7. Use precise wording of questions and directions. Only the mildest of paraphrasing is acceptable occasionally.

8. Be subtle, not distracting, when using a stopwatch.

Breaks during testing are allowed but should be taken only between two subtests, not in the middle of a subtest. If an adult's level of motivation has been clearly lowered during a very difficult subtest, some encouraging comments plus a brief break may be warranted. If, during a challenging subtest, an examinee indicates that he or she will not go on, you may need to provide encouragement, such as "Just try your best" or "Give it your best shot." During administration of timed subtests, you will find it useful to allow examinees to have a few extra seconds past the time limit to work if they are actively involved in the task. These little tips in administration may lessen potential discouragement and will extend rapport throughout the session.

CAUTION

Appropriate Feedback and Encouragement

- Praise and encourage the examinee's level of effort.
- Be careful *not* to give feedback on whether a particular response is right or wrong.
- Give encouragement throughout items, not just when examinee is struggling.

TESTING INDIVIDUALS WITH SPECIAL NEEDS

Adults or adolescents with special needs for testing may include those who have hearing impairment, visual problems, or motor difficulties, or those who are not fluent in English. When testing such adults, special consideration needs to be taken to accommodate the particular examinee while maintaining standardized procedures to the degree possible.

It is important for you to obtain as much information as possible about the adolescent's or adult's impairment prior to the assessment session with the individual. You should ask a caregiver about the examinee's vision, hearing, physical condition, or any other limitations. With this information, you will be able to determine how the test procedures need to be modified. Testing should be done in such a manner that the examinee is not penalized because of sensory or motor deficits. If major modifications in the standardized procedure are made, these changes may impact test scores or invalidate the use of the norms. Clinical judgment must be used to determine whether the examinee's impairment prohibits obtaining valid scores on part or all of the test.

CAUTION

Modifying Standardized Procedure

- Modifications to the standardized procedure to accommodate examinees' limitations may invalidate test scores.
- Clinical judgment is key in determining what quantitative and qualitative data are interpretable from the test administration.
  - Adaptations made in the time limits allowed on speeded subtests will invalidate the use of the norms.
  - Translating the test into another language may also cause problems in interpreting the scores.

Modifications to the test administration to accommodate an examinee's special needs may include:

- Administering the test in American Sign Language to a deaf individual (if you are specially trained)
- Adding printed words to facilitate understanding of directions to hard-of-hearing individuals
- Administering only the Verbal Scale subtests to a blind individual
- Eliminating time limits for adolescents or adults with motor difficulties
- Extending the testing over more than one session for any adult with special needs

When any modification is used, such as translation into another language, problems in interpreting the scores may arise. Careful consideration must be given to determine whether using such modifications is best or whether choosing another instrument or supplemental instruments may provide the most useful information.

ADMINISTRATION CONSIDERATIONS

Starting and Discontinuing Subtests

The administration rules have been simplified from the WAIS-III to the WAIS-IV, which aids in the efficient administration of the tasks. The discontinue rules of many subtests have been reduced by at least one item (e.g., from four consecutive failures to three). The Vocabulary and Information subtests reduced their discontinue rules from six to three consecutive failures. Important rules such as when to begin and end each subtest are clearly listed both in the *Manual* and on the Record Form itself. The general overall rules are described here.

Many of the subtests on the WAIS-IV start at items other than 1; these subtests are clearly listed on the Record Form. This procedure allows examiners to curtail testing time for most adults, but it also enables them to administer earlier, simpler items to adults who cannot correctly answer items at the designated starting point. Most often examinees who are functioning at a low intellectual level will need to go back to these easier items. The rule employed to enable examiners to go back to easier items if the first set of items causes difficulty is called the "reverse rule." Reverse rules require administration of earlier subtest items in reverse order if a perfect score is not obtained on *either* of the first two items administered. Until the examinee obtains perfect scores on two consecutive items, this reversal procedure continues. Sample Items are not part of the reverse-sequence procedure. Figures 2.2, 2.3, and 2.4 in the *WAIS-IV Administration and Scoring Manual* show examples of how the reverse rules are applied. These Verbal Comprehension and Working Memory subtests use a reverse rule: Similarities, Vocabulary, Arithmetic, Information, and Comprehension. The Perceptual Reasoning subtests with a reverse rule are: Block Design, Matrix Reasoning, Visual Puzzles, Figure Weights, and Picture Completion. Rapid Reference 2.1 summarizes the start and reverse rules for the subtests.

≡ Rapid Reference 2.1

Summary of Subtest Start Points and Reverse Rules

Subtest	Start Point	Reverse Rule
Block Design	Sample Item, then Item 5	Score of 0 or 1 on either Item 5 or Item 6, administer preceding items in reverse order until two consecutive perfect scores are obtained
Similarities	Sample Item, then Item 4	Score of 0 or 1 on either Item 4 or Item 5, administer preceding items in reverse order until two consecutive perfect scores are obtained
Digit Span	Forward: Item 1 Backward: Sample Item, then Item 1 Sequencing: Sample Item, then Item 1	None
Matrix Reasoning	Sample Items A and B, then Item 4	Score of 0 on either Item 4 or Item 5, administer preceding items in reverse order until two consecutive perfect scores are obtained
Vocabulary	Item 5	Score of 0 or 1 on either Item 5 or Item 6, administer preceding items in reverse order until two consecutive perfect scores are obtained
Arithmetic	Sample Item, then Item 6	Score of 0 on either Item 6 or Item 7, administer preceding items in reverse order until two consecutive perfect scores are obtained

(continued)

Subtest	Start Point	Reverse Rule
Symbol Search	Demonstration Items, Sample Items, then Test Items	None
Visual Puzzles	Demonstration Item, Sample Item, then Item 5	Score of 0 on either Item 5 or Item 6, administer preceding items in reverse order until two consecutive perfect scores are obtained
Information	Item 3	Score of 0 on either Item 3 or Item 4, administer preceding items in reverse order until two consecutive perfect scores are obtained
Coding	Demonstration Items, Sample Items, then Test Items	None
Letter-Number Sequencing	Demonstration Item A, Sample Item A, then Item 1	None
Figure Weights	Demonstration Items A and B, Sample Item, then Item 4	Score of 0 on either Item 4 or Item 5, administer preceding items in reverse order until two consecutive perfect scores are obtained
Comprehension	Item 3	Score of 0 or 1 on either Item 3 or Item 4, administer preceding items in reverse order until two consecutive perfect scores are obtained
Cancellation	Demonstration Item A, Sample Item A, then Item 1	None
Picture Completion	Sample Item, then Item 4	Score of 0 on either Item 4 or Item 5, administer preceding items in reverse order until two consecutive perfect scores are obtained

Source: From Table 2.7 of the *WAIS-IV Administration and Scoring Manual.* Copyright © 2008 The Psychological Corporation. Adapted and reproduced by permission. All rights reserved.

In contrast, the Verbal subtests that do not use a reverse rule include Digit Span and Letter-Number Sequencing. None of the Processing Speed Subtests uses reverse rules, and these subtests end when a specified time has elapsed. A summary of discontinue rules for each subtest can be found in Rapid

≡ *Rapid Reference 2.2*

· ·

Summary of Subtest Discontinue Rules

Subtest	Discontinue Rule
Block Design	After 2 consecutive scores of 0
Similarities	After 3 consecutive scores of 0
Digit Span	Forward: After scores of 0 on both trials of an item
	Backward: After scores of 0 on both trials of an item
	Sequencing: After scores of 0 on both trials of an item
Matrix Reasoning	After 3 consecutive scores of 0
Vocabulary	After 3 consecutive scores of 0
Arithmetic	After 3 consecutive scores of 0
Symbol Search	After 120 seconds
Visual Puzzles	After 3 consecutive scores of 0
Information	After 3 consecutive scores of 0
Coding	After 120 seconds
Letter-Number Sequencing	After scores of 0 on all three trials of an item
Figure Weights	After 3 consecutive scores of 0
Comprehension	After 3 consecutive scores of 0
Cancellation	After 45 seconds for each item
Picture Completion	After 4 consecutive scores of 0

Source: From Table 2.7 of the *WAIS-IV Administration and Scoring Manual.* Copyright © 2008 The Psychological Corporation. Adapted and reproduced by permission. All rights reserved.

Reference 2.2. More detail is also provided in the Subtest-by-Subtest Guide later in this chapter.

Sometimes during administration of a subtest, it may be unclear how to score a response and, therefore, whether the subtest should be discontinued. This situation occurs most frequently during the Vocabulary, Similarities, and Comprehension subtests that have some subjectivity in their scoring. If it is not possible to determine quickly whether a response is correct, it is best to continue administering further items until you are certain that the discontinue rule has been met. This procedure is safest because the scores can always be reviewed later and items that are passed after the discontinue criterion has been met can (indeed, must) be excluded from the adult's raw score on the subtest (although such successes on hard items may provide you with valuable *clinical* information).

However, if upon review of the scores it is noted that items should have been administered beyond where the subtest was ended, it will be too late, and the test may be unscorable.

CAUTION

Common General Errors in Administration

- Forgetting that if the examinee gets the second item administered *partially* correct, you may have to apply the reverse rule (even though the examinee got the first item administered correct)
- Forgetting that when applying the reverse rule, you administer until *two* consecutive perfect scores are obtained, *including* previously administered items
- Forgetting to administer enough items to meet the discontinue rule

---

Recording Responses

While administering the WAIS-IV, it is crucial to write down responses for all items administered or attempted. This recording is especially important for Verbal Comprehension subtests, such as Vocabulary, Similarities, Information, and Comprehension. However, even brief verbal responses produced in Arithmetic, Digit Span, Letter-Number Sequencing, and Picture Completion are important to record. Some examiners are tempted to write down only *a score* for a subject's response to an item, but this practice is discouraged. Irretrievable information may be lost if only a "0" or "1" is recorded. Useful clinical information and patterns in responding may be apparent when all responses are written down. When recording what an examinee says, you should try to capture most of what is said verbatim. Using abbreviations frequently helps balance the maintenance of rapport with the recording of essential information. At times you will find it necessary to record your own statements. For example, if you probe to clarify an answer by saying "Tell me more about that," you should always record a "(Q)" on the Record Form directly after the response that you queried to indicate that you had to prompt the adult. When interpreting the recorded information clinically, you may then want to note whether many responses were elicited by querying or whether the examinee produced them spontaneously. It is also of clinical value to note adolescents' or adults' response to queries: Did they usually improve the quality of their answers? Did they tend not to add anything to their first responses, saying simply "Don't know"? Did they talk and talk after a query yet fail to improve their item scores?

≡ Rapid Reference 2.3

Abbreviations for Recording Responses

@	At
B	Both
DK	Don't know
EO	Everyone
F	Fail (examinee responded incorrectly)
INC	Incomplete (Response wasn't completed within the time limit)
LL	Looks Like
NR	No Response
OT	Overtime
P	Pass (examinee responded correctly)
Prmt	Prompt
PC	Points correctly
PPL	People
PX	Points incorrectly
Q	Question or Query
R	Are
Shd	Should
SO	Someone
ST	Something
↓	Decrease
↑	Increase
U	You
w/	With
w/o	Without
Wld	Would

Timing

All of the Perceptual Reasoning subtests, except Matrix Reasoning, require a stopwatch for exact timing, as do both of the Processing Speed subtests and Arithmetic on the Working Memory Index. Careful planning is necessary when administering these seven subtests so that the timing is not distracting to the examinee. The watch should be unobtrusive, but if the examinee asks whether he or she is being timed, you may want to say something like: "Yes, but you don't need to worry about that." When giving directions to these subtests, you must have your stopwatch ready to go because properly starting the timing exactly when the examinee is told to begin is critical. Impulsive individuals, for example, may start even sooner than you would anticipate, and you must be ready to time them immediately.

DON'T FORGET

A stopwatch is needed for:
- Block Design
- Arithmetic
- Symbol Search

- Visual Puzzles
- Coding
- Figure Weights

- Cancellation
- Picture Completion

Once the timing for an item has begun, it is important to remember that even if the examinee asks for clarification or repetition of the instructions, the timing is to continue. On some of the subtests, such as Block Design, the examinee may not tell you when he or she is finished (although you request that the examinee do so in the directions). Closely observe the examinees. If it appears that they have completed an item, you should ask, "Are you done?" and immediately record the time. Similarly, if you had stopped the time because you thought the examinee was done, and then the examinee continues working, be sure to restart the stopwatch and to count the entire time during which the examinee was working (which requires you to estimate the number of seconds that the stopwatch was off).

Querying

At times, an examinee's response may be too vague or ambiguous to score. When such answers are given, you need to ask the examinee to clarify his or her response. The *Manual* lists responses to Vocabulary, Similarities, Comprehension, and Information items that should be queried, but these responses are only illustrative. Examiner judgment is necessary to query similar responses to ones listed in the *Manual's* scoring system. The key is incompleteness or ambiguity. Examiners may query even responses that are *not* queried in the *Manual* if the examinee's voice or face suggests confusion or uncertainty. The manner in which you ask for clarification is crucial. Questioning or querying should be done with neutral statements. For example, say: "Tell me more about that," or "Explain what you mean." Be careful not to provide any hints or clues to the answer when you are querying, except when following the *Manual*'s specific queries (e.g., "Tell me another reason why child labor laws are needed."). If the examinee spontaneously produces a completely incorrect answer, you do not want to query. As mentioned earlier when discussing recording responses, queried responses should be indicated on the record form with a "Q." As a rule, it is best to query with a gentle command ("Tell me more") than with a question. The easiest response to "Can you tell me more about it?" is "No."

Repeating Items

The general rule for repeating questions or instructions is that you may do so if the examinee requests it or if the examinee does not seem to understand the task at hand. However, for Digit Span and Letter-Number Sequencing, an item trial may not be repeated, and in Arithmetic, a question may be repeated only one time. When questions are repeated, the entire verbal question, not just a portion of it, should be repeated.

Occasionally you may find that examinees are able to provide answers to more difficult items on a subtest when they responded "I don't know" to earlier, easier items. When this situation occurs, you can readminister the earlier items if you believe that an examinee knows the answers to the items. Anxiety or insecurity may have originally interfered with the subject's responses on the easier items, or the person's behaviors may have been responsible for a few quick "Don't knows" before being able to take a risk. However, you may not readminister timed items or items on the Digit Span subtest.

Teaching the Task

Sample items and the first two items administered on many of the WAIS-IV subtests are included to ensure that examinees understand what they are supposed to do to respond to the items on the subtest. These items afford the opportunity to give extra instruction if an examinee fails one of the first items in the subtest. This teaching after a failed item does not change an adolescent's or adult's score, but it does provide clarification of the directions. The underlying premise of teaching the task is that examinees should be given the opportunity to do as well as possible on items and that the items should be measuring their ability to do the task, not their ability to quickly grasp the instructions.

DON'T FORGET

....

When to Teach the Task

Subtest	Demonstration Item	Sample Item	Test Item
Block Design	No	Yes	No
Similarities	No	Yes	4 & 5
Digit Span	No	Yes	No
Matrix Reasoning	No	Yes	No
Vocabulary	No	No	5 & 6
Arithmetic	No	Yes	I & 2
Symbol Search	Yes	Yes	No
Visual Puzzles	Yes	Yes	No
Information	No	No	3 & 4
Coding	Yes	Yes	No
Letter-Number Sequencing	Yes	Yes	I & 2
Figure Weights	Yes	Yes	No
Comprehension	No	No	3 & 4
Cancellation	Yes	Yes	No
Picture Completion	No	Yes	4 & 5

Note: Teaching the task is allowed only when specified in the directions. The table summarizes when teaching the task is acceptable; typically it is acceptable during the Demonstration Item, Sample Item, or first two items administered. Providing answers beyond what is stated in the instructions will lead to an inaccurate assessment of the examinee's abilities.

SUBTEST-BY-SUBTEST RULES OF ADMINISTRATION

Detailed rules for subtest-by-subtest administration are provided in the WAIS-IV *Manual.* Some important reminders for competent administration of each of the subtests are presented here. This section may be used as a guide or to refresh your memory if you have already learned the details of the test. The subtests are listed in order of administration. During administration of the WAIS-IV, it is important to be an astute observer of an examinee's behavior. Such behavioral observations can give great insight into how to interpret a particular subtest, and patterns of behavior across many subtests may also be critical in the process of interpretation. After the rules of each subtest, key behaviors to watch for are suggested.

Block Design

This Performance subtest has many details to which the examiner needs to attend. Prior to administration, make sure that all of the materials are ready to be used, including: box of 9 blocks, Stimulus Booklet with model forms, stopwatch, *Manual*, and Record Form. Correct positioning of the adult and the blocks is crucial to facilitate proper administration. The block model must be at a distance 7 inches away from the edge of the table, and beside the Stimulus Booklet (see Figure 3.1 in the *WAIS-IV Administration and Scoring Manual*). An important part of this Block Design task is being able to understand the relationship between two-dimensional representations and three-dimensional representations. The first four items provide a model that is three-dimensional (in addition to the two-dimensional figure in the Stimulus Booklet) and that is then recreated by the examinee in three-dimensional space. Items 5 through 14 require the adult to perceive and visually analyze the *two*-dimensional model, and then re-create it in *three*-dimensional space. This type of problem is more complex than those that utilize three dimensions for both the model and the examinees' design. When the two-dimensional models are shown in the Stimulus Book, some of the visual cues are removed, such as the lines that distinguish one block from another. In general, the whole administration procedure is set up as a learning situation that shapes the adult from simple three-dimensional designs to complex 9-block designs depicted in pictures. In fact, the final item removes the square outline of the design such that only the red portions of the design are distinguishable from the white page on which the design is presented.

Blocks must have a variety of faces showing before each administration, so as to not bias or help the examinee. Careful timing is important for scoring. At times, adults may not verbalize when they have completed a design. In such instances, learn to rely on nonverbal cues to determine when to stop timing. If necessary, ask the adult if he or she is done. No credit should be awarded if it takes the examinee longer than the allowed time to complete a given Block Design item.

Lists of important Block Design rules are presented next. Important behaviors to watch for and note while administering the Block Design subtest are listed in Rapid Reference 2.4.

Start, Reverse, Discontinue Rules
- Examinees ages 16 to 90 begin with the Sample Item and then proceed to item 5.
- If scores of 0 are obtained on either Item 5 or 6, then administer the proceeding items in reverse order until two consecutive perfect scores are obtained.
- Discontinue after two consecutive scores of 0.

≡ *Rapid Reference 2.4*
....

Behaviors to Note on Block Design

• Observe problem-solving styles during adults' manipulation of the blocks. Some use a trial-and-error approach whereas others systematically examine and appear to carefully plan before moving any of the blocks.

• Observe whether the subject tends to pair up blocks and then integrates the smaller segments into the whole. On the designs requiring 9 blocks, observe whether examinees work from the outside in or perhaps start in one corner and work their way around the design.

• Motor coordination and hand preference may be apparent during this task. Note whether individuals seem clumsy in their manipulation of the blocks or have hands that are noticeably trembling, or whether they move very quickly and steadily.

• Look to see whether examinees refer back to the model while they are working. This could be indicative of visual memory ability, cautiousness, or other factors.

• Examine whether adults tend to be obsessively concerned with details (such as lining up the blocks perfectly). Such behaviors may negatively impact the examinee's speed.

• Observe how well examinees persist, especially when the task becomes more difficult and they may face frustration. Note how well they tolerate frustration.

• Look to see whether examinees lose the square shape for some designs, even if they have managed to re-create the overall pattern. This kind of response could be indicative of figure-ground problems.

• Note whether adults are noticeably twisting their bodies to obtain a different perspective on the model or are rotating their own designs. Such behaviors may be indicative of visual-perceptual difficulties.

• It is important also to note whether examinees fail to recognize that their designs look different from the models.

Other Rules

• Begin timing after saying the last word of instructions.

• Place the Stimulus Booklet approximately 7 inches from the edge of the table, and place the model of the block design beside the Stimulus Booklet for items 1 to 4.

• Make sure the proper variety of faces of the blocks are showing before each item (i.e., some red, some white, and some red and white).

• Rotations of 30 degrees or more are considered failures. Rotations may be corrected only *once* during the subtest.

• Remember to give the extra 5 blocks for Item 11.

- Record responses by drawing the design of blocks made by the examinee.
- No special administration is necessary for the Block Design No Time Bonus Process score, as the score is simply calculated from the regular administration of Block Design.

Similarities

The Similarities subtest is not difficult to administer. The only materials needed are the *Manual* and the Record Form. It is important to be aware of what types of answers need to be queried (those that are vague and those specifically listed in the *Manual*). When querying, you must present the question to the examinee in a neutral fashion. This verbal subtest also requires careful recording of verbal responses. A detailed description of scoring of each subtest is presented in chapter 3 of this book as well as in the WAIS-IV *Manual.*

To succeed in Similarities, examinees must understand that abstraction is necessary. For this reason, on Items 4 and 5 are teaching items on which corrective feedback is given if an examinee does not spontaneously produce a correct 2-point response. These examples allow opportunity for examinees to hear that a response involving a higher degree of abstraction is more desirable than a purely concrete response.

Lists of important queries and other Similarities rules for the Similarities subtest are presented next. Rapid Reference 2.5 lists behaviors to note on Similarities.

≡ *Rapid Reference 2.5*

Behaviors to Note on Similarities

- Observe whether the adult benefits from feedback on Item 4 (if feedback was given). Adults who learn from the example given by the examiner may have flexibility whereas those who cannot learn from the example may be more rigid or concrete.
- Observe whether the quality of response decreases as the items become more difficult.
- Length of verbal responses gives an important behavioral clue. Overly elaborate responses may suggest obsessiveness.
- Quick responses or abstract responses to easy items may indicate overlearned associations rather than high-level abstract reasoning.

Start, Reverse, Discontinue Rules
- Examinees ages 16 to 90 begin with the Sample Item and then proceed to Item 4.
- If scores of 0 or 1 are obtained on either Item 4 or 5, then administer the proceeding items in reverse order until two consecutive perfect scores are obtained.
- Discontinue after three consecutive scores of 0.

Queries
- Use neutral questions to query vague or incomplete responses.
- Query multiple responses appropriately if wrong answers are included with correct ones or if "differences" are given.
- Do not query a string of responses; rather, score the best one if none is clearly wrong.

Other Rules
- Give an example of a 2-point response if the examinee's responses to either Item 4 or Item 5 are not perfect.
- Use the general distinctions between responses scored 2, 1, or 0 (see pp. 74–75 of *WAIS-IV Administration and Scoring Manual*).

Digit Span

Previous Wechsler scales, including the WAIS-III and WISC-IV, included two sections of Digit Span, the Forward and Backward series. The WAIS-IV added a third section, which requires the individual to repeat the numbers back in ascending order. Thus, WAIS-IV Digit Span is administered in three separate sections: Digit Span Forward, Digit Span Backward, and Digit Span Sequencing. However, the administration of each of these parts is quite similar. To administer this subtest, only the Record Form with the number sequences and the *Manual* are needed, along with a slow, steady voice. The key to administering this subtest is reading the series of digits at the proper rate: one digit per second. At times, some examinees will jump in and begin to respond before all of the numbers in the sequence have been read. Examinees should be encouraged to wait until the entire sequence of numbers has been read before responding. Digit Span Backward and Digit Span Sequencing each provide two examples of what is required before the scored items are administered. If examinees respond correctly to the first sample, then Trial 2 of the Sample Item should be administered immediately; however, if they respond incorrectly to the first trial of the Sample Item on either the Backward or Sequencing task, provide the corrective feedback and explanation from the *Manual* before proceeding to the

≡ *Rapid Reference 2.6*

Behaviors to Note on Digit Span

- Note whether adults are attempting to use a problem-solving strategy such as "chunking." Some examinees will use such a strategy from the beginning, and others will learn a strategy as they progress through the task.
- Note whether errors are due simply to transposing numbers or to completely forgetting numbers.
- Attention, hearing impairment, and anxiety can impact this test; therefore, such difficulties should be noted if present.
- Watch for rapid repetition of digits or beginning to repeat the digits before you have completed the series. Such behavior may be indicative of impulsivity.
- Observe whether there is a pattern of failing the first trial and then correctly responding to the second trial. Such a response pattern may be indicative of learning or may simply be a warm-up effect.

second trial. Careful recording of the subject's individual responses on this subtest can provide useful interpretive information.

Digit Span Forward is measuring a different aspect of memory from that of Digit Span Backward and Sequencing. The Backward and Sequencing tasks require more mental manipulation and visualization of numbers, whereas the Forward task can be done with simple rote recall. Careful attention to processing and problem-solving style can be useful for interpretation.

Lists of important Digit Span rules are presented next. Important behaviors to watch for and note while administering the Digit Span subtest are listed in Rapid Reference 2.6.

Start and Discontinue Rules

- For all ages, begin with Item 1 on the Forward Task but with the Sample Items on the Backward and Sequencing Tasks.
- There are three separate discontinue points (one for Forward, one for Backward, and one for Sequencing). For each task, discontinue after scores of 0 on both trials on an item.

General Rules

- Say the numbers at a steady rate of one per second.
- Do not "chunk" the numbers into small groups.
- Drop your voice on the last digit of each series of items.
- Remember to give the second trial of each item, whether the first trial is passed or not.

- Administer Digit Span Backward even if subject obtains a 0 on Digit Span Forward.
- Administer Digit Span Sequencing even if the examinee obtains a 0 on the Forward and Backward tasks.
- Read directions exactly; do not give extra help on Digit Span Backward or Digit Span Sequencing.

Matrix Reasoning

The Stimulus Booklet, containing four types of nonverbal reasoning tasks, the Record Form, and the *Manual* are necessary for this subtest. Two Sample Items begin Matrix Analogies. The items are included to ensure that the examinee understands what is expected in the task. The standardized procedure includes teaching the task via alternative explanation if necessary. As items become progressively more difficult, some examinees may be tempted to guess for their response. If guessing occurs, such individuals should be instructed to try to reason out the solution rather than taking random guesses. It is important to note that because there is no time limit, some examinees may take a significant amount of time to solve the problems. However, the *WAIS-IV Administration and Scoring Manual* suggests that you should encourage a response after approximately 30 seconds, if the examinee has not responded.

≡ *Rapid Reference 2.7*

. . . .

Behaviors to Note on Matrix Reasoning

- Note whether adults talk their way through the problems, using verbal mediation, or whether they are more apt to simply use mental imagery to work to the solution.
- Observe whether examinees need to touch the Stimulus Booklet to aid in their problem solving. Touching the stimuli may help some adults visualize the solution.
- Although this test is not timed, note whether adults process the information slowly, carefully, and methodically, or whether they work more quickly and impulsively.
- Observe whether examinees are distracted by unessential detail, such as color, if the solution to the problem only requires noting the shape and number of objects.
- Note whether adults attend to part of the stimuli but miss other essential parts to complete the matrix successfully.
- Make note of signs of frustration or anxiety, especially when the problems become more complex.
- Note whether examinees' problem solving includes trying each of the given possible solutions one by one, or first attempting to come up with a solution and then checking the row of choices to find the solution that they had created.

Lists of important Matrix Reasoning rules follow. Important behaviors to watch for and note while administering the Matrix Reasoning subtest are listed in Rapid Reference 2.7.

Start, Reverse, and Discontinue Rules
• Start administration with Samples A and B in forward order.
• Illustrate the correct response if A or B is incorrect. Provide an alternative explanation to the problem if necessary.
• Regardless of performance on Sample Items, proceed to Item 4.
• If examinee scores a 0 on either item 4 or item 5, then administer preceding items in reverse order until 2 consecutive perfect scores are obtained.

General Rules
• Point correctly to the response choices in the Stimulus Booklet when indicating from which ones the examinee may choose.
• No teaching or feedback should be given on Items 1–26.
• Examinee should not be allowed to guess randomly.
• Adults who are color blind will have impaired performance on this subtest. If information about such difficulties is not offered spontaneously by the examinee, be sure to inquire whether color blindness may be affecting the responses.

Vocabulary

This subtest requires Stimulus Booklet 1 for administration of the first three picture items. Stimulus Booklet 1 is also used to present a visual list of vocabulary words as they are read aloud by the examiner for Items 4–30. The *Manual* and Record Form must also be used during administration. Scoring should be completed as responses are recorded, to the degree possible. As mentioned previously, it is best to continue administering items if you are unsure if a difficult-to-score response will affect the discontinue rule. Because it may be necessary to review responses after the test is over, it is critical to record the exact response of the examinee as much as possible. One of the most challenging aspects of Vocabulary is querying vague responses appropriately. Be careful to use only *neutral* queries when prompting for more information. Scoring can also be difficult, as there is some subjectivity. (See chapter 3.)

Lists of important queries and other Vocabulary rules are presented next. Important behaviors to watch for and note while administering the Vocabulary subtest are listed in Rapid Reference 2.8.

Rapid Reference 2.8

Behaviors to Note on Vocabulary

- Make note of "I don't know" responses, as such responses may be indicative of adults with word retrieval problems who struggle with this test. Word fluency can impact an individual's performance as much as his or her word knowledge.

- Hearing difficulties may be apparent on this test. The Vocabulary words are not presented in a meaningful context (although they are presented in written as well as oral form). Because the words are presented both in visual and auditory form, hearing problems may surface for illiterate or dyslexic adults on the WAIS-IV. Note behaviors such as leaning forward during administration to hear better. Other clues to watch are indications of auditory discrimination problems ("confine" rather than "confide").

- Observe when individuals seem to jump ahead and proceed with the visually presented words, thereby disregarding the auditory stimulus. Such behavior may be indicative of a preference for the visual rather than auditory channel

- Note adults who are overly verbose in their responses. They may be attempting to compensate for insecurity about their ability, or they may be obsessive, or they may be inefficient in their verbal expression.

Start, Reverse, and Discontinue Rules
- Start with Item 5, unless the examinee is suspected of an intellectual disability; in that case, begin with Item 1.
- If the examinee obtains a score of 0 or 1 on either Item 5 or 6, administer the preceding items in reverse order until two consecutive perfect scores are obtained. Corrective feedback is also given after imperfect scores on Items 5 and 6.
- Discontinue after three consecutive scores of 0.

Queries
- Use neutral questions to query vague or incomplete responses.
- Query responses that are indicated in the *Manual.*
- Query responses that are similar to those in the *Manual* (scoring rules are illustrative, not exhaustive).

Other Rules
- On the Vocabulary Picture items, the examinee may respond with a marginal response, general response, a functional response, or a hand gesture. In any of these cases, further query of the response is necessary. Specific queries for each of these types of responses are listed on pages 99–100 of the *WAIS-IV Administration and Scoring Manual.*

- After the examinee understands the requirements for the verbal items, the formal directions may be omitted, and the vocabulary word may just be read.
- Use the general distinctions between responses scored 2, 1, or 0 (see pages 102–103 of the *WAIS-IV Administration and Scoring Manual*).
- Probe if the examinee responds to a word that sounds like the stimulus word but is not the word.

Arithmetic

The materials required for this test are the *Manual*, Record Form, Stimulus Booklet 1, and a stopwatch (no paper and pencil). Some examinees may exhibit frustration when they are told they may not use paper or pencil to work out the mathematical problems during this subtest. However, if they choose to write imaginary numbers in the air or on the table, this strategy is perfectly acceptable, and should be noted in behavioral observations. Not allowing paper and pencil on these mathematics problems requires examinees to utilize working memory.

Lists of important Arithmetic rules are presented next. Important behaviors to watch for and note while administering the Arithmetic subtest are listed in Rapid Reference 2.9.

Start, Reverse, and Discontinue Rules
- Start administration with the Sample Item and then proceed to Item 6. However, if examinee is suspected of intellectual deficiency, then begin with Item 1 after the Sample Item is administered.

≡ *Rapid Reference 2.9*

Behaviors to Note on Arithmetic

- Observe examinees for signs of anxiety. Some adults who view themselves as poor at math may be more anxious during this task. Be aware of statements such as "I was never taught that in school," or "I can't do math in my head."
- Watch for signs of distractibility or poor concentration, which are usually noticeable during Arithmetic.
- Note when a subject asks for repetition of a question, as it may be indicative of several things, including poor hearing, inattention, stalling for more time, and more.
- Take note of whether examinees respond quickly and may be impulsive or are rather methodical and careful in their processing of the information.

• If examinees obtain a score of 0 on either item 6 or 7, administer the preceding items in reverse order until two consecutive perfect scores are obtained.
• Discontinue after three consecutive scores of 0.

Other Rules
• Items 1–5 are presented with a corresponding picture in the Stimulus Booklet.
• Repeat an Arithmetic question only once per item.
• Keep the stopwatch going even if repeating a question.
• Paper and pencil are not allowed, but an examinee can use his or her finger to "write" on table.
• Query if an examinee provides multiple responses and you are unsure which is the examinee's intended response.

Symbol Search

Several materials are needed to administer this subtest: *Manual*, Response Booklet 1, stopwatch, and two pencils without erasers. The Scoring template will be needed to score this subtest. The directions to Symbol Search are lengthy. It is important to read them verbatim but also to maintain rapport by not burying your head in the *Manual* while doing so. Thus, become very familiar with the directions. There are both Sample and Practice Items, which are not timed. Sample Items provide an explanation and demonstration of the task for examinees. Practice Items require the examinees to attempt items that are not part of the Symbol Search score. Examinees are given immediate feedback and correction on Practice Items. You are to proceed with the task only when the examinee clearly understands the directions and is able to complete the Practice Items successfully. As examinees are completing the task, you may find it necessary to remind them that they must complete the test items in order.

Lists of important Symbol Search rules are presented next. Important behaviors to watch for and note while administering the Symbol Search subtest are listed in Rapid Reference 2.10.

Start, Reverse, and Discontinue Rules
• Start administration with the Demonstration Items followed by the Sample Items and then proceed to page 2, where the subtest Items begin.

Other Rules
• Do not proceed with the subtest unless the examinee clearly understands the task after the Demonstration and Sample Items are administered.

≋ Rapid Reference 2.10

Behaviors to Note on Symbol Search

- Note how the adult handles the pencil. Is there pressure? Is the pencil dropped? Does the examinee seem coordinated?
- Observe attention and concentration. Is the adult's focus consistent throughout the task, or does it wane as time goes on?
- Look to see whether examinees check each row of symbols only once, or if they go back and recheck the row of symbols in an item more than once. Obsessive concern with detail may be noted.
- Make note of examinees' response styles. Impulsivity and reflectivity are usually observable in this task.

- Read the directions verbatim (with a minimum of paraphrasing) but do not lose rapport with the examinee.
- During administration of the Demonstration and Sample Items, point to the various symbols as you explain the directions (as advised in the *Manual*), which provides additional visual clarification of the task at hand.
- Consider a response incorrect if both a symbol and NO are marked for the same item.
- The raw score is obtained by subtracting incorrect from correct responses.

Visual Puzzles

The materials needed to administer this subtest include the *Manual*, Record Form, Stimulus Booklet 1, and a stopwatch. The object of Visual Puzzles is for the examinee to view a completed puzzle and then select three response options that can be combined to reconstruct the puzzle. The examinee has from 20 to 30 seconds to complete each item. Although there are time limits for each item, it is advisable to let examinees complete their response if they have already begun selecting response options when the time limit expired. Despite the fact that examinees cannot receive credit for responses given in overtime, it is good practice to allow examinees to finish responding without interruption. Giving this extra time will help foster a positive rapport and prevent undue frustration. Record the overtime responses for clinical information. Individuals who tend to respond correctly after the time limit has expired have better problem-solving skills than those who fail regardless of time limit, even if they obtain identical scaled scores.

Some examinees may appear confused after the Demonstration Item is administered. If such confusion is apparent, repeat the explanation of the task with the Demonstration Item and proceed only when the examinee understands the task. At times throughout this task, examinees may select fewer or more than the allowed three pieces to complete the puzzle. In such cases, prompt examinees to select only three pieces, or ask them to clarify which three pieces they intended for their response.

Lists of important Visual Puzzle rules are presented next. Important behaviors to watch for and note while administering the Visual Puzzle subtest are listed in Rapid Reference 2.11.

Start, Reverse, and Discontinue Rules
• Start with the Demonstration and Sample Items and then proceed to Item 5. However, if the examinee is suspected to have an intellectual disability, start with Item 1 after administering the Demonstration and Sample Items.
• If the examinee obtains a score of 0 on either Item 5 or 6, then administer the preceding items in reverse order until two consecutive perfect scores are obtained.
• Discontinue after three consecutive scores of 0.

≡ *Rapid Reference 2.11*

Behaviors to Note on Visual Puzzles

• Observe whether there is verbalization during problem solving.
• Note whether the examinee studies the puzzles for a few moments prior to answering. Such behavior may indicate a careful, reflective style.
• Observe whether examinees visibly turn their heads or twist their bodies in attempting to rotate the pieces rather than simply mentally rotating the pieces. Such behavior may indicate difficulty with visual processing.
• Note if the examinee touches the Stimulus Booklet to aid in the visualization process. For example, some examinees try to pick up the puzzle pieces to aid in the process of mental rotation.
• Notice how the examinee handles frustration on this test. For example, a response such as "None of those responses is correct" may indicate defensiveness or avoidance. A repeated response of "I don't know" may indicate that the examinee is giving up when faced with frustration.
• Note any patterns in the errors. For example, do examinees continually pick only two rather than three pieces to complete the puzzle?
• Note patterns of spontaneously correcting oneself. Examinees who jump to a response and then correct themselves may be impulsive or uncertain of themselves.

Other Rules
- There is a 20-second time limit for Items 1–7 and a 30-second time limit for Items 8–26.
- Provide a "warning" of the time elapsing by saying, "Do you have an answer?" after 10 seconds on items 1–7 and after 20 seconds on Items 8–16.
- Timing should begin after the last word of the instructions is spoken or after the item is presented.
- Remember to point to the completed puzzle and across each of the response options during administration.
- Ensure that the examinee understands the task prior to beginning administration of the test items. If additional explanation is needed, readminister the Demonstration Item.
- Remind examinees as often as necessary that they must choose three pieces to make the puzzle.
- If more than three pieces are selected, ask examinees to clarify which three were the intended responses.

Information

The *Manual* lists a series of short questions to be read orally in this subtest, and the Record Form is needed to record responses. The questions asked in Information were developed to tap knowledge about common events, objects, places, and people. Some examinees may ask for clarification about how to spell a word or may ask for a question to be repeated. It is acceptable to repeat a question, but the wording should not be changed whatsoever. Even if asked, the words should not be spelled or defined for the examinee because this type of help is not part of the standardized procedure. Querying an examinee's response to gain further clarification of vague or incomplete responses is perfectly acceptable but should be done with neutral prompts.

Lists of important Information rules are presented next. Important behaviors to watch for and note while administering the Information subtest are presented in Rapid Reference 2.12.

Start, Reverse, and Discontinue Rules
- Start on Item 3 unless the examinee is suspected of intellectual disability; in that case, begin on Item 1.
- If the examinee scores 0 on either Item 3 or 4, administer items in reverse order until two perfect scores on two consecutive items are obtained. In addition, provide corrective feedback on Items 3 and 4 when one of these items is missed.
- Discontinue after three consecutive scores of 0.

≡ Rapid Reference 2.12

Behaviors to Note on Information

- Note whether adults may provide unnecessarily long responses. If long responses filled with excessive detail are given, it may be indicative of obsessiveness.
- Make note of any observable pattern in a subject's responses. Patterns of responding that include missing early, easier items and having successes on harder items may suggest anxiety, poor motivation, or retrieval difficulties.
- Observe whether items on which errors are made are those that are especially related to examinee's cultural background, such as "Civil War" at a certain time or "Martin Luther King, Jr." Such observations should be incorporated in interpretation.

General Rules
- Do not spell the words or define any words in the questions.
- Items can be repeated as often as necessary
- Note that Items 1, 2, 9, 19, 24, and 26 require a specific query to certain responses. These specific queries are noted in the *Manual* with an asterisk.

Coding

Many materials are needed to administer this subtest: the *Manual*, the Record Form, Response Booklet 1, a stopwatch, and two pencils without erasers. Because there are lengthy verbal directions for this subtest and you must point to certain areas on the Response Booklet, it is highly recommended that examiners rehearse the administration multiple times. Once the examinee has gone through the Sample Items, the test can be started. Timing should be precise—allow *exactly* 120 seconds. Some adults will quickly realize that the best strategy is to fill in one type of symbol at a time; however, skipping numbers is not allowed, and examinees must be corrected immediately if this unacceptable (but quite efficient) strategy is used. Be sure to record the precise symbol the subject completed when the 120 seconds elapsed.

Lists of important Coding rules are presented next. Important behaviors to watch for and note while administering the Coding subtest are listed in Rapid Reference 2.13.

Starting and Discontinue Rules
- All examinees begin with the Demonstration Items, the Sample Items, and then the Test Items.
- Discontinue after 120 seconds. (There is no reverse rule.)

≡ *Rapid Reference 2.13*

Behaviors to Note on Coding

- Watching the eye movements of adults taking the test can be very informative. Consistent glancing back and forth from the Coding key to the response sheet may be indicative of a poor memory or insecurity. In contrast, someone who uses the key infrequently may have a good short-term memory and remember number-symbol pairs readily.

- Impulsivity in responding may be observed when an adult quickly but carelessly fills in symbols across the rows.

- Shaking hands, a tight grip on the pencil, or pressure on the paper when writing may be indicative of anxiety.

- Fatigue, boredom, or inattention may become apparent as the Coding task progresses. Noting the number of symbols copied during 30-second intervals provides helpful behavioral information.

Other Rules

- Try not to paraphrase the directions, yet do not lose rapport with the examinee by burying your head in the *Manual*.
- While the examinee is completing the Sample Items, correct any errors immediately, as they are made.
- If necessary, remind the examinee that he or she must start at the beginning of the row and not skip any.
- If an examinee is left-handed and partially blocks the key with his or her left hand while completing the Sample Items, place an extra Response Booklet (with the Coding subtest key visible) to the right of the examinee's Response Booklet. This arrangement will provide the examinee with an unobstructed view of the Coding key.

Letter-Number Sequencing

The *Manual* and the Record Form are the only materials needed to administer this subtest. Letter-Number Sequencing provides a Demonstration Item and a Sample Item before Items 1 and 3. Be sure to administer all of these Demonstrations and Sample Items. Even if an examinee fails all of the Sample A items, the subtest is to be continued. Some examinees will respond quickly and others more slowly, so you must be prepared to record each response verbatim quickly. In the directions, the examinee is asked to repeat the numbers in order first and then the letters in alphabetical order; however, the examinee

≡ Rapid Reference 2.14

Behaviors to Note on Letter-Number Sequencing

- Observe whether the examinee learns from errors made during the Sample Items. Examinees may also appear to learn from errors made within one item (i.e., miss the first trial but get the second two correct).
- Note whether adults respond by giving the numbers first and then the letters as requested, or whether the opposite pattern is produced in responses.
- Anxiety, distractibility, and concentration may impact performance on this test. Observe any behaviors that may be indicative of such difficulties.
- Observe and note any strategies that may be used during this task. For example, adults may keep track of numbers on one hand and letters on another. Rehearsal and chunking may be other strategies that are observed. Examinees who close their eyes while the items are administered (and, perhaps, while responding) are probably using a visualization strategy.
- Note whether there is a pattern in the errors, such as missing only the letters but getting all of the numbers correct. This may be indicative of stimulus overload.
- Note errors that may be indicative of hearing difficulty, such as incorrectly repeating letters that differ only slightly from the stimuli (i.e., T rather than D).

will be given credit if the letters are said before the numbers, as long as they are in the correct sequence.

Lists of important Letter-Number Sequencing rules are presented next. Important behaviors to watch for and note while administering the Letter-Number Sequencing subtest are listed in Rapid Reference 2.14.

Start and Discontinue Rules
- Do not administer to examinees who are age 70 or older, except for clinical purposes; norms extend only to age 69.
- Begin administration with Demonstration Item A, Sample Item A, and then Item 1.
- Discontinue after scores of 0 on all three of the trials of an item.

General Rules
- Administer all both the Demonstration A and Sample A, and also Demonstration B and Sample B, unless the examinee has met the discontinue criterion on Item 1 or 2.
- Correct the examinee during all Sample Items.
- Say each combination at a rate of one number or letter per second.

- The examinee obtains credit if letters are said before numbers, as long as they are in the correct sequence.
- No additional administration is required to obtain the Longest Letter-Number Sequence (LLNS) process score. This process score is calculated simply based on the regular administration of Letter-Number Sequencing. Chapter 3 of this book provides detail on how to calculate the LLNS score.

Figure Weights

The materials needed to administer this subtest include: the *Administration and Scoring Manual*, Record Form, Stimulus Booklet 2, and a stopwatch. The object of Figure Weights is for the examinee to view a two-dimensional representation of a scale with missing weights and then select the response option that keeps the scale balanced. The examinee has from 20 to 40 seconds to complete each item. If examinees have begun responding but hesitate and do not complete their response before the time limit expires, allow them to complete their response to preserve rapport but do not count that response as correct if it was given after the time limit. As indicated for Visual Puzzles, it is important clinically whether a person tends to solve items correctly over time.

Examinees can respond by either pointing to or saying the number of the selected response option. If another verbal response is given, such as "The red block" or "The three blue balls," you should ask the examinee to show which option was the intended response. Generally, if an examinee does not respond after you have prompted them with "Do you have an answer?" when the time limit expires, you can proceed to the next item with "Let's try another one." Figure Weights provides two Demonstration Items plus one Sample Item to ensure that the examinee understands the task demands before the test items begin.

Lists of important Figure Weights rules are presented next. Important behaviors to watch for and note while administering the Figure Weights subtest are listed in Rapid Reference 2.15.

Start, Reverse, and Discontinue Rules
- Do not administer to examinees who are age 70 or older, except for clinical purposes; norms extend only to age 69.
- Start with the Demonstration Items A and B, the Sample Item, and then proceed to Item 4. However, if the examinee is suspected to have an intellectual disability, start with Item 1 after administering the Demonstration and Sample Items.

≣ *Rapid Reference 2.15*

....

Behaviors to Note on Figure Weights

- Observe whether there is verbalization during problem solving.
- Observe whether the examinee calculates the correct answer with mathematical calculation (done by "writing" in the air or by "writing" on the table.)
- Note if the examinee touches the Stimulus Booklet to aid in the visualization process. Determine if this behavior is present for the higher-level items with 3 scales to compare (e.g., 16–27) versus the earlier, less complex 2-scale items.
- Notice how the examinee handles frustration on this test. For example, a response such as "None of those responses is correct" may indicate defensiveness or avoidance. A repeated response of "I don't know" may indicate that the examinee is giving up when faced with frustration.
- Note any patterns in the errors. For example, do errors indicate that the examinee has begun erroneously matching colors or shapes rather than finding the equivalently weighted shapes?
- Note patterns of spontaneously correcting oneself. Examinees who jump to a response and then correct themselves may be impulsive or uncertain of themselves.

- If the examinee obtains a score of 0 on either Item 4 or 5, administer the preceding items in reverse order until two consecutive perfect scores are obtained.
- Discontinue after three consecutive scores of 0.

Other Rules
- There is a 20-second time limit for Items 1–12 and a 40-second time limit for Items 13–27.
- Provide a "warning" of the time elapsing by asking, "Do you have an answer?" after 10 seconds on items 1–12 and after 30 seconds on Items 13–27.
- Timing should begin after the last word of the instructions is spoken or after the item is presented.
- Remember to point to the visual stimuli, each of the response options, and the question mark during administration.
- If examinees give multiple responses and it is unclear what their intended response is, ask for clarification of their intended response (e.g., "Which one did you mean?")
- Request that examinees clarify their response (either by pointing or by selecting the number of their response choice) if they provide an alternate verbalization as their response.
- Item 16 requires that the instructions be read verbatim.

Comprehension

This subtest requires only questions written in the *Manual* and the Record Form. Examinees may need a question repeated from time to time, and this is allowed. However, the question should be repeated in its entirety and should not be abbreviated in any way. Four of the Comprehension questions require responses from two of the general categories. It is important to remember to query for another response if an examinee spontaneously provides an answer from only one category. When requesting a second response, be sure to restate the question as indicated on pages 169–170 of the *WAIS-IV Administration and Scoring Manual*:

WRONG: "Tell me another reason."
RIGHT: "Tell me another reason why child labor laws are needed."

Whereas most items require the adult to demonstrate deductive reasoning in response to socially relevant questions, note that Items 11, 14, 15, and 18 require the adult to reason inductively in response to proverbs.

≡ *Rapid Reference 2.16*

Behaviors to Note on Comprehension

- Observe whether unusually long verbal responses are an attempt to cover up for not actually knowing the correct response or because the examinee tends to be obsessive about details.

- Some of the Comprehension questions have rather long verbal stimuli. Note whether inattention is impacting adults' responses to such items. For example, only part of the question may be answered.

- Note whether defensiveness is occurring in responses to some Comprehension items. For example, when asked the "democracy" item, if the adult's response does not really answer the question and is something like "We shouldn't have it at all," this may be defensive responding.

- Note whether the adults require consistent prompting for a second response or whether they spontaneously provide enough information in their answer.

- Observe the responses carefully to determine whether poor verbal ability is the cause of a low score or whether it is due more to poor social judgment.

- Note how subjects respond to queries. Some may be threatened or frustrated with the constant interruption, and others may seem quite comfortable with the extra structure. When asked for another reason, some people simply restate the first reason in different words or otherwise do not give a second "idea."

Lists of important Comprehension rules are presented next. Important behaviors to watch for and note while administering the Comprehension subtest are listed in Rapid Reference 2.16.

Start, Reverse, and Discontinue Rules
- Start with Item 3, unless the examinee is suspected of an intellectual disability, in which case begin with Item 1.
- If the examinee obtains a score of 0 or 1 on either Items 3 or 4, administer the preceding items in reverse order until two consecutive perfect scores are obtained. In addition, corrective feedback is given if the examinee does not give a 2-point response on either Item 3 or 4.
- Discontinue after three consecutive scores of 0.

General Rules
- You may repeat a question, but it must be repeated verbatim.
- Items 5, 8, 9, and 10 require two general concepts for a 2-point response; prompt for another response if only one general concept is given in the examinee's response.
- Query vague or incomplete responses.
- Do not explain the meaning of any words in the questions.

Cancellation

Administration of this subtest requires Response Booklet 2, a stopwatch, the *Administration and Scoring Manual,* the Record Form, and a #2 pencil without an eraser. The Cancellation subtest requires the examinee to scan both a structured arrangement of shapes and mark target shapes within a specified time limit. Like the other Processing Speed subtests, the directions for Cancellation are lengthy. Be sure to be well rehearsed prior to attempting administration of this task.

There are two items contained in the Cancellation Response Booklet 2: Item A with red squares and yellow triangles and Item B with orange stars and blue circles. On each item, the goal is for the examinee to mark the target shapes within 45 seconds. If the examinee fails to mark a target or marks a distractor item during the Sample Items, the examiner should provide corrective feedback. It is important not to proceed to Item 1 until the examinee fully understands the task. Spontaneous corrections should not be discouraged, unless such corrections occur frequently enough to impede performance.

Lists of important Cancellation rules are presented next. Important behaviors to watch for and note while administering the Cancellation subtest are listed in Rapid Reference 2.17.

≋ Rapid Reference 2.17

Behaviors to Note on Cancellation

- Watch for shaking hands, a tight grip on the pencil, or pressure on the paper when writing. These behaviors may indicate anxiety.
- Note whether examinees have difficulty with or resistance to working quickly. This behavior may relate perfectionism.
- Observe attention and concentration. Is the examinee's focus consistent throughout the task, or does it wane as the task progresses?
- Observe signs of fatigue, boredom, or inattention as the subtest progresses. Noting the number of responses produced during 15-second item intervals within the 45-second limit may provide helpful behavioral information in this regard.
- Observe whether the examinee's response rate is consistent throughout the subtest.
- Note whether the examinee quickly but carelessly circles responses. This behavior may suggest impulsivity.
- Note the effect of distractors on the examinee's performance. Remember that the target items are identically placed on both the items.

Source: Adapted from D. P. Flanagan & A. S. Kaufman, *Essentials of WISC-IV Assessment.* Copyright © 2009 John Wiley & Sons, Inc. This material is used by permission of John Wiley & Sons, Inc.

Start and Discontinue Rules
- All examinees begin with the Demonstration Items, the Sample Items, and then the Test Items.
- On each item, discontinue after 45 seconds. (There is no reverse rule.)

Other Rules
- Do not administer to examinees who are age 70 or older, except for clinical purposes; norms extend only to age 69.
- Try not to paraphrase the directions, yet do not lose rapport with the examinee by burying your head in the Manual.
- While the examinee is completing the Sample Items, correct any errors immediately as they are made.
- Only slash marks are allowed for marking the target shapes.
- If necessary, remind the examinee that he or she must start at the beginning of the row and not skip any.
- Some examinees attempt to complete the left half of the 11×17 booklet (as you would if reading a book). In such cases, remind the examinee to work all the way across each of the 18 shapes in a row.

Picture Completion

This subtest requires the use of the *Manual*, Stimulus Booklet 2 with incomplete drawings, a stopwatch, and the Record Form to record responses. This subtest is generally easy to administer and is viewed as fun and game-like by most adolescents and adults. The most common mistakes in administering Picture Completion concern the three queries that are each allowed to be given only *once* during the entire subtest, if needed:

- "Yes, but what is missing?"
- "A part is missing in the picture. What is it that is missing?"
- "Yes, but what is the most important part that is missing?"

Although these prompts are listed on the Record Form, common examiner errors are to forget to use these queries or to use each one several times instead of the mandated "once." Other types of administration errors may occur if an adult or adolescent produces a verbal response that is unclear or ambiguous. If this type of response is given, it is necessary to query for clarification of the response. Responses may be verbal or nonverbal (pointing), as both are considered acceptable. It is important to keep in mind that this test's main focus is not on verbal ability but on visual perception, spatial ability, and holistic processing. However, important information about verbal ability may be gleaned in this last-administered test. Interestingly, although Picture Completion is intended as a nonverbal subtest, the Sample Item's instructions to the adult subtly encourage verbalization by instructing adults to "Look at each picture and TELL me what is missing." The word *tell* suggests a verbal response, whereas *show* would have prompted a nonverbal response. However, the directions for the remaining test items remove the word *tell* and simply state: "Look at this picture. What part is missing?"

Lists of important queries and other Picture Completion rules are present next. Important behaviors to watch for and note while administering the Picture Completion subtest are listed in Rapid Reference 2.18.

Start, Reverse, and Discontinue Rules
- Start with the Sample Item and then proceed to Item 4. However, if an individual is suspected of intellectual disability, start with Item 1 after the Sample is administered.
- If a score of 0 is obtained on either Item 4 or Item 5, administer the preceding items in reverse order until two consecutive perfect scores are obtained. If the examinee does not give a correct response on Item 4 or 5, provide corrective feedback.
- Discontinue after four consecutive scores of 0.

≡ Rapid Reference 2.18

Behaviors to Note on Picture Completion

- The speed at which an adult or adolescent responds is noteworthy. A reflective individual may take more time in responding (but most likely can respond within the 20-second time limit), whereas an impulsive individual may respond very quickly but incorrectly.
- Note whether the examinee is persistent in stating that nothing is missing from the picture (rather than responding "I don't know"), as it may reflect oppositionality or inflexibility.
- If nonverbal responses (pointing) are consistently observed, it may be evidence of a word retrieval problem in adults. Although it is acceptable to give a nonverbal response, it is far more common to give a verbal response.
- Verbal responses that are imprecise ("the connector") or overly elaborative ("the small piece of material that forms a connection between the two sections of the eyeglasses which hold the lenses in place") are also noteworthy.
- Note whether adults give responses that consistently indicate a focus on details ("the grain" on the door, "the flakes on the pie crust" on the pie crust weave, or "the pollen" on the roses).
- After individuals have been redirected (i.e., "Yes, but what is the *most important* part that is missing?"), it is important to note whether they still continue to respond with the same quality of response. This persistence in approach may be indicative of not understanding the task or inflexibility in thinking.

Queries
- Give each of the three queries only *once* for the entire administration of Picture Completion.

Other Rules
- The time limit for each item is 20 seconds. Begin timing after you have spoken the last word of the instruction or after the item itself has been presented.
- If verbal response is ambiguous, say, "Show me where you mean."
- On Items 8, 10, and 19, get clarification about where in the picture the examinee's verbal response is referring, if necessary.
- The Record Form provides a place to record the examinee's verbal response and the pointing response. Mark "PC" if the examinee pointed correctly and "PX" if the examinee pointed incorrectly in response to the item.
- Some verbal responses must be accompanied by a correct pointing response to earn credit. Those verbal responses are listed in the right-hand column of

the table on pages 202–204 of the *Administration and Scoring Manual* and should be clarified by asking, "Show me where you mean."

- If the examinee points to the correct place but spoils the response by giving a clearly incorrect verbal response, the item is failed.

Pitfalls of Subtest Administration

The basic rules of subtest administration have been reviewed in this chapter. Several areas are found to be continually problematic for most examiners when they administer the WAIS-IV. A list of such problems is shown in the Common Pitfalls of Subtest Administration Caution box. By reviewing this box, you can ensure that you are especially aware of the most prominent administration pitfalls, whether you are learning the WAIS-IV in a graduate level-assessment course or are starting with prior experience administering the WAIS-III and are now learning the WAIS-IV.

CAUTION
....
Common Pitfalls of Subtest Administration

1. *Block Design*
   - Neglecting to make sure that the proper variety of block faces are showing before the item is begun
   - Placing the model or Stimulus Booklet in an incorrect position
   - Correcting block rotations more than once during the subtest
   - Remembering to use the reverse rule when adults score is 0 on Design 6, even if they earn 4 points on Design 5

2. *Similarities*
   - Forgetting to give an example of a 2-point response if the examinee's response to Item 4 or 5 is not perfect
   - Overquerying or underquerying vague responses

3. *Digit Span*
   - Reading the sequence of digits too quickly
   - Inadvertently chunking the numbers as they are read
   - Giving extra help on Digit Span Backward or Sequencing
   - Forgetting to administer Digit Span Backward to adults who score 0 on Digit Span Forward
   - Forgetting to administer Digit Span Sequencing to adults who score 0 on Digit Span Backward

4. Matrix Reasoning

- Not continuing on to Item 4 if Sample Items are incorrect
- Moving to Item 1 after the Samples if the Samples were correct
- Giving feedback on items beyond the Sample
- Allowing examinees to guess randomly

5. Vocabulary

- Not recording exact verbal responses
- Not querying vague responses appropriately
- Forgetting to use the Stimulus Booklet to allow adults to see the words they are defining
- Forgetting to provide corrective feedback if necessary on Item 5 or 6

6. Arithmetic

- Repeating the questions more than one time
- Stopping the stopwatch when a question is repeated
- Allowing paper and pencil to be used if asked

7. Symbol Search

- Proceeding with the task before the examinee clearly understands what is required
- Burying your head in the *Manual* while reading directions

8. Visual Puzzles

- Losing rapport with the examinee by burying your head in the *Manual* while reading long directions
- Forgetting to start the stopwatch after the item is presented
- Forgetting to prompt the examinee when 10 seconds remain in Items 1–7 with "Do you have an answer?" (or after 20 seconds for Items 8–26)
- Forgetting that the time limit increases from 20 to 30 seconds at Item 8
- Forgetting to tell examinees "Show me" what their selected response was if they verbalize a response other than the numbers of their selections
- Forgetting to remind examinees to select three pieces if they select fewer than that in their response

9. Information

- Defining words if asked by the examinee
- Forgetting to give required prompts (e.g., "What unit of distance?") to an incomplete answer
- Being unaware that it is permissible to give neutral queries (e.g., "Tell me more") to Information responses that are incomplete or ambiguous (Queries are not limited to responses on Similarities, Comprehension, and Vocabulary.)

10. Coding

- Losing rapport with the examinee by burying your head in the *Manual* while reading long directions

(continued)

- Forgetting to start the stopwatch when the examinee begins
- Not paying attention to examinees and allowing them to skip over items
- Allowing a left-handed examinee to partially block the key with their left hand and forgetting to provide them with an extra Coding Key

11. Letter-Number Sequencing

- Reading items too slowly or too quickly
- Neglecting to correct an examinee on any missed practice item
- Repeating a trial of an item if the examinee asks for repetition
- Counting a response as an error if the letters are read in sequence before the numbers
- Forgetting to give corrective feedback on teaching Items 1 and 2 if the examinee responds incorrectly or does not respond within about 30 seconds
- Allowing over 30 seconds for a response

12. Figure Weights

- Losing rapport with the examinee by burying your head in the *Manual* while reading long directions
- Forgetting to start the stopwatch after the item is presented
- Forgetting to prompt the examinee when 10 seconds remain in Items 1–12 with "Do you have an answer?" (or after 30 seconds for Items 13–27)
- Forgetting that the time limit increases from 20 to 40 seconds at Item 13
- Forgetting to tell examinees "Show me" what their selected response was if they verbalize a response such as "the two red stars."
- Forgetting to read the instructions verbatim on Item 16 to introduce the items with three scales

13. Comprehension

- Forgetting to give corrective feedback on Item 3 or 4 if the examinee does not obtain a perfect score
- Forgetting to query for a second response (Items 5, 8, 9, and 10) if necessary
- Explaining the meaning of a word if asked (No explanations or definitions are allowed to be given.)
- Neglecting to write down the exact verbal response

14. Cancellation

- Forgetting to time the examinee
- Forgetting to discontinue after 45 seconds
- Forgetting to administer the second item
- Forgetting to provide corrective feedback when the examinee marks incorrect responses during the Sample Items
- Forgetting to carefully watch examinees during the test items and remind them to not skip any items or not to go back and mark a missed item

15. Picture Completion

- Forgetting to provide the correct answer to Item 4 or 5 if the examinee does not give correct response
- Giving the allowed queries too often
- Forgetting to time the Picture Completion items (20-second limit)
- Forgetting to administer in reverse sequence if a 0 score is obtained on either Item 4 or 5
- Forgetting to circle PC or PX to record a pointing response
- Forgetting to query when the examinee does not spontaneously point when providing a response from the right-hand-column items (that require pointing in addition to a verbal response)

⚜ TEST YOURSELF ⚜

1. List the materials that are not included in the WAIS-IV kit that the examiner should be prepared to bring him- or herself.

2. The examiner must memorize all directions in order to administer the test appropriately. TRUE or FALSE?

3. In establishing rapport with the examinee during the administration of the WAIS-IV, you may tell him or her:

   (a) You got that answer correct, nice work.

   (b) Most test takers find some questions easy and some questions quite difficult.

   (c) We won't be able to complete the test unless you refrain from using the restroom during the evaluation.

   (d) That wasn't quite right, let's do another one.

4. If you find you need to adapt the test to accommodate an individual with special needs, it is better not to administer the test altogether. TRUE or FALSE?

5. List some modifications that may be made in the test administration procedures to accommodate individuals with special needs.

6. Which of these subtests do NOT use a "reverse rule"?

   (a) Block Design

   (b) Similarities

   (c) Digit Span

   (d) Matrix Reasoning

   (e) Vocabulary

   (f) Arithmetic

   (g) Symbol Search

(h) Visual Puzzles

(i) Information

(j) Coding

(k) Letter-Number Sequencing

(l) Figure Weights

(m) Comprehension

(n) Cancellation

(o) Picture Completion

7. **When applying the reverse rule, you must**

(a) Go back to Item 1 and administer all items sequentially until you get to where you started.

(b) Go back to administer items until one earlier item is correct.

(c) Go back to administer items until two consecutive items are correct, not including the item with which you initially started.

(d) Go back to administer items until two consecutive items are correct, including the item with which you initially started.

8. **Which is the only subtest in which all items must be administered?**

9. **If you are administering a subtest with subjective scoring and are unsure of what score an examinee's response should get, it is best to take a few minutes to carefully review that item's scoring rules and tell the examinee to wait quietly. TRUE or FALSE?**

10. **To preserve the balance of maintaining rapport and getting necessary clinical information, it is best to:**

(a) Record only the examinee's score if it can save some time and quicken the pace of the evaluation.

(b) Record the examinee's responses verbatim, but using abbreviations when possible.

(c) Record only incorrect responses to analyze clinically.

(d) Tell the examinee to wait just a few minutes while you very carefully write down every single word that is said.

11. **Which subtests require the use of a stopwatch?**

(a) Block Design

(b) Similarities

(c) Digit Span

(d) Matrix Reasoning

(e) Vocabulary

(f) Arithmetic

(g) Symbol Search

(h) Visual Puzzles

(i) Information

(j) Coding

(k) Letter-Number Sequencing

(l) Figure Weights

(m) Comprehension

(n) Cancellation

(o) Picture Completion

12. **Give examples of queries that you may use to obtain more information about a vague, ambiguous, or incomplete response.**

13. **You may repeat questions or instructions only on Verbal Comprehension subtests and never on Perceptual Reasoning subtests. TRUE or FALSE?**

THOUGHT QUESTIONS

14. **Why was it wise for the test developers to include Sample Items and allow teaching the task on the first two items?**

15. **What are some of the benefits and weaknesses of using a standardized instrument?**

16. **What may cause a disruption in the rapport between examiner and examinee, and what might you do to preserve it?**

17. **What areas of administration are likely to cause the most difficulty for novice examiners?**

Answers: 1. Two No. 2 pencils without erasers, stopwatch, clipboard, extra paper, and writing implements; 2. False; 3. B; 4. False; 5. Administering the test in American Sign Language, adding printed words, administering only one scale, eliminating time limits, extending the testing over more than one session. 6. C, H, J, L, M, N; 7. D; 8. Cancellation; 9. False; 10. B; 11. A, E, F, G, J, L, N, O; 12. "Tell me more about that." "Explain what you mean."; 13. False.

Chapter 2 Thought Question Answers:

14. Allowing examiners to teach the task ensures that the examinee understands the task; therefore, allowing the examiner to determine when the examinee does not know the answer as opposed to when he or she does not understand the task.

15. Benefits of standardized instruments include being able to compare an individual to a similar group of people to gain an understanding of how he or she functions. You can obtain standardized scores, which are a common metric that is readily compared across many measures. A disadvantage of standardized instruments is that the normative sample may not always be appropriate to compare a particular individual to (i.e., if the ethnic background is very dissimilar to the normative group). Another disadvantage is that when testing patients with special needs, the standardized instruments do not offer flexibility in procedures, which are often needed with these groups. Not all standardized tests offer good reliability and validity, so the values obtained from these tests may not offer completely valuable information.

16. If the examinee is terribly shy, rapport may be difficult to establish. More time may need to be spent developing a relationship with the examinee prior to

beginning testing. If the examinee is terribly frustrated with a particular subtest, he or she may become disinterested in the testing. The examiner may need to give the examinee extra encouragement or a break before continuing testing. If the examinee has a variable attention span, rapport may be disrupted as well. The examiner may have to be extra vigilant in keeping the subject on track and offer more frequent breaks, or extend the testing over more than one day.

17. Novice examiners are likely to have difficulty with scoring subjective subtests, such as Vocabulary, Similarities, and Comprehension. Difficulty with utilizing multiple testing materials during some Perceptual Reasoning subtests, such as Block Design, while accurately recording the time with the stopwatch is also problematic for novices. Subtests which have very lengthy directions, such as Visual Puzzles, Figure Weights, Coding, and Symbol Search, can often cause problems to those that are new to the WAIS-IV.

Three

HOW TO SCORE THE WAIS-IV

TYPES OF SCORES

The WAIS-IV provides three types of scores: Raw Scores, scaled scores, and IQ/Index scores. The Raw Score is the first obtained and is simply the sum of points earned on a subtest. The Raw Score alone is meaningless, as it is not a norm-referenced score. To interpret an examinee's performance, you must translate the Raw Scores into standard scores (either scaled scores or IQ/Indexes). Rapid Reference 3.1 lists the metrics for various types of standard scores. The subtest scaled scores have a mean of 10 and a standard deviation of 3 (ranging from 1 to a maximum of 19). The IQs and factor indexes have a mean of 100 and a standard deviation of 15 (ranging from 40 to 160 for Full Scale IQ [FSIQ] and from 50 to 150 for indexes).

Most individuals earn scores on the WAIS-IV that are within 1 standard deviation from the mean. Specifically, about two-thirds of the examinees earn IQs or Indexes between 85 and 115. The number of examinees whose

≡ Rapid Reference 3.1

Metrics for Standard Scores

Type of Standard Score	Mean	Standard Deviation	Range of Values
Scaled Score	10	3	1–19
FSIQ	100	15	40–160
Index	100	15	50–150

scores are 2 standard deviations from the mean (from 70–130) jumps up to about 95%. A very small number earn scores that are higher than 130 (about 2.2%) or lower than 70 (also about 2.2%). For the subtest scaled scores, corresponding values are: about 66% score between 7 and 13 and about 95% score between 4 and 16; the extreme 2.2% in each "tail" earn scaled scores of 1–3 (very low functioning) and 17–19 (very high functioning).

STEP-BY-STEP: HOW THE WAIS-IV IS SCORED

Raw Scores

The first step in the process of scoring is obtaining Raw Scores for each of the administered subtests. Much of the scoring for this test is straightforward and lacking in ambiguity, but there are a few subtests (mainly on the Verbal Comprehension Index) in which subjectivity presents constant thorns to examiners during the scoring process. Later in this chapter we review some suggestions on how to properly score the more tricky types of responses. For the most part, all that is necessary to calculate the subtests' Raw Scores is careful addition. The Caution box displays common errors in the process of calculating Raw Scores that you need to avoid.

CAUTION

Common Errors in Raw Score Calculation

- Neglecting to add points earned from the first few items that were not administered to the total Raw Score
- Neglecting to add the points recorded on one page of the Record Form to the points recorded on the next page (i.e., Digit Span, Vocabulary, Information, and Comprehension)
- Forgetting to subtract the number of incorrect responses from correct responses on Symbol Search and Cancellation
- Transferring total Raw Scores incorrectly from inside the Record Form to Score Conversion summary tables on the front page of Record Form
- Miscalculating the Raw Score sum via an addition mistake
- Including points earned on items that were presented after the discontinue criterion was met

Scaled Scores

To determine an examinee's scaled scores, you will need: (1) the individual's chronological age; (2) his or her subtest Raw Scores from the Record Form; and (3) Table A.1 from the *WAIS-IV Administration and Scoring Manual*. The steps to convert Raw Scores into scaled scores are listed in the Rapid Reference 3.2. In addition to the 15 subtest scaled scores that can be calculated, the WAIS-IV yields scaled scores for four process tests: Block Design No Time Bonus (BDN), Digit Span Forward (DSF), Digit Span Backward (DSB), and Digit Span Sequencing (DSS). These process scores are calculated in a similar manner to the core and supplemental subtest scaled scores (see Rapid Reference 3.3) but require referencing a different table in the *WAIS-IV Administration and Scoring Manual* (Table C.1; Wechsler, 2008). Four additional process scores yield only Raw Scores: Longest Digit Span Forward (LDSF), Longest Digit Span Backward (LSDB), Longest Digit Span Sequence (LDSS), and Longest Letter-Number Sequence (LLNS). Thus, for LDSF, LDSB, LDSS, and LNSS, the scoring process stops with Raw Scores, but the interpretation of these scores continues in Chapter 5 of this book.

CAUTION

Process Scores that Yield Only Raw Scores

Process Score	Raw Score Available	Scaled Score Available
Block Design No Time Bonus (BDN)	Yes	Yes
Digit Span Forward (DSF)	Yes	Yes
Digit Span Backward (DSB)	Yes	Yes
Digit Span Sequencing (DSS)	Yes	Yes
Longest Digit Span Forward (LDSF)	Yes	No
Longest Digit Span Backward (LSDB)	Yes	No
Longest Digit Span Sequence (LDSS)	Yes	No
Longest Letter-Number Sequence (LLNS)	Yes	No

The tables used to obtain the scaled scores are "user-friendly" and easy to find in the tabbed format of the WAIS-IV Manual. Examiners commonly make errors when they are rushed to look up scores or when they do not take the time to double-check their work.

≡ Rapid Reference 3.2

Converting Raw Scores to Scaled Scores

1. Transfer the total Raw Scores from the bottom right corner of each subtest on the Record Form to the appropriate spot on the **Score Summary Page** (page 1 of the Record Form).

2. For each subtest, find the scaled score equivalent to the obtained raw score. These scores should be obtained by looking in Table A.1 of the *Administration and Scoring Manual*, on the page that lists the appropriate norms group based on each examinee's chronological age.

3. Record each subtest's scaled score under all of the possible columns on the Record Form (VCI, PRI, WMI, PSI, and FSIQ).

4. **Optional Step:** If you wish to compare scores to the reference group of adults ages 20–34, obtain scaled scores from Table A.2 and record them in the right-hand column of the Score Summary Page. However, these optional scaled scores are not used to compute Indexes or FSIQ. They are primarily of interest to examiners who administered the WAIS or WAIS-R, which based scaled scores for individuals of all ages on the 20- to 34-year-old reference group. (IQ on those tests, however, was always based on the person's chronological age.)

≡ Rapid Reference 3.3

Process Scores: Converting Raw Scores to Scaled Scores

1. For the four process scores that yield scaled scores—Block Design No Time Bonus, Digit Span Forward, Digit Span Backward, and Digit Span Sequencing—transfer the total raw scores from the bottom right corner of each process subtest on the Record Form to the appropriate spot on the Process Analysis table (inside cover of the Record Form).

2. For each subtest's process score, find the scaled score equivalent to the obtained Raw Score. These scores should be obtained by looking in Table C.1 of the *Manual*, on the page that lists the examinee's age.

3. Record each subtest's scaled score beside the appropriate subtest's process score in the table.

4. To prepare for interpretation of the process scores, transfer the scaled scores from BDN, DSF, DSB, DSS, and Block Design onto the table labeled "Scaled Score Discrepancy Comparison." (Calculations for interpretation are discussed in Chapter 6 of this book.)

CAUTION

Common Errors in Obtaining Scaled Scores

- Miscalculating a sum when adding scores to obtain the Raw Score or the Sum of Scaled Scores
- Writing illegibly, leading to errors
- Using a score conversion table that references the wrong age group
- Misreading across the rows of the score conversion tables

IQs and Factor Indexes

Once the scaled scores have been obtained, you are ready to find the FSIQ and factor indexes. Care should be taken in the next steps to ensure that calculation errors are not made.

Converting Scaled Scores to IQ/Indexes

1. Calculate the sum of the scaled scores for the appropriate subtest scores for the four Indexes and the Full Scale IQ (see Figure 2.10 of the *WAIS-IV Administration and Scoring Manual*). **NOTE:** The supplemental subtests, Letter-Number Sequencing, Figure Weights, Comprehension, Cancellation, and Picture Completion are not used in the Sums of Scaled Scores for the Indexes or the FSIQ *unless* they are replacing another subtest.
2. Record the sums of the scaled scores on the bottom row of the respective column for each of the indexes and the FSIQ on the **Summary Page** of the record form (i.e., the Record Form's front page). Rapid Reference 3.4 reviews the subtests that comprise each Composite.
3. Copy the Sums of Scaled Scores to the **Sum of Scaled Scores to Composite Score Conversion table** at the bottom of the first page of the Record Form, where it is labeled **Sums of Scaled Scores.**
4. For each index and the FSIQ, determine the appropriate composite score based on the Sum of Scaled Scores. (See Tables A.3–A.7 of the *Administration and Scoring Manual*).
5. In addition, record the Percentiles and Confidence Intervals for each of the scales; they are also found in Tables A.3–A.7 of the Manual.

Raw Scores of Zero May Invalidate Composite

If an examinee obtains a total Raw Score of 0 (zero) on a subtest, you must make special considerations when converting that Raw Score to a scaled score, Index

≡ Rapid Reference 3.4

. . . .

Subtests Comprising WAIS-IV Index Scores, FSIQ, and GAI

Subtest	Scale	FSIQ	GAI
Similarities	VCI	FSIQ	GAI
Vocabulary	VCI	FSIQ	GAI
Information	VCI	FSIQ	GAI
(Comprehension)	(VCI)		
Digit Span	WMI	FSIQ	
Arithmetic	WMI	FSIQ	
(Letter-Number Sequencing)	(WMI)		
Block Design	PRI	FSIQ	GAI
Matrix Reasoning	PRI	FSIQ	GAI
Visual Puzzles	PRI	FSIQ	GAI
(Figure Weights)	(PRI)		
(Picture Completion)	(PRI)		
Symbol Search	PSI	FSIQ	
Coding	PSI	FSIQ	
(Cancellation)	(PSI)		

Key: Verbal Comprehension Index (VCI); Perceptual Reasoning Index (PRI); Working Memory Index (WMI); Processing Speed Index (PSI), Full Scale IQ (FSIQ); General Ability Index (GAI).
    Subtests in parentheses are supplemental and may be substituted for a core subtest on a scale if a core subtest is spoiled.

score, and FSIQ. The difficulty with a Raw Score of zero is that the score does not indicate the examinee's true ability; rather it indicates that the examinee's ability cannot be determined by the particular set of subtest items. Ultimately, a Raw Score of zero indicates that the subtest did not have enough low-level (or easy) items ("floor items") to adequately assess the individual's skills. The Don't Forget box lists the situations in which Raw Scores of zero will invalidate a composite.

Prorating and Scoring Options

Options are available for calculating the Indexes or FSIQ if not all 10 core subtests were administered or if some of the subtests were spoiled during the administration. Some of the subtests may be replaced by others to calculate the composite scores. Comprehension may substitute for Similarities, Vocabulary, or Information. Letter-

DON'T FORGET

When Raw Scores of Zero Invalidate a Composite

Total Raw Scores of Zero	Effect on Composite
On two of the three subtests that contribute to the VCI (including potential substitutions)	No VCI, GAI, or FSIQ can be derived
On two of the three subtests that contribute to the PRI (including potential substitutions)	No PRI, GAI, or FSIQ can be derived
On both subtests that contribute to the WMI (including potential substitutions)	No WMI or FSIQ can be derived
On both subtests that contribute to the PSI (including potential substitutions)	No PSI or FSIQ can be derived

Key: Verbal Comprehension Index (VCI); General Ability Index (GAI); Full Scale IQ (FSIQ); Perceptual Reasoning Index (PRI); Working Memory Index (WMI); Processing Speed Index (PSI).

Note: If a supplemental subtest score is available to replace the subtest on which a Raw Score of zero was earned, it would be appropriate to substitute the supplemental subtest in order to derive a composite (that otherwise would have been invalid because too many zero scores would not allow calculation of that composite).

Number Sequencing may substitute for Digit Span or Arithmetic. Picture Completion may substitute for Block Design, Matrix Reasoning, or Visual Puzzles. Figure Weights may also substitute for Block Design, Matrix Reasoning, or Visual Puzzles. For individuals age 70 or older, Figure Weights, Letter-Number Sequencing, and Cancellation are not administered, and therefore cannot be used to substitute for a core subtest at these older age ranges.

CAUTION

Minimal Subtest Substitution Is Allowed

- Only one subtest substitution is allowed when deriving each Index score.
- No more than two substitutions from different Index scales are allowed when deriving the FSIQ.

The choice to substitute one subtest for another is not one that can be made randomly. You certainly would not want to substitute one subtest for another because a client performed better (or worse) on one or the other. The decision to substitute one subtest for another must be based on solid reasons. For example, if Digit Span was spoiled because of distracting noises that were present during the administration, this would be a valid reason to substitute Letter-Number Sequencing. An a priori decision to substitute Cancellation for Coding may be made if adults' fine motor control is so poor that it would be unreasonable for them to draw small symbols, but they could write simple slashes through the Cancellation responses. Picture Completion or Figure Weights may be substituted for Block Design, for example, if it was clear that the examinee had motor challenges that prevented him or her from manipulating the blocks. In this case, a decision may be made ahead of time to utilize Picture Completion or Figure Weights in the PRI score because they require no motor manipulation.

DON'T FORGET

Substituting Certain Subtests

VCI Subtest	⟷	Replacement Subtest
Similarities	⟷	Comprehension
Vocabulary	⟷	Comprehension
Information	⟷	Comprehension
WMI Subtest		
Digit Span	⟷	Letter-Number Sequencing*
Arithmetic	⟷	Letter-Number Sequencing*
PRI Subtest		
Block Design	⟷	Figure Weights* or Picture Completion
Matrix Reasoning	⟷	Figure Weights* or Picture Completion
Visual Puzzles	⟷	Figure Weights* or Picture Completion
PSI Subtest		
Symbol Search	⟷	Cancellation*
Coding	⟷	Cancellation*

*Letter-Number Sequencing, Figure Weights, and Cancellation can be administered only to examinees under age 70.

Prorating scores becomes necessary when only two PRI subtests or two VCI are available. In the prorating process, an estimated sum of the VCI or PRI scale is used to derive the composite score. The WMI and the PSI should never be prorated because proration requires at least two valid subtest scaled scores, and these two Indexes each comprise only two subtests. The Full Scale IQ can be computed after either the VCI or the PRI (or both) have been prorated.

The process of prorating the VCI or PRI can be easily be undertaken by utilizing Table A.8 in the *WAIS-IV Administration and Scoring Manual*. Simply determine the prorated score by referencing the sum of the two subtests administered. If you would like to determine the prorated score manually, you may do so by using a simple formula. On the Verbal Scale, you multiply the sum of the scaled scores by $^3\!/_2$ and round to the nearest whole number, which is then your prorated score. It is important to always indicate on the Record Form when a score has been prorated. You may do so by using the abbreviation "PRO."

There are special considerations for the FSIQ when proration is completed. If either the VCI or the PRI (or both) is prorated, then the FSIQ should be calculated using these newly prorated Sums of Scaled Scores. However, if only one subtest score is available for either the WMI and/or PSI, then the prorated FSIQ must be calculated differently. The prorated score for the FSIQ may be derived from Table A.9 of the *Administration and Scoring Manual* if nine subtest scores are available. The second section of Table A.9 is used to derive the FSIQ if eight subtests are available.

CAUTION

Requirements when Simultaneously Substituting and Prorating

If you must use both substitution and proration when deriving the FSIQ or the GAI, be aware of these rules:

1. One substitution and one prorated sum of scaled scores are allowed.

2. The substitution and proration must occur on different index scores.

   Example: You can derive the FSIQ from a prorated VCI and a WMI calculated with Letter-Number Sequencing Substituting for Digit Span, plus a normally calculated PRI and PSI.

Scoring Subtests Requiring Judgment

The core and supplemental subtests of the Verbal Comprehension Index require some level of judgment in their scoring due to the nature of examinees' highly variable verbal responses. Most often Vocabulary, Similarities, and Comprehension require such judgment, but some responses to Information questions can also require prudence in scoring. For each of these four Verbal subtests, the

WAIS-IV Administration and Scoring Manual provides sample responses in addition to scoring criteria. Because it is impossible to list every possible answer that an examinee may state, the Manual must be used only as a guide; it is up to each examiner to interpret the scoring system for each of the unique responses.

Often Verbal responses seem to fall in a borderline area, fitting neither a 1- or 2-point response clearly. Indeed, some answers seem to be perfect 1 $\frac{1}{2}$ point responses. Because variable verbal responses occur commonly, it is important to be familiar with both the specific scoring examples and the general scoring criteria for these Verbal subtests. In general, the examinee's ability to express him- or herself properly should not be included in the scoring of a response. For example, if poor grammar or improper pronunciation is used, an examinee should not be penalized. The content of what is said is what is most important. For example, the response to the Vocabulary item *PLAGIARIZE* "to stole somebody's writin' and preten' like it yours" would earn full credit even though it contains poor grammar. For the Similarities item, *ACCEPTANCE and DENIAL,* the response "Reactivating to situations" uses poor grammar, but the content and thoughts behind it are correct, again earning full credit.

Some adults or adolescents may spontaneously give long responses that actually contain two or more responses in one. Examinees may also elaborate responses after being queried. When such elaboration occurs, a fundamental misconception about the item may be apparent in the response. This is termed a spoiled response, and the item is then scored 0 points. For example, if a response to the Similarities item *PIANO-DRUM* is "music," the examiner should then query (*Q*) the response. If the examinee elaborates by saying, "You make the rhythm by hitting the drum, but you make the melody by tapping on the piano keys," the response should be considered spoiled. Although the original response, "music," fell under the 1-point category, the examinee's elaboration clearly showed a misconception of how the two were *alike.* Therefore, the entire response is scored 0 because of spoilage.

Another case of elaboration or multiple responses to a Verbal subtest item may occur when an adult gives a series of responses in which the *second* or *third* response is intended be the actual response. If this is the case, the *final* answer should be scored. However, if multiple responses are given—some incorrect and some correct—but it is unclear which answer is the final answer, the examinee should be asked to clarify the intended final response. Then the only response scored should be whichever answer is indicated to be the designated final answer. Subtle cues in adults' responses must be used to determine which response is intended as the actual response. Usually if a string of responses is given, with the last phrase being the intended response, examinees will accentuate the last response by dropping their voice at the end of the last word or giving a nonverbal nod of the head. Other adults will give many responses, all equally accentuated and all separated by equal pauses, which tends to lead to a lack of clarity about which response was the intended final response. A helpful, but not leading, manner in which to prompt the examinee is by saying "You said ___, ___, and ___. Which one was your answer?"

On other occasions, many responses may be given that vary greatly in their quality. For example, 0-, 1-, and 2-point responses may occur in one long answer. If this case occurs, and no spoiled responses are present, then simply score the best response. For example, if an examinee spontaneously responds "to build up . . . to start some thing . . . to create" to the Vocabulary item *GENERATE*, then each part of the response is worth different point values. In this response, "to build up" earns 0 points, "to start some thing" earns 1 point, and "to create" earns 2 points. None of these responses spoils another or reveals misconceptions about the word "generate," so the best response ("to create") should be scored; therefore, the examinee earns 2 points.

General Scoring Criteria for Verbal Subtests

Vocabulary, Similarities, and Comprehension all include a set of general scoring criteria, along with the specific examples listed in the manual. The fine points of each of the scoring guidelines are highlighted in Rapid References 3.5, 3.6, and 3.7.

Subtest-by-Subtest Scoring Keys

Some subtests require 0- and 1-point scoring and others require 0-, 1-, and 2-point scoring. The overall scoring rules are consistent throughout the WAIS-IV, but there are also subtle nuances of which the examiner should be aware. The Don't Forget box includes important keys to remember for scoring each subtest.

Computer Scoring Procedures

Examiners can save time scoring and reporting results with the computerized WAIS-IV Scoring Assistant and Report Writer Software. The WAIS-IV Scoring Assistant is available for $235.00 on www.pearsonassess.com. The software

≡ Rapid Reference 3.5

Vocabulary Scoring Rules

2 points	• Shows a good understanding of the word
	• Good synonym
	• Major use
	• One or more definitive features of an object
	• General classification to which the word belongs
	• Correct figurative use of the word
	• Several less definitive but correct descriptive features that cumulatively indicate understanding of the word
	• For verbs, a definitive example of action or a causal relation
1 point	• Response is generally correct, but shows poverty of content
	• A vague or less pertinent synonym
	• A minor use, not elaborated
	• An attribute that is correct but not definitive nor not a distinguishing feature
	• An example using the word itself, not elaborated
	• A concrete instance of the word, not elaborated
	• A correct definition of a related form of the word
0 points	• Obviously wrong responses
	• Verbalizations that show no real understanding even after query
	• A demonstration that is not elaborated with words
	• Not totally incorrect responses, but ones that, even after questioning, are vague or trivial or show a great poverty of content

program requires examiners to enter Raw Scores, and the software generates concise score reports and statistical reports with graphs and tables. It also provides the Raw to Scaled Score conversions and strength and weakness discrepancies. The WAIS-IV scores may also be integrated with other scoring applications, such as the WMS-IV and WIAT-II, and can produce cross-battery analysis of scores. The WAIS-IV Report Writer software includes all capabilities of the Scoring Assistant but also produces individualized, comprehensive reports that go beyond scores, tables, and graphs. For example, this Report Writer

≡ *Rapid Reference 3.6*

Similarities Scoring Rules

2 points	• A general, major classification of the pair • A universal property of the pair • A concept pertinent to both members of the pair
I point	• A specific property common to both that is a minor or less pertinent similarity • A major classification that is less pertinent for both members of the item, but correct general classifications
0 points	• A property that is not pertinent to both members of the pair • A property that is too general in nature • Description of differences between members of the item pair • Clearly wrong responses

software provides a nontechnical client report, a comprehensive narrative report with narrative interpretations, and a clinical and background review. The WAIS-IV Report Writer software is available for $399.00 on www.pearsonassess.com. Rapid Reference 3.8 lists the minimum software requirements for WAIS-IV Scoring Assistant and Report Writer.

≡ *Rapid Reference 3.7*

Comprehension Scoring Rules

2 points	• Expression of the 2-point general concept indicated in the *Manual* • Expression of two general responses on items 5, 8, 9, and I0
I point	• Expression of the I-point general concept indicated in the *Manual* • For items that require two general concepts, I point is awarded if the examinee's queried response refers to the same general concept as the initial response
0 points	• In general, are vague or trivial responses, or not addressing the question

DON'T FORGET

....

Scoring Keys

Subtest	Range of Item Scores	Scoring Pointers
1. Block Design	0–2 (items 1–4)	• For designs 1–4, successful completion within the time limit on the first Trial earns 2 points.
	0 or 4 (items 5–8)	• For designs 1–4, successful completion within the time limit on the second Trial earns 1 point.
	0 or 4–7 (items 9–14)	• For designs 5–8, successful completion within the time limit earns 4 points
		• For designs 9–14, points ranging from 4–7 are awarded on the basis of completion time.
		• For items 1–14, designs completed correctly *after* the allowed time limit has expired are scored 0.
		• If designs 1–4 are not administered, then award 2 points for each of those items.
		• Partially correct responses are scored 0.
Process Score: Block Design No Time Bonus (BDN)	0–2 (items 1–4)	• For designs 1–4, successful completion within the time limit on the first trial earns 2 points.
	0 or 4 (items 5–14)	• For designs 5–14, successful completion within the time limit earns 4 points. (No bonus points are awarded.)
		• For items 1–14, designs completed correctly *after* the allowed time limit has expired are scored 0.
2. Similarities	0–2	• Utilize the general 0–2-point scoring criteria and specific examples.
		• Score spontaneous improvement in responses.
		• Degree of abstraction is key in assigning credit to responses.
		• Add 2 points to the raw score for each of the unadministered reversal items.
3. Digit Span	0–2	• Exact correct repetition is given 1 point per trial (2 points per item possible).
		• Self-corrections are given credit.

Subtest	Range of Item Scores	Scoring Pointers
		• Score 0 points if the examinee gives an incorrect response.
		• Score 0 points if the examinee does not respond within approximately 30 seconds.
		• The Raw Scores from Digits Forward, Digits Backward, and Sequencing are combined to create the Digit Span raw score.
Process Score: Digit Span Forward (DSF)	0–16	• Sum of the Forward item scores.
Process Score: Digit Span Backward (DSB)	0–16	• Sum of the Backward item scores.
Process Score: Digit Span Sequence (DSS)	0–16	• Sum of the Sequencing item scores.
Process Score: Longest Digit Span Forward (LDSF)	0–9	• Number of digits recalled on the last Forward trial scored 1 point.
Process Score: Longest Digit Span Backward (LDSB)	0–8	• Number of digits recalled on the last Backward trial scored 1 point.
Process Score: Longest Digit Span Sequence (LDSS)	0–9	• Number of digits recalled on the last Sequencing trial scored 1 point.
4. Matrix Reasoning	0–1	• Do not add score from Sample Items A or B into calculation of the Raw Score. • Examinees are not penalized due to speediness of responding. • The correct answers are printed in bold blue font on the Record Form. Score 1 point for correct response.
5. Vocabulary	0–1 (items 1–3) 0–2 (items 4–30)	• For Picture Items 1–3, score 1 point for correct response. • For Picture Items 1–3, score 0 points for incorrect response or no response within approximately 30 seconds.

(continued)

Subtest	Range of Item Scores	Scoring Pointers
		• For Items 4–30, utilize the general 0–2-point scoring criteria and specific examples.
		• Slang or regionalisms not in the dictionary are scored 0.
		• Any meaning found in a standard dictionary is scored correct.
		• Poor grammar is not penalized in scoring.
		• Add 1 point to the raw score for each of the unadministered reversal items 1–3, and 2 points for item 4.
6. Arithmetic	0–1	• If subject gets the numeric value correct but does not give the unit, score 1 point.
		• If subject gives a correct response with an alternate unit (e.g., 1 hour = 60 seconds), score 1 point.
		• Problems completed correctly *after* the 30-second time limit has expired are scored 0.
		• Add 1 point to the raw score for each of the unadministered reversal items.
7. Symbol Search	0–60	• Use the Symbol Search Scoring Template to score responses.
		• If both YES and NO are marked for the same item, the response is incorrect.
		• The Symbol Search Total Raw Score is calculated by subtracting the Number Incorrect from the Number Correct.
		• Any items left blank are not included in the score computation.
		• Any item completed after the 120-second time limit should not be counted in the score calculation.
8. Visual Puzzles	0–1	• Items completed after the time limit are scored 0 points.
		• The three correct responses for each item are printed in bold blue font on the Record Form.

Subtest	Range of Item Scores	Scoring Pointers
		• All three responses for each item must be correct to earn 1 point.
		• If an examinee does not choose three correct responses or does not know the answer, score 0 points.
9. Information	0–1	• The list of possible responses in the *Manual* is not exhaustive. Give credit for any response that is of the same caliber as the samples.
		• Add 1 point to the raw score for each of the unadministered reversal items.
10. Coding	0–135	• Use the Coding scoring template to check the examinee's responses.
		• One point is given for each correctly drawn symbol (completed within 120 seconds).
		• Spontaneous correction of an incorrect symbol is scored 1.
		• A response that is imperfect but a clearly identifiable symbol is scored 1.
		• Skipped items are not counted.
11. Letter Number Sequencing	0–3 (0 = fail all trials 1 = pass one trial 2 = pass 2 trials 3 = pass all three trials)	• If a letter or number is omitted in the response, it is incorrect.
		• For items 1–2, there is only one correct response for each trial.
		• For items 3–10, credit is given if letters are given in the correct sequence and then numbers in the correct sequence.
		• Each of the three trials in an item is worth 1 point.
		• Practice items are not included in the Raw Score.
Process Score: Longest Letter-Number Sequence (LLNS)	0–8	• The number of letters and numbers recalled on the last trial are scored 1 point.
12. Figure Weights	0–1	• Responses completed after the time limit are scored 0.

(continued)

Subtest	Range of Item Scores	Scoring Pointers
		• Correct responses are printed in bold blue font in the Record Form.
		• Correct responses within the time limit are scored 1.
		• Incorrect responses or "I don't know" responses are scored 0.
13. Comprehension	0–2	• Utilize the general 0–2-point scoring criteria and specific examples.
		• The Administration and Scoring Manual is not all-inclusive and must be used only as a guide.
		• Score spontaneous improvement in responses.
		• Degree of understanding expressed by the examinee is scored.
		• For responses that require two general concepts, only 1 point is earned if both ideas stated by the examinee are included in the same general concept.
		• Add 1 point to the Raw Score for each of the unadministered reversal items.
14. Cancellation	0–36 (items 1 & 2)	• Use the Cancellation scoring template to score the responses.
		• Marks on target shapes are correct, and marks on nontarget shapes are incorrect.
		• If a mark on one shape inadvertently extends through an adjacent shape, score only the originally marked shape.
		• Subtract the number incorrect from the number correct for each item score
		• Total Raw Score is the sum of the scores from the two items
15. Picture Completion	0–1	• Score 0 if examinee responds after 20 seconds.
		• Correct verbal responses earn 1 point.
		• Certain verbal responses earn 1 point only if accompanied by a correct pointing response. Those verbal responses are

Subtest	Range of Item Scores	Scoring Pointers
		listed in the right column of the Sample Responses table in the *Manual*.
		• If only a pointing response is given, 1 point is awarded for correctly pointing.
		• If examinee points to the correct place but gives an incorrect verbal response, score 0.
		• Correct description using a synonym or examinee's own words, score 1.
		• Add 1 point to the Raw Score for each of the unadministered reversal items.

≡ *Rapid Reference 3.8*

System Requirements for WAIS-IV Scoring Assistant and Report Writer

Minimum System Requirements
• Windows Vista/XP/2000

• 400 MHz processor

• 256 MB RAM; more memory improves performance

• 2 MB video card capable of 800 × 600 resolution (16-bit color)

• 175 MB free hard disk space when installing PsychCorpCenter®–II for the first time

• Internet Explorer 6.0

• CD-ROM drive

Recommended System Requirements
• Windows Vista/XP (SP 2)/2000 (SP 4)

• 1 GHz processor

• 512 MB RAM; more memory improves performance

• 2 MB video card capable of 1024 × 768 resolution (32-bit color)

• 175 MB free hard disk space when installing PsychCorpCenter®–II for the first time

• Internet Explorer 6.0 or higher

• CD-ROM drive

• Microsoft Word

🐢 TEST YOURSELF 🐢

1. Like earlier editions of Wechsler's adult tests, the WAIS-IV scaled scores are determined by comparing an individual's performance to that of the reference group of adults ages 20–34. TRUE or FALSE?

2. Unless replacing another subtest, none of the following subtests are used in the calculation of the FSIQ except

   (a) Letter-Number Sequencing.

   (b) Symbol Search.

   (c) Comprehension.

   (d) Figure Weights.

3. If Digit Span is a spoiled subtest, which of the following subtests can replace it?

   (a) Letter-Number Sequencing

   (b) Symbol Search

   (c) Cancellation

   (d) Arithmetic

4. At what age can Figure Weights no longer be substituted for other PRI subtests?

   (a) Age 50

   (b) Age 60

   (c) Age 65

   (d) Age 70

5. Which one of the following scales is NOT safe to prorate?

   (a) Full Scale IQ

   (b) Perceptual Reasoning Index

   (c) Verbal Comprehension Index

   (d) Processing Speed Index

6. What is the mean and standard deviation of scaled scores?

   (a) 100 and 15

   (b) 50 and 10

   (c) 10 and 3

   (d) 5 and 2

   (e) 500 and 100

7. Of the WAIS-IV process tasks, which ones yield a Scaled Score in addition to the Raw Score?

   (a) Block Design No Time Bonus (BDN)

   (b) Digit Span Forward (DSF)

   (c) Digit Span Backward (DSB)

   (d) Digit Span Sequencing (DSS)

   (e) Longest Digit Span Forward (LDSF)

    (f) Longest Digit Span Backward (LSDB)

    (g) Longest Digit Span Sequence (LDSS)

    (h) Longest Letter-Number Sequence (LLNS)

8. **If you forget to administer the Digit Span Sequencing portion of the Digit Span subtest, you can simply calculate the Digit Span Scaled Score based on the Raw Score sum of Digit Span Forward and Digit Span Backward because that was how Digit Span was calculated on previous versions of the WAIS. TRUE or FALSE?**

9. **As long as an examinee points to the correct location of the missing object in Picture Completion, score the response "1," even if the verbal response is incorrect. TRUE or FALSE?**

Answers: 1. False; 2. b; 3. a; 4. d; 5. d; 6. c; 7. a, b, c, d; 8. False; 9. False.

Four

HOW TO INTERPRET THE WAIS-IV: CONCEPTUAL AND CLINICAL FOUNDATIONS

Your philosophy toward the interpretation of individually administered clinical tests should be an intelligent one. The basic premise of test interpretation that we put forth in this book is one that we and others have advocated before (Kamphaus & Reynolds, 1987; Kaufman, 1979a, 1990, 1994a; Kaufman & Lichtenberger, 1999, 2000, 2006; Kaufman, Lichtenberger, Fletcher-Janzen, & Kaufman, 2005; Reynolds & Fletcher-Janzen, 1989). We begin this chapter by clearly articulating the tenets of the intelligent testing philosophy. We then segue into a description of qualitative and clinical factors that may influence performance on the WAIS-IV and that should be considered when using an intelligent approach to test interpretation. The final section of this chapter includes a discussion of Watkins and Canivez's (2004) critiques of our previous approach to interpreting Wechsler scales, our response to their arguments and methodology, and an articulation of how and why we created our current system of WAIS-IV interpretation.

INTELLIGENT TESTING PHILOSOPHY

We believe that it is critical that examiners use an intelligent approach to testing and understand our basic philosophy before proceeding with the specifics of test interpretation. Assessment should be of the individual and for the individual. The examiner's role in assessment is more than simply examining the scores; rather, he or she must bring together research knowledge, theoretical sophistication, and solid clinical skill when interpreting tests. The intelligent testing philosophy that we follow is fivefold, as shown in the Don't Forget box.

DON'T FORGET

....

Tenets of the Intelligent Testing Philosophy

....

1. Subtests measure what the individual has learned.

2. Subtests are samples of behavior and are not exhaustive.

3. Standardized, individually administered tests assess mental functioning under fixed experimental conditions.

4. Test batteries are optimally useful when interpreted from a theoretical model.

5. Hypotheses generated from the test profile should be supported with data from multiple sources.

1. *Subtests measure what the individual has learned.* This concept comes directly from Wesman's (1968) introduction of the intelligent testing approach. The content of all tasks, whether verbal or nonverbal, is learned within a culture. The learning may take place formally in the school, casually in the home, or incidentally through everyday life. As a measure of past learning, the IQ test is best thought of as a kind of achievement test, not as a simple measure of aptitude. Plain and simple, cognitive tests measure prior learning. Thus, the strong relationships between cognitive tests and achievement measures are not surprising. However, even though the predictive validity of cognitive test scores is strong, the relationship between cognitive test scores and school achievement need not indicate a predetermined fate for an individual. That is, if results from a cognitive test are appropriately interpreted and translated to helpful recommendations, positive change in academic achievement may occur, thereby changing one's IQ-determined "destiny."

The interaction between learning potential and availability of learning experiences is too complex to ponder for any given person, making the whole genetics–environment issue of theoretical value but impractical and irrelevant for the interpretation of that person's test profile. Issues of heredity versus environment and the validity of the IQ construct are meaningful for understanding the multifaceted intelligence construct; the accumulating research helps test developers, practitioners, and theoreticians appreciate the foundation of the tests used to measure intelligence; and the IQ tests, as vehicles for the research, are essential sources of group data for use in scientific study of these topics. But all of the controversy loses meaning for each specific person referred for evaluation when the clinician administers an IQ test to study and interpret just what the person has or has not learned and to help answer the practical referral questions.

2. *Subtests are samples of behavior and are not exhaustive.* This tenet is relevant to the generalizability of the test findings. Since test results usually are obtained within 1 or 2 hours and include samples of behavior from a select set of tasks, caution needs to be exercised in generalizing the results to other behaviors in different circumstances. The individual Wechsler subtests, or the subtests that compose the Woodcock-Johnson (third edition; WJ III), Kaufman tests, and other cognitive tests, do not reflect the essential ingredients of intelligence whose mastery implies some type of ultimate life achievement. They, like tasks developed originally by Binet, are more or less arbitrary samples of behavior. Teaching people how to solve similarities, assemble blocks to match abstract designs, or repeat digits backward will not make them smarter in any broad or generalizable way. What we are able to infer from the person's success on the tasks and style of responding to them is important; the specific, unique aspect of intellect that each subtest measures is of minimal consequence.

Limitations in the selection of tasks necessarily mean that one should be cautious in generalizing the results to circumstances that are removed from the one-on-one assessment of a finite number of skills and processing strategies. Intelligence tests should, therefore, be routinely supplemented by other formal and informal measures of cognitive, clinical, and neuropsychological functioning to facilitate the assessment of mental functioning as part of a more thorough evaluation. In addition, theoretical models of intelligence should be used as a guide for selecting cognitive tasks to administer during an evaluation, and examiners should not be wedded to a single instrument, even one as popular as the WAIS-IV. Dawn Flanagan's cross-battery assessment provides a wonderful methodology for ensuring that any comprehensive evaluation of a person's intelligence measures a diversity of key broad and narrow Cattell-Horn-Carroll (CHC) abilities (Flanagan, Ortiz, & Alfonso, 2007).

To the degree that tasks are chosen to meet theoretical constructs, the array of cognitive subtests in a comprehensive test battery is systematic and not arbitrary. Nonetheless, even when using cross-battery assessment, neither a global IQ nor a thorough profile of CHC abilities should be interpreted as an estimate of a person's "total" or "complete" level of intellectual functioning. Examination of one's individual cognitive strengths and weaknesses obtained from IQ test data is more fruitful when combined with supportive data from other samples of behavior such as those data obtained from supplemental measures. These measures might include behavioral assessment, personality assessment, neuropsychological assessment, adaptive behavior assessment, and even informal assessment of abilities that are not easily tested by standardized instruments (such as measures of the creative and practical intelligence components of Sternberg's triarchic theory of successful human intelligence; Sternberg, Kaufman, & Grigorenko, 2008).

3. *Standardized, individually administered tests assess mental functioning under fixed experimental conditions.* Strict adherence to the standardized procedures of administration and scoring of standardized tests is important to ensure the comparability of obtained test results to those of the normative group. However, these same formal procedures for administration and scoring add to the artificial nature of the testing situation. Very infrequently in real life does someone sit across from you with an easel and stopwatch and ask you to perform a task while your every move is being observed, scrutinized, and recorded. Thus, awareness of the experimental nature of the testing process will help prevent over-interpreting a person's IQ as their maximum capacity.

Standardized administration and scoring means conducting an experiment with $N = 1$ every time an examiner tests someone on an intelligence test. For the results of this experiment to be meaningful, the experimenter-examiner must adhere precisely to the wording in the *Manual*, give appropriate probes as defined in the instructions, time each relevant response diligently, and score each item exactly the way comparable responses were scored during the normative procedure. Following these rules prevents examiners from applying a flexible clinical investigatory procedure during the administration (as Piaget always advocated with his *méthode clinique*), from giving feedback to a person who urgently desires it, or from cleverly dislodging from the crevices of a person's brain his or her maximum response to each test item.

It is necessary to be an exceptional clinician to establish and maintain rapport and to weave the standardized administration into a natural, pleasant interchange between examiner and subject. Clinical skills are also essential when observing and interpreting a person's myriad behaviors during the examination and when integrating all available information and data to interpret the profile of test scores. But it is vital for an examiner to follow the standardized procedures to the letter while administering the test; otherwise, the standard scores yielded for the person will be invalid and meaningless. To violate the rules is to negate the value of the meticulous set of norms obtained under experimental conditions by major test-publishing companies for their tests.

The testing situation has a certain built-in artificiality by virtue of the stopwatch, the precise words to be spoken, and the recording of almost everything spoken by the examinee. A person with excellent visual-spatial and manipulative skills might perform slowly and ineffectively on Block Design because of anxiety caused by the time pressure; or a person with a good commonsense understanding of social situations (coupled with limited word knowledge) may fail several Comprehension items because of failure to understand some of key words used in the questions. It is tempting to give credit to a design solved "just 2 or 3 seconds overtime" or to simplify the wording of a question that the person "certainly knows the answer to." But the good examiner will resist these temptations, knowing that the people in the reference group did not receive such help.

Testing the limits on a subtest often can give valuable insight into the reasons for failure or confusion, so long as this flexible, supplemental testing occurs *after* the score has been recorded under appropriate conditions. In an experiment, the empirical results are of limited value until they are interpreted and discussed in the context of pertinent research and theory by a knowledgeable researcher. By the same token, the empirical outcomes of an IQ test are often meaningless until put into context by the examiner. That is the time for a clinician's acumen and flexibility to be displayed. Interpreting test scores in the context of observed behaviors can aid in the appropriate interpretation of the scores. For example, when an adolescent's oppositionality during testing has led to a low level of motivation on timed tasks, this behavior is crucial to understanding that the obtained scores may be a gross underestimate of the adolescent's abilities. In addition, such observations can be useful in translating test results into practical recommendations. Kaufman (1990) states:

The value of the scores increases when the examiner functions as a true experimenter and tries to determine *why* the child earned the particular profile revealed on the record form; the IQs become harmful when they are unquestioningly interpreted as valid indicators of intellectual functioning and are misconstrued as evidence of the child's maximum or even typical performance. (p. 9)

4. *Test batteries are optimally useful when interpreted from a theoretical model.* This tenet is an important notion to remember when attempting to organize test data in a meaningful way. Using the appropriate theoretical model is crucial when trying to understand the reasons underlying the peaks and valleys of a person's cognitive profile to facilitate the translation of the scores to pragmatic, fundamental, theoretically meaningful areas of deficit and strength. As will be discussed in chapter 5, the WAIS-IV has foundations in cognitive neuroscience theory and research, and its scores can be interpreted from a variety of theoretical models, ranging from the CHC model (Flanagan et al., 2007) to neuropsychological approaches such as Luria's (1973, 1980).

In addition to these theoretical foundations, alternate models may be applied to interpret the profile of test scores. For example, an information-processing model that features input, integration, storage, and output (Silver, 1993) could be helpful frameworks for test interpretation (see Figure 4.1). This model was used in the next section on Qualitative and Clinical Analyses of the WAIS-IV when developing the sections on Influences Affecting Subtest Scores and Clinical Considerations for each subtest. For example, consider Block Design, which is influenced by visual-perceptual problems (Input), the cognitive style of field dependence–field independence (Integration), and working under time pressure (Output). Or consider some of the clinical considerations that pertain to Similarities: (a) creativity and visual imagery may be used to come up with the relationship between two concepts (Integration); (b) clinically rich information can be gleaned from the nature of the verbal response, such as overelaboration or overly general responses (Output); and (c) correct responses on the easier items may simply reflect overlearned, everyday associations rather than true abstract thought (Storage).

Whether test results are interpreted within a test's own theoretical model or by reorganizing the subtests to better fit another theoretical framework, the results will be best explained and translated into practical recommendations if presented within a theoretical framework.

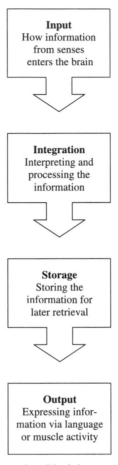

Figure 4.1. Information Processing Model

5. *Hypotheses generated from the test profile should be supported with data from multiple sources.* This tenet is a key postulate to prevent misuse of test results, and is related to all of the previous four tenets of intelligent testing. Results from one instrument should not be interpreted alone as the gospel truth about an individual. Rather, when hypotheses are created from an individual's profile, supplemental information should be found that could confirm or disconfirm the hypotheses. Test score profiles are optimally meaningful when interpreted in the context of known background information, observed behaviors, and approach to each problem-solving task.

Virtually any examiner can deduce that the WAIS-IV Verbal Comprehension Index (VCI) is not a very good measure of the crystallized intelligence of a person raised in a foreign culture, a person who understands Spanish or Vietnamese far better than English, or a person with a hearing impairment, and that the WAIS-IV Processing Speed Index (PSI) does not measure speed of mental processing very well for a person with crippling arthritis or a visual handicap. The goal of the intelligent tester is to deduce when one or more subtests or indexes may be an invalid measure of a person's intellectual functioning for more subtle reasons: distractibility, poor arithmetic achievement in school, subcultural differences in language or custom, emotional content of the items, suspected or known lesions in specific regions of the brain, fatigue, boredom, extreme shyness, bizarre thought processes, inconsistent effort, and the like.

Being a great detective, able to follow up leads and hunches about peaks and valleys in a profile, is the hallmark of an intelligent tester. Such a tester will integrate IQ test profiles with background information, clinical observations of behaviors, and other tests administered in order to more fully understand the examinee's profile.

The importance of this fifth tenet is probably best explained through an example. Consider an adult female who has a WAIS-IV-inspired hypothesis of weak short-term memory. The memory hypothesis is based on a grouping of WAIS-IV subtests that includes low scores on the Digit Span, Arithmetic, and Letter-Number Sequencing scores. Her low scores on these subtests may be due to poor short-term memory but may also be due to anxiety, distractibility, lack of concentration, or other factors. What was the woman like during the evaluation? Did she appear focused and remain on task? Did she seem nervous, fidgety, or exhibit other signs of anxiety? Did she score low on other tests of short-term memory, such as the Short-Term Memory Tests of the WJ III? Did her background include a history of difficulty remembering people's names or phone numbers or forgetting appointments? The answers to questions such as these will support or disconfirm the hypothesis of poor short-term memory. With multiple sources of data backing a hypothesis, you can feel much more confident in stating a person's abilities. Thus, in this book we present an interpretive approach to analyzing the WAIS-IV as part of a comprehensive battery that integrates many sources of data.

TYING TOGETHER THE TENETS OF INTELLIGENT TESTING

The principles discussed in the preceding sections direct our attention to one important point: The focus of any assessment is the person being assessed, not the test. Many psychological reports stress what the scales or subtests measure instead of what aspects of the person are particularly well developed or in need of improvement; many reports are so number-oriented that the reader loses sight of the person's uniqueness. The WAIS-IV enables psychologists to better understand a person's cognitive functioning, but other facets of an individual are also revealed during an assessment and should be fully integrated to represent that person as a whole. Although the section of an assessment report that systematically reports and interprets the FSIQ and index scores is valuable, the behavioral observations section of a case report is often more revealing, and ultimately of more value, if it helps to explain how or why examinees arrived at the scores that they did. The content of the responses and the person's style of responding to various types of tasks can be more important as a determinant of developmental level and intellectual maturity than the scores assigned to the items or tasks.

When several tests are administered to a person (intelligence, language, achievement, personality, neuropsychological), the results must be integrated from one test battery to the other. Intelligent testing does not apply only to the interpretation of intelligence tests. The examiner's main role is to generate hypotheses that pertain mostly to assets and deficits within the CHC, neuropsychological, or information-processing models, and then confirm or deny these hypotheses by exploring multiple sources of evidence. This integrative, flexible, clinical-empirical methodology and philosophy, as outlined in the preceding tenets, represents the approach taken in this book for the interpretation of the WAIS-IV. The guidelines for interpreting WAIS-IV test profiles and the illustrative case reports in chapter 10 rest solidly on the intelligent testing framework.

QUALITATIVE AND CLINICAL ANALYSES OF THE WAIS-IV

In order to maintain focus on the examinee, rather than on the test itself during test interpretation, as the examiner, you must consider the results in the context of what is observed during the testing. Test-taking behaviors may exert a negative or positive influence on WAIS-IV performance. Behavioral factors have the potential to affect the reliability and validity of test scores, although they are essentially unrelated to the test construct being measured (Sattler, 2008).

Qualitative analyses of performance on WAIS-IV tasks serve several functions during the interpretation process.

DON'T FORGET

Summary of the Functions of Qualitative Analyses

- Provide a cross-check for you to evaluate the reliability of the person's test scores obtained during test sessions
- Provide a cross-check of the validity of the test scores obtained during test sessions
- Help determine definitions of standards of test performance
- Provide supplemental information for interpreting scores when test-taking behaviors systematically interfere with performance
- Help ensure that positive as well as negative influences of various test-taking behaviors are observed
- May assist with making decisions about abilities or constructs that should be investigated further

1. *Qualitative analyses provide a cross-check for you to evaluate the* reliability *of the person's test scores obtained during any test sessions.* Therefore, if the reliability of test-taking behavior is called into question in the initial session, you may want to schedule additional sessions at different times and places to see if maladaptive test-taking behaviors are consistently present. If the behaviors are present during other testing sessions then the examiner will need to check for the same behaviors across settings. (Kaufman et al., 2005, pp. 143–144; emphasis added)

It is key to determine if the observed behaviors are *consistently present* during test sessions and alternate settings. The Caution box lists the types of questions that concern the reliability of behaviors examined in qualitative analyses.

CAUTION

Types of Questions that Concern the Reliability of Observed Behaviors

- Does the examinee act this way every time he or she is tested?
- Does the examinee act this way only when being tested in a standardized fashion, or is it in any testing situation?
- Does the examinee act this way when in other structured situations?
- Does the examinee exhibit these test-session behaviors with other examiners or authority figures?

Within a testing session, examiners need to determine whether a person exhibits different test-session behaviors when different modalities are required. For example, some people display poor attention and distractibility when subtests are presented with only auditory stimuli (e.g., Digit Span and Similarities) but are able to sustain attention and exhibit less distractibility with subtests that measure similar constructs with both visual and auditory cues (e.g., Vocabulary). If you notice such a pattern on these WAIS-IV subtests, you may want to verify the observation of the qualitative analyses of behaviors with other tests and with other personnel to see if the inattentive and distractible behaviors are consistently present. If the behaviors are indeed consistently present, then determine the validity of the behavior as it relates to the impact on test performance.

2. *Qualitative analyses of behaviors provide a cross-check of the* validity *of the test scores obtained during test sessions.* If you determine that the behavior is reliably present, then determine the impact of the behavior. For a behavior to be valid, it must exert a moderate to severe impact on test performance in a consistent way. "One of the implicit goals of any cognitive ability battery is to obtain results that are not unduly affected by a person's conduct during the test session (Glutting & Oakland, 1993). In other words, qualitative analyses of behaviors help determine if the person's obtained (*quantitative*) scores reflect the intended cognitive constructs as opposed to the constructs within the context of other extraneous behavioral (*qualitative*) variables" (Kaufman et al., 2005, p. 145).

Hebben and Milberg (2002) suggest that an examiner "should try to document any behaviors that seem unusual or rare within his or her own typical experience, and then decide whether this information is relevant to clinical decision making" (p. 77). Validity, in this sense, is concerned with the *relevance* of the behavior, and relevance pertains especially to the question of whether behaviors observed during the test session *interfered* with test performance. The specific questions that concern the validity of qualitative analyses of behaviors are addressed in the Caution box.

CAUTION

Types of Questions that Concern the Validity of Observed Behaviors

- Did the test-session behavior help or hurt the examinee's performance on a specific item or subtest?
- Did the test-session behavior appear to have a mild, moderate, or severe impact on test performance?

3. *Qualitative analyses of behaviors* "*help ensure that the positive as well as negative influences of various test-taking behaviors are observed. These analyses also aid in understanding the* process *of the test situation as well as the* products" (Kaufman et al., 2005, p. 147). For example, many people who have poor visual-spatial skills will encounter great difficulty on the Block Design subtest of the WAIS-IV. Some people will become frustrated and give up easily, others will verbally mediate their way through the test, and others will simply stay with the task until it is finished regardless of how long it takes. All three of these approaches to working the designs on Block Design give valuable clues about what behaviors sustain eventual success for a given person. The luxury of large batteries like the WAIS-IV is that they provide multiple opportunities to observe not only a person's behavioral weaknesses and trouble areas but also the basic strengths of the person that contribute to good test scores and, it is hoped, to success in other environments as well.

4. *Qualitative analyses of behaviors may assist with making decisions about follow-up testing, including assessment of abilities or constructs that are not generally measured by a cognitive ability battery such as the WAIS-IV.* As Kaufman et al. (2005) indicate, these difficulties suggest weaknesses in executive functioning: "(1) independently orienting and sustaining attention, (2) demonstrating impulsivity when reflection is needed, (3) staying still and orienting to test materials, (4) entertaining competing answers, (5) demonstrating rigidity when flexibility is needed, and (6) checking answers" (p. 147). If you observe these behaviors and believe that they are interfering with scores on the WAIS-IV, then investigate further or recommend further testing in the area of executive functioning. However, these same behaviors might be associated with excessive anxiety or depression rather than poor executive functioning.

The factors that we believe are most likely to influence performance on the WAIS-IV are listed in the pages that follow, but they are not exhaustive, and are intended primarily to alert you to a diversity of possible behaviors to observe and interpret. In chapter 6 of this book, Dr. George McCloskey's description of neuropsychological test interpretation of the WAIS-IV provides additional information related to qualitative analysis in his process approach to examining test data. Be sure to make decisions about qualitative observations that are specific to the person being examined. The information must make sense in light of the person's background information, observations made by other professionals who work with the person on a daily basis, and other tests administered in the comprehensive assessment. Determining the validity of test scores in this context relies on your skillful clinical interpretation of behaviors as well as your willingness to form hypotheses about test-taking behaviors and to test those hypotheses.

In addition to the listing of possible influencing factors for the WAIS-IV are various clinical suggestions to aid in interpreting each subtest. These clinical points come from clinical experience (our own as well as generations of Wechsler lore and feedback from colleagues), and the literature (e.g., Kamphaus, 1993; Kaufman, 1990, 1994a; Reitan & Wolfson, 1992; Sattler, 1998; Zimmerman & Woo-Sam, 1985).

The clinical considerations are meant to be suggestions of hypotheses to consider, not as definite causes for performance on particular subtests. Each psychologist must employ his or her own theoretical framework to provide the best interpretation of any particular clinical evidence.

Although many have suggested clinical hypotheses about Wechsler profiles, empirical research has not supported hypotheses initially proposed by Rapaport and other clinicians. This lack of validation is likely because of the very complicated nature of interpreting pieces of clinical information in isolation. Even two top-notch clinicians may not have exactly the same interpretation of clinical data after testing the same individual (Lipsitz, Dworkin, & Erlenmeyer-Kimling, 1993).

SUBTEST-BY-SUBTEST QUALITATIVE AND CLINICAL ANALYSES

BLOCK DESIGN: Influences Affecting Subtest Scores
• Cognitive style (field dependence-field independence)
• Visual-perceptual problems
• Working under time pressure

BLOCK DESIGN: Clinical Considerations
• Scores may be substantially lowered by obsessive concern with detail or reflectivity. Bonus points can be earned for quick, perfect performance. The comparison between Block Design and Block Design No Time Bonus can help determine the influence that speed of performance had on the person's score.
• Visual-perceptual problems are often apparent on this subtest. If a low score occurs, the input of the visual material may be related to inaccurate perception rather than due to problem-solving ability or motor output. Testing the limits often can help to determine whether the adult is having perceptual difficulties or other problems.

- Scores should be interpreted in light of problem-solving approaches that were observed. Some adults use a trial-and-error approach, some a systematic and planned approach. Factors such as rigidity, perseveration, speed of mental processing, carelessness, self-concept, cautiousness, and ability to benefit from feedback impact the test.
- Some individuals may have little motivation to try and give up easily; others learn as they take the test and sometimes catch on just when they discontinue. In such cases, testing the limits by administering further items can be of great clinical value (although any extra items administered beyond the discontinue rule cannot be counted in the score).
- Performance on this test is vulnerable to any kind of cerebral brain damage (especially right hemisphere). Lesions to the posterior region of the right hemisphere, especially the parietal lobes, can strongly impact Block Design.

SIMILARITIES: Influences Affecting Subtest Scores
- Flexibility
- Interests
- Negativism ("They're not alike")
- Overly concrete thinking
- Outside reading

SIMILARITIES: Clinical Considerations
- Degree of abstractness should be evaluated; responses may be *abstract* (table and chair are "furniture"), *concrete* (coat and suit are "made of cloth"), or *functional* (north and west "tell you where you are going").
- Clinically rich information can be gleaned from the nature of the verbal response: Overelaboration, overly general responses, overly inclusive responses, or self-references should be noted. Overelaboration may suggest obsessiveness. Overly inclusive responses may suggest a thought disorder. Self references are unusual during Similarities and may be indicative of personal preoccupation.
- Obsessive adults may provide responses that vary in quality by embedding a 2-point response among 1- or 0-point responses. This may lead to unusually high scores, as long as no response spoils the answer.
- The pattern of responses should be examined. An adult who earns a raw score by accumulating several 1-point responses may differ substantially in potential from an adult who earns the same raw score with some 2-point and 0-point responses. The individual who mixes the 2s and 0s probably has a greater capacity for excellent performance.

- Creativity may be exhibited in trying to come up with the relationship between two concepts. Sometimes visual imagery may be used. The creativity does not invariably mean a wrong response.
- Correct responses on the easier items may simply reflect overlearned, everyday associations rather than true abstract thought.
- Individuals who miss the first item administered provide the opportunity to see how they benefit from feedback. The examiner gives an example of a correct answer if the examinee does not provide a perfect answer to the first item administered. Adults who catch on quickly to these prompts demonstrate flexibility and adaptability. Rigidity may be evident if the adult continues to insist that certain pairs are "not alike."
- Formal learning is less emphasized than new problem solving. The adult's task is to relate to verbal concepts, but the individual concepts tend to be simple and well known (table-chair).

DIGIT SPAN: Influences Affecting Subtest Scores
- Ability to receive stimuli passively
- Attention span
- Anxiety
- Distractibility
- Flexibility (when switching among forward, backward, and sequencing)
- Learning disabilities
- Attention-Deficit/Hyperactivity Disorder (ADHD)
- Negativism (refusal to try to reverse digits, to exert effort until the more challenging Backward or Sequencing items, or to take a "meaningless" task)

DIGIT SPAN: Clinical Considerations
- The Process-level scores of Digit Span Forward, Backward, and Sequencing will help to discern whether failure is due to poor sequential ability (right numbers in wrong order) or due to poor rote memory (forgetting digits, but otherwise correctly repeating the series). Problems with inattention, distractibility, or anxiety may be evident in responses that bear little relationship to the actual stimuli.
- After the task, testing the limits and questioning whether any strategy can be employed to help differentiate between poor strategy generation (e.g., chunking), low motivation, anxiety, distractibility, sequencing problems, or memory problems.
- Digit Span Backward and Sequencing, which require mental manipulation or visualization of the numbers, are more impacted by number ability than is

Digits Forward. Thus, those who have better number ability may perform better on Digits Backward or Sequencing.

- Typically adults and adolescents produce Forward spans that are 1 digit longer than sequencing spans. Longer sequencing than forward spans (by 2 or more digits) occurs relatively rarely within the normal population of adults and is therefore noteworthy: less than 5% of the time (averaging across all ages) (Wechsler, 2008, Table C.5). One explanation for a longer Sequencing span is that individuals may find it to be more challenging and worthy of sustaining effort, or individuals may have better skill at representational (high level) tasks than at automatic (overlearned) tasks such as Digits Forward.
- Conversely, most adults have longer sequencing spans than backward spans. Less than 5% of adults have a backward span that is longer than their sequencing span by 2 or more points. Although both the sequencing and backward tasks require working memory, the process of sequencing numbers is typically a more well-learned task than repeating numbers backward.
- Typically adults and adolescents produce Forward spans that are 1 to 2 digits longer than backward spans. Longer Backward than Forward spans occur relatively rarely within the normal population of adults and are therefore noteworthy: less than 4% of the time (averaging across all ages) (Wechsler, 2008, Table C.5). One explanation for a longer Backward span is that individuals may find it to be more challenging and worthy of sustaining effort, or individuals may have better skill at representational (high level) tasks than at automatic (overlearned) tasks such as Digits Forward.
- Less-than-ideal testing conditions may adversely affect performance on this subtest (visual or auditory distractions), and hearing impairment may make examinees vulnerable to failure.
- Repeating digits seems to be more impaired by state anxiety (or test anxiety) than by chronic (trait) anxiety.
- Impulsivity may be evident when adults begin to respond before the examiner has completed the series of digits, or when the examinee repeats the digits very rapidly.
- Learning ability may be evident when adults make errors on the first trial but then are able to pass the second trial. Look for this pattern in other subtests as well (Letter-Number Sequencing, Block Design).

MATRIX REASONING: Influences Affecting Subtest Scores
- Ability to respond when uncertain
- Cognitive style (field dependence–field independence)

- Color blindness (for some items, the use of several colors may confuse color-blind individuals)
- Flexibility
- Motivation level
- Negativism ("None of them go there")
- Overly concrete thinking
- Persistence
- Visual-perceptual problems

MATRIX REASONING: Clinical Considerations

- Since this subtest is not timed, response time may vary widely for adults. Those who are mentally retarded or neurologically impaired may take longer to respond. Impulsivity may be indicated by extremely quick, incorrect responses. Failure to respond within a reasonable amount of time (45 seconds) is of potential diagnostic value, as it may be indicative of reflective style, obsessiveness, or confusion.
- Some items have complex visual stimuli. Individuals with visual-perceptual problems may display stimulus overload in attempting to input the multi-colored, spatially complex items.
- A holistic processing approach is most common in solving the matrices. Some individuals choose to answer the problem with a trial-and-error approach by testing each of the possible choices one by one. Others may use a more planful approach to the problem, first mentally creating a solution to fill in the answer and then searching the given responses to see if one matches the solution they had envisioned.
- Perseveration may be apparent on this subtest if an individual repeatedly chooses the same number response for each item (e.g., number 5).
- Color blindness must be ruled out as a potential cause for poor performance. If such information is not offered spontaneously by the examinee, consider probing for information on color blindness if there is less difficulty on items that depend on form versus those that depend on color.
- Indecisiveness (e.g., "It is either 1 or 3") may indicate insecurity or need for feedback.

VOCABULARY: Influences Affecting Subtest Scores

- Cultural opportunities at home
- Foreign language experience
- Intellectual curiosity and striving
- Interests
- Outside reading

- Richness of early environment
- School learning

VOCABULARY: Clinical Considerations

- Repression may lead to poor performance by pushing out of consciousness any word meanings that are even mildly conflict-laden. Repression may also impair the acquisition of new word meanings as well as recall of specific words on the Vocabulary subtest.
- Similar to Information, high scores relative to other Verbal subtests can reflect intellectual ambitiousness or stress for achievement in one's life.
- The content presented in an adult's or adolescent's response lends itself to analysis regarding the person's fears, guilt, preoccupations, feelings, interests, background, cultural milieu, bizarre thought processes, perseveration, and clang associations (ponder-yonder, remorse-of course). Themes in response content may occur also in conjunction with Comprehension or Similarities as well as during spontaneous conversation during the assessment.
- Perseveration is sometimes evidenced when individuals give the same opening line for each response ("Confide, that's a hard one to define...").
- Responses that are overlearned, almost booklike definitions, should be distinguished from those that appear to be responses driven by intellectual vigor and personalization of the responses with current experiences.
- The open-ended nature of the Vocabulary responses make it possible to glean information about an individual's verbal fluency, not just word knowledge. Some words are easily defined by one-word synonyms, but some individuals may give excessive verbiage in their response or may give a response in a roundabout manner.
- Hearing difficulties may become apparent for those individuals who are illiterate (cannot read the visually presented word list) or for those who focus only on the auditory stimuli. Because the words are presented in isolation, the examinee has no context clues that could help him or her understand the word.
- Level of abstract thinking can also be evaluated in Vocabulary items. Some responses may be abstract (confide is "to entrust") or more concrete (confide is "talking to a person").

ARITHMETIC: Influences Affecting Subtest Scores

- Attention span
- Anxiety
- Concentration
- Distractibility

- Learning disabilities/ADHD
- School learning
- Working under time pressure

ARITHMETIC: Clinical Considerations

- Inferring the cause of the error is useful: whether it was computational, reasoning, failure to attend, or misunderstanding the meaning of a question. For example, in response to a question about the number of hours it takes to walk 25 miles at the rate of 5 miles per hour, the answer "7" reflects a computational error, while "30" reflects a reasoning error, and "5000" is bizarre. This type of bizarre response may suggest inattention, lack of comprehension, or a thought disorder. Such an unusual response on Arithmetic should be explored further.
- Because Arithmetic has a strong factor loading (.77) on the Fluid Reasoning Cluster (T. Keith, personal communication, January 30, 2009), if difficulties with reasoning are suspected, consider comparing Arithmetic to the other fluid reasoning tasks of Matrix Reasoning and Figure Weights. If the scores are reasonably consistent, then reasoning ability is likely related to performance on Arithmetic.
- Testing the limits by removing the time limit and with paper and pencil is often helpful to help assess the roles of anxiety and concentration on test performance.
- For developmentally disabled adults, the subtest measures a portion of adaptive functioning, as items involve money, counting, and other real-life situations.
- Adolescents or adults who have struggled with mathematics in school may become anxious when asked to respond to school-like Arithmetic questions. Their response to the anxiety and frustration may be clinically interesting: Can they compose themselves? Do they respond with hostility? Do they reject the test?
- It is important to consider when individuals are able to respond correctly to the questions but failed to do so within the time limits. Those who tend to be reflective, compulsive, obsessive, or neurologically impaired may exhibit this pattern of responding.
- Observe for signs of trying to compensate for the auditory nature or memory requirements of the task: for example, finger writing on the table, or asking for a pencil and paper or a calculator.

SYMBOL SEARCH: Influences Affecting Subtest Scores

- Anxiety
- Distractibility

- Learning disabilities/ADHD
- Motivation level
- Obsessive concern with accuracy and detail
- Persistence
- Visual-perceptual problems
- Working under time pressure

SYMBOL SEARCH: Clinical Considerations

- Similar to most Processing Speed and Perceptual Reasoning subtests, visual impairment should be ruled out before interpreting a low Symbol Search score.
- As noted in chapter 2, it is important to be an astute observer during this task, as many observed behaviors can help to interpret the Symbol Search score. Concentration, distractibility, obsessive concern with detail, impulsiveness, reflectivity, motivation level, visual-perceptual problems, or anxiety are just some of the factors that may be inferred to be related to a person's performance on Symbol Search.
- A learning curve may be present on this test. Individuals who begin to answer later items more quickly may have developed a plan or strategy after completing earlier items. To note whether speed of responding is, in fact, increasing, you can track how many items were answered during each of the four 30-second intervals during the subtest.
- Visual memory ability sometimes can be inferred from observations on this task. Some adults may look at the Target symbols only once and then find the response in the Search Group, and others may look back and forth several times between the Target and Search groups before marking their response. The repeated referring back and forth between the symbols may be indicative of poor visual memory (or of insecurity).
- After the entire test has been administered, you may test the limits to help discern why certain responses were made. Point to some items answered correctly and some that were wrong, and ask the adult to explain why they choose their response.

VISUAL PUZZLES: Influences Affecting Subtest Scores

- Ability to respond when uncertain
- Flexibility
- Motivation level
- Negativism ("It's impossible. That design can't be made.")
- Overly concrete thinking
- Persistence
- Visual-perceptual problems

- Worries about time limits
- Impulsivity in responding
- Ability to self-correct

VISUAL PUZZLES: Clinical Considerations

- Response time may vary widely for adults on this task (although there is a time limit). Those who are developmentally disabled or neurologically impaired may take longer to respond. Impulsivity may be indicated by extremely quick, incorrect responses. Failure to respond within a reasonable amount of time (before the time limit) is of potential diagnostic value, as it may be indicative of reflective style, obsessiveness, or confusion.
- As with Matrix Reasoning, some items have complex visual stimuli. Individuals with visual-perceptual problems may display stimulus overload in attempting to input the multicolored, spatially complex items.
- A holistic processing approach is most common in solving the puzzles. Some individuals choose their answer the problem with a trial-and-error approach by testing each of the possible choices one by one before deciding which three work best. Others may use a more planful approach to the problem, first mentally creating a solution and then searching the given responses to see which triad matches the solution they had envisioned.
- Perseveration may be apparent on this subtest if an individual repeatedly chooses the same number response for each item (e.g., responds with numbers 1, 2, 3 every time).
- Indecisiveness may indicate insecurity or need for feedback.

INFORMATION: Influences Affecting Subtest Scores

- Alertness to the environment
- Cultural opportunities at home
- Foreign language background
- Intellectual curiosity and striving
- Interests
- Outside reading
- Richness of early environment
- School learning

INFORMATION: Clinical Considerations

- Items are generally nonthreatening and emotionally neutral.
- Rationalizations and excuses may be produced in response to this test (i.e., "That isn't important").

- Effortless, automatic responding facilitates good performance. Adults or adolescents with chronic anxiety may suffer early failures and depressed scores in general.
- Retrieval difficulties may be revealed on this test when success on harder items is proceeded by failure on easy items.
- Alertness to the environment in addition to formal schooling together are the source of most of the factual knowledge needed for success.
- Unnecessary detail and trivial responses may suggest obsessiveness.
- Intellectual ambitiousness can be reflected in high scores and often is coupled with high Vocabulary scores.
- A perfectionistic approach may be evident when no response is preferred to an imperfect answer.
- An adolescent's or adult's pattern of responses may be indicative of cultural background. For example, questions pertaining to U.S. history or other famous leaders in America may pose more difficulty than those on general geography or science for individuals who are not originally from the United States.
- Bizarre or odd responses can shed light on an individual's mental state. For example, a response such as "There are 1000 weeks in a year," or "Gandhi is the guy I saw at the supermarket" may indicate a need to explore mental functioning further.

CODING: Influences Affecting Subtest Scores
- Anxiety
- Distractibility
- Learning disabilities/ADHD
- Motivation level
- Obsessive concern with accuracy and detail
- Persistence
- Visual-perceptual problems
- Working under time pressure

CODING: Clinical Considerations
- Visual or motor impairment must be ruled out before interpreting a low score.
- Individuals who have demonstrated perfectionistic or compulsive tendencies prior to Coding should be told *during the sample items* that they need to copy the symbols legibly but not perfectly.
- Changes in rate of responding during the subtest can be related to motivation, distraction, fatigue, boredom, and so forth. Thus, it is a good

idea to note the number of symbols copied during each of the four 30-second periods within the 120-second limit.

- Astute observation is key to interpreting scores on this subtest. Include these points in your interpretation of the score: coordination (grip on the pencil), attention/concentration, distractibility, motivation level, visual perceptual problems (rotating or distorting symbols), perfectionistic tendencies, perseveration (copying the same symbol for a whole line), or anxiety.
- Some individuals appear to have to search for each number in the row of stimulus pairs, seemingly unaware that the "5" is always right before the "6." This behavior could be indicative of sequencing problems.
- Short-term visual memory deficits may be evident if adults keep referring back to the key before copying symbols (or these individuals may be insecure). Those who have memorized several pairs of symbols are likely to have a good visual memory (if they are not making errors in their response).

LETTER-NUMBER SEQUENCING: Influences Affecting Subtest Scores
- Ability to receive stimuli passively
- Attention span
- Anxiety
- Concentration
- Distractibility
- Flexibility
- Illiteracy or dyslexia (does not know letters and alphabet at an automatic level)
- Learning Disabilities
- Attention-Deficit/Hyperactivity Disorder (ADHD)
- Negativism (Refusal to take a "meaningless" task)
- Persistence

LETTER-NUMBER SEQUENCING: Clinical Considerations
- Sequencing, poor short-term memory, inattention, distractibility, or anxiety may be causative factors for trouble on Letter-Number Sequencing. Similar to Digit Span, sequencing problems can be evident from correctly remembering the numbers and letters but in the wrong sequence. Short-term memory may be implicated if part of the sequence is correct but some of the numbers or letters are forgotten.
- Observe the examinee for signs of stimulus overload, which can lead to frustration. Statements such as "That is too much to remember at once" or "How about just the numbers?" can be indicative of an examinee's being overwhelmed with the amount of auditory stimuli.

- Digit Span Backward and Digit Span Sequencing are more conceptually related to Letter-Number Sequencing (LNS) than Digits Forward. The backward and sequencing items, like LNS, require the examinee to mentally manipulate or visualize the stimuli. (Some examinees who rely on visualization strategies will close their eyes during the administration of the items and/or during their response.) If strategies were generated to respond to the Backward or Sequential items on Digit Span, the examinee may benefit from using those or similar strategies on LNS.
- As there are three trials for each item, subjects have an opportunity to develop and test strategies. Test the limits or question the examinee after the test is complete to gather information about any strategies that may have been generated to complete the task.
- Like Digit Span, the skills required for this test are impaired more by state (test) anxiety than by chronic anxiety.
- Whereas number sequences are automatic for most adolescents and adults, the precise alphabetic sequence has not been adequately "overlearned" for many individuals. Note whether some examinees consistently make errors on the letters but get all numbers right. Do these individuals have reading problems (e.g., illiteracy or dyslexia)?
- LNS is a novel task, not likely to be encountered in the real world, and requires a good, flexible approach to succeed. Adolescents and adults who do poorly may display problems on other tasks that depend on fluid ability (e.g., Matrix Reasoning) or flexibility (e.g., Similarities).

FIGURE WEIGHTS: Influences Affecting Subtest Scores
- Ability to respond when uncertain
- Flexibility
- Motivation level
- Negativism ("None of them go there")
- Overly concrete thinking
- Persistence
- Ability to shift sets
- Executive functioning problems
- Worries about time limits
- Impulsivity in responding
- Ability to self-correct

FIGURE WEIGHTS: Clinical Considerations
- Examinees who are mathematically minded or who are skilled in the concepts of algebra may be more likely to view this as a mathlike test.

- Response time may vary widely for adults on this task (although there is a time limit). Those who are developmentally disabled or neurologically impaired may take longer to respond. Impulsivity may be indicated by extremely quick, incorrect responses. Failure to respond within a reasonable amount of time (before the time limit) is of potential diagnostic value, as it may be indicative of reflective style, obsessiveness, or confusion.
- Figure Weights places a great demand on executive functioning skills because the examinee must sustain attention while using several different cognitive processes at the same time.
- Individuals who have difficulty shifting sets may have trouble because the shapes represent different "weights" on every item, so this task requires continual set shifting. An increased difficulty may be noticed when the examinee is required to shift from examining two to three scales beginning with Item 16.
- A flexible problem-solving approach in which an individual examines the problem from left to right, but can also view it from right to left, can be beneficial on this task.
- Some individuals choose their answer to the problem with a trial-and-error approach by testing each of the possible choices one by one before deciding which one works best. Others may use a more planful approach to the problem, first mentally creating a solution when examining the scales and then searching the given responses to see which response matches the solution they had envisioned.
- Perseveration may be apparent on this subtest if an individual repeatedly chooses the same number response for each item.
- Indecisiveness may indicate insecurity or need for feedback.

COMPREHENSION: Influences Affecting Subtest Scores
- Cultural opportunities at home
- Development of conscience or moral sense
- Flexibility (ability to shift from social reasoning to proverb items and ability to give a "second reason")
- Negativism ("We shouldn't have to pay taxes")
- Overly concrete thinking

COMPREHENSION: Clinical Considerations
- A stable and emotionally balanced attitude and orientation are necessary for success on this subtest. Any type of maladjustment may lower scores.
- A high score on Comprehension alone is not enough evidence to interpret strong social adjustment. Corroborating evidence must be obtained from

clinical observations, background information, or adaptive behavior inventories.

- Responses offer clues about a disturbed individual's social-adaptive functioning in practical, social situations, but be cautious about generalizing from single-issue questions to the complexities of the real world.
- When responses appear overlearned, stereotypical, or parroted, test the limits to determine the level of real understanding and reasoning ability.
- Like responses to Similarities and Vocabulary, responses to Comprehension may vary in their degree of abstractness. This ability to reason may be especially evident in the explanation of the proverbs. Ability to think in abstract terms (*swallow* means "Don't generalize from a single instance") is distinct from more concrete types of responses (*brooks* means "if the brook is so shallow and you throw a rock in, it makes noise").
- Five of the Comprehension items require further questioning if only one response is given, and all questions allow querying for clarification of responses. Analyze how individuals respond to follow-up questioning. Do they become defensive? Are they inflexible and unable to move beyond their original response? Clinically relevant bits of information can be obtained from observing the difference between someone who is spontaneously able to produce two concise responses versus someone who needs constant structure and prodding.

CANCELLATION: Influences Affecting Subtest Scores
- Attention span
- Concentration
- Distractibility
- Visual acuity
- Reflectivity/impulsivity
- Planning
- Ability to perform under time pressure

CANCELLATION: Clinical Considerations
- As this is one of the last subtests administered, fatigue and boredom should be ruled out as possible explanations for a low score.
- Anxiety may be notable on this subtest. Shaking hands, a tight pencil grip, or pressure on the paper when writing could be signs of nervousness.
- The pace at which an individual works may be related to impulsivity (quick, careless responding) or relate perfectionism (slower, more careful responding).
- Attention and concentration may impact this brief task. It is a monotonous task that requires sustained attention for success. Inconsistent responding

(or an inconsistent response rate) across the two items may be indicative of difficulties sustaining attention or concentration.

- Executive functioning can impact performance on this task. Along with maintaining attention, examinees must ignore distractor stimuli while marking the targets. In addition, examinees must shift sets from between Items 1 and 2 when the target items shift.

PICTURE COMPLETION: Influences Affecting Subtest Scores
- Ability to respond when uncertain
- Alertness to the environment
- Cognitive style (field dependence–field independence)
- Concentration
- Negativism ("Nothing is missing")
- Working under time pressure

PICTURE COMPLETION: Clinical Considerations
- This test typically serves as a good icebreaker, as it is the first test administered. Usually adults find it nonthreatening and consider it enjoyable.
- Although this subtest is timed, usually the 20-second limit is ample time for adults who are neither mentally retarded nor neurologically impaired. Impulsivity may be indicated by extremely quick, incorrect responses. Failure to respond within the limit is of potential diagnostic value, as even reflective individuals typically respond within the limit.
- Verbal responses are far more common than nonverbal responses on this Performance task, especially since the directions explicitly say "TELL me what is missing." Although nonverbal responses are also considered correct, the frequency of such responses should be evaluated and may possibly be indicative of word retrieval problems. Verbal responses that are imprecise or vague may also be indicative of word retrieval problems.
- Negativity or hostility may be noted in persistent "Nothing is missing" responses.
- Obsessiveness or concentration problems may be evident in responses that are focused on trivial details of a picture (i.e., brand name on the glasses). Similarly, confabulatory responses (indicating that something not in the picture is missing—e.g., feet in the tennis shoes, blood on the knife) are of clinical interest. Giving trivial or confabulatory responses several times during the subtest is of potential diagnostic interest, especially because examiners are instructed to redirect individuals the first time they give a trivial response or a confabulatory response.

• This task appears to be relatively resilient to the impact of brain damage. It is not able to consistently or reliably indicate right cerebral damage, which perhaps may be related to the nature of verbal responding by most adults, and "it is entirely possible that the nature of the task is not as heavily demanding of adequate brain functions as are some of the other subtests" (Reitan & Wolfson, 1992, p. 107).

WATKINS AND CANIVEZ'S CRITIQUE OF OUR INTERPRETIVE SYSTEM AND ARTICULATION OF A NEW THEORY-BASED APPROACH TO PROFILE INTERPRETATION

Watkins and Canivez (2004) published a study in *Psychological Assessment*, "Temporal Stability of WISC-III Subtest Composite Strengths and Weaknesses." They used 3-year WISC-III reevaluation data to evaluate the method of profile interpretation that we have advocated in the past (Kaufman & Lichtenberger, 2000) and concluded that ipsative strengths and weaknesses were unstable over time and that our approach was not valid. However, Watkins and Canivez failed to demonstrate understanding of the crucial aspect of the interpretive method that emphasizes integration of multiple sources of evidence before reaching any conclusions about the meaningfulness of an individual's strengths and weaknesses. They also did not take into account other mitigating factors that might account for the low kappa statistics that their analysis yielded. In this section, we provide specific criticisms of the Watkins-Canivez article and offer a rationale in support of our clinical approach to profile interpretation. Nonetheless, we acknowledge that some of the published concerns about using a purely ipsative approach to profile interpretation are valid, impelling us and our colleagues to develop a new approach for interpreting profiles of test scores (Flanagan & Kaufman, 2004; Kaufman & Lichtenberger, 2006, Appendixes A, B, & C; Kaufman et al., 2005). In this section we discuss the guiding principles for this new approach to profile interpretation that is more theory-based, integrates ipsative with normative interpretation, and is applied to the WAIS-IV in chapter 5 on of this volume.

Watkins and Canivez (2004) used 3-year reevaluation data obtained on a sample of 579 students tested twice on the WISC-III (at age 9 and age 12) to evaluate our former method of profile interpretation (Kaufman & Lichtenberger, 2000). They concluded that ipsative strengths and weaknesses (i.e., high and low

---

This section on Watkins and Canivez's critique of our interpretive system is an edited version of Appendix D in Kaufman and Lichtenberger (2006) that was written by Alan Kaufman and Dawn Flanagan.

scores relative to a person's own ability level) were unstable over time. Based on their analysis, they concluded that our approach was not valid.

Watkins and Canivez (2004) argued that the WISC-III reevaluation data that they obtained from school psychologists' files "have unambiguous implications for psychological practice. . . . [B]ecause ipsative subtest categorizations are unreliable, recommendations based on them will also be unreliable" (p. 137). However, they assumed incorrectly that all cognitive abilities represent enduring traits and, therefore, ought to remain stable over time. They further assumed that interpretations of test data are made in a vacuum—that data from multiple sources, no matter how compelling, cannot influence the findings generated from an ipsative analysis of scores from a single intelligence battery. Furthermore, because their methodology for examining the stability of cognitive strengths and weaknesses over time is questionable, their conclusions are ambiguous. Finally, the method of test interpretation initially developed by Kaufman (1979a) changed considerably in recent years (Kaufman & Lichtenberger, 2002; Lichtenberger & Kaufman, 2003), even before Watkins and Canivez (2004) published their critique. Such changes reflect, in part, the research of Glutting and colleagues (e. g., McDermott, Fantuzzo, Glutting, Watkins, & Baggaley, 1992). However, these researchers continued their cries of "Just Say No" to *any* type of interpretation of test scores beyond a global IQ and offered *no* recommendations with regard to how clinicians can make sense out of an individual's scaled-score profile. In contrast, we have recognized the onerous task facing clinicians in their daily work of identifying the presumptive cause of a child's learning difficulties or an adult's problems in college, at home, or in the workplace. As such, we and our colleagues continue to provide clinicians with guidance in the test interpretation process that is based on theory, research, psychometrics, and clinical experience. What Watkins and Canivez (2004) failed to accept is that our interpretive method extends far beyond the identification of intra-individual strengths and weaknesses.

Following is a discussion of the most salient flaws in Watkins and Canivez's evaluation of our method.

Not All Cognitive Abilities Remain Stable over Time

Watkins and Canivez (2004) stated that intelligence is presumed to be an enduring trait. However, although this statement is generally true of global ability (e.g., Wechsler FSIQ), it is not necessarily true of specific or narrow cognitive abilities (Carroll, 1993), as reflected by subtest scores, for example. Because all traits are not enduring, some test authors have attempted to correct for *trait instability* when reporting test-retest reliability coefficients (McGrew, Werder, & Woodcock, 1991). Watkins and Canivez (2004) did not account for trait instability or even consider known neurological and developmental changes that occur between the average age of the test (9 years) and retest (12 years) in their investigation. At age 9, children are in Piaget's stage of concrete operations whereas at age 12, they are in the stage of formal operations. Coinciding with the onset of formal operational thought is the rapid development at about ages 11–12 of the tertiary areas of the prefrontal lobes, associated with planning ability. These new developments for average children between test 1 and test 2 change the way they approach the solving of problems and make them qualitatively different children at age 12 compared to age 9. Their different performance on specific abilities the second time around may relate to their mental development at about age 11, which will not be a constant from child to child; some children will benefit from the neurological and cognitive advances more than others. And there are other differences between 9- and 12-year-olds. For example, they differ in their problem-solving speed. Several WISC-III Performance subtests give bonus points for quick, perfect performance. At age 9, bonus points do not contribute very much to children's scores on Block Design, Picture Arrangement, and Object Assembly; at age 12, bonus points contribute heavily (Kaufman, 1994a). Hence, the same subtests are quite different at older than younger ages, conceivably affecting the level of the child's performance at two distinctly different points in time.

In addition to trait instability, Watkins and Canivez did not consider the fact that because some abilities are amenable to change, interventions can and often do improve performance on some tests. Watkins and Canivez (2004) stated, "Psychologists often proffer interventions and remedial recommendations based on hypotheses about WISC-III subtest and subtest composite score information" (p. 136). They are correct. Therefore, with respect to their sample, it is entirely possible that interventions have already taken place during the 3-year interval between test and retest—not at all surprising in view of the fact that all retest data are for children enrolled in special education. Indeed, the authors noted that "the use of reevaluation cases means that those students who were no longer enrolled in special education were not reevaluated and thus not part of the sample" (p. 137).

Intervention, whether based on our method of profile interpretation or not, will have an impact on the person's cognitive functioning. Areas of strength or weakness may no longer be as extreme on a retest, 3 years later, if the interventions have been successful to some extent. Certainly, several Wechsler subtests might be directly affected by educational intervention (e. g., Information, Vocabulary), while others are conceivably affected by pharmaceutical intervention (e. g., Symbol Search, Digit Span). Not only have the children tested 3 years later changed in unknown ways, their cognitive ability and behavioral profiles have conceivably been modified due to specific interventions or experiences. And if interventions have not been successful, then children who previously performed adequately on WISC-III measures of acquired knowledge may now display a weakness in these and related areas. Yet the authors have no way of assessing the amount or effectiveness of intervention for each individual child because of the haphazard way in which the cases were obtained from around the country.

Interpretation of Test Data Is Not Done in a Vacuum: The Meaningfulness of Relative Strengths and Weaknesses Is Dependent on Other Data Sources

Watkins and Canivez (2004) were careful to point out that "the ipsative methods detailed by Kaufman and Lichtenberger (2000) were precisely followed to identify WISC-III subtest ability patterns" (p. 134). They should have been just as conscientious in reading what we said about ipsative methods: "The process of ipsative comparison is not intended to be the ending of profile interpretation; rather it is just the beginning point for practical, clinical analysis. From the ipsative comparison, hypotheses are generated and then may be supported or disconfirmed with further information" (Kaufman & Lichtenberger, 2000, p. 3). But they apparently misunderstood or ignored that statement. Although we stated unambiguously that any application of our ipsative comparison method is for the purpose of generating hypotheses, to be supported or disconfirmed with additional data, Watkins and Canivez (2004) argued that the cross-validation approach is "contradicted by the research literature" (p. 137). They cavalierly dismissed the value of cross-validating test results with multiple sources of data by citing a few articles that are tangential to the issue. In fact, their refusal even to consider the context in which test scores are obtained suggests that they are content to interpret test results in total isolation, disdaining the potential benefits of corroboration or refutation by real-life variables. That is their right, when they choose to define their *own* approach to test interpretation. But Watkins and Canivez's goal was to challenge our interpretive approach; therefore, they needed to evaluate test data *within the context of our methodology, not their own methodology*. And our system clearly involves a merger of ipsative analyses with multiple-source cross-validation.

Diagnostic decisions should not be made based on test scores alone; nor should they be based on clinical judgment alone. Rather, as discussed in the section called "Intelligent Testing," diagnostic decisions should be based on test data, clinical observations during the testing session, background information, data from other assessments, and referral questions geared specifically to the person being evaluated. No rational clinician would interpret low scores on the Wechsler subtests associated with the Working Memory Index (referred to in days gone by as the Freedom from Distractibility factor) as reflecting a person's distractibility without also having observed the person's behaviors during the test session, in the classroom (or workplace), and perhaps in other environments as well. One would be foolish to infer that a person's relatively high scores on Picture Arrangement and Comprehension reflected well-developed "Common Sense, Social Comprehension, or Social Judgment" if the person was known to have difficulties getting along with peers; or to infer that relatively low scores on Similarities and Vocabulary reflected a weakness in "Handling Abstract Verbal Concepts, Verbal Concept Formation, and Degree of Abstract Thinking" if the person's spontaneous conversations during the evaluation indicated appropriate usage of abstract concepts; or to infer that relatively low scores on Coding and Block Design denoted a weakness in "Visual Perception of Abstract Stimuli" if the person performed well on a test of design copying; or that relatively high scores on Digit Span, Coding, and Symbol Search reflected a good "Short-term Memory (Auditory or Visual)" if the person kept asking for questions to be repeated and misplaced the pencil during the evaluation. The hypotheses just quoted are among the numerous "Strengths and Weaknesses" included in Watkins and Canivez's (2004) Table 1, and were rejected as unreliable because of trivial kappa statistics.

Because we recognize that variation in cognitive abilities is commonplace in the general population (e.g., McGrew & Knopik, 1996), we and our colleagues make it clear in our writings that intra-individual differences alone are insufficient grounds upon which to base diagnostic, classification, or treatment decisions (Flanagan & Ortiz, 2001; Kaufman, 1994a; Kaufman & Lichtenberger, 2006; see also Reschly & Grimes, 1995). When statistically significant intra-individual differences are found, a judgment with regard to their meaningfulness is made based on other sources of information. We believe that any outlier score or significant intra-individual difference gains diagnostic meaning only when it converges with other data sources in a manner suggested by existing research. For example, consider an example with a child tested on the WJ III. The fact that auditory processing emerged as a relative weakness for an individual (following ipsative analysis) is not meaningful in and of itself. However, the fact that the individual is in second grade and has not learned how to read—and her score on an auditory processing composite (which consists of phonetic coding tests) is within the deficient range compared to same-age peers—provides the clinician with information to hypothesize that the observed auditory processing deficit is the presumptive cause of her inability to read. The clinician's hypothesis is strengthened by the results of numerous investigations that have shown that phonological processing is the core deficit in individuals who are reading disabled (see Flanagan, Ortiz, Alfonso, & Mascolo, 2002, for a review). After ruling out other potential causes for deficient reading and phonological processing, such as hearing impairment, history of ear infections, poor instruction, deficient speed of lexical access, and so forth, the clinician can reasonably conclude that the individual's reading difficulties were due to a core phonological processing deficit. The clinician's evaluation of the types of errors made on the tests of phonological processing administered inform his or her recommendations with regard to intervention and remediation. The detective-work procedure used here to interpret test scores for a child tested on the WJ III applies to adolescents and adults tested on the WAIS-IV and, indeed, to individuals of all ages, referred for evaluation for any number of reasons, who are tested on the wide array of excellent psychometric tools that are available to today's clinicians.

The belief that test findings, however unusual, gain diagnostic meaning only when they converge with other data sources, including findings from relevant research, is not unique to the field of psychological assessment. Indeed, most disciplines that use measurement tools, including medicine, undoubtedly share the same philosophy. Consider this example of the thought processes of a veterinarian evaluating a cat who presented with a history of not eating and vomiting. Blood work revealed a blood urea nitrogen (BUN) of 54 (normal range = 14–36) and a creatinine of 2.7 (normal range = .6–2.4). Based on the presenting symptoms and the elevated kidney values (BUN and creatinine), a presumptive diagnosis is that the cat is in renal (kidney) failure—a condition that has a very poor prognosis. However, in order to test the hypothesis of renal failure, additional testing was deemed necessary. After receiving the results of a urinalysis, the veterinarian found that the cat's urine specific gravity was normal at 1.065. With this additional information, the veterinarian concluded that the cat's increased BUN and creatinine levels were due to dehydration, not renal failure. How is the psychologist's approach to using assessment tools and interpreting test results different? It is not. The reader is referred to the work of Rohling and his colleagues on the benefits of integrating test results from multiple sources (e.g., Miller & Rohling, 2001).

Tests do not think for themselves, nor do they directly communicate with patients. Like a stethoscope, a blood pressure gauge, or an MRI scan, a psychological test is a dumb tool, and the worth of the tool cannot be separated from the sophistication of the clinician who draws inferences from it and then communicates with patients and professionals. (Meyer et al., 2001, p. 128)

Likewise, the worth of a test interpretation method, such as intra-individual analysis, cannot be separated from the sophistication of the clinician who draws conclusions from it.

Questionable Methodology

Psychometrics has an important place in clinical assessment, as do analyses of group data. Reliability, validity, understanding of group differences in cognitive ability, development of appropriate norms, and item bias statistics are just a few areas that require psychometric analysis and group data. Investigating individual children's or adults' ipsative strengths and weaknesses is not such an area. We believe that Watkins and Canivez have applied a questionable statistical "test" of our method. Apparently, they either do not understand the method or choose to ignore the fact that the method is a clinical, individual approach.

In the Watkins and Canivez (2004) study, the kappa statistics were based on group data and basically answer the question "Did a large sample of children have a data-based strength, weakness, or neither, on a WISC-III assessment, and did this group of children maintain their same categorizations (strength, weakness, neither) on a retest administered about three years later?" The kappas, based on *group* data, do not answer the question about the stability of the strength or weakness for any particular *individual* in the sample (Cicchetti, 1994). This statistic does not address the validity of the strength or weakness for an individual. Statistics alone do not interpret the possible area of integrity or deficit. To do this, clinical behaviors, referral and background information, and other data sources must be taken into account. *That is precisely what we instruct clinicians to do if they use the intra-individual method. We do not want them ever to apply the method blindly, out of context, without integrating the statistical findings with all other pertinent formal and informal data.* Therefore, rather than using kappa to examine the stability of categories over time, which does not adequately capture the decision-making process that underlies our method, Watkins and Canivez should have examined the inter-rater reliability of clinicians trained in our interpretive method to determine agreement with regard to interpretation of areas of integrity and deficit at Time 1 and then again at Time 2—that is, different clinicians rating the same person's areas of integrity and deficit at time 1 and then again at time 2 using our method of intra-individual analysis. Consider this example: A scaled score of 5 on Block Design (for example) at Time 1 emerges as a weakness based on ipsative analysis. At Time 2, Block Design yields a scaled score of 6 and is no longer considered a weakness based on ipsative analysis. A well-trained clinician would conclude that the ability underlying Block Design is deficient, regardless of a nonsignificant finding based on ipsative analysis at Time 2. This example demonstrates that an evaluation of the reliability of our method must focus on the conclusions that clinicians who are trained in their method draw from the data.

Two other methodological issues with the Watkins and Canivez (2004) study require mention. First, quite obviously, there will be statistical regression to the mean for all shared abilities identified on the initial test as strengths or weaknesses. For any person with an identified strength, that strength will regress toward the mean, as will any identified weakness. Of course, positive chance errors contribute to any area of ability that is identified as a strength, and negative chance errors contribute to any area of ability that is identified as a weakness. That is built into the method. It is not only because of sound clinical practice that we tell examiners to cross-validate each possible strength and weakness with clinical behaviors and other data; it is also to help ensure that the putative strengths and weaknesses are not just a function of the chance error. The authors did not account for predictable regression effects in their analyses, which would lower the kappas. In contrast, intelligent application of our clinical method will help control for chance.

The second additional methodological issue is that Watkins and Canivez took a continuous variable (deviation from the mean) and turned it into a categorical variable (strength, weakness, neither). Apparently, they were trying to mimic clinical practice. However, empirical analysis and clinical practice are not synonymous. By taking a continuous variable and turning it into a categorical variable, Watkins and Canivez effectively reduced the statistical power of their analysis, thereby reducing the kappa (Cohen, 1983). Thus, Watkins and Canivez's chances of finding a lack of agreement in classifications over time were maximized.

Overview of Criticisms of the Watkins and Canivez (2004) Study

In short, a great deal happens in 3 years. The effects of intervention. Developmental changes. Regression to the mean. Changes in what some subtests measure at different ages. The group data provided by Watkins and Canivez do not have implications for the individual method of profile interpretation that we advocate. The strengths and weaknesses that we believe might have useful applications for developing educational interventions are based on cognitive functioning at a particular point in time. They need to be cross-validated at that time to verify that any supposed cognitive strengths or weaknesses are consistent with the wealth of observational, referral, background, and other-test data that are available for each person who is evaluated. Only then will those data-based findings inform diagnosis and be applied to help answer the individual person's referral questions.

The simple finding that reevaluation data at age 12 do not support the stability of children's data-based strengths and weaknesses at age 9 says *nothing* about the validity of our former interpretive approach. If one's blood pressure is "high" when assessed in January and is "normal" when assessed 3 months later, does this suggest that the physician's categories (e.g., high, normal, low) are unreliable? Does it suggest that the blood pressure monitor is unreliable? Or does it suggest that the medication prescribed to reduce the individual's blood pressure was effective?

FLANAGAN AND KAUFMAN'S (2004) REVISIONS OF TRADITIONAL IPSATIVE ANALYSIS

We believe that, despite its inherent flaws, intra-individual or ipsative analysis has not fared well because it historically has not been grounded in contemporary theory and research, and it has not been linked to psychometrically defensible procedures for interpretation (Flanagan & Ortiz, 2001). When theory and research are used to guide interpretation and when psychometrically defensible interpretive procedures are employed, *some* of the limitations of the intra-individual approach are circumvented, resulting in the derivation of useful information. Indeed, when an interpretive approach is grounded in contemporary theory and research, practitioners are in a much better position to draw clear and useful conclusions from the data (Carroll, 1998; Daniel, 1997; Kamphaus, 1993; Kamphaus, Petosky, & Morgan, 1997; Keith, Cool, Novak, White, & Pottebaum, 1988). The findings of an intra-individual analysis are not the end of the interpretation process, they are only the beginning. We do find many flaws with the purely empirical approach that Watkins and Canivez used to evaluate our approach to profile interpretation. Nonetheless, we took quite seriously many of the criticisms of a purely ipsative method of profile analysis that have appeared in the literature in articles by Watkins, Glutting, and their colleagues (e.g., McDermott et al., 1992). Indeed, our collaborators have been frankly critical of ipsative analysis that ignores normative analysis (Flanagan, Ortiz, Alfonso, & Dynda, 2008), and Flanagan and Kaufman (2004) relied on all of these criticisms to modify and enhance WISC-IV interpretation methods. Following are a few of the most salient ways in which we and our colleagues have attempted to improve the practice of ipsative analysis of the WISC-IV and Kaufman Assessment Battery for Children (2nd Edition; KABC-II) (Flanagan & Kaufman, 2004, 2009; Kaufman & Kaufman, 2004; Kaufman et al., 2005). In chapter 5, we apply these principles to WAIS-IV interpretation.

1. *We recommend interpreting test data within the context of a well-validated theory.* Use of the Cattell-Horn-Carroll theory of the structure of cognitive abilities is becoming commonplace in test construction and interpretation because it is the best-supported theory within the psychometric tradition (Daniel, 1997; Flanagan & Ortiz, 2001; Horn & Blankson, 2005; McGrew, 2005). Without knowledge of theory and an understanding of its research base, there is virtually no information available to inform interpretation. For the KABC-II, that theoretical base broadens to include Luria's neuropsychological theory. For the WAIS-IV, we base our interpretive approach on CHC theory, neuropsychological theory, and the theoretical and research basis from cognitive neuroscience that researchers at The Psychological Corporation used to develop the WAIS-IV and WISC-IV.

2. *We recommend using composites or clusters, rather than subtests, in intra-individual analysis.* Additionally, the clusters that are used in the analysis must represent *unitary* abilities, meaning that the magnitude of the difference between the highest and lowest score in the cluster is not uncommon in the general population.

3. *The clusters that are included in the interpretive analysis should represent basic primary factors in mental organization (e.g., visual processing, auditory short-term memory).* There are exceptions to this generalization; for example, in chapter 6 of this book, specific subtests are included as part of the interpretive process. But, as a general guiding principle, WAIS-IV interpretation should focus primarily on theoretically relevant clusters of subtests rather than on interpreting the unique abilities purportedly measured by individual subtests. When the variance that is common to all clusters (as opposed to subtests) is removed during "ipsatization" (i.e., identifying strengths and weaknesses compared to a person's own mean score), *proportionately more reliable variance remains.* And it is precisely this shared, reliable variance that we believe ought to be emphasized during profile interpretation because it represents the construct that was intended to be measured by the cluster.

4. *If a relative weakness revealed through ipsative analysis falls well within the average range of functioning compared to most people, then its meaningfulness is called into question.* For example, despite presumptions of disability, average ability is achieved by most people, and most people are not disabled. Therefore, a relative weakness that falls in the average range of ability compared to same-age peers will suggest a different interpretation than a relative weakness that falls in the deficient range of functioning relative to most people (see Flanagan & Kaufman, 2009).

Despite the pains taken to elevate the use of ipsative analysis to a more respectable level, by linking it to normative analysis and recommending that unitary, theoretically derived clusters be featured, one undeniable fact remains. The intra-individual analysis does not diagnose, clinicians do. Clinicians, like medical doctors, will not cease to compare scores, nor should they.

> Would one want a physician, for example, not to look at patterns of test results just because they in and of themselves do not diagnose a disorder? Would you tell a physician not to take your blood pressure and heart rate and compare them because these two scores in and of themselves do not differentially diagnose kidney disease from heart disease? (Prifitera, Weiss, & Saklofske, 1998, p. 6)

Comparing scores from tests, whether psychological or medical, is a necessary component of any test interpretation process. Why? We believe it is because comparing scores assists in making diagnoses when such comparisons are made using psychometric information (e.g., base rate data) as well as numerous other sources of data as described previously.

CONCLUDING COMMENTS

This is not the first place that the flaws of the purely empirical approaches advocated by Watkins and his colleagues have been articulated, especially regarding the power of their group-data methodology for dismissing individual-data assessment. Anastasi and Urbina (1997) state:

> One problem with several of the negative reviews of Kaufman's approach is that they seem to assume that clinicians will use it to make decisions based solely on the magnitude of scores and score differences. While it is true that the mechanical application of profile analysis techniques can be very misleading, this assumption is quite contrary to what Kaufman recommends, as well as to the principles of sound assessment practice. (p. 513)

✒ TEST YOURSELF ✒

1. **All of the following are principles of the intelligent testing philosophy EXCEPT:**

   (a) Subtests measure what the individual has learned.

   (b) Subtests are samples of behavior and not exhaustive.

   (c) Behavioral observations and background information are of little importance in interpreting a person's test profile.

   (d) Test batteries are optimally useful when interpreted from a theoretical model.

   (e) IQ tests assess mental functioning under fixed experimental conditions.

2. **Which one of the following WAIS-IV subtests is NOT especially vulnerable to distractibility?**

   (a) Digit Span

   (b) Symbol Search

   (c) Picture Completion

   (d) Coding

   (e) Arithmetic

3. **Which WAIS-IV subtest is affected by a person's visual-perceptual problems and also has a long research history as being especially vulnerable to brain damage?**

   (a) Vocabulary

   (b) Block Design

   (c) Visual Puzzles

   (d) Arithmetic

   (e) Digit Span Forward

4. **Which of the following WAIS-IV subtests BEST provides clinical information about a person's ability to express his or her ideas in words and to provide possible insight into the person's fears, guilt, preoccupations, feelings, interests, and cultural background?**

   (a) Information

   (b) Picture Completion

   (c) Letter-Number Sequencing

   (d) Vocabulary

   (e) Block Design

5. **Which WAIS-IV subtest (apart from Arithmetic) is most likely to be viewed as a math-like test by examinees who are "mathematically minded" or who are skilled in the concepts of algebra?**

   (a) Figure Weights

   (b) Block Design

   (c) Visual Puzzles

(d) Symbol Search

(e) Information

6. **A major limitation of Watkins and Canivez's critique of the Kaufman-Lichtenberger ipsative approach to Wechsler interpretation is their failure to**

(a) take into account that hypotheses are generated from multiple sources of data, not just by test scores.

(b) use an adult test like the WAIS-III instead of the WISC-III, a children's test.

(c) perform any type psychometric analysis of their data.

(d) emphasize the importance of global IQs.

Answers: 1. c; 2. c; 3. b; 4. d; 5. a; 6. a

Five

HOW TO INTERPRET THE WAIS-IV: STEP-BY-STEP

INTRODUCTION TO INTERPRETATION

Examining and interpreting the 50-plus values on the Profile Page and Analysis Page of the WAIS-IV Record Form requires a very systematic plan. Just randomly grabbing interesting-looking scores is not a useful approach. In this chapter, we present an approach that guides you through the most global score to the most specific, to determine the most meaningful hypotheses about the examinee's abilities. Using this approach will set up a logical outline to follow when writing the Test Results and Interpretations sections of your WAIS-IV reports.

The steps of interpretation presented in this chapter begin with an analysis of the WAIS-IV indexes to determine the best way to summarize a person's overall intellectual ability. Next, both Normative and Personal Strengths and Weaknesses among the indexes (or alternative factors) are identified. Interpretation of fluctuations in the person's Index or Factor profile offers the most reliable and meaningful information about WAIS-IV performance because it identifies strong and weak areas of cognitive functioning relative to both same-age peers from the normal population (interindividual or normative approach) and the person's own overall ability level (intra-individual or ipsative approach). We also offer additional interpretive steps involving WAIS-IV composites (called Clinical Clusters) for examiners who choose to go beyond the FSIQ and index or factor profile in an attempt to uncover additional information about a person's cognitive capabilities as well as generate potentially meaningful hypotheses about areas of integrity or dysfunction.

Our interpretive approach reflects numerous modifications of and enhancements to prior methods of Wechsler test interpretation, including our own (Flanagan & Kaufman, 2004, 2009; Kaufman, 1979a, 1994a; Kaufman & Lichtenberger, 1999, 2000, 2002). Previously, Kaufman (1979a, 1994a) stressed ipsative methods for identifying areas of strength and weakness, whereas others emphasized normative approaches (e.g., Flanagan & Ortiz, 2001; Flanagan, Ortiz, Alfonso, & Mascolo, 2002, 2006). Like Flanagan and Kaufman's (2009) approach to WISC-IV interpretation and our approach to both KABC-II and WAIS-III interpretation (Kaufman & Lichtenberger, 2006; Kaufman, Lichtenberger, Fletcher-Janzen, & Kaufman, 2005), our current method for the WAIS-IV links ipsative analysis with normative analysis rather than focusing exclusively on either one or the other. In addition, our method:

1. Emphasizes cluster scores and deemphasizes individual subtest scores in the interpretive steps
2. Uses base rate data to evaluate the clinical meaningfulness of cluster and index score variability
3. Grounds interpretation in theories of cognitive abilities (e.g., Cattell-Horn-Carroll's (CHC) theory and neuropsychological theory) and in the cognitive neuroscience research that forms the theoretical basis for the WAIS-IV
4. Provides guidance on the use of supplemental measures to test hypotheses about significant subtest variation or outlier scores

As we discussed in chapter 4, during the process of interpretation, the step-by-step *quantitative* analysis of WAIS-IV data should be examined in the context of *qualitative* factors that may help to explain a person's test performance. Qualitative information on each of the subtests was presented in chapter 4 to aid in interpreting WAIS-IV performance, and additional information on qualitative analysis is presented in chapter 6, which focuses on neuropsychological test interpretation. Qualitatively analyzing a person's performance can facilitate the selection of supplementary measures to augment the WAIS-IV when necessary. So, too, can basing test selection on a theoretical model such as Flanagan et al.'s (2007) cross-battery approach that is rooted in CHC theory. *All interpretations of test performance gain diagnostic meaning when they are corroborated by other data sources and when they are empirically or logically related to the area or areas of difficulty specified in the referral.*

The interpretive steps described here are illustrated using a WAIS-IV profile of Laura, a 17-year-old 12th grader who was referred for an assessment of her neurocognitive and psychological functioning. (Laura's full case report is included in chapter 10.) In addition, a comprehensive WAIS-IV Interpretive Worksheet (included in Appendix A.1 on the CD-ROM in this book and designed to be completed by hand) walks the examiner through our interpretation method step by step. A software program, also included on the CD-ROM, called the WAIS-IV Data Management and Interpretive Assistant v1.0 (WAIS-IV DMIA) automates our interpretive system and is described alongside the worksheet. The WAIS-IV Interpretive Worksheet and the WAIS-IV DMIA have some stylistic differences but yield identical information. It is recommended that users of this book complete a few interpretive worksheets by hand in order to fully understand the interpretive steps prior to using the automated WAIS-IV DMIA. Also, while practicing the WAIS-IV interpretive steps, you can use the automated program to check the accuracy of the information you filled out by hand on the interpretive worksheet. Note that the WAIS-IV Interpretive Worksheet can be downloaded from the CD-ROM.

Administration Tips for Using the Step-by-Step Interpretive System

WAIS-IV examiners administer 10 subtests to obtain a person's FSIQ (assuming they do not opt to obtain a prorated FSIQ), and they have the option of administering 5 supplemental subtests to obtain further data. Of these 5 supplemental subtests, 3 are normed only for ages 16 to 69 and are not administered to adults ages 70 to 90 (except for clinical purposes): Figure Weights, Letter-Number Sequencing, and Cancellation. Only two of the supplemental tasks span the full 16–90 range: Comprehension and Picture Completion. The basic interpretive system presented here can be used for individuals of all ages who are administered the core group of 10 subtests. That system incorporates FSIQ, the 4 indexes, and 2 special scores (GAI and Cognitive Proficiency Index [CPI]). But the system also includes a valuable theory-based interpretive option in Steps 4–9 that focuses on five factor scores instead of the four indexes. *That special Five-Factor option is applicable only for individuals ages 16 to 69, and it requires the administration of 2 supplemental subtests, Figure Weights and Letter-Number Sequencing.*

In addition, Step 10 examines comparisons of pairs of clusters, many of which are theory based, to gain a deeper understanding of the person's WAIS-IV profile of strengths and weaknesses. Six of these comparisons include one or more of these supplemental subtests: Figure Weights, Letter-Number Sequencing, and Picture Completion. These six comparisons are applicable (a) only to individuals who are between the ages of 16 and 69 years and (b) who were administered these supplemental subtests. The remaining two comparisons are suitable for individuals of all ages but require the administration of the supplemental Comprehension subtest. The Cancellation subtest is excluded from our interpretive system, although it may provide useful clinical information to examiners who opt to administer it.

To make full use of our step-by-step interpretive system, we recommend that examiners routinely administer these supplemental subtests:

- Ages 16–69: Figure Weights, Letter-Number Sequencing, Comprehension, and Picture Completion
- Ages 70–90: Comprehension, and Picture Completion

If it is not feasible to administer all four, examiners who test individuals ages 16 to 69 should endeavor to administer Figure Weights and Letter-Number Sequencing because (a) they permit interpretation of the Five-Factor interpretation of the WAIS-IV, and (b) they permit making comparisons that involve fluid reasoning and working memory, two of the key constructs that pertain to the theoretical constructs from cognitive neuroscience research that were used by the test publisher's scientists to develop the WAIS-IV. Examiners who want to follow up our step-by-step interpretive system with the neuropsychological analysis of subtests detailed in chapter 6 should also make special effort to administer Picture Completion because of its unique contributions to neuropsychological analysis of the WAIS-IV, as Dr. George McCloskey explains in that chapter.

STEPS 1–3: ANALYZE THE FSIQ AND THE INDEX PROFILE

Step 1: Report the Person's WAIS-IV Standard Scores (FSIQ and Indexes) and Subtest Scaled Scores

For Step 1, create a table of the person's standard scores (FSIQ and four Wechsler indexes) as well as the person's scaled scores on all subtests administered. Report the name of each index and subtest along with the person's obtained score on each one. For the FSIQ and indexes *only*, report the confidence interval, percentile rank, and descriptive category associated with the person's obtained standard scores. For subtests, report the percentile associated with the person's obtained scaled scores. (See Rapid Reference 5.1.) Examiners need to select whether to use the 90% or 95% confidence interval for standard scores, namely the FSIQ and the four indexes. Examiners should always report standard scores with their associated confidence intervals. (Although most of the information obtained in Step 1 is found on the cover of the WAIS-IV Record Form, examiners may choose to create a similar table for inclusion in a psychological report.)

Traditional descriptive category systems consider Average functioning to be 90–109 and include other categories, such as Low Average (80–89) and Superior (120–129). A traditional category system is included in the *WAIS-IV Technical and Interpretive Manual* (Psychological Corporation, 2008, Table 6.3), and those descriptive labels appear frequently in case reports (see, e.g., Lichtenberger, Mather, Kaufman, & Kaufman, 2004). However, we suggest using an alternative category approach known as the Normative Descriptive System (shown in Rapid

≡ Rapid Reference 5.1

National Percentile Ranks Corresponding to Scaled Scores

Percentile Rank	Scaled Score	Corresponding IQ
99.9	19	145
99.6	18	140
99	17	135
98	16	130
95	15	125
91	14	120
84	13	115
75	12	110
63	11	105
50	10	100
37	9	95
25	8	90
16	7	85
9	6	80
5	5	75
2	4	70
1	3	65
0.4	2	60
0.1	1	55

Reference 5.2) that is based on the distance, in standard deviation (SD) units, from the mean. The Average Range in the Normative system is 85 to 115, which corresponds to 100 ±1 SD. Although either system may be used to classify a person's overall intellectual functioning on the WAIS-IV, Flanagan and Kaufman (2004) recommend the Normative Descriptive System, a general approach that "is commonly used by neuropsychologists and is becoming more widespread among clinical and school psychologists" (p. 123). Figure 5.1 shows an example of Step 1 using Laura's profile.

Step 2: Determine the Best Way to Summarize Overall Intellectual Ability

Two composites are available for the WAIS-IV—the traditional FSIQ and the General Ability Index (GAI), composed only of the subtests that constitute the VCI and PRI (Psychological Corporation, 2008). The GAI, which excludes subtests associated with a person's working memory and processing speed, has also been used as an alternate measure of global intelligence for the WISC-III

≡ Rapid Reference 5.2

Alternative "Normative" Descriptive System for WAIS-IV

Standard Score Range	WAIS-IV Descriptive Classification	Alternative Description of Performance
140+		
139		Upper Extreme/
135	Very Superior	Normative Strength
131	130+	131+
130		
129		
125	Superior	Above Average/
120	120 to 129	Normative Strength
119		116 to 130
116		
115	High Average	
111	110 to 119	
110		
109		
105		
100		Average Range/
99	Average	Normal Limits
95	90 to 109	85 to 115
90		
89		
85	Low Average	
84	80 to 89	
80		
79		Below Average/
75	Borderline	Normative Weakness
70	70 to 79	70 to 84
≤ 69		
	Extremely Low	Lower Extreme/
	≤ 69	Normative Weakness
		≤ 69

Examinee Name:	Laura O.		Date of Birth:	3/22/1992		
Date of Assessment:	10/22/2009		Age:	17 yr 7 mo		

Enter the scores in cells bordered in red with examinee's scores.
The program will automatically calculate the next steps for you.

Index/IQ Subtest	Score	Conf. Interval	Percentile Rank	Descriptive Category	Is Index/IQ/Cluster Interpretable?
Verbal Comprehension	96	91-101	39	Average Range/Within Normal Limits	Yes
Similarities	9		37		
Vocabulary	11		63		
Information	8		25		
(Comprehension)	10		50	*Does not contribute to Index or IQ*	
Perceptual Reasoning	79	74-84	8	Below Average/Normative Weakness	Yes
Block Design	5		5		
Matrix Reasoning	7		16		
Visual Puzzles	7		16		
(Figure Weights)	4		2	*Does not contribute to Index or IQ*	
(Picture Completion)	6		9	*Does not contribute to Index or IQ*	
Working Memory	95	90-100	37	Average Range/Within Normal Limits	Yes
Digit Span	11		63		
Arithmetic	7		16		
(Letter-Number Sequencing)	4		2	*Does not contribute to Index or IQ*	
Processing Speed	97	92-102	42	Average Range/Within Normal Limits	Yes
Symbol Search	10		50		
Coding	9		37		
(Cancellation)	9		37	*Does not contribute to Index or IQ*	
Full Scale IQ	83	78-88	13	Below Average/Normative Weakness	Yes
GAI	86	82-93	18	Average Range/Within Normal Limits	Yes
CPI	96	90-102	39	Average Range/Within Normal Limits	Yes
Keith Factor *(roll cursor over the red triangle to see which subtests comprise each cluster)*					
Crystallized Intelligence (Gc)	97	92-102	42	Average Range/Within Normal Limits	Yes
Short-Term Memory (Gsm)	86	81-93	18	Average Range/Within Normal Limits	No
Fluid Reasoning (Gf)	75	71-83	5	Below Average/Normative Weakness	Yes
Visual Processing (Gv)	78	73-86	7	Below Average/Normative Weakness	Yes
Processing Speed (Gs)	97	90-104	42	Average Range/Within Normal Limits	Yes

Figure 5.1. Illustration of Step 1 Using Laura's WAIS-IV Profile with the WAIS-IV Data Management and Interpretive Assistant (DMIA)

(Prifitera, Weiss, & Saklofske, 1998), WISC-IV (Flanagan & Kaufman, 2004; Prifitera, Saklofske, Weiss, & Rolfhus, 2005), and WAIS-III (Kaufman & Lichtenberger, 2006). The three VCI and three PRI subtests that compose the WAIS-IV GAI are usually the best measures of g, whereas the Working Memory and Processing Speed subtests are often among the worst measures (Tulsky et al., 2001). Because the GAI is composed of strong measures of general ability, it is especially useful for estimating general ability for individuals whose scores on memory and speed subtests deviate significantly from their scores on measures of verbal and nonverbal tasks (Psychological Corporation, 2008).

Steps 2a and 2b, described next, help determine whether the FSIQ or GAI provides the best measure of a person's global intellectual ability (or whether neither global score should be used).

Step 2a. Consider the person's four WAIS-IV Indexes. Subtract the lowest index from the highest index. Answer this question: *Is the size of the standard score difference less than 1.5 SDs (< 23 points)?*

- If YES, then the FSIQ may be interpreted as a reliable and valid estimate of a person's global intellectual ability. Proceed directly to Step 3.
- If NO, then the variation in the indexes that compose the FSIQ is considered too great (i.e., > 23 Points) for the purpose of summarizing global intellectual ability in a single score (i.e., the FSIQ). Proceed to Step 2b.

Step 2b. When the FSIQ is not interpretable, determine whether the General Ability Index (GAI) may be used to describe overall intellectual ability. Answer this question: *Is the size of the standard score difference between the VCI and PRI less than 1.5 SDs (< 23 points)?*

- If YES, then the GAI may be calculated and interpreted as a reliable and valid estimate of a person's general intellectual ability. To calculate the GAI and obtain its 90% or 95% confidence intervals, simply sum the scaled scores on the six subtests that compose the GAI (Similarities, Vocabulary, Information, Block Design, Matrix Reasoning, and Visual Puzzles) and enter this sum into the appropriate table (see Appendix C of the *WAIS-IV Technical and Interpretive Manual*). After calculating GAI, proceed to Step 3.
- If NO, then the variation in the indexes that compose the GAI is considered too great (i.e., > 23 points) for the purpose of summarizing global ability in a single score (i.e., GAI). Therefore, neither FSIQ nor GAI is appropriate, suggesting that the person's global ability cannot be meaningfully conveyed as a single score. Proceed to Step 3.

As we explained in our interpretive system for the WAIS-III (Kaufman & Lichtenberger, 2006, Appendix A), the FSIQ, as originally conceptualized by Wechsler, should be the global score of choice *unless it includes so much variability that it cannot be meaningfully interpreted.* In that instance, it is sensible to substitute the GAI for the FSIQ. But, again, we believe that the GAI should be interpreted as an estimate of a person's overall cognitive ability only if it does not contain too much variability. We therefore recommend that the GAI be interpreted only when two conditions are met: (a) there is too much variability among the four Indexes to permit meaningful interpretation of FSIQ; *and* (b) standard scores on the two scales that compose GAI (VCI and PRI) differ by less than 1.5 SDs, indicating that GAI provides a meaningful summary of the person's global ability. Rapid References 5.3, 5.4, and 5.5 provide examples of how to describe the FSIQ and the GAI in a written report. Figure 5.2 shows an example of Step 2 using Laura's profile.

≡ Rapid Reference 5.3

Example of How to Describe an Interpretable FSIQ in a Psychological Report

An interpretable FSIQ means that the size of the difference between the highest and lowest indexes does not equal or exceed 1.5 SDs (23 points). In the case of Laura, the difference between her highest index (97 on the PSI) and her lowest index (79 on the PRI) = 18 points. This value is less than 23 points, so her FSIQ is interpretable.

Laura earned a FSIQ of 89, classifying her overall intellectual ability, as measured by the WAIS-IV, as Average Range/Within Normal Limits. The chances are good (95%) that Laura's true FSIQ is somewhere within the range of 85 to 93. Her FSIQ is ranked at the 23rd percentile, indicating that she scored higher than 23% of other individuals the same age in the standardization sample.

Step 3: Determine Whether the Difference Between the Person's GAI and Cognitive Proficiency Index is Unusually Large

When the two Working Memory core subtests are combined with the two Processing Speed core subtests, a special index standard score may be computed and interpreted: the Cognitive Proficiency Index (CPI) (Dumont & Willis, 2001; Weiss, Saklofske,

≡ Rapid Reference 5.4

Example of How to Describe the GAI in a Psychological Report

Miguel's WAIS-IV Full Scale IQ (FSIQ) could not be interpreted because he demonstrated too much variability in his performance across the four Indexes that make up this score: the Verbal Comprehension, Perceptual Reasoning, Working Memory, and Processing Speed Indexes. However, because Miguel's performance on the Verbal Comprehension (98) and Perceptual Reasoning (90) Indexes was similar, these indexes can be combined to yield a General Ability Index (GAI). The GAI differs from the FSIQ in that it is not influenced directly by Miguel's performance on working memory and processing-speed tasks.

Miguel earned a GAI of 93, classifying his general level of intellectual ability as Average Range/Within Normal Limits. The chances are good (95%) that Miguel's true GAI is somewhere within the range of 87 to 99. His GAI is ranked at the 33rd percentile, indicating that he scored higher than 33% of other individuals of the same age in the standardization sample.

≡ Rapid Reference 5.5

Example of How to Describe in a Psychological Report the Finding of Both a Noninterpretable FSIQ and a Noninterpretable GAI

A noninterpretable FSIQ means that the size of the difference between the highest and lowest indexes equals or exceeds 1.5 SDs (23 points). A noninterpretable GAI means that the size of the difference between the VCI and PRI equals or exceeds 1.5 SDs (23 points). In the case of Susan, the difference between her highest index (98 on the VCI) and her lowest index (70 on the PSI) = 28 points. This value is more than 23 points, so her FSIQ is noninterpretable. In addition, the difference of 25 points between Susan's VCI (98) and PRI (73) equals or exceeds 1.5 SDs (23 points). Consequently, her GAI is also noninterpretable.

Susan earned a Full Scale IQ (FSIQ) of 76, but this estimate of her overall intellectual ability cannot be interpreted meaningfully because she displayed too much variability in the four indexes that compose this full-scale score. Therefore, Susan's intelligence is best understood by her performance on the separate WAIS-IV indexes—namely, Verbal Comprehension, Perceptual Reasoning, Working Memory, and Processing Speed.

Exception to the Rule: Always interpret a person's overall score on the WAIS-IV whenever a global score is essential for diagnosis (e.g., of intellectual disability) or placement (e.g., in a gifted program). Even if both the FSIQ and GAI are noninterpretable based on our empirical criteria, select the one that provides the most sensible overview of the child's intelligence for use in the diagnostic or placement process. Use clinical judgment to make this decision. For example, if the examinee was impulsive or distractible when administered the working memory and/or the processing speed subtests, then select the GAI (which excludes the WMI and PSI).

STEP 2. The Best Way to Summarize Overall Intellectual Ability is Determined

Step 2a. To determine whether the FS-IQ is interpretable, the lowest index is subtracted from the highest index .

	97	-	79	=	18
Index Standard Scores:	Highest		Lowest		Difference

Is the size of the difference less than 1.5 standard deviations (i.e., < 23 points)?
YES, FS-IQ may be interpreted as a reliable and valid estimate of a person's overall intellectual ability.

Step 2b. To determine whether the General Ability Index (GAI) may be used to summarize overall intellectual ability, the absolute difference between the VCI and PRI is calculated.

	96	-	79	=	17
Index Standard Scores:	VCI		PRI		Absolute Difference

Is the size of the difference less than 1.5 standard deviations (i.e., < 23 points)?
YES, GAI may be interpreted as a reliable and valid estimate of a person's overall intellectual ability.

Core VCI and PRI subtest scaled scores are summed, and the GAI that corresponds to this sum is located.

	9	+	11	+	8	+	5	+	7	+	7	=	47	=	86
Scaled Scores:	SI		VC		IN		BD		MR		VP		Sum		GAI

Figure 5.2. Illustration of Step 2 Using Laura's Profile with the WAIS-IV DMIA

Schwartz, Prifitera, & Courville, 2006). The CPI, a term coined by Dr. Larry Weiss, reflects the person's proficiency for processing certain types of information. As Weiss and colleagues (2006) indicate, "Proficient processing, through quick visual speed and good mental control, facilitates fluid reasoning and the acquisition of new material by reducing the cognitive demands of novel tasks" (p. 170). Although the computation of the CPI is supported from a psychometric perspective, it has been questioned from a neuropsychological basis (Hebben, 2009).

This step uses sound psychometric procedures to compare the CPI and GAI. (See Table 5.1 for the reliability coefficients of these indexes.) The result of the comparison has practical and clinical benefits, especially for individuals with learning disabilities, traumatic brain injuries, and Asperger's disorder (Weiss et al., 2006); however, deficits in specific neurological substrates should not be inferred even when the person's GAI is unusually larger than his or her CPI.

Table 5.1. Internal Consistency Reliability Coefficients of WAIS-IV GAI and CPI by Age and Overall Sample

Age Group	GAI $SI+VC+IN+BD+MR+VP$	CPI $DS+AR+CD+SS$
6–17	.96	.93
18–19	.97	.94
20–24	.97	.94
25–29	.97	.94
30–34	.97	.93
35–44	.97	.94
45–54	.98	.94
55–64	.97	.94
65–69	.98	.95
70–74	.97	.95
75–79	.97	.95
80–84	.97	.95
85–90	.97	.95
All	.97	.94

Note: The subtest abbreviations underneath the GAI and CPI represent the subtests that comprise each index.
Source: Standardization data and analysis results from the Wechsler Adult Intelligence Scale—Fourth Edition (WAIS-IV). Copyright © 2008 by NCS Pearson, Inc. Used with permission. All rights reserved.

As detailed in Step 2b, the GAI (composed of the core VCI and PRI subtests) sometimes serves as the best estimate of a person's global ability when the FSIQ is not interpretable. The CPI-GAI comparison is an especially useful interpretive step for those individuals whose global ability is best represented by GAI (based on Step 2a and 2b computations). However, examiners may compare the CPI and GAI (even when FSIQ is interpretable) so long as both the GAI and CPI are found to be interpretable.

Step 3a. Prior to conducting the GAI-CPI comparison, you must first determine whether the two indexes represent unitary abilities or processes.

For the GAI, answer this question: *Is the size of the difference between VCI and PRI less than 1.5 SDs (i.e., < 23 points)?* (If this question has already been answered in Step 2b, use that result for Step 3a.)

- If YES, then the GAI can be calculated and interpreted as a reliable and valid estimate of the person's overall intellectual ability. Proceed to the next part of this step to determine whether the CPI can be interpreted.
- If NO, then the GAI-CPI comparison cannot be made.

For the CPI, answer this question: *Is the size of the difference between WMI and PSI less than 1.5 SDs (i.e., < 23 points)?*

- If YES, then the CPI and GAI can both be calculated and interpreted as reliable and valid estimates of the person's functioning. Proceed to Step 3b.
- If NO, then the GAI-CPI comparison cannot be made.

Step 3b. Calculate the GAI and CPI. (If the GAI has already been calculated in Step 2b, use that value for Step 3 and calculate CPI.)

To compute GAI: (a) sum the person's scaled scores on the three core VCI and three core PRI subtests, and (b) enter this sum into Appendix C of the *WAIS-IV Technical and Interpretive Manual* to determine the GAI, percentile rank, and confidence interval (select either 90% or 95% confidence).

To compute CPI: (a) sum the person's scaled scores on the two core WMI and two core PSI subtests, and (b) enter this sum into Appendix A.2 (see the CD-ROM in this book) to determine the person's CPI, percentile rank, and confidence interval (select either 90% or 95% confidence).

Step 3c. Determine whether the size of the difference between the GAI and CPI (regardless of direction) is significant. The difference needed for significance at the $p < .05$ level is 8.8 points, and difference needed for significance at the $p < .01$ level is 11.6 points.

Step 3d. Determine whether the size of the difference between the GAI and CPI (regardless of direction) is unusually large or uncommon, occurring less than 10% of the time in the WAIS-IV standardization sample. If the difference is 19

Table 5.2. Differences between GAI and CPI Required for Statistical Significance (at $p < .05$ and $p < .01$) and to Be Considered Uncommon

	Difference Required for Significance		Difference Required for an Unusually Large or Uncommon Discrepancy			
	$p < .05$	$p < .01$	10% Base Rate	5% Base Rate	2% Base Rate	1% Base Rate
Difference between GAI and CPI	8.8	11.6	19	23	27	30

Source: Standardization data and analysis results from the Wechsler Adult Intelligence Scale—Fourth Edition (WAIS-IV). Copyright © 2008 by NCS Pearson, Inc. Used with permission. All rights reserved.

Note: "Unusually large or uncommon" denotes differences estimated to occur infrequently in the WAIS-IV standardization sample. We suggest using 10% of the normative population to denote uncommonly large discrepancies, but values are also shown for the 5%, 2%, and 1% levels for examiners who prefer a more stringent criterion. The uncommon differences in this table were estimated by the formula provided by Sattler (1982, Table C-11) for computing the percentage of a population obtaining discrepancies between two standard scores. This formula includes the correlation between GAI and CPI, which was kindly provided by Pearson Assessments (J. J. Wang, personal communication, March 23, 2009). The correlation used in the formula was the value for the total sample, ages 16–90 years.

points or more, it should be considered uncommonly large. Table 5.2 reviews the values necessary for GAI versus CPI differences to be considered significantly large and uncommonly large. Examiners who prefer a more stringent criterion than 10% for determining uncommonly large differences can select the 5%, 2%, or 1% levels, as reported in Table 5.2. Figure 5.3 shows an example of Step 3 using Laura's profile.

INTRODUCTION TO STEPS 4–9: TWO PATHS OF INTERPRETATION

In the next five steps, examiners may choose to evaluate the WAIS-IV in one of two ways:

A. Interpret the four indexes that the WAIS-IV yields (i.e., Wechsler Four-Index model).

B. Interpret a Five-Factor model of the WAIS-IV (i.e., Keith Five-Factor model).

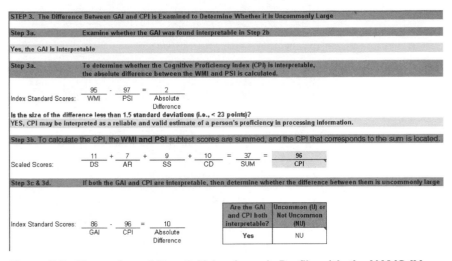

Figure 5.3. Illustration of Step 3 Using Laura's Profile with the WAIS-IV DMIA

The confirmatory factor-analytic data in the *WAIS-IV Technical and Interpretive Manual* support the validity of the four WAIS-IV indexes (i.e., VCI, PRI, WMI, and PSI). However, new WAIS-IV confirmatory factor analysis reported in chapter 1 of this book has also supported the validity of a Five-Factor model (T. Keith, personal communication, January 30, 2009). Keith's analyses supported separate Fluid Reasoning and Visual Processing Factors, which makes the Five-Factor model an especially good choice when there is variability in the person's scaled scores on the core and supplemental subtests associated with the PRI. The Five-Factor model that we have assembled for interpretation includes these clusters:

1. Crystallized Intelligence (*Gc*) = Vocabulary + Information
2. Short-Term Memory (*Gsm*) = Digit Span + Letter-Number Sequencing
3. Fluid Reasoning (*Gf*) = Matrix Reasoning + Figure Weights
4. Visual Processing (*Gv*) = Block Design + Visual Puzzles
5. Processing Speed (*Gs*) = Symbol Search + Coding

We decided in advance to limit each factor to two subtests such that both the traditional four-index Wechsler model and our alternate Keith Five-Factor model are composed of 10 subtests. Rapid Reference 5.6 explains how we

≡ Rapid Reference 5.6

Development of the Five Two-Subtest Factors

In chapter 1, we reported preliminary findings from Tim Keith's WAIS-IV confirmatory factor analyses (CFA) (pers. comm., January 30, 2009). Figure 1.2 displays the results of this CFA. Five factors resulted, with two to three subtests loading on each factor. We examined the subtest loadings, and considered each subtest from a clinical and a CHC theoretical perspective to determine the best combination of subtests to compose each factor.

- The Gc factor had four subtests load on it: Similarities (.83), Vocabulary (.89), Comprehension (.84), and Information (.80). We chose the combination of Vocabulary and Information to represent the Gc factor because, theoretically, they well represent the Gc construct, are excellent measures of a person's knowledge base, and are less influenced by fluid reasoning than are Similarities and Comprehension.

- Three subtests—Picture Completion (.64), Block Design (.76) and Visual Puzzles (.73)—loaded on the Gv factor. We chose Visual Puzzles and Block Design to represent the Gv factor because of their strong factor loadings and their strong representation of the Gv construct. In addition, Picture Completion is a supplemental rather than a core subtest, and its items often elicit verbal (rather than nonverbal) responses.

- Matrix Reasoning (.72), Figure Weights (.77), and Arithmetic (.77) loaded on the Gf factor. We chose Matrix Reasoning and Figure Weights to represent the Gf construct because of their strong factor loadings and strong representation of the Gf construct. Although Arithmetic also has a strong Gf factor loading, it has been shown to be influenced by other cognitive and behavioral variables, such short-term memory, crystallized knowledge, distractibility, and anxiety.

- The Gs factor had two subtests that strongly loaded on it—Coding (.81) and Symbol Search (.80)—and these two tasks are strong theoretical and clinical representations of the construct. Thus, those two tasks were chosen to represent this factor. Cancellation also loaded on the Gs Factor, but its loading (.56) was not as strong as that of the other two subtests.

determined which two subtests would represent each of the five Keith factors. The internal consistency reliability coefficients for the new WAIS-IV Keith factors are shown in Table 5.3.

Note that although the names of the five Keith factors reflect terminology consistent with CHC theory—consistent with Keith's own personal orientation—there are alternate ways to interpret the Keith Five-Factor model in addition to CHC theory. For example, these Five Factors can be interpreted from a neuropsychological approach based on Luria's (1973, 1980) theory. This theoretical foundation for interpretation is similar to the bases for NEPSY-II (Korkman,

Table 5.3. Internal Consistency Reliability Coefficients for the New WAIS-IV Five Factors, by Age and Overall Sample

	FACTOR				
Age Group	Crystallized Knowledge (*Gc*) VC+IN	Short-Term Memory (*Gsm*) LN+DS	Fluid Reasoning (*Gf*) MR+FW	Visual Processing (*Gv*) BD+VP	Processing Speed (*Gs*) CD+SS
16–17	.95	.94	.93	.93	.88
18–19	.95	.94	.93	.93	.90
20–24	.96	.93	.92	.92	.90
25–29	.95	.95	.94	.94	.90
30–34	.95	.96	.95	.94	.87
35–44	.96	.94	.93	.93	.87
45–54	.97	.95	.94	.95	.87
55–64	.97	.94	.93	.93	.91
65–69	.97	.94	.94	.94	.91
70–74	.97	—	—	.93	.91
75–79	.97	—	—	.91	.92
80–84	.97	—	—	.88	.92
85–90	.98	—	—	.89	.92
All	.96	.94	.93	.93	.90

Source: Standardization data and analysis results from the *Wechsler Adult Intelligence Scale—Fourth Edition* (WAIS-IV). Copyright © 2008 by NCS Pearson, Inc. Used with permission. All rights reserved.

Note: The subtest abbreviations underneath the factors represent the subtests that comprise each factor. The Processing Speed Factor (*Gs*) is identical to the WAIS-IV Processing Speed Index (PSI). *Gc* = Crystallized Knowledge; *Gsm* = Short-Term Memory; *Gf* = Fluid Reasoning; *Gv* = Visual Processing; and *Gs* = Processing Speed.

Kirk, & Kemp, 2007), Cognitive Ability System (CAS; Naglieri & Das, 1997), and the KABC-II (Kaufman & Kaufman, 2004). Luria (1970) believed that the brain's basic functions can be represented by three main blocks (or functional systems), which form the framework of Naglieri and Das's (1997) PASS model. These three blocks are responsible for arousal and attention (Block 1); the use of one's senses to analyze, code, and store information (Block 2); and the application of executive functions for formulating plans and programming behavior (Block 3). Using Lurian theory, cognitive functions are viewed as complex capacities with interactive subcomponents that contribute to performance within and across functional domains. As Kemp, Kirk, and Korkman (2001) summarize:

> Cognitive functions, such as attention and executive functions, language, sensory perception, motor function, visuospatial abilities, and learning and memory are complex capacities in the Lurian tradition. They are composed of flexible and interactive subcomponents that are mediated by equally flexible, interactive, neural networks. (p. 6)

Rapid Reference 5.7 demonstrates how Keith's Five Factors may be interpreted from either a CHC or Lurian-based neurological perspective, depending on one's personal theoretical focus. The Lurian complex capacities provide a theoretical explanation of Keith's Five-Factor solution that is no less defensible than CHC theory: Attention & Executive Functions (*Gf*), Language (*Gc*), Sensorimotor (*Gs*), Visuospatial Functions (*Gv*), and Memory & Learning (*Gsm*).

≋ *Rapid Reference 5.7*

Suggested Interpretation of Keith Five-Factor Model from CHC and Lurian-Based Neurological Perspectives

Lurian Neuropsychological Perspective	CHC Perspective
Short-Term Memory (*Gsm*) Keith Factor	
Performing the complex capacities that involve conceptualizing, categorizing, and making associations (Memory & Learning). On the WAIS-IV, these capacities closely resemble Luria's Block 2 "successive" or sequential processing, namely arranging input in sequential or serial order to solve a problem, where each idea is linearly and temporally related to the preceding one.	Taking in and holding information, and then using it within a few seconds.
Visual Processing (*Gv*) Keith Factor	
Performing the complex capacities of integrating visuospatial and motor skills and using nonmotor visuospatial processing (Visuospatial Abilities). These capacities closely resemble Luria's Block 2 "simultaneous" processing, in which stimuli must be integrated and synthesized in holistic fashion to solve a complex visual-spatial problem.	Perceiving, storing, manipulating, and thinking with visual patterns.

Lurian Neuropsychological Perspective	CHC Perspective
Fluid Reasoning (*Gf*) Keith Factor	
Performing the high-level, decision-making, executive processes often associated with Block 3, where the emphasis is on the use of flexible strategies and planning, especially the ability to adopt and shift cognitive sets, monitor behavior, and maintain impulse control (Attention & Executive Processes). However, as Reitan (1988) states, "Block 3 is involved in no sensory, motor, perceptual, or speech functions and is devoted exclusively to analysis, planning, and organization of programs for behavior" (p. 335). Therefore, integration of the three blocks is especially important to solve these problems efficiently.	Solving novel problems by using reasoning abilities, such as induction and deduction.
Crystallized Ability (*Gc*) Keith Factor	
Performing complex linguistic capacities associated with speech and language that place special demands on both receptive and expressive functions (Language). On the WAIS-IV, the person must demonstrate his or her store of verbal-conceptual and factual knowledge as well as the ability to process the linguistic stimuli.	Demonstrating the breadth and depth of knowledge acquired from one's culture.
Processing Speed (*Gs*) Keith Factor	
Performing complex perceptual and motor capacities that involve integrating visual perception and eye-hand coordination, most notably graphomotor precision and speed (Sensorimotor).	Fluently and automatically performing cognitive tasks, especially when under pressure to maintain focused attention and concentration.

Note: The subtests that compose each Keith factor can be interpreted in a manner parallel to certain scales and subtests on other tests, such as the NEPSY-II, CAS, and KABC-II. Keith *Gsm* Factor subtests are similar conceptually to NEPSY-II Memory and Learning, CAS Successive, and KABC-II Sequential/*Gsm*. The Keith *Gv* Factor subtests are similar conceptually to NEPSY-II Visuospatial Abilities, CAS Simultaneous, and KABC-II Simultaneous/*Gv*. The Keith *Gf* Factor subtests are similar conceptually to the NEPSY-II Tower subtest in the Attention and Executive Functioning Domain, CAS Planning, and KABC-II Planning/*Gf*. The Keith *Gc* Factor subtests are similar conceptually to NEPSY-II Language and KABC-II Knowledge/*Gc*. The Keith *Gs* Factor subtests are similar conceptually to NEPSY-II Sensorimotor, except that the WAIS-IV subtests have a clear-cut cognitive component and the NEPSY-II subtests do not.

Examiners who prefer to interpret the four WAIS-IV Wechsler indexes, based on their personal theoretical and clinical orientations, need not use the Keith Five-Factor system for any of the individuals they test; however, the Five-Factor approach will be especially appealing to examiners who favor the CHC theory and enjoy using cross-battery assessment (Flanagan, Ortiz, & Alfonso, 2007) as well as those who want to examine the profile from a Lurian neuropsychological perspective. As we mentioned earlier, the Five-Factor approach is suitable only for individuals ages 16 to 69 because two of the subtests needed for the analysis are not normed for adults who are 70 or older.

The next steps will assist you in deciding which interpretive model to use. The text walks you through the steps to perform accurate and psychometrically sound interpretation of the data.

Step 4: Selecting the Wechsler Four-Index Model or the Keith Five-Factor Model

This step is designed to help you determine if use of the Keith Five-Factor model is appropriate or if the Wechsler Four-Index model should be your choice for interpretation. Answering the next three questions will help you select the appropriate model.

Step 4a. Answer this question: *Is the person you tested between the ages of 16 and 69?*

- If NO, proceed to Step 5 to interpret data with the Wechsler Four-Index Model.
- If YES, go to Step 4b.

Step 4b. Answer this question: *Did you administer the supplementary subtests, and Letter-Number Sequencing, and Figure Weights?*

- If NO, proceed to Step 5 to interpret data with the Wechsler Four-Index Model.
- If YES, go to Step 4c.

Step 4c. Answer this question: *Considering your personal theoretical and clinical foundations, do you choose to interpret the WAIS-IV data with the Keith Five-Factor model?*

- If NO, proceed to Step 5 to interpret data with the Wechsler Four-Index model.
- If YES, continue to Step 6 to interpret the data with the Keith Five-Factor model.

Note that even if you do choose to interpret the WAIS-IV profile from the perspective of Keith Five-Factor model, you should always report the scores from the four Wechsler indexes in your case report as well. This reporting of information should include the Index standard scores, confidence intervals, and percentile ranks. Professionals and organizations familiar with the Wechsler tests will want to be informed of those four index scores, even if your interpretation is based on a reorganization of the data into the Keith Five-Factor model. Also note that it is acceptable to report standard scores for both the Wechsler Four Indexes and the Keith Five Factors; however, you need to be mindful that these two sets of scores combine to yield many numbers. Be particularly careful with how you choose to write your report to clarify which scores you are writing about in the test results section. Many of the scores from the two models have similar labels, so it is important to emphasize the most salient aspects of the Wechsler indexes and Keith factors so that the reader is not overwhelmed with the information that you are presenting or confused by the wealth of data. Although we do not especially advise it, examiners certainly have the option of interpreting *both* the Wechsler index profile (Step 5) and the Keith factor profile (Step 6) to see which result provides the richest source of hypotheses about the person's pattern of strengths and weaknesses. In that instance, it is absolutely essential to be prudent and concise when writing the case report. Sometimes less is more when conveying important highlights of a person's cognitive test profile. Figure 5.4 shows an example of Step 4 using Laura's profile.

DON'T FORGET

Recommendations for Report Writing when Using the Keith Five-Factor Model

- When the Keith Five-Factor model is used as the basis of your interpretation, always report the scores from the four Wechsler indexes in your case report as well.
- Include the index standard scores, confidence intervals, and percentile ranks.
- It is acceptable to report standard scores for both the Wechsler Four Indexes and the Keith Five Factors.
- Be mindful to write with clarity because many of the scores from the two models have similar labels.
- Emphasize the most salient aspects of the Wechsler indexes and Keith factors to distinguish the differences between the scores.

Step 5: Determine Whether Each of the Four Wechsler Indexes Is Unitary, and Thus Interpretable

Skip this step if you are interpreting the person's profile via the Keith Five-Factor Approach. Proceed to Step 6.

When the variability among subtest scaled scores within an index is unusually large, then the standard score does not provide a good estimate of the ability it is

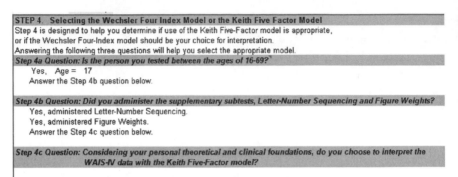

STEP 4. Selecting the Wechsler Four Index Model or the Keith Five Factor Model
Step 4 is designed to help you determine if use of the Keith Five-Factor model is appropriate,
or if the Wechsler Four-Index model should be your choice for interpretation.
Answering the following three questions will help you select the appropriate model.
Step 4a Question: Is the person you tested between the ages of 16-69?
 Yes, Age = 17
 Answer the Step 4b question below.

Step 4b Question: Did you administer the supplementary subtests, Letter-Number Sequencing and Figure Weights?
 Yes, administered Letter-Number Sequencing.
 Yes, administered Figure Weights.
 Answer the Step 4c question below.

*Step 4c Question: Considering your personal theoretical and clinical foundations, do you choose to interpret the
    WAIS-IV data with the Keith Five-Factor model?*

 If no, proceed to Step 5 to interpret data with the Wechsler Four-Index model.
 If yes, continue to Step 6 to interpret the data with the Keith Five-Factor model.

Figure 5.4. Illustration of Step 4 Using Laura's Profile with the WAIS-IV DMIA

intended to measure and, therefore, is not interpretable. In other words, when a substantial difference between the scaled scores composing an index is found, the index cannot be interpreted as representing a unitary ability. The notion of unitary abilities was also a guiding principle in our approach for interpreting other Wechsler scales as well (Flanagan & Kaufman, 2004, 2009; Kaufman, 1994a; Kaufman & Lichtenberger, 2000, 2006; Lichtenberger & Kaufman, 2004). Rapid Reference 5.8 shows an example of how to interpret a unitary index (or factor) in a psychological report. Rapid Reference 5.9 shows an example of how to interpret a nonunitary index (or factor) in a psychological report.

≡ *Rapid Reference 5.8*

Example of How to Interpret a Unitary Index in a Psychological Report

The Processing Speed Index (PSI), a measure of Processing Speed (Gs), represents Laura's ability to perform simple, clerical-type tasks quickly. Laura's Gs ability was assessed with two tasks: One required her to quickly copy symbols that were paired with numbers according to a key (37th percentile), and the other required her to identify the presence or absence of a target symbol in a row of symbols (50th percentile). The difference between Laura's performances on these two tasks was not unusually large, indicating that her PSI is a good estimate of her processing speed. Laura obtained a PSI of 97 (89–106), which is ranked at the 42nd percentile and is classified as in the Average Range/Within Normal Limits.

≡ Rapid Reference 5.9

Example of How to Interpret a Nonunitary Index in a Psychological Report

The Verbal Comprehension Index (VCI), a measure of Crystallized Intelligence (Gc), represents Stephan's ability to reason with previously learned information. Crystallized intelligence develops largely as a function of both formal and informal educational opportunities and experiences and is highly dependent on exposure to mainstream U.S. culture. Stephan's Gc was assessed by tasks that required him to define words (16th percentile), draw conceptual similarities between words (37th percentile), and answer general factual questions (84th percentile). The variability among Stephan's performances on these tasks was unusually large, indicating that his overall Crystallized knowledge or ability to reason with previously learned information cannot be summarized in a single score (i.e., the VCI).

Note: Subsequent steps of interpretation may be used to provide additional information about Stephan's Gc performance.

Step 5a. Determine whether the size of the difference among subtest scaled scores within the VCI (composed of three subtests) is too large. Subtract the lowest subtest scaled score from the highest subtest scaled score. Answer this question: *Is the size of the difference less than 1.5 SDs (< 5 points)?*

- If YES, then the ability presumed to underlie the VCI is unitary and may be interpreted. (The Don't Forget box provides the definition of a unitary ability.)
- If NO, then the difference is too large (≥ 5 points), and the VCI cannot be interpreted as representing a unitary ability.

DON'T FORGET

Definition of a Unitary Ability

A unitary ability is an ability (such as Crystallized Intelligence or Processing Speed) that is represented by a cohesive set of scaled scores, each reflecting slightly different or unique aspects of the ability. Thus, when the variability among the subtest scaled scores that compose a WAIS-IV Index is not unusually large, the ability presumed to underlie the Index is considered unitary and may be interpreted. For example, a person obtaining scaled scores of 9, 5, and 8 on Similarities, Vocabulary, and Information, respectively, has a difference score of 4 associated with the VCI

(continued)

(9 – 5 = 4). A difference of less than 1.5 SDs (i.e., < 5 points) between the highest and lowest subtest scaled score is needed for an index to be considered as representing a unitary ability. Therefore, in this example, the VCI represents a unitary ability and may be interpreted as a reliable and valid estimate of verbal reasoning, concept formation, and acquired knowledge, or Crystallized Intelligence (Gc).

Step 5b. Follow the same procedure as in Step 5a to determine the interpretability of the PRI (also composed of three subtests).

Step 5c. Determine whether the size of the difference between the subtest scaled scores that compose the two-subtest WMI is too large. Subtract the lower scaled score from the higher one. Answer this question: *Is the size of the difference less than 1.5 SDs (< 5 points)?*

- If YES, then the ability presumed to underlie the WMI is unitary and may be interpreted.
- If NO, then the difference is too large (≥ 5 points), and the WMI cannot be interpreted as representing a unitary ability.

Step 5d. Follow the same procedure as in Step 5c to determine the interpretability of the PSI (also composed of two subtests).

Although an index is considered uninterpretable when the variability among the subtests that comprise it is too large, in some instances it makes sense to look at the normative classifications of the scaled scores to determine whether a general conclusion may be made about a person's range of observed functioning in the ability presumed to underlie the index (Flanagan & Kaufman, 2004, 2009; Kaufman & Lichtenberger, 2006). Specifically, when all subtest scaled scores within an index are consistently low (≤ 8) or consistently high (≥ 12), that fact should be noted and explained in a report. The Don't Forget box provides information on how to describe a notable integrity in the ability that the index represents. Figure 5.5 shows an example of Step 5 using Laura's profile.

DON'T FORGET

Subtests with Unusual Variability, But All ≥ 12

If the variability among subtest scaled scores composing an index is unusually large and all scaled scores are 12 or greater, then describe the examinee's range of observed functioning in the ability presumed to underlie the index as a notable integrity in this way:

The Perceptual Reasoning Index (PRI), a measure of Fluid Reasoning and Visual Processing (Gf/Gv), represents Susan's ability to reason using visual stimuli. Susan's fluid reasoning and visual processing abilities were assessed by tasks that required her to recreate a series of modeled or pictured designs using blocks (84th percentile), identify the missing portion of an incomplete visual matrix from one of several response options (98th percentile), and select three puzzle pieces that would combine to recreate a puzzle (99.9th percentile). The variability among Susan's performances on these tasks was unusually large, indicating that her overall fluid reasoning and visual processing ability cannot be summarized in a single score (i.e., the PRI). However, it is clear that Susan's fluid reasoning and visual processing ability is a notable integrity for her because her performance on the tasks that compose the PRI ranged from Average Range/Within Normal Limits to Upper Extreme/Normative Strength.

Step 6: Determine Whether Each of the Five Keith Factors Is Unitary, and Thus Interpretable

Skip this step if you interpreted the person's profile via the Wechsler Four-Index Approach. Proceed to Step 7.

STEP 5. The Four Indexes are Examined to Determine Whether they are Unitary

Step 5a. The difference between the highest and lowest core VCI subtest scaled scores is calculated.

VCI Subtest
Scaled Scores: __11__ - __8__ = __3__
       Highest   Lowest   Difference

Is the size of the difference less than 5 points?
YES, interpret the VCI as representing a unitary Index

Step 5b. The difference between the highest and lowest core PRI subtest scaled scores is calculated.

PRI Subtest
Scaled Scores: __7__ - __5__ = __2__
       Highest   Lowest   Difference

Is the size of the difference less than 5 points?
YES, interpret the PRI as representing a unitary Index

Step 5c. The difference between the highest and lowest core WMI subtest scaled scores is calculated.

WMI Subtest
Scaled Scores: __11__ - __7__ = __4__
       Highest   Lowest   Difference

Is the size of the difference less than 5 points?
YES, interpret the WMI as representing a unitary Index

Step 5d. The difference between the highest and lowest core PSI subtest scaled scores is calculated.

PSI Subtest
Scaled Scores: __10__ - __9__ = __1__
       Highest   Lowest   Difference

Is the size of the difference less than 5 points?
YES, interpret the PSI as representing a unitary Index

Figure 5.5. Illustration of Step 5 Using Laura's Profile with the WAIS-IV DMIA

Similar to examining variability within a Wechsler index, when the variability among subtest scaled scores within a Keith factor is unusually large, then the standard score does not provide a good estimate of the ability it is intended to measure and, therefore, is not interpretable. In other words, when a substantial difference between the scaled scores factor is found, the factor cannot be interpreted as representing a unitary ability.

Step 6a. Calculate the standard scores for the five Keith factors by summing the scaled scores for the two subtests that comprise each cluster and converting the sum to a standard score using the norms in Appendixes A.3–A.6 on the CD-ROM. (Use the WAIS-IV Manual's *Table A.6 PSI Equivalents Sums of Scaled Score* to obtain the Gs standard score.)

Step 6b. Determine whether the size of the difference among subtest scaled scores within the Crystallized Intelligence (*Gc*) factor (Vocabulary and Information) is too large. Subtract the lowest subtest scaled score from the highest subtest scaled score. Answer this question: *Is the size of the difference less than 1.5 SDs (< 5 points)?*

- If YES, then the ability presumed to underlie the *Gc* factor is unitary and may be interpreted.
- If NO, then the difference is too large (≥ 5 points) and the *Gc* factor cannot be interpreted as representing a unitary ability.

DON'T FORGET

What Do I Do with a Noninterpretable Index or Factor?

When an index is found to be noninterpretable, the variability among the subtest scaled scores composing the index is too large to allow for the interpretation of a single ability. For example, when the variability among the VCI subtest scaled scores is unusually large, the VCI cannot be interpreted as representing the ability of Crystallized Intelligence (*Gc*). However, the subtests composing the noninterpretable index may be combined with other subtests in different ways to allow for meaningful interpretations of more specific abilities at later steps in the interpretive process (e.g., Step 8).

Step 6c. Follow the same procedure as in Step 6a to determine the interpretability of the Short-Term Memory (*Gsm*) factor (comprised of Digit Span and Letter-Number Sequencing).

Step 6d. Follow the same procedure as in Step 6a to determine the interpretability of the Fluid Reasoning (*Gf*) factor (comprised of Matrix Reasoning and Figure Weights).

Step 6e. Follow the same procedure as in Step 6a to determine the interpretability of the Visual Processing (*Gv*) factor (comprised of Block Design and Visual Puzzles).

Step 6f. Follow the same procedure as in Step 6a to determine the interpretability of the Processing Speed (*Gs*) factor (comprised of Symbol Search and Coding).

Step 6g. Determine how many of Keith's Five Factors are interpretable by reviewing the results of Steps 6b–6f. If three or more of the factors are interpretable, proceed with your interpretation of the WAIS-IV data using the Keith Five-Factor model. However, if only one or two of Keith's five factors are interpretable, we strongly recommend using the Wechsler Four-Index model to interpret the WAIS-IV data. Thus, if only one or two of Keith's five factors are interpretable (i.e., three or more Keith factors are not unitary and cannot be meaningfully interpreted), go back to Step 5 and complete interpretation of the Wechsler Four-Index model. (However, remember that we do recommend always listing the four Wechsler index scores in your written report, even when you do interpret the profile from the perspective of the Keith Five-Factor Model.)

CAUTION

Three or More Keith Factors Needed for Interpretation

Number of Interpretable Keith Factors	Recommendation
5	Proceed with interpretation of Keith Five-Factor model
4	Proceed with interpretation of Keith Five-Factor model
3	Proceed with interpretation of Keith Five-Factor model
2	Stop interpretation of Keith Five-Factor model, and instead interpret Wechsler Four-Index model
1	Stop interpretation of Keith Five-Factor model, and instead interpret Wechsler Four-Index model

Similar to what we suggested with uninterpretable indexes, in some instances of an uninterpretable factor, it makes sense to look at the normative classifications of the subtest scaled scores to determine whether a general conclusion may be made about a person's range of observed functioning in the ability presumed to underlie the factor. Specifically, when all subtest scaled scores within a Factor are consistently low (≤ 8) or consistently high (≥ 12), that fact should be noted and explained in a report. The Don't Forget box provides information on how to describe a notable limitation in the ability that the Factor represents. Figure 5.6 shows an example of Step 6 using Laura's profile.

DON'T FORGET

....

Subtests with Unusual Variability, But All ≤ 8

If the variability among subtest scaled scores composing a factor is unusually large and all scaled scores are 8 or greater, then describe the examinee's range of observed functioning in the ability presumed to underlie the Factor as a notable limitation:

The Short-Term Memory (Gsm) factor, a measure of the working memory aspect of short term memory, represents Amy's ability to apprehend and hold information in immediate awareness, manipulate the information, and produce a result. Amy's working memory was assessed by tasks that required her to repeat numbers verbatim, to repeat numbers in reverse order, or to sequence numbers (9th percentile); and to listen to a sequence of numbers and letters and repeat the numbers in ascending order, followed by the letters in alphabetical order (0.1st percentile). The variability among Amy's performances on these tasks was unusually large, indicating that her overall short-term memory ability cannot be summarized in a single score. However, Amy's working memory ability is a notable limitation for her because her performance on the tasks that compose the Short-Term Memory Factor ranged from Below Average/Normative Weakness to Lower Extreme/Normative Weakness.

Step 7: Determine *Normative Strengths* and *Normative Weaknesses* in the Index (or Factor) Profile

Whether you have pursued the Wechsler Four-Index model (Step 5) or the Keith Five-Factor model (Step 6) to guide your analysis of the WAIS-IV data, you should complete Steps 7, 8, and 9. These steps provide a method for interpreting unitary Wechsler indexes and unitary Keith factors.

Only unitary Wechsler indexes or unitary Keith factors identified in the previous steps are included in this analysis. To determine Normative Strengths and Normative Weaknesses in a person's index or factor profile, review the exact value of the interpretable Indexes. If the index or factor standard score is greater than 115, the ability measured by the index or factor is a Normative Strength. If

STEP 6. The Five Keith Factors are Examined to Determine Whether they are Unitary

Step 6a. Calculate the standard scores for the five Keith Factors
Step 6b-f. Determine if the size of the difference between subtest scores Is less than 1.5 SDs (< 5 points)

Keith Factor		Scaled Score 1		Scaled Score 2		Sum of Scaled Scores	Factor Standard Score	Absolute Difference between Scores 1 & 2	Is the difference < 5 points?	
Gc	VC	11	+ IN	8	=	19	97	3	Yes	The ability presumed to underlie the Factor is unitary & may be interpreted.
Gsm	DS	11	+ LN	4	=	15	86	7	No	Factor cannot be interpreted as representing a unitary ability.
Gf	MR	7	+ FW	4	=	11	75	3	Yes	The ability presumed to underlie the Factor is unitary & may be interpreted.
Gv	BD	5	+ VP	7	=	12	78	2	Yes	The ability presumed to underlie the Factor is unitary & may be interpreted.
Gs	SS	10	+ CD	9	=	19	97	1	Yes	The ability presumed to underlie the Factor is unitary & may be interpreted.

Step 6g. Determine how many of Keith's Five Factors are interpretable

Number of interpretable Keith Factors = 4
Are less than 3 factors interpretable? = No   Then proceed to Step 7 to interpret the Five Keith Factors.

Figure 5.6. Illustration of Step 6 Using Laura's Profile with the WAIS-IV DMIA

STEP 7. *Normative Strengths* and *Normative Weaknesses* in the Index or Factor Profile are Determined

The standard score of each interpretable Wechsler Index is entered in the table below.
An "X" is placed in the box corresponding to the appropriate normative category for each Index.

Wechsler Index	Standard Score	Normative Weakness <85	Within Normal Limits 85-115	Normative Strength >115
VCI	96		X	
PRI	79	X		
WMI	95		X	
PSI	97		X	

The standard score of each interpretable Keith Factor is entered in the table below.
An "X" is placed in the box corresponding to the appropriate normative category for each Index.

Keith Factor	Standard Score	Normative Weakness <85	Within Normal Limits 85-115	Normative Strength >115
Gc	97		X	
Gsm				
Gf	75	X		
Gv	78	X		
Gs	97		X	

Figure 5.7. Illustration of Step 7 Using Laura's Profile with the WAIS-IV DMIA

the Index or Factor standard score is less than 85, the ability measured by the index or factor is a Normative Weakness. If the index or factor standard score is between 85 and 115 (inclusive), the ability measured by the index or factor is Within Normal Limits. For example, a client's PRI of 123 is a Normative Strength. However, her WMI of 115 and PSI of 114 are both in the Average Range and, therefore, Within Normal Limits. Figure 5.7 shows an example of Step 7 using Laura's profile.

Step 8: Determine *Personal Strengths* and *Personal Weaknesses* in the Index (or Factor) Profile

The Normative Strengths and Normative Weaknesses discussed in Step 7 indicate a person's abilities relative to other individuals of about the same age. In contrast, Personal Strengths and Personal Weaknesses, which are identified in Step 8, refer to indexes or factors that differ significantly from the person's own mean index or factor. Rapid Reference 5.10 provides descriptions of these terms as well as other terms that are pertinent for understanding Step 8.

Rapid Reference 5.10

Terms Used to Describe Fluctuations in a Person's WAIS-IV Index Profile

Term (Abbreviation)	Definition
Index	A standard score with a mean of 100 and standard deviation of 15.
Normative Strength (NS)	An index that is above 115.
Normative Weakness (NW)	An index that is below 85.
Normal Limits (NL)	An index that is 85–115 (inclusive).
Personal Strength (PS)	An index that is significantly higher than the examinee's own mean index, using the .05 level of significance.
Personal Weakness (PW)	An index that is significantly lower than the examinee's own mean index, using the .05 level of significance.
Uncommon Personal Strength (PS/Uncommon)	A Personal Strength that is not only statistically significant but also substantially different from the examinee's own mean. That is, the size of the difference between the index and the examinee's mean of all four indexes is unusually large, occurring less than 10% of the time in the WAIS-IV standardization sample.
Uncommon Personal Weakness (PW/Uncommon)	A Personal Weakness that is not only statistically significant but also substantially different from the examinee's own mean. That is, the size of the difference between the index and the examinee's mean of all four indexes is unusually large, occurring less than 10% of the time in the WAIS-IV standardization sample.
Key Asset (KA)	An index that is an Uncommon Personal Strength and a Normative Strength.
High Priority Concern (HPC)	An index that is an Uncommon Personal Weakness and a Normative Weakness.

Source: Adapted from Flanagan and Kaufman (2004, Rapid Reference 4.10), with permission.

Step 8a. Compute the mean of the person's index or factor standard scores and round to the nearest tenth of a point. Note that all indexes or factors (interpretable and noninterpretable) are included in the computation of the mean for practical reasons. Excluding any index or factor would result in the need for numerous tables for determining both statistical significance and uncommon index/factor variation (i.e., mean indexes based on 2, 3, and 4 index combinations).

DON'T FORGET

··

Identifying Personal Strengths and Weaknesses

When determining the examinee's Personal Strengths and Personal Weaknesses, compare only interpretable indexes (or factors) to the examinee's mean index (or factor). Noninterpretable indexes (or factors) ARE included in the computation of the examinee's mean index (or factor), but they ARE NOT compared to that mean or interpreted. Follow parallel processes when identifying personal strengths and weaknesses among the four indexes and five factors.

Step 8b. Subtract the mean of all index or factor standard scores from each *interpretable* index or factor standard score. Use the values reported in Table 5.4 to determine whether the size of the difference between an interpretable index and the mean of all indexes is significant. Use the values reported in Table 5.5 to determine whether the size of the difference between an interpretable factor and the mean of all factors is significant. These tables include differences required for statistical significance at both the .05 and .01 levels. We recommend using the .05 level that appears in the shaded rows of the appropriate table, but examiners may choose either the .05 or .01 level. Because some of the values for specific age levels differ from those reported for the total sample, we recommend using the differences reported by age. In order to be considered statistically significant, the difference must be equal to or greater than the value required for significance.

Table 5.4. Differences Required for Statistical Significance (at $p < .05$ and $p < .01$) between an Index and the Mean of all Four Indexes, by Age and Overall Sample

Age	p Value	VCI	PRI	WMI	PSI
16–17	.05	6.5	6.1	6.8	8.3
	.01	8.5	8.1	9.0	10.8
18–19	.05	5.6	6.3	6.3	7.6
	.01	7.4	8.3	8.3	9.9
20–24	.05	5.7	6.4	7.0	7.6
	.01	7.5	8.4	9.3	10.0
25–29	.05	5.5	5.5	5.8	7.5
	.01	7.2	7.2	7.7	9.8
30–34	.05	5.6	5.6	6.0	8.4

Age	p Value	VCI	PRI	WMI	PSI
	.01	7.4	7.4	7.8	11.0
35–44	.05	5.6	6.0	6.0	8.4
	.01	7.4	7.9	7.9	11.1
45–54	.05	5.1	5.5	5.9	8.3
	.01	6.8	7.3	7.8	11.0
55–64	.05	5.0	5.8	6.2	7.2
	.01	6.6	7.7	8.1	9.4
65–69	.05	5.0	5.8	6.2	7.2
	.01	6.6	7.7	8.1	9.4
70–74	.05	5.1	5.9	6.6	7.2
	.01	6.7	7.7	8.6	9.5
75–79	.05	5.5	6.2	5.8	6.9
	.01	7.2	8.1	7.7	9.0
80–84	.05	5.1	6.9	6.3	6.9
	.01	6.8	9.1	8.3	9.1
85–90	.05	4.6	6.6	6.6	6.9
	.01	6.1	8.6	8.6	9.1
All[a]	.05	5.5	5.9	6.3	7.5
	.01	7.3	7.8	8.3	9.9

[a] All = overall WAIS-IV standardization sample (p. 16–90).

Source: Naglieri, Lichtenberger, & Kaufman (2009).

Note: Only use this table with interpretable indexes. To use this table, calculate the mean of all four indexes (rounded to the nearest 10th). Subtract this mean value from each interpretable Index and obtain difference scores. Select a significance level (.05 or .01). We recommend using .05 (the shaded portions of the table). Compare the difference score to the value in the appropriate row (.01 or .05) and the appropriate Index column. If the difference score is equal to or greater than this value, the difference is statistically significant. If the difference score is less than this value, the difference is not statistically significant. For example, if a 57-year-old obtained an interpretable WMI of 85 and the mean of all four Indexes was 93.2, you would subtract the mean of all four Indexes from the WMI. The difference score of 8.2 (85 − 93.2 = −8.2) is compared to the value for the WMI at the .05 level for a 57-year-old (i.e., 6.2). Because the difference score is equal to or greater than the value listed in the table, you would interpret the difference as statistically significant. Additionally, because the WMI was lower than the mean, it is considered a Personal Weakness.

Table 5.5. Differences Required for Statistical Significance (at $p < .05$ and $p < .01$) Between Factor and the Mean of All Five CHC Factors, by Age and Overall Sample

Age Group	p Value	Crystallized Knowledge (GC) V+I	Fluid Reasoning (GF) MR+FW	Visual Processing (GV) BD+VP	Short-Term Memory (GSM) DS+LN	Processing Speed (GS) CD+SS
16–17	.01	8.2	9.2	9.2	8.7	11.4
	.05	6.2	7.0	7.0	6.6	8.7
18–19	.01	7.8	8.9	8.9	8.4	10.3
	.05	6.0	6.8	6.8	6.4	7.8
20–24	.01	7.3	9.4	9.4	9.0	10.3
	.05	5.6	7.2	7.2	6.8	7.9
25–29	.01	7.8	8.3	8.3	7.8	10.2
	.05	5.9	6.3	6.3	5.9	7.8
30–34	.01	7.8	7.8	8.4	7.2	11.5
	.05	5.9	5.9	6.4	5.5	8.8
35–44	.01	7.3	9.0	9.0	8.5	11.6
	.05	5.6	6.8	6.8	6.4	8.8
45–54	.01	6.6	8.4	7.8	7.8	11.5
	.05	5.0	6.4	5.9	5.9	8.8
55–64	.01	6.5	8.8	8.8	8.3	9.8
	.05	4.9	6.7	6.7	6.3	7.4
65–69	.01	6.4	8.2	8.2	8.2	9.7
	.05	4.9	6.3	6.3	6.3	7.4

Source: Naglieri, Lichtenberger, & Kaufman (2009).

Note: Only examinees ages 16 to 69 can be administered the subtests necessary to calculate the five CHC factors. The subtest abbreviations underneath the factor names represent the subtests that comprise each factor. Only use this table with interpretable indexes. To use this table, calculate the mean of all four indexes (rounded to the nearest 10th). Subtract this mean value from each interpretable index and obtain difference scores. Select a significance level (.05 or .01). We recommend using .05 (the shaded portions of the table). Compare the difference score to the value in the appropriate row (.01 or .05) and the appropriate index column. If the difference score is equal to or greater than this value, the difference is statistically significant. If the difference score is less than this value, the difference is not statistically significant.

Note that the Bonferroni correction has not been applied to values in Tables 5.4 and 5.5, to be consistent with the method that we advocated for the WAIS-III (Kaufman & Lichtenberger, 2006, Appendix A) and that Flanagan and Kaufman (2004, 2009) advocate for the WISC-IV. Although others, such as Longman (2004), have applied the Bonferroni correction when conducting similar analyses, we prefer not to apply this conservative procedure for the same reason we prefer the .05 to the .01 level of significance—to permit the identification of more, rather than fewer, hypotheses to explore.

Use these criteria for identifying personal strengths and weaknesses:

i. If the difference is significant and the interpretable index or factor is higher than the mean, then the index or factor is a Personal Strength for the person.

ii. If the difference is significant and the interpretable index or factor is lower than the mean, than the index or factor is a Personal Weakness for the person.

Step 8c. Determine whether Personal Strengths and Personal Weaknesses are uncommon using the less than 10% base rate criterion. Because statistical significance means only that an observed difference is "real" (i.e., not due to chance), it is necessary to determine whether the difference is also unusually large or uncommon. Differences among indexes or factors that occur infrequently in the standardization sample may be valuable in making diagnoses and generating educational recommendations when corroborated by other data. If the magnitude of the observed difference between an interpretable index and the mean of all indexes (or between a factor and the mean of all factors) is *equal to or greater than 15 points*, the difference is uncommon.[1]

Step 8d. Identify "Key Assets" and "High Priority Concerns" in the person's profile using the next criteria to identify personal strengths and weaknesses that are of greatest importance, diagnostically and educationally:

i. Significant Personal Strengths that are also uncommon and greater than 115 are labeled *Key Assets*.

---

1. The data needed to conduct the analysis of estimating the size of difference to be considered uncommon were not available for either the Wechsler indexes or the Keith factors. However, we were able to estimate the size of an uncommon difference by examining the data from the WAIS-III and WISC-IV. On both of these tests, the size of uncommon discrepancies between an index and the mean of all indexes was consistently about 1 standard deviation (15 points), using a 10% base rate.

Step 8. Determine Personal Strengths and Personal Weaknesses in the Index or Factor Profile								
Wechsler Index	Standard Score	Rounded Mean of All Indexes or Factors	Difference Score	Critical Value Needed for Significance (p<.05)	Personal Strength or Personal Weakness (PS or PW)	Uncommon (U) or Not Uncommon (NU) (base rate <10%)	Normative Strength or Normative Weakness (NS or NW)	Key Asset (KA) or High Priority Concern (HPC)
VCI	96	91.8	4.3	6.5		NU		
PRI	79	91.8	-12.8	6.1	PW	NU	NW	
WMI	95	91.8	3.3	6.8		NU		
PSI	97	91.8	5.3	8.3		NU		
Keith Factor								
Gc	97	84.0	13.0	6.2	PS	NU		
Gsm		84.0		6.6				
Gf	75	84.0	-9.0	7	PW	NU	NW	
Gv	78	84.0	-6.0	7		NU	NW	
Gs	97	84.0	13.0	8.7	PS	NU		

Figure 5.8. Illustration of Step 8 Using Laura's Profile with the WAIS-IV DMIA

ii. Significant Personal Weaknesses that are also uncommon and less than 85 are labeled *High Priority Concerns.*

Figure 5.8 shows an example of Step 8 using Laura's profile.

Step 9: Interpret Fluctuations in the Person's Index or Factor Profile

Reliable and useful information for making diagnostic and educational decisions can be obtained from interpreting a person's index or factor profile (Flanagan & Kaufman, 2004). To provide clarity about the meanings of the descriptive terms (e.g., High Priority Concern, Key Asset) used in your psychological reports, you may include a section that defines these terms. Rapid Reference 5.10 provides a description of all the terms that are used to classify indexes or factors. Rapid Reference 5.11 gives examples of how to describe indexes or factors that are classified as strengths. Rapid Reference 5.12 gives examples of how to describe indexes or factors that are classified as weaknesses. To properly interpret the person's profile using the interpretive system described here, it is important for examiners to understand theories related to cognitive assessment such as CHC theory or concepts of neuropsychological theory. The Broad Abilities and Narrow Abilities that form the essence of CHC theory are particularly useful concepts to understand. For an in-depth discussion of CHC theory, consult the writings of Flanagan and her colleagues (Flanagan et al., 2007; Flanagan et al., 2005; Flanagan & Kaufman, 2004, 2009; Flanagan, McGrew, & Ortiz, 2000). Basic definitions of CHC Broad and Narrow Abilities are also summarized in

Appendix A.7 on the CD-ROM. An overview of neuropsychological theory and CHC theory related to the interpretation of the Keith Five-Factor model was presented in Rapid Reference 5.7. The information in Rapid Reference 5.7 can also provide a useful outline for neuropsychologically based and CHC-based interpretation of the Wechsler Four-Index model: the VCI Index measures CHC constructs of Gc; PRI measures CHC constructs of both Gv and Gf; WMI measures CHC constructs of Gsm; and PSI measures CHC constructs of Gs.

CAUTION

Interpretation of Scores

No single score, including an interpretable index or factor, should be used in isolation to make a diagnosis or to develop an individualized education program (IEP).

≡ Rapid Reference 5.11

Interpretation of Index or Factor Scores that Are Classified as a Strength

	Normative Strength	With Normal Limits*
Uncommon Personal Strength	*Key Asset (Normative Strength and Personal Strength/Uncommon):* Sierra's processing speed is considered a significant strength as compared to other individuals her age in the normal population. In addition, her ability in this area is significantly higher than her abilities in other areas. In fact, the difference between Sierra's processing speed and her abilities in other areas is so large that it is not commonly achieved by other individuals her age in the normal population. Therefore, Sierra's processing speed is a Key Asset and a notable integrity, a finding that should play an essential role in developing specialized interventions. Note that the latter part of this interpretive statement	*Personal Strength/ Uncommon but Not a Normative Strength:* Sierra's processing speed is considered a significant strength compared to her abilities in other areas. In fact, the difference between her processing speed and her abilities in other areas is so large that it is not commonly achieved by other individuals her age in the normal population. Therefore, Sierra's processing speed is a notable Personal Strength, a finding that should play an essential role in developing specialized interventions. [Note that the latter part of this interpretive statement may be germane only when other abilities (cognitive or academic) are either in the lower end of the Average

(continued)

	Normative Strength	With Normal Limits*
Uncommon Personal Strength	may be germane only when other abilities (cognitive or academic) are either in the lower end of the Average range or lower, suggesting that intervention is indeed warranted.	range or lower, suggesting that intervention is indeed warranted. Also, in this scenario, Sierra's processing speed may be considered a notable integrity, as it was in the first two scenarios, if her Processing Speed standard score is at the upper end of the Average Range (i.e., 110–115). Finally, it is also possible for Sierra's processing speed to be a Personal Strength/Uncommon but a Normative Weakness (i.e., if the Personal Strength/Uncommon is associated with a standard score of < 85).]
Personal Strength	**Normative Strength and Personal Strength/Not Uncommon:** Sierra's processing speed is considered a significant strength as compared to other individuals her age in the normal population. In addition, her ability in this area is significantly higher than her abilities in other areas. Therefore, Sierra's processing speed is a notable integrity, a finding that may play an essential role in developing specialized interventions. [Note that the latter part of this interpretive statement may be germane only when other abilities (cognitive or academic) are either in the lower end of the Average range or lower, suggesting that intervention is indeed warranted.]	**Personal Strength/Not Uncommon but Not a Normative Strength:** Sierra's processing speed is considered a significant strength compared to her abilities in other areas. Her processing speed is a notable Personal Strength, a finding that should play an essential role in developing specialized interventions. [Note that the latter part of this interpretive statement may be germane only when other abilities (cognitive or academic) are either in the lower end of the Average Range or lower, suggesting that intervention is indeed warranted.
Not Personal Strength	**Normative Strength but Not a Personal Strength:** Sierra's processing speed is considered a significant strength compared to other individuals her age in the normal population. Her processing speed is a notable integrity, a finding that may play an essential role in developing specialized interventions. [Note that the latter part of this interpretive statement	**Interpretation of an index that is unitary but is neither a strength nor a weakness:** The Processing Speed Index (PSI), a measure of Processing Speed (Gs), represents Sierra's ability to fluently and automatically perform cognitive tasks, especially when under pressure to maintain focused attention and concentration. Sierra's Gs was assessed by

	Normative Strength	With Normal Limits*
Not Personal Strength	may be germane only when other abilities (cognitive or academic) are either in the lower end of the Average Range or lower, suggesting that intervention is indeed warranted.]	tasks that required her to copy a series of symbols that are paired with numbers using a key (Coding) and indicate the presence or absence of a target symbol within a search group (Symbol Search). Sierra obtained a PSI standard score of 100, which is ranked at the 50th percentile and is classified as Average Range/Within Normal Limits.

*Also, it is possible for Sierra's processing speed to be a Personal Strength/Not Uncommon but a Normative Weakness (i.e., if the Personal Strength/Not Uncommon is associated with a standard score of < 85).

Source: Adapted from Flanagan & Kaufman (2004).

≡ *Rapid Reference 5.12*

Interpretation of Index or Factor Scores that Are Classified as a Weakness

	Normative Weakness	With Normal Limits*
Uncommon Personal Weakness	**High-Priority Concern (Normative Weakness and Personal Weakness/Uncommon):** Sierra's processing speed is considered a significant weakness as compared to other individuals her age in the normal population. In addition, her ability in this area is significantly lower than her abilities in other areas. In fact, the difference between her processing speed and her abilities in other areas is so large that it is not commonly found in the normal population. Therefore, Sierra's processing speed is a High-Priority Concern and suggests that she has a disorder in this basic psychological process, a finding that	**Personal Weakness/ Uncommon but not a Normative Weakness:** Sierra's processing speed is considered a significant weakness compared to her abilities in other areas. In fact, the difference between her processing speed and her abilities in other areas is so large that it is not commonly found in the normal population. Therefore, Sierra's processing speed is a notable Personal Weakness, a finding that may play an essential role in developing specialized interventions. [Note that the latter part of this interpretive statement may be germane only when the actual Processing Speed standard

(continued)

	Normative Weakness	With Normal Limits*
Uncommon Personal Weakness	should play an essential role in developing specialized interventions.	score is in the lower end of the Average Range (i.e., 85–90), suggesting that intervention may indeed be warranted. The finding of a Personal Weakness that is uncommon in the normal population does not provide de facto evidence of a processing disorder. It is feasible for an individual to have a Personal Weakness/Uncommon that is associated with a standard score that falls in either the Average/Within Normal Limits range or the Above Average/Normative Strength Range.]
Personal Weakness	**Normative Weakness and Personal Weakness/Not Uncommon:** Sierra's processing speed is considered a significant weakness as compared to other individuals her age in the normal population. In addition, her ability in this area is significantly lower than her abilities in other areas. Therefore, Sierra's processing speed is a notable weakness and suggests that she has a disorder in this basic psychological process, a finding that should play an essential role in developing specialized interventions.	**Personal Weakness/Not Uncommon but not a Normative Weakness:** Sierra's processing speed is considered a significant weakness compared to her abilities in other areas. Her processing speed is a notable Personal Weakness, a finding that may play an essential role in developing specialized interventions. [Note that the finding of a Personal Weakness, in and of itself, does not provide de facto evidence of a processing disorder. A Personal Weakness that is associated with a standard score that falls Within Normal Limits or higher does not, in and of itself, provide evidence of a disorder.]
Not Personal Weakness	**Normative Weakness but not a Personal Weakness:** Sierra's processing speed is considered a significant weakness compared to other individuals her age in the normal population. Her processing speed is a notable weakness and suggests that she has a disorder in this basic psychological process, a finding that should play an essential role	**Interpretation of an index that is unitary but is *neither* a strength nor a weakness:** The Processing Speed Index (PSI), a measure of Processing Speed (Gs), represents Sierra's ability to fluently and automatically perform cognitive tasks, especially when under pressure to maintain focused attention and concentration. Sierra's Gs was assessed by tasks that required her to copy a

	Normative Weakness	With Normal Limits*
Not Personal Weakness	in developing specialized interventions.	series of symbols that are paired with numbers using a key (Coding) and indicate the presence or absence of a target symbol within a search group (Symbol Search). Sierra obtained a PSI standard score of 100, which is ranked at the 50th percentile and is classified as Average Range/Within Normal Limits.

* Also, it is feasible for an individual to have a Personal Weakness/Not Uncommon that is associated with a standard score that falls in the Above Average/Normative Strength range.

Source: Adapted from Flanagan & Kaufman (2004).

Before considering whether to conduct Step 10 of the interpretive system, it is useful to summarize the results of all index or factor analyses (Steps 4–8) and record your clinical impressions. In addition, you should specify whether any Planned Clinical Comparisons (conducted in Step 10) might be useful to conduct in order to gain a better understanding of the person's cognitive capabilities.

ANALYZE PLANNED CLINICAL COMPARISONS WHEN THE REQUISITE WAIS-IV SUBTESTS ARE ADMINISTERED

Step 10: Conduct Planned Clinical Comparisons

Based on the theoretical foundations of the WAIS-IV, knowledge of the abilities measured by the WAIS-IV, CHC theory, neuropsychological theory, and relevant research on the relationships between specific cognitive abilities and learning/ achievement, a select number of additional comparisons may provide potentially meaningful hypotheses about cognitive capabilities. Such information would go beyond that generated from the Index Profile Analysis or Factor Profile Analysis in the earlier interpretive steps. Flanagan and Kaufman (2004, 2009) developed eight theory-based clinical clusters, composed of two or three WISC-IV subtests, and Kaufman and Lichtenberger (2006) adapted those clusters for the WAIS-III.

We have adapted those WISC-IV and WAIS-III cluster comparisons to the WAIS-IV and created new cluster comparisons specifically focused on the WAIS-IV's theoretical underpinnings. Rapid References 5.13, 5.14, and 5.15 list the clinical clusters, the subtests that comprise them, and a brief definition of each cluster derived from the perspective of the WAIS-IV's theoretical foundations (Rapid Reference 5.13) and from the perspective of CHC theory (Rapid

≡ Rapid Reference 5.13

Clinical Clusters from WAIS-IV Theoretical Model

Clinical Cluster	Subtests Comprising Cluster

Visual-Motor Speed — *Block Design + Coding + Symbol Search*

Definition: The Visual-Motor Speed Cluster consists of three subtests, all of which require visual-motor speed and quick information processing. Coding and Symbol Search compose the Processing Speed Index. Block Design is the one Perceptual Reasoning subtest that also requires visual-motor coordination and speed of processing. Processing speed has been shown to be related to aging in adults (Finkel, Reynolds, McArdle, & Pederson, 2007; Kaufman & Lichtenberger, 2006) and has a dynamic relationship to mental capacity (Kail & Hall, 1994) and to other fluid reasoning tasks (Fry & Hale, 1996; Kail, 2000).

Problem-Solving without Visual Motor Speed — *Matrix Reasoning + Visual Puzzles + Picture Completion + Figure Weights*

Definition: The Problem-Solving without Visual-Motor Speed Cluster includes the four Perceptual Reasoning tasks (two Core, two supplemental) that do not require a motor response. The WAIS-IV increased the emphasis on the theoretical constructs of fluid reasoning and visual problem solving by adding two new subtests: Visual Puzzles and Figure Weights (Psychological Corporation, 2008). On the WAIS-III, most nonverbal Problem-Solving subtests required visual-motor coordination and speed. However, with Object Assembly and Picture Arrangement eliminated from the WAIS-IV, Block Design is now the only remaining PRI subtest that demands coordination and speed. Therefore, by excluding Block Design and considering the remaining PRI subtests as a cluster, it is possible to measure a person's fluid reasoning and visual-spatial problem solving without the "contamination" of either the person's motor coordination or speed. *This cluster requires administration of the supplemental Figure Weights and Picture Completion subtests and may be calculated only for examinees ages 16–69 because Figure Weights is not normed for individuals ages 70 and above.*

Mental Manipulation — *Letter-Number Sequencing + Digit Span*

Definition: The Mental Manipulation Cluster consists of two subtests that measure the ability to actively maintain information in conscious awareness and perform some operation or manipulation with it (an ability commonly referred to as working memory but labeled here as Mental Manipulation to avoid confusion with the WAIS-IV Working Memory Index). Letter-Number Sequencing, Digit Span Backward, and Digit Span Sequencing tap one's ability to temporarily store and perform a set of cognitive operations on information that requires divided attention and the management of the limited capacity of short-term memory. Digit Span Forward does not require mental manipulation but does demand the ability to attend to and immediately recall temporally ordered elements in the correct order after a single presentation. Unlike the WMI, the Mental Manipulation Cluster does not include Arithmetic because of Arithmetic's additional demands on verbal comprehension, fluid reasoning, and mathematical knowledge. Research has shown that working memory is an essential component of higher order cognitive processes such as fluid reasoning (Psychological Corporation, 2008). This Mental Manipulation Cluster consists of the same two subtests as the Short-Term Memory (*Gsm*-MW) cluster described under CHC theory, reflecting different nomenclature because of the varying theoretical perspectives. *This cluster requires administration of the supplemental Letter-Number Sequencing subtest and may be calculated only for examinees ages 16–69 because Letter-Number Sequencing is not normed for individuals ages 70 and above.*

≡ *Rapid Reference 5.14*

Clinical Clusters from a CHC Theoretical Model

Clinical Cluster	Subtests Comprising Cluster

Fluid Reasoning (*Gf*) Cluster   Matrix Reasoning + Figure Weights

CHC Definition: The Fluid Reasoning (*Gf*) Cluster consists of two subtests that measure the Broad *Gf* ability in CHC theory. *Gf* is defined as encompassing the mental operations that an individual uses when faced with a novel task that cannot be performed automatically. These mental operations include forming and recognizing concepts, perceiving relationships among patterns, drawing inferences, problem solving, and so forth. Matrix Reasoning measures the narrow *Gf* ability of *General Sequential Reasoning (Deduction)*, which is defined as the ability to start with stated rules, premises, or conditions, and to engage in one or more steps to reach a solution to a novel problem. Figure Weights is primarily a measure of *Quantitative Reasoning*, and also involves the fluid reasoning abilities of induction and deduction (Psychological Corporation, 2008). *This cluster requires administration of the supplemental Figure Weights subtest and may be calculated only for examinees ages 16–69 because Figure Weights is not normed for individuals ages 70 and above.*

Visual Processing (*Gv*) Cluster   Block Design + Visual Puzzles

CHC Definition: The Visual Processing (*Gv*) Cluster consists of two subtests that measure the Broad *Gv* ability in CHC theory. *Gv* is defined as the ability to generate, perceive, analyze, synthesize, store, retrieve, manipulate, and transform visual patterns and stimuli. Block Design measures the narrow *Gv* ability of *Spatial Relations*, which is defined as the ability to perceive and manipulate visual patterns rapidly, or to maintain orientation with respect to objects in space. Visual Puzzles involves *Gv*—especially the narrow abilities of *Visualization* and *Spatial Relations*—and some aspects of Fluid Reasoning (*Gf*). Unlike Block Design, Visual Puzzles does not involve any motor manipulation.

Verbal Fluid Reasoning   Similarities + Comprehension
(*Gf*-Verbal) Cluster

CHC Definition: The Verbal Fluid Reasoning (*Gf*-verbal) Cluster is comprised of two subtests that involve the Broad *Gc* ability in CHC theory. *Gc* is defined as the

(continued)

Clinical Cluster	Subtests Comprising Cluster

breadth and depth of a person's accumulated knowledge of a culture and the effective use of that knowledge. Notwithstanding their primary Gc classifications, Similarities and Comprehension, to some extent, both require the use of the narrow Gf ability of Induction. Because Similarities and Comprehension (although primarily verbal or Gc subtests) both require the ability to reason (inductively) with verbal stimuli, this cluster is labeled Verbal Fluid Reasoning. For the WISC-IV, this cluster consists of Similarities and Word Reasoning (Flanagan & Kaufman, 2004). *This cluster requires administration of the supplemental Comprehension subtest.*

Lexical Knowledge (Gc-VL) Cluster   Vocabulary + Similarities

CHC Definition: The Lexical Knowledge (Gc-VL) Cluster consists of two subtests that measure the Broad Gc ability in CHC theory. Gc is defined as the breadth and depth of a person's accumulated knowledge of culture and the effective use of that knowledge. Both Vocabulary and Similarities measure the narrow Gc ability of Lexical Knowledge, which is defined as the extent of vocabulary that can be understood in terms of correct word meanings. (Lexical Knowledge is a primary ability for Vocabulary and a secondary ability for Similarities.) Therefore, this cluster was labeled Lexical Knowledge. For the WISC-IV, this cluster consists of Vocabulary and Word Reasoning, both of which are considered primary measures of Lexical Knowledge (Flanagan & Kaufman, 2004).

General Information (Gc-K0) Cluster   Comprehension + Information

CHC Definition: The General Information (Gc-VL) Cluster consists of two subtests that measure the Broad Gc ability in CHC theory. Gc is defined as the breadth and depth of a person's accumulated knowledge of culture and the effective use of that knowledge. These subtests, Comprehension and Information, primarily measure the narrow Gc ability of General Information, which is defined as an individual's range of general knowledge. Therefore, this cluster is labeled General Information. This cluster consists of the same two subtests on the WAIS-III and WISC-IV (Flanagan & Kaufman, 2004). *This cluster requires administration of the supplemental Comprehension subtest.*

Long-Term Memory (Gc-LTM) Cluster   Vocabulary + Information

CHC Definition: The Long-Term Memory (Gc-LTM) Cluster consists of two subtests that measure the Broad Gc ability in CHC theory. These subtests, Vocabulary and Information, measure to a greater or lesser extent the narrow Gc ability of General Information. Vocabulary also measures the narrow Gc ability of Lexical Knowledge. However, because both Vocabulary and Information represent knowledge that is typically stored in long-term memory, this cluster was labeled Long-Term Memory. Note that "Long-Term Memory" is not a CHC label per se and therefore should not be confused with the broad Long-Term Retrieval (Glr) ability in CHC theory. This cluster consists of the same two subtests on the WAIS-III and WISC-IV (Flanagan & Kaufman, 2004).

Clinical Cluster	Subtests Comprising Cluster
Short-Term Memory (*Gsm-MW*) Cluster	**Letter-Number Sequencing + Digit Span**

CHC Definition: The Short-Term Memory (*Gsm-MW*) Cluster consists of two subtests that measure the Broad *Gsm* ability in CHC theory. *Gsm* is defined as the ability to apprehend and hold information in immediate awareness and to use it within a few seconds. Letter-Number Sequencing and Digit Span (Backward) measure the narrow *Gsm* ability of *Working Memory*, which is defined as the ability to temporarily store and perform a set of cognitive operations on information that requires divided attention and the management of the limited capacity of short-term memory. Digit Span also measures the narrow *Gsm* ability of *Memory Span*, which is defined as the ability to attend to and immediately recall temporally ordered elements in the correct order after a single presentation. This cluster consists of the same two subtests on the WAIS-IV and WISC-IV (Flanagan & Kaufman, 2004). *This cluster requires administration of the supplemental Letter-Number Sequencing subtest and may be calculated only for examinees ages 16–69 because Letter-Number Sequencing is not normed for individuals ages 70 and above.*

Reference 5.14). Note that if you have conducted the analysis of the Keith Five Factors in Steps 4 through 8, some of the clinical clusters described here in Step 10 will be redundant with the five factors analyzed in earlier steps.

Internal consistency reliability coefficients for each clinical cluster for the overall WAIS-IV standardization sample are available in Table 5.6.

Step 10a. Prior to conducting clinical comparisons, you must first determine whether the clusters in the comparison represent unitary abilities. To do this, compute the difference between the highest and lowest scaled scores that make up the clinical Cluster. Answer this question: *Is the size of the scaled score difference less than 5?*

- If YES, the clinical cluster represents a unitary ability and the clinical comparison that includes this cluster may be made *only* if the other cluster in the comparison also represents a unitary ability. Proceed to Step 10b.
- If NO, the clinical cluster does not represent a unitary ability and the clinical comparisons that include this cluster should not be made.

Figure 5.9 shows an example of Step 10a using Laura's profile.

DON'T FORGET

When Can I Make a Planned or Post Hoc Clinical Comparison?

Clinical comparisons can be made only when both clusters in the comparison represent unitary abilities.

≡ Rapid Reference 5.5

Subtests that Comprise the Clinical Clusters

Subtest/Composite Score	Abbreviation	Visual-Motor Speed	Problem Solving Without Visual-Motor Speed	Mental Manipulation	Verbal Fluid Reasoning	Lexical Knowledge	General Information	Long-Term Memory	Short-Term Memory	Fluid Reasoning	Visual Processing
Block Design	BD	BD									BD
Similarities	SI				SI	SI					
Digit Span	DS			DS					DS		
Matrix Reasoning	MR		MR							MR	
Vocabulary	VC					VC		VC			
Arithmetic	AR										
Symbol Search	SS	SS									
Visual Puzzles	VP		VP								VP
Information	IN						IN	IN			
Coding	CD	CD									
Letter-Number Sequencing	LN			(LN)					(LN)		
Figure Weights	FW		(FW)							(FW)	
Comprehension	CO				(CO)		(CO)				
Cancellation	CA										
Picture Completion	PCm		(PC)								

Note: Subtests in parentheses are supplementary subtests.

Table 5.6. Internal Consistency Reliability Coefficients for the New WAIS-IV Clinical Clusters, by Age and Overall Sample

Age Group	Visual-Motor Speed BD +CD +SS	Problem Solving Without Visual-Motor Speed MR+VP +PC+FW	Mental Manipulation LN+DS	Verbal Fluid Reasoning SI+CC	Lexical Knowledge VC+SI	General Information CO+IN	Long-Term Memory VC+IN	Short-Term Memory LN+DS	Fluid Reasoning MR+FW	Visual Processing BD+VP
16–17	.91	.94	.94	.89	.92	.91	.95	.94	.93	.93
18–19	.92	.95	.94	.92	.94	.93	.95	.94	.93	.93
20–24	.91	.94	.93	.92	.94	.94	.96	.93	.92	.92
25–29	.93	.95	.95	.92	.94	.93	.95	.95	.94	.94
30–34	.91	.96	.96	.92	.94	.93	.95	.96	.95	.94
35–44	.90	.95	.94	.93	.95	.94	.96	.94	.93	.93
	.91	.96	.95	.92	.95	.94	.97	.95	.94	.95

(continued)

Table 5.6. (Continued)

Age Group	Visual-Motor Speed BD +CD +SS	Problem Solving Without Visual-Motor Speed MR+VP +PC+FW	Mental Manipulation LN+DS	Verbal Fluid Reasoning SI+CO	Lexical Knowledge VC+SI	General Information CO+IN	Long-Term Memory VC+IN	Short-Term Memory LN+DS	Fluid Reasoning MR+FW	Visual Processing BD+VP
45–54										
55–64	.93	.95	.94	.92	.94	.95	.97	.94	.93	.93
65–69	.93	.96	.94	.93	.95	.94	.97	.94	.94	.94
70–74	.93	—	—	.92	.95	.93	.97	—	—	.93
75–79	.93	—	—	.92	.94	.94	.97	—	—	.91
80–84	.92	—	—	.94	.96	.94	.97	—	—	.88
85–90	.94	—	—	.95	.96	.96	.98	—	—	.89
All	.92	.95	.94	.92	.95	.94	.96	.94	.93	.93

Step 10a. This step determines whether each clinical cluster is unitary and, therefore, interpretable. The difference between the highest and lowest subtest scaled scores in a cluster is calculated. *If the size of the difference is less than 5 points, then the clinical cluster is unitary.*

Cluster	Subtests	Highest Scaled Score		Lowest Scaled Score		Difference	Is Cluster Interpretable?
Visual Motor Speed	BD+CD+SS	10	-	5	=	5	No
Problem Solving without Visual Motor Speed	MR+VP+PC+FW	7	-	4	=	3	Yes
Mental Manipulation	LN+DS	11	-	4	=	7	No
Verbal Fluid Reasoning	SI+CO	10	-	9	=	1	Yes
Lexical Knowledge	VO+SI	11	-	9	=	2	Yes
General Information	CO+IN	10	-	8	=	2	Yes
Long-Term memory	VO+IN	11	-	8	=	3	Yes
Short Term Memory	LN+DS	11	-	4	=	7	No
Fluid Reasoning	MR+FW	7	-	4	=	3	Yes
Visual Processing	BD+VP	7	-	5	=	2	Yes

Figure 5.9. Illustration of Step 10a Using Laura's Profile with the WAIS-IV DMIA

Subtest	Visual Motor Speed	Problem Solving without Visual Motor Speed	Mental Manipulation	Verbal Fluid Reasoning	Lexical Knowledge	General Information	Long-Term memory	Short Term Memory	Fluid Reasoning	Visual Processing
Block Design	5									5
Similarities				9	9					
Digit Span			11					11		
Matrix Reasoning		7							7	
Vocabulary					11		11			
Arithmetic										
Symbol Search	10									
Visual Puzzles		7								7
Information						8	8			
Coding	9									
Letter-Num. Sequen.			4					4		
Figure Weights		4							4	
Comprehension				10		10				
Cancellation										
Picture Completion		6								
Sum of Scaled Scores	24	24	15	19	20	18	19	15	11	12
Cluster Standard Score	87	76	86	97	100	94	97	86	75	78
Percentile Rank	19	5	18	42	50	34	42	18	5	7
Confidence Interval	82-94	72-82	81-93	91-104	95-105	89-100	92-102	81-93	71-83	73-86
Subtest	Visual Motor Speed	Problem Solving without Visual Motor Speed	Mental Manipulation	Verbal Fluid Reasoning	Lexical Knowledge	General Information	Long-Term memory	Short Term Memory	Fluid Reasoning	Visual Processing

Figure 5.10. Illustration of Step 10b Using Laura's Profile with the WAIS-IV DMIA

Step 10b. Calculate the clinical cluster by summing the scaled scores for the two subtests that comprise the clinical cluster and converting the sum to a standard score using the norms in Appendixes A.9–A.17 on the CD-ROM. Figure 5.10 shows an example of Step 10b using Laura's profile.

Step 10c. Determine whether the size of the difference between the clusters in the comparison is unusually large or uncommon, occurring less than 10% of the time in the WAIS-IV standardization sample. To do this, calculate the difference between the clusters in the comparison. (Rapid Reference 5.16 reviews the suggested planned clinical cluster comparisons from a Wechsler theoretical model, and Rapid Reference 5.17 reviews the suggested planned clinical comparisons from a CHC theoretical model). If the size of the difference is equal to or greater than the value reported for the comparison in Table 5.7, the difference is uncommon. If the size of the difference between the two clusters in the comparison is less than the table value, the difference is not uncommon. Specifically, a comparison between two interpretable clinical clusters can have either one of two outcomes:

1. The size of the difference between the two interpretable clinical clusters is uncommon in the normative population.

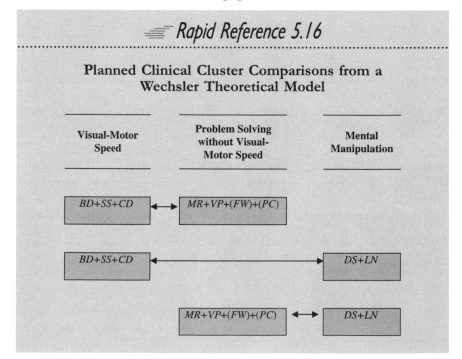

≡ *Rapid Reference 5.16*

Planned Clinical Cluster Comparisons from a Wechsler Theoretical Model

Visual-Motor Speed	Problem Solving without Visual-Motor Speed	Mental Manipulation

BD+SS+CD ←→ MR+VP+(FW)+(PC)

BD+SS+CD ←————————→ DS+LN

MR+VP+(FW)+(PC) ←→ DS+LN

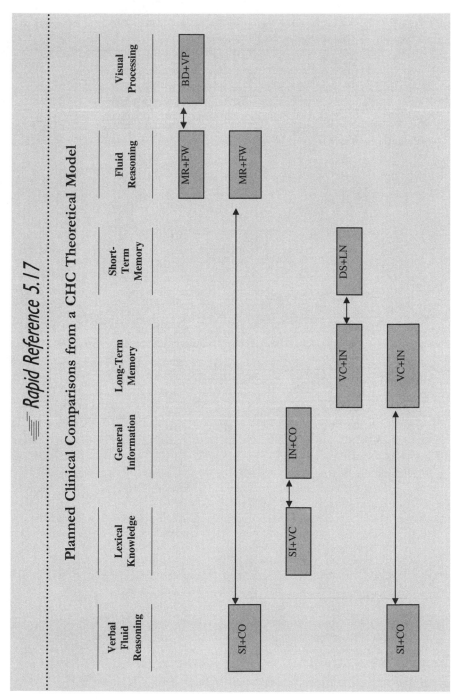

Rapid Reference 5.17

Planned Clinical Comparisons from a CHC Theoretical Model

Table 5.7. Size of Difference between Pairs of Clinical Clusters Needed to Be Considered Unusually Large or Uncommon

Cluster Comparison			Amount of Difference
Visual-Motor Speed (BD+CD+SS)	vs.	Problem Solving without Visual-Motor Speed (MR+VP+PC+FW)	20
Visual-Motor Speed (BD+CD+SS)	vs.	Mental Manipulation (LN+DS)	24
Mental Manipulation (LN +DS)	vs.	Problem Solving without Visual-Motor Speed (MR+VP+PC+FW)	22
Fluid Reasoning (MR+FW)	vs.	Visual Processing (BD+VP)	20
Verbal Fluid Reasoning (SI+CO)	vs.	Fluid Reasoning (MR+FW)	22
Lexical Knowledge (VC+SI)	vs.	General Information (CO+IN)	15
Long-Term Memory (VC+IN)	vs.	Short-Term Memory (LN+DS)	24
Verbal Fluid Reasoning (SI+CO)	vs.	Long-Term Memory (VC+IN)	16

Source: Standardization data and analysis results from the *Wechsler Adult Intelligence Scale—Fourth Edition* (WAIS-IV). Copyright © 2008 by NCS Pearson, Inc. Used with permission. All rights reserved.

Note: "Unusually large or uncommon" denotes differences estimated to occur less than 10% of the time in the WAIS-IV standardization sample. The differences in this table were estimated by the formula provided by Sattler (1982, Table C-11) for computing the percentage of a population obtaining discrepancies between two standard scores. This formula includes the correlations between the two standard scores for each comparison, which were kindly provided by Pearson Assessments (J. J. Wang, personal communication, March 23, 2009). Two comparisons are based on data for the total WAIS-IV standardization sample (ages 16–90): Lexical Knowledge vs. General Information and Verbal Fluid Reasoning vs. Long-Term Memory. All other comparisons are for ages 16–69 only and are based on correlations for ages 16–69. The two comparisons involving Problem Solving without Visual-Motor Speed can be conducted with only Matrix Reasoning and Visual Puzzles when Figure Weights or Picture Completion (or both) are not administered. In such instances, the values shown in the table for these two comparisons apply even when the cluster comprises only Matrix Reasoning and Visual Puzzles. One of those two comparisons (Visual-Motor Speed vs. Problem Solving without Visual-Motor Speed) can be administered to adults ages 70–90 when the two-subtest

2. The size of the difference between the two interpretable clinical clusters is not uncommon in the normative population.

Figure 5.11 shows an example of Step 10c using Laura's profile.

Step 10d. Regardless of the outcome of Step 10c, describe the results of the planned clinical comparisons. Although there are many ways to describe the results of these planned clinical comparisons, in Rapid Reference 5.18 we provide samples of interpretive statements that can be used to describe the results of the individual's clinical cluster comparisons. Keeping in mind the tenets of intelligent testing, all hypotheses that are derived from the post hoc planned clinical comparisons should be supported with additional sources of data (e.g., behavioral observations, other test results, referral concerns). Suggested hypotheses for the meanings of patterns of findings from the clinical comparisons are provided in Rapid Reference 5.19.

Interpretation of the WAIS-IV profile (from the global ability, to the indexes, to these clinical clusters) must consider other factors than true differences in ability. Chapter 4 reviewed many of these clinical and behavioral factors that may elucidate an examinee's WAIS-IV profile. In addition, chapter 6 provides detailed information from a neuropsychological approach to interpretation that can provide more insight into understanding peaks and valleys in a person's abilities. Interpretation of the process scores that the WAIS-IV offers is detailed in chapter 6. Integration of all of these quantitative and qualitative aspects of the WAIS-IV profile will provide the most accurate portrait of an individual's cognitive abilities.

Cluster 1	vs.	Cluster 2	Score 1	–	Score 2	=	Differ- ence	Critical Value	Uncomm on (U) or Not Uncomm on (NU)
Visual Motor Speed (BD+CD+SS)	vs.	Problem Solving w/o Visual Motor Speed (MR+VP+PC+FW)		–	76	=		20	
Visual Motor Speed (BD+CD+SS)	vs.	Mental Manipulation (LN+DS)		–		=		24	
Mental Manipulation (LN+DS)	vs.	Problem Solving w/o Visual Motor Speed (MR+VP+PC+FW)		–	76	=		22	
Fluid Reasoning (MR+FW)	vs.	Visual Processing (BD+VP)	75	–	78	=	3	20	NU
Verbal Fluid Reasoning (SI+CO)	vs.	Fluid Reasoning (MR+FW)	97	–	75	=	22	22	U
Lexical Knowledge (VC+SI)	vs.	General Information (CO+IN)	100	–	94	=	6	15	NU
Long-Term Memory (VC+IN)	vs.	Short-Term Memory (LN+DS)	97	–		=		24	
Verbal Fluid Reasoning (SI+CO)	vs.	Long-Term Memory (VC+IN)	97	–	97	=	0	16	NU

Figure 5.11. Illustration of Step 10c Using Laura's Profile with the WAIS-IV DMIA

≡ Rapid Reference 5.18

Examples of How to Describe the Findings of Planned and Post Hoc Clinical Comparisons in a Psychological Report

Planned Clinical Comparison	Both SS < 85	One SS < 85 One SS ≥ 85	Both SS 85–115 (Inclusive)	One SS < 115 One SS ≥ 115	Both SS > 115
Difference Not Un-common	Interpretive Statement 1	Interpretive Statement 2	Interpretive Statement 3	Interpretive Statement 4	Interpretive Statement 5
Difference Uncommon	Interpretive Statement 6	Interpretive Statement 7	Interpretive Statement 8	Interpretive Statement 9	Interpretive Statement 10

Note: SS = Standard Score.

Interpretive Statement (the Numbers that Follow Correspond to Numbers in Table)

1. **Example: *Verbal Fluid Reasoning (Gf-verbal) Cluster = 80; Fluid Reasoning (Gf-nonverbal) Cluster = 75.*** The difference between Roberto's Verbal Fluid Reasoning Cluster of 80 (9th percentile) and his Fluid Reasoning Cluster of 75 (5th percentile) was not unusually large, indicating that it is not uncommon to find a difference of this magnitude in the normative population. Nevertheless, it is important to recognize that Roberto's abilities to reason with both verbal and nonverbal information are Below Average and therefore represent Normative Weaknesses relative to his age mates.

2. **Example: *Long-Term Memory (Gc-LTM) Cluster = 90; Verbal Fluid Reasoning (Gf-verbal) Cluster = 84.*** The difference between Roberto's Long-Term Memory Cluster of 90 (25th percentile) and his Verbal Fluid Reasoning Cluster of 84 (14th percentile) was not unusually large, indicating that it is not uncommon to find a difference of this magnitude in the normative population. Nevertheless, it is important to recognize that Roberto's ability to reason with knowledge (Gf-verbal) fell within the Below Average range of functioning and represents a Normative Weakness relative to his age mates.

3. **Example: *Long-Term Memory (Gc-LTM) Cluster = 106; Short-Term Memory (Gsm-WM) Cluster = 100.*** The difference between Roberto's Long-Term Memory Cluster of 106 (65th percentile) and his Short-Term Memory Cluster of 100 (50th percentile) was not unusually large, indicating that it is not uncommon to find a difference of this magnitude in the

normative population. Relative to his age mates, Roberto's performances in these areas are within the Average Range of functioning or Within Normal Limits.

4. **Example: Nonverbal Fluid Reasoning (Gf-nonverbal) Cluster = 118; Visual Processing (Gv) Cluster = 112.** The difference between Roberto's Fluid Reasoning Cluster of 118 (88th percentile) and his Visual Processing Cluster of 112 (79th percentile) was not unusually large, indicating that it is not uncommon to find a difference of this magnitude in the normative population. Relative to his age mates, Roberto's Gv ability is within the Average Range of functioning, and his Gf-nonverbal ability is Above Average and therefore represents a Normative Strength.

5. **Example: Lexical Knowledge (Gc-VL) Cluster = 125; General Information (Gc-K0) Cluster = 120.** The difference between Roberto's Lexical Knowledge Cluster of 125 (95th percentile) and his General Information Cluster of 120 (91st percentile) was not unusually large, indicating that it is not uncommon to find a difference of this magnitude in the normative population. Relative to his age mates, Roberto's lexical knowledge and general information abilities are Above Average (or if scores are > 130, then "in the Upper Extreme") and therefore represent Normative Strengths.

6. **Example: Visual Processing (Gv) Cluster = 84; Fluid Reasoning (Gf) Cluster = 60.** The difference between Roberto's Visual Processing Cluster of 84 (14th percentile; Below Average/Normative Weakness) and his Fluid Reasoning Cluster of 60 (< 1st percentile; Lower Extreme/Normative Weakness) is unusually large. (Differences as large as Roberto's discrepancy of 24 points occur less than 10% of the time in the normative population.) Higher standard scores on Visual Processing than Fluid Reasoning can occur for many reasons. For example, some individuals might have a better ability to analyze or manipulate isolated aspects of visual stimuli than to reason with such stimuli. Although Roberto's visual processing is better developed than his fluid reasoning, it is important to recognize that Roberto demonstrated Normative Weaknesses in both domains. Note that Roberto's fluid reasoning ability, in particular, represents a disorder in a basic psychological process—but only when this Lower Extreme performance is corroborated by other data sources.

7. **Example: Problem Solving Without Visual-Motor Speed Cluster = 110; Visual-Motor Speed Cluster = 83.** The difference between Roberto's Problem Solving without Visual-Motor Speed Cluster of 110 (75th percentile; Average Range/Within Normal Limits) and his Visual-Motor Speed Cluster of 83 (13th percentile; Below Average/Normative Weakness) is unusually large. (Differences as large as Roberto's discrepancy of 27 points occur less than 10% of the time in the normative population.) Higher standard scores on Problem Solving without Visual-Motor Speed compared to Visual-Motor Speed can occur for many reasons. For example, some individuals might have the ability to reason with nonverbal stimuli but have difficulty when required simply to provide a speedy visual-motor response to a problem. Not only is Roberto's visual-motor speed ability less well developed than his ability to problem solve without visual-motor speed, it is also Below Average relative to his age mates and therefore is a Normative Weakness.

(continued)

8. **Example: Long-Term Memory (Gc-LTM) Cluster = 115; Verbal Fluid Reasoning (Gf-verbal) Cluster = 85.** The difference between Roberto's Long-Term Memory Cluster of 115 (84th percentile; Average Range/Within Normal Limits) and his Verbal Fluid Reasoning Cluster of 85 (16th percentile; Average Range/Within Normal Limits) is unusually large. (Differences as large as Roberto's discrepancy of 30 points occur less than 10% of the time in the normative population.) Higher standard scores on Long-Term Memory than Verbal Fluid Reasoning can occur for many reasons. For example, some individuals might have a well-developed fund of information but are unable to reason well with this information. Although Roberto's performance in both domains falls Within Normal Limits relative to his age mates, it would not be unusual for Roberto to become easily frustrated when required to reason with general information (e.g., drawing inferences from text).

9. **Example: Problem Solving Without Visual-Motor Speed Cluster = 116; Mental Manipulation Cluster = 86.** The difference between Roberto's Problem Solving without Visual-Motor Cluster of 116 (86th percentile; Above Average/ Normative Strength) and his Mental Manipulation Cluster of 86 (17th percentile; Average Range/Within Normal Limits) is unusually large. (Differences as large as Roberto's discrepancy of 30 points occur less than 10% of the time in the normative population.) Higher standard scores on the Problem Solving without Visual-Motor Speed Cluster than the Mental Manipulation Cluster can occur for many reasons. For example, some individuals might have the ability to problem solve when not required to use speedy visual-motor responses but may have difficulty encoding information in immediate awareness long enough to manipulate or transform it. Although Roberto's performance in Mental Manipulation falls within Normal Limits relative to his age mates, he may benefit from strategies designed to improve his initial encoding of information or his attention. (Note: When the standard score on the lower cluster in the comparison is < 85, replace the last sentence with "Not only is Roberto's ability to mentally manipulate information less well developed than his problem solving without visual-motor speed, but it is also in the Below Average [or Lower Extreme, depending on the score] range of functioning relative to his age mates and therefore represents a Normative Weakness." Also note that Roberto's Below Average [or Lower Extreme] performance in mental manipulation represents a disorder in a basic psychological process [but only when such performance is corroborated by other data sources].)

10. **Example: Visual-Motor Speed Cluster = 146; Mental Manipulation Cluster = 116.** The difference between Roberto's Visual-Motor Speed cluster of 146 (> 99th percentile; Upper Extreme/Normative Strength) and his Mental Manipulation Cluster of 116 (86th percentile; Above Average/Normative Strength) is unusually large. (Differences as large as Roberto's discrepancy of 30 points occur less than 10% of the time in the normative population.) Nevertheless, it is important to recognize that Roberto's speed of visual-motor processing and ability to mentally manipulate information are very well developed, falling in the Upper Extreme and Above Average ranges, respectively, compared to his age mates and therefore represent Normative Strengths.

Source: Adapted from Flanagan and Kaufman (2004).

≋ Rapid Reference 5.19

Hypotheses for Observed Differences between Clinical Clusters

Fluid Reasoning (Gf) Cluster > Visual Processing (Gv) Cluster

Hypotheses: This difference may indicate that the individual's overall reasoning ability is good and that, despite difficulty with visual processing, the individual can solve problems by focusing on characteristics that are less visual in nature. For example, on Matrix Reasoning, the individual may not focus on the spatial aspects of the pattern to arrive at an answer (e.g., the pattern shifts from top to bottom, then left to right, then back to the top), but rather he or she may focus on the number of dots in a pattern to complete the matrix. Also, an individual with such a pattern of abilities may do well when he or she uses a strategy such as verbal mediation to solve problems with substantial visual information. That is, an individual may be able to solve a problem involving visual stimuli only after translating the visual information into verbal information.

Visual Processing (Gv) Cluster > Fluid Reasoning (Gf) Cluster

Hypotheses: This difference may indicate that the individual has good concrete visual skills but experiences difficulty when asked to reason with visual information. Implications may include difficulty with mathematical application tasks, such as making predictions based on visual stimuli (e.g., graphs, charts). An individual with this pattern of performance may also have difficulty interpreting visual information. That is, an individual with higher visual processing skills than visual reasoning skills may be able to see specific details in visual information but may have difficulty integrating visual information to solve problems.

Fluid Reasoning (Gfl) Cluster > Verbal Fluid Reasoning (Gf-verbal) Cluster

Hypotheses: This difference may indicate that the individual can reason better with visually based stimuli as compared to verbal stimuli. An individual with this pattern of performance may learn best when new information is presented visually.

Verbal Fluid Reasoning (Gf-verbal) Cluster > Fluid Reasoning (Gf) Cluster

Hypotheses: This difference may indicate that the individual can reason better with verbally based stimuli as compared to visual stimuli. An individual with this pattern of performance may learn best when new information is presented verbally. Moreover, an individual with this pattern of performance may do well with lecture formats that are primarily verbal in nature but may get lost when too many visual aids are used (e.g., graphs, diagrams) to teach a new concept.

(continued)

Lexical Knowledge (*Gc*-VL) Cluster > General Information (*Gc*-K0) Cluster

Hypotheses: This difference may indicate that the individual has facility with words and can reason with words but has minimal knowledge of factual information or has difficulty applying knowledge in specific situations. An individual with this pattern of performance may have difficulty with written expression, in terms of breadth and depth of content, despite an appropriate vocabulary. On reading tasks, the individual may be able to read (decode) well and generally comprehend what he or she is reading but may not be able to make meaningful connections or draw inferences due to a lack of background knowledge.

General Information (*Gc*-K0) Cluster > Lexical Knowledge (*Gc*-VL) Cluster

Hypotheses: This difference may indicate that the individual has good knowledge of factual information but lacks facility with words and may have difficulty reasoning with words. On writing assignments, an individual with this pattern of performance may have good content but may be unable to communicate his or her thoughts well. That is, the individual's writing may appear poorly developed (e.g., writing is bland, lacks variety with regard to adjectives). On reading tasks, an individual with this pattern of performance may have good comprehension when reading about familiar topics, but he or she may have poor comprehension when reading about topics that are novel or that contain several unknown words. Thus, it is not unusual for an individual with this pattern of performance to be described as having inconsistent comprehension skills.

Long-Term Memory (*Gc*-LTM) Cluster > Short-Term Memory (*Gsm*-WM) Cluster

Hypotheses: This difference may indicate that the individual can retrieve information but has trouble encoding the information. In other words, the individual's stores of knowledge are likely the result of repeated practice using a number of meaningful associations. On reading and writing tasks, an individual with this pattern of performance may do well with known topics but poorly on new ones. Additionally, due to difficulty with holding information in immediate awareness long enough to use it, an individual with this pattern of performance may have difficulty efficiently copying information from written material or recording information from a lecture or from the board. Finally, an individual with this pattern of performance may have difficulty with a bottom-up learning approach in which the component parts of a general concept are presented separately and sequentially. This learning approach may cause particular difficulty for the individual primarily because he or she cannot hold the component parts in memory long enough to be able to synthesize them into the whole concept.

Short-Term Memory (*Gsm*-WM Cluster) > Long-Term Memory (*Gc*-LTM) Cluster

Hypotheses: This difference may indicate that the individual can encode information but has trouble retrieving it. Individuals with this pattern may do well with new topics in the short term, but if there is a delay between their learning of information and the need to demonstrate their knowledge, they may demonstrate a poor outcome. A classic example is when an employer or instructor indicates that the individual demonstrated an understanding of a particular topic while it was being presented but did not remember it later in the day. Also, an individual with this pattern of performance is often described as knowing information shortly after studying it but not being able to demonstrate that knowledge later (e.g., on a cumulative exam). It is likely that these individuals are not forgetting information per se; rather, they are not encoding information at a level that is necessary for efficient retrieval.

Long-Term Memory (*Gc*-LTM) Cluster > Verbal Fluid Reasoning (*Gf*-verbal) Cluster

Hypotheses: This difference may indicate that the individual has an adequate fund of knowledge but cannot reason well with that knowledge.

Verbal Fluid Reasoning (*Gf*-verbal) Cluster > Long-Term Memory (*Gc*-LTM) Cluster

Hypotheses: This difference may indicate that the individual can reason well but that he or she has an insufficient amount of information to reason with.

Visual-Motor Speed > Problem Solving Without Visual-Motor Speed

Hypotheses: This difference may indicate that an individual has a strong ability to quickly encode and respond to visually presented information by giving a motor response (e.g., either by manipulating blocks or writing with a pencil) but has more difficulty responding to visual information that requires processing through nonverbal reasoning when speed of responding is not a critical factor. Individuals with strong manual-motor dexterity or motor coordination may reveal a well-developed ability on the Visual-Motor Speed Cluster while not performing as well on the Problem Solving without Visual-Motor Speed Cluster. Such individuals may also perform well because they are highly motivated to beat the clock but may be overwhelmed with stimuli that is spatially complex or that requires a higher level of cognitive processing. Individuals who do not employ verbal mediation strategies when working may struggle more with tasks on the Problem Solving without Visual-Motor Speed Cluster while still being able to perform adequately on the Visual-Motor Speed Cluster.

Problem Solving Without Visual-Motor Speed > Visual-Motor Speed

Hypotheses: This difference may indicate that an individual has a strong ability to perceive and process visual information using nonverbal reasoning when speed of responding is not a critical factor but has more difficulty quickly encoding and responding to visually presented information by responding motorically (e.g., either by manipulating blocks or writing with a pencil). Individuals with weaker manual-motor dexterity or motor coordination may reveal a poorly developed ability on the Visual-Motor Speed Cluster while performing well on the Problem Solving without Visual-Motor Speed Cluster. Such an individual may also demonstrate signs of anxiety when required to beat the clock but may be less anxious and more motivated to work spatially complex stimuli or stimuli that require a higher level of cognitive processing. Individuals who employ verbal mediation strategies when

(continued)

working may show enhanced performance on tasks from the Problem Solving without Visual-Motor Speed Cluster while still struggling on the Visual-Motor Speed Cluster, which lends itself less to verbal mediation.

Visual-Motor Speed > Mental Manipulation

Hypotheses: This difference may indicate that the individual's attention to visual stimuli is better developed than his or her auditory attention abilities. The output required for the tasks on the Visual-Motor Speed Cluster differs greatly from that of the tasks on the Mental Manipulation Cluster. Specifically, an individual with such a difference may have a better ability to respond by using visual-motor coordination than by using expressive language skills. Although working memory is employed with both of these clinical clusters, an individual with higher visual-motor speed may have a better-developed ability to apply working memory to visual stimuli (Visual-Motor Speed Cluster) than to auditory stimuli (Mental Manipulation Cluster). If an individual has difficulty with auditory processing speed (or the speed at which auditory information is registered), he or she may display weaker performance on the Mental Manipulation Cluster than on the Visual-Motor Speed Cluster, which requires quick encoding of and response to visual stimuli.

Mental Manipulation > Visual-Motor Speed

Hypotheses: This difference may indicate that the individual's auditory attention abilities are better developed than his or her ability to attend to visual stimuli. The output required for the tasks on the Mental Manipulation Cluster differs greatly from that of the tasks on the Visual-Motor Speed Cluster. Specifically, an individual with such a difference may have a better ability to respond by using expressive language skills than by using visual-motor coordination. Although working memory is employed with both of these clinical clusters, an individual may have a more well developed ability to apply working memory to auditory stimuli (Mental Manipulation Cluster) than to visual stimuli (Visual-Motor Speed Cluster). If an individual has difficulty with encoding and responding rapidly to visual stimuli, he or she may display weaker performance on the Visual-Motor Speed Cluster than on the Mental Manipulation Cluster, which benefits from speedy auditory processing (i.e., the speed at which auditory information is registered).

Problem Solving Without Visual-Motor Speed > Mental Manipulation

Hypotheses: This difference may indicate that the individual's attention to visual stimuli is better developed than his or her auditory attention abilities. Although working memory may enhance performance on both of these clinical clusters, an individual with poor auditory working memory (Mental Manipulation Cluster) will be more likely to show this pattern of performance. If an individual has difficulty with auditory processing speed (or the speed at which auditory information is registered), he or she may display weaker performance on the Mental Manipulation cluster than the Problem Solving without Visual-Motor Speed Cluster that has more emphasis on reasoning and less emphasis on speed of processing.

Mental Manipulation > Problem Solving Without Visual-Motor Speed

Hypotheses: This difference may indicate that the individual's auditory attention abilities are better developed than their ability to attend to visual stimuli. Although working memory is employed with both of these clinical clusters, an individual with a strong auditory working memory (Mental Manipulation Cluster) may be more likely to display this pattern of performance. If an individual has difficulty with nonverbal reasoning (even without emphasizing speed), he or she may display weaker performance on the Problem Solving without Visual-Motor Speed Cluster than on the Mental Manipulation cluster, which benefits from speedy auditory processing (without requiring reasoning).

Source: Adapted from Flanagan & Kaufman (2004). Additional hypotheses may be developed from using a neuropsychological approach, which is described in chapter 6.

Note: Per the intelligent testing approach that we advocate in this book, all hypotheses based on observed differences between clinical cluster scores should be validated with other sources of data.

🪶 TEST YOURSELF 🪶

1. **If the FSIQ is not interpretable,**
   (a) the GAI should automatically be designated as the best representation of a person's general intellectual ability.
   (b) determine if the GAI can be calculated and interpreted as a reliable and valid estimate of a person's general intellectual ability.
   (c) the WAIS-IV is not a good test to measure the person's IQ.
   (d) the CPI should be considered as the best measure of the person's general intellectual ability.

2. **If the examinee is age 75, you should select the interpretation of the Keith Five Factors over the Wechsler Four Indexes. TRUE or FALSE?**

3. **A personal strength in visual processing ability may be evident from**
   (a) a Visual Processing (Gv) Cluster score of 90 that is uncommonly higher than the mean factor score of 74.
   (b) a Visual Processing (Gv) Cluster score of 120 that is uncommonly higher than the mean factor score of 95.
   (c) a Visual Processing (Gv) Cluster score of 82 that is uncommonly higher than the mean factor score of 65.
   (d) All of the above.

4. **Using the normative descriptive system to describe the WAIS-IV Index scores, a score of 84 should be described as**
   (a) a Normative Strength.
   (b) within normal limits.
   (c) a Normative Weakness.
   (d) None of the above.

5. Alex obtained a PRI of 79, which is significantly lower than his other indexes and is uncommon in the normal population. Alex's PRI is best described as a

   (a) Key Asset.

   (b) Personal Strength.

   (c) Personal Weakness.

   (d) High Priority Concern.

6. An abnormally large discrepancy between PRI and VCI means it is

   (a) rare among the normal population.

   (b) equivalent to a statistically significant discrepancy.

   (c) at least 50-point discrepancy.

   (d) at least 5-point discrepancy.

7. If the PRI is not a unitary ability, then examiners may consider interpreting the profile from the Keith Five-Factor model. TRUE or FALSE?

8. If an individual has a WMI less than 85, that person has a possible deficit in

   (a) working memory.

   (b) auditory attention.

   (c) expressive language.

   (d) speed of auditory processing.

   (e) any or all of the above areas.

9. Wechsler indexes, Keith factors, and clinical clusters

   (a) must be interpreted from a CHC theoretical model.

   (b) must be interpreted from a neuropsychological perspective.

   (c) must be interpreted from the perspective of the test publishers.

   (d) must consider theory, behavior, and the background of the client in interpretation.

10. A low score on the Keith factor of Short-Term Memory (*Gsm*) may be interpreted as all of the following EXCEPT

    (a) distractibility or attentional difficulties.

    (b) difficulty with numbers.

    (c) poor visual-motor ability.

    (d) excessive anxiety.

11. A low score on PSI or Keith's Processing Speed (*Gs*) Factor is LEAST likely to be due to

    (a) fine motor control difficulty.

    (b) reflective processing style.

    (c) poor visual memory.

    (d) poor nonverbal reasoning.

12. In calculation of an individual's personal strengths and weaknesses in the index or factor profile, you compare each of their interpretable index or factor scores to the person's own mean index or factor score. **TRUE or FALSE?**

Answers 1. b; 2. False; 3. d; 4. c; 5. d; 6. a; 7. True; 8. e; 9. d; 10. c; 11. d; 12. True.

Six

CLINICAL APPLICATIONS I: A NEUROPSYCHOLOGICAL APPROACH TO INTERPRETATION OF THE WAIS-IV AND THE USE OF THE WAIS-IV IN LEARNING DISABILITY ASSESSMENTS

George McCloskey, PhD

INTRODUCTION

This chapter applies neuropsychological concepts to the interpretation of performance on the WAIS-IV. The approach described here is an extension of the process-oriented approach that has been applied in the interpretation of the WISC-IV (McCloskey, 2009; McCloskey & Maerlender, 2005) and reflects the clinical interpretation methods of Edith Kaplan and her colleagues (Kaplan, 1988; Kaplan, Fein, Morris, Kramer, & Delis, 1999). The approach described here is consistent with the intelligent testing approach described in chapter 4 of this book and is also compatible with the cognitive hypothesis testing model offered by Hale and Fiorello (2004). The focus of this approach is on how examinees perform the items of each WAIS-IV subtest as well as the scores they earn on each of those subtests. Therefore, the key to effective interpretation of test performance *after* administration is careful observation of test performance *during* administration. Integration of what was observed during administration with what is scored after administration enables the clinician to characterize more accurately the specific cognitive strengths and weaknesses of the examinee.

The approach presented in this chapter is best summarized through the Interpretive Levels Framework shown in Figure 6.1 and summarized in Rapid References 6.1 through 6.5. Interpretation of the WAIS-IV can occur on multiple levels. Each of these levels represents a particular degree of aggregation, or disaggregation, of the information gathered during administration and assembled after administration. Each successive level, from bottom to top, represents an

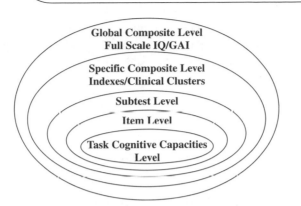

Figure 6.1. Interpretive Levels Framework Applied to the WAIS-IV

aggregation of information that obscures the details revealed by the levels below it. The Full Scale IQ obscures variability that may be present at the index level. Each index score obscures the contribution of individual subtest scores to the index. Each subtest score obscures the contribution of individual item scores to the subtest. Each item score obscures the contribution of variability in task cognitive capacity use that may be observed during item administration. Although interpretation at each level can be viewed from a neuropsychological perspective, some levels are more suited to the application of a wide range of neuropsychological concepts than others. While there is merit in the interpretation of FSIQ, Wechsler's Index scores, Keith's five theory-based factors, and assorted clusters of subtests (as explained thoroughly in chapter 5), the premise of this chapter is that the most effective neuropsychological interpretation of WAIS-IV performance will be found at the subtest, item, and cognitive capacities levels.[1]

This chapter focuses on WAIS-IV interpretation at the subtest, item, and cognitive capacities levels with some treatment of subtest clusters at the specific

---

1. From the perspective of the authors of this book, the tenets expressed in this chapter on neuropsychological interpretation are valuable as a follow-up to the step-by-step approach delineated in chapter 5, not as a replacement for that approach. As such, the book authors consider this Kaplan-based approach to WAIS-IV interpretation as a key *clinical* and *qualitative* supplement to the chapter 5 quantitative system (despite the fact that much of the neuropsychological approach is data based). In particular, the book authors believe that interpretation of subtests and items should always be a second line of interpretation, following the first line—namely, the step-by-step analyses of FSIQ, GAI, CPI, the four Wechsler Indexes, the five Keith factors, and the diverse clinical clusters. The author of this chapter would undoubtedly reverse the order of the "first line" and "second line," which the book authors believe enriches the breadth and quality of the WAIS-IV interpretation system presented in this book.

composite level. The final section of this chapter discusses a model for the assessment of learning disabilities and how the WAIS-IV interpreted from a neuropsychological perspective can be used in the assessment of adolescent and adult learning disabilities.

LEVELS OF INTERPRETATION

Global Composite Level of Interpretation

At the global composite level, all of the subtests from two or more indexes are summed together to yield a broader composite score. The WAIS-IV offers two such global-level composite scores: FSIQ and GAI. GAI and FSIQ interpretations assume that performance across the multiple indexes they encompass was relatively uniform and that a closely related group of cognitive capacities was used by the examinee while performing the index-specific tasks comprising the global composite. A GAI or FSIQ standard score is thought to be a homogeneous indication of the examinee's degree of capability, relative to a standardization sample comparison group, in using the cognitive capacities thought to be assessed by the index-specific tasks aggregated to form the global composite. Global composite-level interpretation obscures the contribution of the separate indexes to the global score, assuming that variations in index-level performance represent random fluctuations that are unimportant or impossible to interpret meaningfully in an empirically valid manner.

Although some psychologists might argue that the FSIQ or the GAI offer a neuropsychological perspective on overall level of cognitive functioning, even the most diehard globalist must admit that the FSIQ and GAI greatly obscure the contribution of various cognitive capacities to the overall level of performance. When these various sources are out of balance in a dramatic way (i.e., the differences between index scores are statistically significant and highly unusual relative to standardization sample performance), the FSIQ and GAI are masking information that is critical to a neuropsychological interpretation of performance. The only situation in which the FSIQ and/or GAI can be justified even marginally as a reflection of overall neuropsychological functioning is when index-level and subtest-level scores all cluster within a very restricted score range showing minimal and nonsignificant variation. That approach to global scores is entirely consistent with the step-by-step interpretive approach spelled out in chapter 5. Even cases where index and subtest scores do not vary significantly, however, significant variation at the item level may offer a much richer source of neuropsychological interpretation, especially in cases where some form of cognitive impairment is suspected. When significant

≡ *Rapid Reference 6.1*
....

Key Facts about the Global Composite Level of Interpretation

• All of the subtests from two or more Indexes are summed together to yield a broader composite score.
• The WAIS-IV offers the FSIQ and GAI.
• When the differences between Index scores are statistically significant and uncommonly large, the FSIQ and GAI are masking information that is critical to a neuropsychological interpretation of performance.

variations in index- and/or subtest-level scores are present, neuropsychological interpretation must focus at levels below the global composite level.

Specific Composite (Index) Level of Interpretation

At the specific composite level, various subtest scaled score triads and dyads are aggregated together to form composite scores called Indexes that are represented normatively by standard scores. Each index standard score represents an aggregation of performance across multiple subtests. Index level interpretation assumes that performance across the multiple subtests was relatively uniform and that a closely related group of cognitive capacities was used by the examinee while performing the subtests comprising the index. An index standard score is thought to be a homogeneous indication of the examinee's degree of capability, relative to a standardization sample comparison group, in using the cognitive capacities thought to be assessed by the cluster of subtests that form the index. Index level interpretation obscures the contribution of individual subtests to the Index, assuming that variations in subtest-level performance represent random fluctuations that are unimportant or impossible to interpret meaningfully in an empirically valid manner.

Index-level interpretation provides a more varied perspective on cognitive function than the FSIQ or GAI, acknowledging that performance is likely to vary across four (or two) general cognitive domains labeled Verbal Comprehension, Perceptual Reasoning, Working Memory, and Processing Speed. This is an improvement over FSIQ and GAI in that variations among the indexes can offer a richer source for neuropsychological interpretation when these variations are significant and unusually large. The index level of interpretation is likely to pick up on glaring imbalances that might be present among the four general domains represented on the WAIS-IV. Contrasting performance on the VCI and PRI with performance on the WMI and PSI is certainly a step in the right direction in acknowledging the need for a neuropsychological perspective on interpretation. Stopping at this level of analysis when significant and unusual differences among index scores are found, however, significantly limits the potential effectiveness of a neuropsychological approach to interpretation of WAIS-IV test performance.

Limiting interpretation to the index level is problematic because there are more than just four broad cognitive capacities that should be considered when applying a cognitive neuropsychological perspective to interpretation of the WAIS-IV. The seeming unitary nature of each of the four WAIS-IV indexes is not an accurate representation of the multiple cognitive capacities that are needed to perform the aggregated tasks of each of the indexes. This is especially apparent in cases where subtest scores within an Index differ significantly. Focusing interpretation at the index score level can result in erroneous neuropsychological interpretations of performance.

A more valid approach to aggregation of subtest score information at the specific composite level is the subtest cluster method, which combines scores from one or more subtests only after interpretive analysis supports the contention that the clustered subtests are measuring similar cognitive capacities at the level of specificity needed for effective interpretation.

Subtest Level of Interpretation

Individual subtest scores are obtained by summing performance across all the items of the subtest producing an aggregate raw score that is converted into a

---

≣ *Rapid Reference 6.2*

Key Facts about the Specific Composite (Index) Level of Interpretation

- Subtest scaled score triads and dyads form composite scores called Indexes that are represented normatively by Standard Scores.
- Index-level interpretation assumes that performance across the multiple subtests was relatively uniform.
- Interpretation at this level assumes that the examinee used a closely related group of cognitive capacities while performing the subtests comprising the index.
- An alternative to index-level interpretation is the subtest cluster method, which combines scores from subtests only after interpretive analysis indicates that subtests are measuring similar cognitive capacities.

norm-referenced scaled score. Subtest-level interpretation assumes that performance across the multiple subtests was relatively uniform and that the same set of cognitive capacities was used by the examinee while performing the items comprising the subtest. A subtest scaled score is thought to be a homogeneous indication of the examinee's degree of capability, relative to a standardization sample comparison group, in using the cognitive capacities thought to be assessed by the items of that subtest. Subtest-level interpretation obscures the contribution of item response patterns, item clusters, or individual items to subtest performance, assuming that variations in item-level performance represent random fluctuations that are unimportant or impossible to interpret meaningfully in an empirically valid manner.

Clinicians seeking to interpret WAIS-IV assessment from a neuropsychological perspective are on somewhat firmer ground when attention is focused at the subtest level. The need for subtest-level interpretation is clear when significantly large differences are present between or among the subtests that comprise an index. In these instances, a clear pattern of difference in the use of cognitive capacities might be readily apparent.

Although subtest-level interpretation can be more specific than index- or global-level interpretation, clinicians attempting to interpret the WAIS-IV from a neuropsychological perspective using the subtest scaled score profile are at risk of missing important aspects of performance that would significantly alter the interpretation of a subtest score profile. In the majority of cases, interpretation of subtest differences is not particularly straightforward due to the fact that performance on each of the subtests of the WAIS-IV always involves the use of multiple cognitive capacities. Additionally, the multiple cognitive capacities used to perform a subtest can vary

≡ Rapid Reference 6.3

Key Facts about the Subtest Level of Interpretation

- Subtest scores are an aggregate raw score that is converted into a norm-referenced scaled score.
- Interpretation at the subtest level assumes that the same set of cognitive capacities was used by the examinee while performing the items comprising the subtest.
- The contribution of item response patterns, item clusters, or individual items to subtest performance is obscured at this level of interpretation.
- Subtest-level performance involves multiple cognitive capacities, so test hypotheses on a case-by-case basis in order to develop stronger inferences about how specific cognitive capacities are affecting subtest performance.

from one examinee to another. Because subtest-level performance involves multiple cognitive capacities, it is necessary to test hypotheses on a case-by-case basis in order to develop stronger inferences about how specific cognitive capacities are affecting subtest performance. If interpretation remains focused solely on the subtest score level, then the clinician must use additional subtests to test hypotheses about the contribution of various cognitive capacities to subtest performance. The greater the number of possible cognitive capacities required for subtest performance, the greater the number of competing hypotheses that require further testing.

Item Level of Interpretation

All WAIS-IV items are scored individually using predetermined criteria. Each item score represents an aggregate statement about the cognitive capacities used to perform the item. The methods used to assign scores to items assume that only the cognitive capacities thought to be required for item performance are being assessed as intended and are contributing equally to the performance of each item. A correct response indicates that the examinee demonstrated effective use of the cognitive capacities intended to be assessed with the item. An incorrect response indicates the ineffective use of the cognitive capacities intended to be assessed with the item. It is also assumed that examinee item responses will follow a specific pattern throughout the subtest where consistently correct performance on a subset of items in the "easy range" will be followed by variable performance on a subset of items in the "challenging range," which will be followed by incorrect responses on a subset of items in the "too-difficult range."

Taken at face value, item scores obscure the possible differential contribution of multiple cognitive capacities to item success or item failure, and deviations from the expected pattern of item performance represent random fluctuations that are unimportant or impossible to interpret meaningfully in an empirically valid manner. Rather than taking an examinee's set of item-level scores at face value, item-level interpretation attempts to identify and understand unusual patterns of item performance, such as easy items answered incorrectly or hard items answered with ease, or performance on a cluster of items that is inconsistent with the expected pattern. When performed effectively, item-level interpretation will draw on knowledge obtained at the task cognitive capacities level to generate hypotheses about the cognitive capacities that are, or are not, being used in the performance of individual items or subsets of items.

Although subtest-level interpretation is much more likely to yield valuable information from a neuropsychological perspective than index scores, specific subtests that can be used to test hypotheses about the contribution of different

≡ Rapid Reference 6.4

Key Facts about the Item Level of Interpretation

- Item scores are aggregate statements about the cognitive capacities used to perform the item.
- An examinee's response indicates whether he or she effectively used the cognitive capacities intended to be assessed with the item.
- Item scores obscure the possible differential contribution of multiple cognitive capacities to item success or item failure.
- Deviations from the expected pattern of item performance represent random fluctuations that are unimportant or impossible to interpret meaningfully in an empirically valid manner.
- Analyzing item response patterns, item cluster performance, and individual item performance often will yield information useful in testing hypotheses about the specific cognitive capacities involved in subtest performance.

cognitive capacities to WAIS-IV subtest performance are not always available and/or clinicians often cannot devote the time needed to thoroughly test every hypothesis using additional subtests. In these instances, neuropsychological interpretation of subtest performance can be greatly enhanced through careful inspection of item-level performance. Item level analysis focused on item response patterns, item cluster performance, and individual item performance often will yield information that can be very useful in testing hypotheses about the specific cognitive capacities likely to be involved in subtest performance.

Task Cognitive Capacities Level of Interpretation

The task cognitive capacities level of interpretation acknowledges the fact that an examinee's attempt to complete any single item from any subtest of the WAIS-IV will require an attempt to make use of multiple cognitive capacities. Although each item is constructed in a manner that assumes that the use of a specific cognitive capacity, or set of capacities, will be the most efficient and effective way to perform the item, there is no guarantee that individual examinees will chose to use those specific cognitive capacities in their efforts to complete the item. Individual examinees will use their own decision-making processes to determine what cognitive capacities they draw on to perform an item. The cognitive capacities chosen by the examinee are likely to reflect inherent preferences or biases of the examinee, and may not be consistent with the cognitive capacities the item was intended to assess. Careful observation of how the examinee performs an item is therefore critical to the accurate understanding of what cognitive capacities are actually being assessed by that item. No matter what efforts are made to try to ensure that a specific task is assessing a specific cognitive capacity, most examinees' specific neural capabilities will enable them to choose for themselves the cognitive capacities they wish to engage in their efforts with a task. This fact will continue to frustrate the efforts of researchers and clinicians who desire to identify and make use of tasks that are "pure" measures of a single cognitive capacity. This fact also confounds the standard view of subtest reliability in which all sources of unexplained variability in task perform-ance are considered "measurement error." Unfortunately, such misguided conceptions of reliability are used to support the argument against the use of subtest-level interpretation of test performance and to discourage clinicians from attempting to understand the individual variation observed in task performance. In many cases, careful clinical observation of task performance can identify and explain how examinees are using cognitive capacities, thereby increasing the interpretive validity as well as the reliability of the assessment process by explaining the unexplained sources of variability in performance that would have been identified only as measurement error.

A cognitive neuropsychological approach to WAIS-IV interpretation requires a solid understanding of the various cognitive capacities that could be involved in the performance of the individual items of each subtest and knowledge of the kinds of

═ *Rapid Reference 6.5*

Task Cognitive Capacities Level of Interpretation

- Individual examinees determine what cognitive capacities they draw on to perform an item.
- Careful observation of how the examinee performs an item is critical to the accurate understanding of what cognitive capacities are actually being assessed by that item.
- The interpretive validity and the reliability of the assessment process are increased by illuminating the unexplained sources of variability in performance that may be inferred from careful clinical observations of how examinees are using cognitive capacities.
- Effective interpretation of the cognitive capacities used during individual items informs all subsequent levels of interpretation, thereby increasing the likelihood of an accurate characterization of the examinee from a neuropsychological perspective.

behaviors that are most likely to indicate the use of these cognitive capacities. This level of analysis requires more than simply looking for item response patterns, performance on item clusters, or knowing whether a specific item was scored as right or wrong. As noted earlier, examinees determine for themselves what cognitive capacities they choose to use to perform test items, necessitating careful observation of examinee performance and an understanding of how specific behaviors can reflect the use of specific cognitive capacities. Effective interpretation of the cognitive capacities used during individual items informs all subsequent levels of interpretation, thereby increasing the likelihood of an accurate characterization of the examinee from a neuropsychological perspective.

NEUROPSYCHOLOGICAL INTERPRETATION OF WAIS-IV PERFORMANCE

To effectively use and interpret the WAIS-IV from a neuropsychological perspective, it is necessary to understand the multifactorial nature of the WAIS-IV subtests. Specifically, examiners should consider what cognitive capacities the subtests assess and how these cognitive capacities are reflected in item-level performance and subtest- and composite-level scores. (Because the neuropsychological interpretation of WAIS-IV Performance is so complex, we warn against deriving hypotheses of neurological pathology by the simple presence of significant differences between scores.)

CAUTION

Overinterpretation of VCI-PRI Difference

Perhaps the most notable erroneous interpretation of index-level scores is the conception that significant and unusual differences between the VCI and PRI Index scores (and comparable differences between VIQ-PIQ scale scores on the WAIS, WAIS-R, and WAIS-III) consistently represent a pathognomonic sign of some form of neuropsychological impairment or a general form of "hemispheric imbalance." The legitimate research studies that have reported the neuropsychological implications of VIQ-PIQ differences (and more recently on VCI-PRI differences) and hemispheric functioning imbalances typically offer caveats such as: "It is cautioned that these VIQ-PIQ discrepancies in isolation are ineffective indexes of cerebral dysfunction and that patterns of performance must be viewed in the context of a complete neuropsychological examination and relevant medical and educational historical data" (Bornstein, 1983, p. 779).

Despite such prudent cautionary statements, overstatement of the neuropsychological implications of VCI-PRI differences in either direction still occurs in many psychological reports and professional and popular literature sources. As

(continued)

shown in the next table, the WAIS-IV standardization data do not support a general interpretation of cognitive impairment based solely on VCI-PRI significant differences.

Percentage of the WAIS-IV Standardization Sample Displaying a VCI-PRI or PRI-VCI Discrepancy This Size or Larger for Various FSIQ Score Ranges

	FSIQ Score Range				
Size of Discrepancy	< 79	80–89	90–109	110–120	>119
10	40.8	45.9	45.9	45.7	53.5
15	19.0	21.9	26.2	31.2	35.5
20	7.4	10.1	15.1	17.3	18.5
25	3.7	3.6	6.7	9.1	9.5

These data reveal a picture of cognitive functioning that is in direct contradiction to the well-entrenched myth that the greater the VCI-PRI difference, the greater the likelihood that some form of cerebral dysfunction is present. Applying the "VCI-PRI significant difference equals cognitive impairment" argument to the data from the WAIS-IV standardization sample leads one to the absurd conclusion that the more capable a person is (based on FSIQ), the more likely it is that he or she is demonstrating hemispheric imbalance and brain dysfunction, since the proportion of VCI-PRI differences rises as the FSIQ increases. Considering the fact that most types of brain dysfunction tend to have the effect of lowering FSIQ, it is curious to note that the frequency of occurrence of VCI-PRI differences decreases proportionately with the drop in FSIQ level, therefore producing the situation where individuals in the general population most likely to be affected with some form of undetected neurological complications (i.e., those scoring below FSIQ 90) that would produce hemispheric imbalances or cognitive impairment actually display less variability in their score profile than those who are more often thought of as being neurologically intact (i.e., those scoring above FSIQ 120). While it is certainly possible that a person with a high FSIQ and a large difference between VCI and PRI scores is suffering from a neurological disorder, the idea that a VCI-PRI difference of 10 points, or even 20 points, denotes pathology is unwarranted and unsupportable from the standardization data. It is important to note that the pattern of cumulative percentages of VCI-PRI differences shown in the WAIS-IV standardization data was also present in the WAIS-III and the WISC-IV standardization sample data.

Although some examiners choose to administer only the core 10 WAIS-IV subtests that comprise the four indexes, cognitive neuropsychological interpretation can be greatly enhanced when one or more of the five supplemental subtests are administered along with the core subtests, as the additional subtests offer a more varied perspective on the examinee's use of cognitive capacities. The next section discusses the subtests of the WAIS-IV from a neuropsychological perspective, organized by the four indexes. The goal will be to demonstrate how the Index-level scores often mask important variations in test performance and how information from the levels of the subtest clusters, subtests, items, and cognitive capacities can be used to enhance test interpretation from a neuropsychological perspective.

WHAT DO THE VERBAL COMPREHENSION SUBTESTS MEASURE?

The Verbal Comprehension Index (VCI) subtests were designed primarily to assess the use of specific cognitive capacities applied with orally presented verbal content. These capacities are the primary focus of interpretation of the VCI as well as each individual subtest, and include retrieval of verbal information from long-term storage and reasoning with verbal information. The roles of these primary cognitive capacities in task performance are described in Appendix B.1. Examiners who are interested in knowing as much as possible about the examinee's ability to reason with verbal information are strongly encouraged to administer the supplementary Comprehension subtest, even though it is not a core subtest of the VCI.[2]

DON'T FORGET
....
Cognitive Capacities Most Likely to Be Involved in Verbal Comprehension Tasks
Primary Capacities Targeted for Assessment
  Retrieval of verbal information from long-term storage
  Retrieval of word meanings (Vocabulary)
  Retrieval of facts from various content areas (Information)
Reasoning with orally presented verbal information
  Reasoning with conceptually related words (Similarities)
  Reasoning with real-world cause-effect relationships (Comprehension)
Secondary Capacities Not Targeted for Assessment
  Auditory Acuity
  Auditory Attention
  Auditory Discrimination
  Auditory Comprehension (Receptive Language)
  Auditory Processing Speed

(continued)

---

2. The book authors also recommended administering Comprehension (chapter 5) because two of the comparisons that involve the clinical clusters depend on the person's performance on Comprehension.

Initial Registration of auditorily presented verbal information
Working Memory applied with auditorily presented verbal information
Expressive Language Production
Executive Function cueing and directing of receipt of input, internal processing of input, and production of responses

Beyond the two primary cognitive capacities targeted for assessment with the VCI, the specific formats of each VCI subtest make demands on the examinee that require the engagement of additional cognitive capacities in order to achieve success. While these capacities are required for effective subtest performance, they are not considered to be the primary target of the assessment (i.e., the intention of the subtest is not to quantitatively assess the examinee's use of these cognitive capacities). These secondary cognitive capacities include Auditory Attention, Auditory Discrimination, Auditory Comprehension, Auditory Processing Speed, Expressive Language, Working Memory applied to verbal content, and multiple Executive Functions applied to cue and direct the mental processing of language and working with verbal content. The roles of these secondary cognitive capacities in subtest performance are described in detail in Appendix B.2.

When VCI subtest scores are interpreted, either collectively using the VCI or individually, it is often assumed that the subtests are measuring the primary capacities intended to be assessed. The secondary capacities required for effective performance are either ignored or assumed to be intact and functioning as expected, allowing the focus of interpretation to be on the primary capacities. For example, if an examinee cannot respond effectively to Similarities and Comprehension items, the assumption often is that the examinee has poor reasoning abilities; if the examinee cannot provide adequate responses to the Vocabulary and Information subtests, the assumption is that the examinee does not know the meanings of the words or does not know the specific facts about which he or she is being asked. In many cases where low performance is observed, however, such assumptions are not necessarily warranted. To know if these assumptions about the primary capacities are valid, the role of the secondary cognitive capacities in task performance must be explored in detail. Secondary cognitive capacities can interfere with task performance to a significant degree when not accessed or when applied ineffectively. Thus, it is inappropriate to focus subtest score interpretation exclusively on the primary capacities that are thought to be assessed.

When low scores or scores that are not consistent with what is known about the examinee are obtained with one or more of the VCI subtests, careful analysis of the shared and/or unique contributions of secondary cognitive capacities and more detailed analysis of item responses and the ways in which the responses were delivered should be undertaken. As indicated in the earlier discussion, poor performance on the VCI subtests is thought to reflect a lack of reasoning and/or a lack of stored knowledge (i.e., a lack of verbal intelligence). Clinicians who appreciate that a low score on one or more VCI subtests could be due to many different sources can draw on their knowledge of cognitive capacities shared by subtests and observations about the manner in which the responses were delivered to help obtain a better understanding of the cognitive capacities most likely to have contributed to the poor performance.

Appendix B.3 provides an interpretive summary table that can be used to assist with the analysis of VCI subtests in terms of cognitive capacities that could be contributing to performance on each subtest. Appendix B.5 provides a summary of the interpretations associated with behaviors observed during administration of the VCI subtests that can be used to enhance hypothesis testing about what cognitive capacities are, or are not, being used to perform subtests.

When VCI subtest scores vary greatly and/or when the examiner observes behaviors that suggest that secondary cognitive capacities are influencing task performance, subtest cluster analysis may be helpful in identifying specific strengths and weaknesses in the use of various cognitive capacities. Appendix B.5 outlines the general interpretation of subtest clusters and illustrates the application of the subtest cluster analysis method with the VCI subtests.

When you are engaged in subtest interpretation at the composite level with subtest cluster analysis or at the subtest level, subtest comparisons should include the determination of whether a statistically significant difference exists between the scores earned on the subtests being compared. Use a rounded value of 3 scaled score points to signify a statistically significant difference for any of the comparisons between pairs of VCI subtests or between subtest clusters. Appendix B.5 provides guidelines for interpreting comparisons between specific VCI subtests, and Appendix B.6 provides a worksheet to aid in the interpretation of VCI subtest scaled score comparisons. Appendix C.1 provides a case study example that illustrates the application of subtest cluster-, subtest-, item-, and cognitive capacity–level interpretation of Verbal Comprehension subtest performance.

WHAT DO THE PERCEPTUAL REASONING SUBTESTS MEASURE?

The Perceptual Reasoning Index (PRI) subtests were designed primarily to assess the application of reasoning with nonverbal, visual stimuli including the ability to "analyze and synthesize abstract visual stimuli" (Wechsler, 2008, pp. 13–14). Assessment of these reasoning capacities is intended to be the primary focus of interpretation of the PRI as well as the individual PRI subtests. The role of the primary cognitive capacity of reasoning in task performance is described in detail in Appendix B.7.

DON'T FORGET

....

Cognitive Capacities Most Likely to Be Involved in Perceptual Reasoning Tasks

Primary Capacities Targeted for Assessment

Reasoning with visually presented nonverbal stimuli

Reasoning with visual quantitative information (Figure Weights)

Reasoning with conceptually related concrete visual stimuli

Reasoning with conceptually related abstract visual stimuli

Reasoning about how to integrate visual elements to create a model

Secondary Capacities Not Targeted for Assessment

Visual Acuity

Visual Discrimination

Visual Processing Speed

Initial registration of nonverbal visual stimuli

Working memory applied with nonverbal visual stimuli

Executive Function cueing and directing of receipt of input, internal processing, and production of responses

---

Beyond the primary cognitive capacity targeted for assessment with the PRI subtests, the specific formats of each subtest make demands on the examinee that require the engagement of additional cognitive capacities in order to achieve success. While these capacities typically are required for effective subtest performance, they are not considered to be the primary target of the assessment (i.e., the intention of the subtest is not to quantitatively assess the examinee's use of these cognitive capacities). These secondary cognitive capacities include Visual Perception and Representation; Visual Discrimination; Visualization; Motor Dexterity; Visual, Motor, and Visuo-motor Processing Speed; Working Memory applied to visual nonverbal content; and multiple Executive Functions applied to cue and direct the mental processing of nonverbal visual stimuli. The roles of these secondary cognitive capacities in subtest performance are described in detail in Appendix B.7.

Contrary to the claim of the test publisher, the replacement of the Picture Completion subtest with the Visual Puzzles subtest did not increase the likelihood that the cognitive capacity of primary concern (i.e., reasoning with visual stimuli) would be the cognitive capacity having the greatest impact on performance of the PRI subtests. As noted in Appendix B.7, the capacities most likely to be assessed with the Visual Puzzles subtest focus on basic visual processing and visual processing speed capacities rather than reasoning with visual stimuli.

The wording used here to describe the primary cognitive capacity of the Perceptual Reasoning tasks (i.e., reasoning with nonverbal, visual stimuli) was very purposefully chosen. The phrase "Reasoning with nonverbal visual stimuli" is not synonymous with the term *nonverbal reasoning*. Placing nonverbal visual materials in front of an examinee is not a guarantee that the examinee will reason nonverbally with those materials, especially when clinicians use standardized directions that include verbal explanations of how to perform items when introducing PRI subtests. While it may be advantageous to reason without engaging language abilities when attempting PRI subtests, it is not necessary to do so. Clinicians are likely to observe examinees who engage language abilities to "talk themselves through" some or all aspects of specific Matrix Reasoning, Figure Weights, or Picture Completion items. Such verbal mediation can be helpful, or even essential, to the success of the efforts of some examinees with these tasks. Less likely to be observed is the examinee who attempts to verbally mediate most or all of his or her work with the Block Design and/or Visual Puzzles subtests, but even such a mismatched allocation of mental capacities, though unusual, is not entirely without occurrence.

In contrast to the previous discussion, when PRI subtest scores are interpreted, either collectively using the PRI or individually, it is assumed often that scores reflect the primary capacity of reasoning with nonverbal, visual material. In such cases, the secondary capacities required for effective performance are either ignored or assumed to be intact and functioning as expected, thereby allowing the focus of interpretation to be on reasoning capacity. From this perspective, if an examinee cannot respond effectively to Visual Puzzles, Block Design, and/or Matrix Reasoning items, the assumption is that the examinee has poor nonverbal reasoning ability. In many cases where low performance is observed, however, such an assumption is not necessarily warranted. To know if the assumption about the primary capacity is valid, the role of the secondary cognitive capacities in task performance must be understood and explored in more detail. When not accessed, or when applied ineffectively, these secondary cognitive capacities can interfere with task performance to a significant degree, making it inappropriate to focus subtest score interpretation exclusively on the primary capacity thought to be assessed.

Clinicians should take note of the variety of secondary cognitive capacities assessed with the Picture Completion and Figure Weights subtests. Knowing how an examinee performs with these two supplemental subtests can greatly enhance interpretation of Perceptual Reasoning performance. Examiners are strongly encouraged to include these two supplemental tasks as part of their standard administration of the WAIS-IV.[3]

When low scores or scores that are not consistent with what is known about the examinee are obtained with one or more of the PRI subtests, careful analysis of the shared and/or unique contributions of the secondary cognitive capacities and more detailed analysis of item responses and the ways in which responses were delivered should be undertaken. As indicated in the previous discussion, poor performance on the PRI subtests is thought to reflect a lack of reasoning with nonverbal visual material (i.e., a lack of nonverbal intelligence). Clinicians who appreciate that a low score on one or more PRI subtests could be due to many different sources can draw on the subtest cluster-, item-, and cognitive capacity–level analyses to help obtain a better understanding of why the examinee performed poorly and the implications of such poor performance.

Appendix B.8 provides an interpretive summary table that can be used to assist with the analysis of PRI subtests in terms of cognitive capacities thought to be assessed by each subtest. Appendix B.9 provides a summary of the interpretations associated with behaviors observed during administration of the PRI subtests that can be used to enhance hypothesis testing about what cognitive capacities are, or are not, being used to perform subtests.

The Block Design No Time Bonus Process Score (BDN) score offers a unique opportunity to contrast performance on the Block Design subtest with and without bonus points added for speed of completion of the final six most difficult items on the subtest. The BDN score is a formalized, norm-referenced application of the cognitive capacities level of interpretation applied to the items of the Block Design subtest. The BDN score acknowledges the fact that speed of performance is a capacity unique from the capacities required for accurate solution of the more difficult items, and provides a quantitative means of testing the extent to which speed affected an examinee's overall level of subtest performance.

---

3. The book authors strongly encourage administering Figure Weights and Letter-Number Sequencing (chapter 5) because many aspects of the step-by-step system depend on the person's scores on these two supplemental subtests. They are less enthusiastic about administering Picture Completion. Examiners who wish to conduct the kind of neuropsychological interpretation recommended in this chapter should always administer Picture Completion.

When engaged in subtest interpretation at the composite level with subtest cluster analysis or at the subtest level, subtest comparisons should include the determination of whether a statistically significant difference exists between the scores earned on the subtests being compared. Use a rounded value of 3 scaled score points to signify a statistically significant difference for any of the comparisons between pairs of PRI subtests or between subtest clusters (see Appendix B.10).

When PRI subtest scores vary greatly and/or when the examiner observes behaviors that suggest that secondary cognitive capacities are influencing task performance, subtest cluster analysis may be helpful in identifying specific strengths and weaknesses in the use of various cognitive capacities. Appendix B.9 illustrates the application of the subtest cluster analysis method with the PRI subtests, and Appendix B.11 provides a worksheet to aid in the interpretation of Perceptual Reasoning task scaled score comparisons. Appendix C.1 provides a case study example that illustrates the application of item- and cognitive capacity–level procedures in the interpretations of PRI subtest performance.

WHAT DO THE WORKING MEMORY SUBTESTS MEASURE?

The Working Memory Index (WMI) subtests were designed primarily to assess the capacities involved in the initial registration and holding of information (sometimes referred to as short-term memory) and the mental manipulation of information that is being held in mind (often referred to as working memory). All three of the WMI subtests assess these capacities using auditorily presented verbal and verbal-quantitative stimuli. Assessment of these capacities is the primary focus of interpretation of the WMI as well as the individual WMI subtests. The roles of these primary cognitive capacities in task performance are described in detail in Appendix B.12.

DON'T FORGET
....
Cognitive Capacities Most Likely to Be Involved in Working Memory Tasks

Primary Capacities Targeted for Assessment
  Initial registration of stimuli
  Mental Manipulation of stimuli
Secondary Capacities Not Targeted for Assessment
  Auditory discrimination

(continued)

Attention to auditory stimuli
Auditory processing speed
Mental processing speed
Retrieval of verbal information from long-term storage
Organization/sequencing ability
Math skills
Expressive language ability
Executive Function cueing and directing of receipt of input, internal processing, and production of responses

Beyond the primary cognitive capacities targeted for assessment with the WMI subtests, the specific formats of each subtest make demands on the examinee that require the engagement of additional cognitive capacities in order to achieve success. While these capacities are required for effective subtest performance, they are not considered to be the primary target of the assessment (i.e., the intention of the subtest is not to quantitatively assess the examinee's use of these cognitive capacities). These secondary cognitive capacities include Auditory Acuity, Auditory Discrimination, Auditory Processing Speed, Attention to Auditorily Presented Verbal Information, Language Expression, and multiple Executive Functions applied to cue and direct the use of initial registration and working memory resources. The roles of these secondary cognitive capacities in subtest performance are described in detail in Appendix B.12.

In many cases where low performance is observed on one or both of the WMI core subtests, the generalized assumption of poor initial registration and/or poor working memory capacities is not necessarily warranted. To know if the assumption about these primary capacities is valid, the role of the secondary cognitive capacities in task performance and the effect of input and response formats must be understood and explored in more detail. When not accessed, or when applied ineffectively, secondary cognitive capacities can interfere with task performance to a significant degree, making it inappropriate to focus Index or subtest score interpretation exclusively on the primary capacities that are thought to be assessed. Additionally, without knowing how the examinee performs when input and response formats are varied, the clinician is in danger of over-interpreting the generalizabiity of the WMI score.

When low scores or scores that are not consistent with what is known about the examinee are obtained from one or more of the WMI subtests, careful analysis of the shared and/or unique contributions of the secondary cognitive capacities and more detailed analysis of item responses and the ways in which responses were delivered should be undertaken. As indicated in the previous discussion, poor performance on WMI subtests is thought to reflect a lack of effective initial registration and manipulation of information in working memory. Clinicians who appreciate that a low score on one or more of the WMI subtests could be due to many different sources can draw on the item- and cognitive capacity–level analyses to help obtain a better understanding of why the examinee performed poorly and the implications of such poor performance.

Appendix B.13 provides an interpretive summary table that can be used to assist with the comparison of registration and mental manipulation tasks in terms of the cognitive capacities that may be involved in the performance of test items. Appendix B.14 provides a summary of the interpretations associated with behaviors observed during administration of the WMI subtests that can be used to enhance hypothesis testing about what cognitive capacities are, or are not, being used to perform subtests.

Meaningful interpretation of WMI subtest and Digit Span Process Task comparisons should include the determination of whether a statistically significant difference exists between the scores earned on the subtests and/or tasks being compared. Use a rounded value of 3 scaled score points to signify a statistically significant difference for any of the comparisons of the WMI subtests (see Appendix B.15).

When WMI subtest scores vary greatly and/or when the examiner observes behaviors that suggest that secondary cognitive capacities are influencing task performance, subtest cluster analysis may be helpful in identifying specific strengths and weaknesses in the use of various cognitive capacities. Appendix B.16 provides a worksheet to aid in the interpretation of Working Memory Domain task scaled score comparisons. Appendix C.1 provides a case study example that includes the use of the interpretive worksheet and illustrates the application of the item and cognitive capacities levels in the interpretations of Working Memory task performance.

The addition of Digit Span Sequencing to the Digit Span subtest and the pairing of the Digit Span subtest with the Arithmetic subtest to form a two-subtest WMI substantially increased the likelihood that the primary cognitive capacity of applying working memory with auditorily presented verbal and verbal/quantitative information would be reflected in the WMI score. Attempting to assess an examinee's use of working memory capacities solely through the lens of the WMI, however, still has a number of drawbacks. Interpretation can be strengthened to some degree with the addition of the supplemental Letter-Number Sequencing Subtest and the use of the Digit Span Process Task scaled scores for Digit Span Forward (DSF), Digit Span Backward (DSB), and Digit Span Sequencing (DSS).

Without an understanding of the role that secondary cognitive capacities play in task performance, clinicians frequently will have difficulty effectively interpreting an examinee's performance. For example, it is a neuropsychological fact that stimuli must be effectively registered before they can be manipulated in mind (i.e., no manipulation of information can occur if the information was not initially registered and/or is no longer being held in mind). How then does a clinician explain the performance of an examinee who repeats only four digits forward but is able to repeat six digits in reverse? The former result suggests a capacity for initially registering and holding only four digits, but in order to perform Digit Span Backward, the examinee had to first register and hold six digits and then mentally manipulate those six digits to provide a correct response. In such cases, although the examinee has the capacity to initially register and hold six digits, difficulties in the use of one or more secondary capacities reduced the examinee's ability to demonstrate that capacity in a consistent manner.

Clinicians interested in examining in more detail the relationship between performance on Digit Span Forward, Digit Span Backward, and Digit Span Sequencing will find cumulative frequency (Base Rates) tables comparing longest digit span values among these three digit span process tasks in Appendix C, Table C.6 of the *WAIS-IV Administration and Scoring Manual.*

When WMI subtest scores are interpreted either collectively using the WMI or individually, it is typically assumed that the WMI and the WMI subtest scores reflect a general level of working memory capacity. The secondary capacities required for effective performance are either ignored completely or are assumed to be intact and functioning as expected to allow for the focus of interpretation to be on the primary capacities of initial registration and mental manipulation of stimuli.

WHAT DO THE PROCESSING SPEED SUBTESTS MEASURE?

The Processing Speed Index (PSI) subtests were designed primarily to assess processing speed with nonverbal, visual stimuli. Assessment of processing speed therefore is the primary focus of interpretation of the PSI as well as for the individual PSI subtests. The WAIS-IV includes a new supplementary subtest called Cancellation. The role of processing speed in PSI subtest performance is discussed in Appendix B.17.

Beyond the primary cognitive capacity targeted for assessment with the PSI subtests, the specific formats of each subtest make demands on the examinee that require the engagement of additional cognitive capacities in order to achieve success. While these capacities typically are required for effective subtest performance, they are not considered to be the primary target of the assessment (i.e., the intention of the subtest is not to quantitatively assess the examinee's use of these cognitive capacities). These secondary cognitive capacities include Visual Discrimination, Graphomotor abilities/skills, Attention to Visually Presented Information, and multiple Executive Functions applied to cue and direct the use of visual processing and processing speed resources. The roles of these secondary cognitive capacities in subtest performance are described in detail in Appendix B.17. Clinicians familiar with the WISC-IV Cancellation subtest should make note of the substantial difference in the kind of executive functions most likely to be involved in performance of the WAIS-IV Cancellation subtest compared to those involved with the WISC-IV Cancellation subtest.

DON'T FORGET

....

Cognitive Capacities Most Likely to Be Involved in Processing Speed Tasks

Primary Capacities Targeted for Assessment

    Visual processing speed

    Motor processing speed

    Visual-motor processing speed

Secondary Capacities Not Targeted for Assessment

    Visual perception

    Visual discrimination

    Attention to visual details

    Multitasking

    Organization ability/skills

    Graphomotor ability/skill

    Use of working memory with visual stimuli

    Language representation of visual stimuli

    Executive Function cueing and directing of receipt of input, internal processing, and production of responses

It is important to recognize that the PSI comprised of the Coding and Symbol Search subtests offers a fairly limited measure of processing speed. All three of the PSI subtests employ a visual presentation format that requires the processing of nonverbal visual stimuli and graphomotor responses. The WAIS-IV PSI subtests do not address processing speed directly applied to academic tasks such as the fluent reading or writing of words or the completion of math problems. As a result of this narrow focus of input, processing, and output demands, PSI scores have limited generalizability to academic settings or work settings involving these academic skills. Clinicians who wish to know about an examinee's processing speed for reading cannot infer this from the PSI score or the individual Symbol Search, Coding, or Cancellation subtest scores. Such information needs to be obtained from one or more specific measures of reading speed. From a process approach perspective, however, there is a link between performance on the Coding subtest and written expression production. Because effective performance of both Coding and written expression tasks involve basic graphomotor ability or skills, an examinee who experiences extreme difficulties with graphomotor production on the Coding subtest is likely to experience somewhat similar difficulties with the graphomotor demands of written expression tasks. Additionally, the multitasking demands of the Coding subtest are similar to the multitasking demands of written expression tasks, and both require the effective use of executive function capacities to direct and coordinate such multitasking performance. When an examinee earns a low score on the Coding subtest, performance with written expression production should be assessed. Use of a testing-the-limits Coding Copy Process procedure also can offer important insights into how an examinee responds to reduced graphomotor and multitasking demands. Because of the increased complexity involved in producing words and sentences in writing, however, a high score on the Coding subtest is no guarantee that an examinee will not experience graphomotor or other kinds of difficulties with written expression tasks.

When PSI subtest scores are interpreted, either collectively using the PSI or individually, it is typically assumed that score levels reflect a general level of processing speed. It is often the case that the secondary capacities required for effective performance are either ignored completely or assumed to be intact and functioning as expected to allow for the focus of interpretation to be on the primary capacity. For example, if an examinee earns a low score on the Coding subtest, the assumption often is that the examinee's processing speed is slower than that of same-age peers. In many cases where low performance is observed, such an assumption is not necessarily warranted. To know if the assumption about the primary capacity is valid, the role of the secondary cognitive capacities in task performance must be understood and explored in detail. When not accessed, or when applied ineffectively, these secondary cognitive capacities can interfere with task performance to a significant degree, making it inappropriate to focus subtest score interpretation exclusively on the primary capacities thought to be assessed.

When low scores or scores that are not consistent with what is known about the examinee are obtained from one or more of the PSI subtests, careful analysis of the shared and/or unique contributions of the secondary cognitive capacities and more detailed analysis of item responses and the ways in which responses were delivered should be undertaken. As indicated in the prior discussion, poor performance on PSI subtests is thought to reflect a general lack of processing speed. Clinicians who appreciate that a low score on one or more of the PSI subtests could be due to many different sources can draw on the item- and cognitive capacity–level analyses to help obtain a better understanding of why the examinee performed poorly and the implications of such poor performance.

Appendix B.18 provides an interpretive summary table that can be used to assist with the comparison of PSI subtests in terms of the cognitive capacities that may be involved in the performance of test items. Appendix B.19 provides a summary of the interpretations associated with behaviors observed during administration of the PSI subtests that can be used to enhance hypothesis testing about what cognitive capacities are, or are not, being used to perform subtests.

Meaningful interpretation of PSI subtest comparisons should include the determination of whether a statistically significant difference exists between the scores earned on the subtests being compared. Use a rounded value of 3 scaled score points to signify a statistically significant difference for any of the comparisons of the Working Memory subtests (see Appendix B.20).

When PSI subtest scores vary greatly and/or when the examiner observes behaviors that suggest that secondary cognitive capacities are influencing task performance, subtest cluster analysis may be helpful in identifying specific strengths and weaknesses in the use of various cognitive capacities. Appendix B.21 provides a worksheet to aid in the interpretation of Processing Speed scaled score comparisons. Appendix C.1 provides a case study example that includes the use of the interpretive worksheet and illustrates the application of the item and cognitive capacities levels in the interpretations of Processing Speed task performance.

LEARNING DISABILITY ASSESSMENT AND THE WAIS-IV

The long history of the controversies regarding exactly what constitutes a learning disability and whether intellectual assessments are relevant to the identification and classification of individuals with learning disabilities has been most recently summarized by Fletcher, Lyon, Fuchs, and Barnes (2007) and Flanagan, Kaufman, Kaufman, and Lichtenberger (2008). Much of the controversy appears to stem more from confusions about operational definitions of terms such as *intelligence, ability, process, reading, writing,* and *mathematics* than from actual evidence that does, or does not, link cognitive capacities with learning disabilities. When interpretation of cognitive capacities remains at the global composite level, is referred to as intelligence, and is operationally defined as the Full Scale IQ, it should come as no surprise that many researchers have found little or no relationship between this overgeneralized summation of cognitive capacities and specific skill-related learning disabilities (Fletcher et al., 2007). Consistent with the rest of this chapter, this section focuses on a neuropsychologically oriented interpretation of the WAIS-IV at the clinical cluster, subtest, item, and cognitive capacity levels and attempts to show how information obtained from the WAIS-IV can be useful in the assessment of examinees thought to have a learning disability. To accomplish this goal, it is essential that a more specific set of operational definitions, such as those presented in Rapid Reference 6.6, be used when discussing the issue of learning disabilities.

CONSTRAINTS ON LEARNING AND PRODUCTION

The concepts presented in Rapid Reference 6.6 can be used to construct a model of learning and production such as that shown in Appendix B.22 for reading, Appendix B.23 for written expression, Appendix B.24 for math, and Appendix B.25 for listening and oral expression. Some cognitive capacities act as constraints on learning; that is, the amount of learning that takes place will be limited by the amount of the capacity that is available for use.

Constraints on learning that result from the presence of process deficits are most likely to impact the acquisition of basic level reading, writing, math, and oral communication skills. In the case of reading (Appendix B.22), phonological, orthographic, or oral-motor process deficits will make it difficult for a person to develop the reading skills of sight word recognition, word decoding, and fluency (rapid rate of reading). Development of these basic skills can also be impacted by executive function deficits that make it difficult to coordinate the use of the various processes involved in skill acquisition. Deficits in the ability to reason with verbal information, to use language to comprehend meaning, or to grasp the visuospatial implications of what is read will constrain the acquisition of the more complex reading comprehension skills. Reading comprehension can also be constrained by inadequate access to, or availability of, working memory resources; difficulty with accessing, or lack of development of, various knowledge lexicons; executive function difficulties with the coordination of the use of multiple capacities during the reading process; and difficulties with the cueing and directing of mental resources needed for sustained attention to, and active engagement with, what is being read. In a manner similar to that described here for reading and illustrated in Appendixes B.23–B.25, cognitive capacities act as constraints on both basic and complex skill development in writing, mathematics, and oral communication.

Most models of learning disability, including those used to craft the definitions that appear in public law (Individuals with Disabilities Education Improvement Act of 2004) and professional practice references (American Psychiatric Association, 2000), posit an absence of ability constraints on learning (i.e., the ability to reason, to use language, and to grasp visuospatial relations is not interfering with learning, but deficits in cognitive capacities other than abilities are contributing to problems with the acquisition of reading, writing, math, and oral communication skills).

An important goal of assessment with the WAIS-IV in cases where learning disabilities are suspected is to help identify cognitive capacities that are, or are not, likely to be constraining learning and/or production. The questions that clinicians using the WAIS-IV need to ask are:

• Do WAIS-IV results reflect the presence or the absence of ability constraints that would impact learning to read, write, calculate, and orally communicate?
• Do WAIS-IV results reflect the presence or the absence of process deficits or deficits in the use of cognitive capacities other than abilities that would impact learning to read, write, calculate, and orally communicate?

In order to answer these questions, the clinician must know what specific abilities could act as constraints on academic skills acquisition and where in the WAIS-IV they are assessed. Likewise, the clinician must know what specific processes and cognitive capacities other than abilities could act as constraints on academic skills and where in the WAIS-IV they are assessed.

Knowledge of cognitive capacities and their potentially constraining effects does not come from the FSIQ or even from each of the four Index scores of the WAIS-IV. As shown in Appendix B.1 and discussed throughout this chapter, the WAIS-IV Index scores each represent the possible use of an amalgam of various processes, abilities, skills, and lexicons, only some of which would act as constraints on learning to communicate orally, read, write, or calculate and solve math problems. If the WAIS-IV is to be used to provide indicators of cognitive capacity constraints on learning, the accurate identification and description of these constraints will occur through interpretation at the subtest cluster, subtest item, and cognitive capacity levels. Appendixes B.26–B.29 offer guidelines for how the WAIS-IV can be used to indicate the presence or absence of cognitive capacity constraints.

CONCEPTIONS OF LEARNING DISABILITY

Using the concepts just introduced, a learning disability can be operationally defined in two different ways.

Ability-Achievement Discrepancy Conception of Learning Disability

The first definition is more consistent with the original conception of a learning disability in that it reflects a discrepancy between levels of abilities and levels of achievement. The ability-achievement model represented here differs from the traditional conception in the consideration of the effects of other cognitive capacities on learning and in what the term *achievement* represents. The model, as shown in Figure 6.2, defines a learning disability as a condition wherein:

1. There is an absence of any specific ability constraints that would interfere with learning in a specific academic skill domain (i.e., at least average levels of abilities known to act as constraints on learning of that skill).
2. There is a presence of
   a. One or more processing deficits (i.e., there is a deficit in the engagement of one or more basic processes in conjunction with the necessary lexicons and the necessary executive function capacities) and/or
   b. Memory capacity deficits (especially working memory deficits).

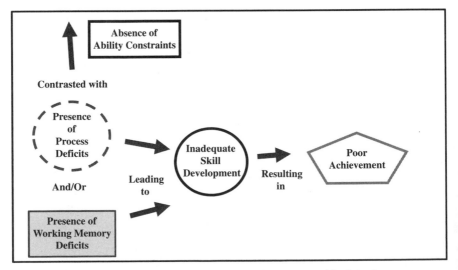

Figure 6.2. Modified Ability-Achievement Discrepancy Model of Learning Disability

3. The processing and/or working memory deficits have a negative impact on basic skill development and acquisition (i.e., basic skills have not been acquired or are being acquired at a very slow rate).
4. The lack of basic skill development may be preventing, disrupting, or slowing the development of complex skills.
5. The lack of basic skill development is reflected in poor performance on measures of achievement.

Note that the ability constraints referred to in this model are skill specific (i.e, they refer only to those abilities that act as constraints on the specific academic skill domain). For example, reasoning with verbal information would be a direct constraint on the development of more complex reading and writing skills, but reasoning with nonverbal visual information would not be a direct constraint on reading and writing skills. The need for identifying direct ability constraints nullifies the use of the WAIS-IV Full Scale IQ and the Perceptual Reasoning Index standard scores as indicators of ability. Even use of the Verbal Comprehension Index score is somewhat problematic since the VCI is composed of subtests that assess retrieval of long-term storage (Vocabulary and Information) much more than reasoning with verbal information (Similarities). The best indicators of reasoning ability constraints related to the development of reading skills would be the Similarities and Comprehension subtest scores (provided item- and cognitive capacity–level analysis confirmed that both of these tasks were assessing the use of reasoning ability).

An additional ability constraint on reading skill development would be the ability to understand language. Although the VCI could be used in this case as an indicator of the absence of a language constraint, the Comprehension, Information, and Arithmetic subtests are the best indicators of the ability to comprehend language, followed by the Similarities and Vocabulary subtests. A composite of these five subtests, with the greatest weight placed on the first three mentioned, would be a better indicator of receptive language ability than the VCI. Thus, the elements of the WAIS-IV that could be used most reasonably as indicators of ability constraints on applying reading skills are found at the subtest cluster level rather than the index level.

Appendixes B.26–B.29 offer guidelines for using information from the WAIS-IV to identify ability constraints and/or deficits in basic process and/or memory capacity use. Figure 6.2 shows how patterns of scores from the WAIS-IV and WIAT-II could be used in the identification of learning disabilities in reading.

ABILITY AND ACHIEVEMENT DEFICIT MODEL OF LEARNING DISABILITY

An alternate model for identifying a learning disability has emerged more recently. This newer model is based on the consistency of ability constraints and academic skill deficits (i.e., in the presence of ability constraints a person has difficulty learning new skills and achieving, regardless of whether process deficits are, or are not, present). Although now referred to as a model of learning disability, this conception traditionally has been referred to as the "slow learner" model, or in cases where the impairment of abilities such as reasoning is severe, as mental retardation.

The model, as shown in Figure 6.3, defines a learning disability as a condition wherein:

1. There is a presence of one or more specific ability constraints that would interfere with learning in a specific academic skill domain (i.e., below-average levels of abilities known to act as constraints on learning of that skill).
2. The ability constraints have a negative impact on basic, complex, and content domain skill development and acquisition (i.e., basic skills have not been acquired or are being acquired at a very slow rate).

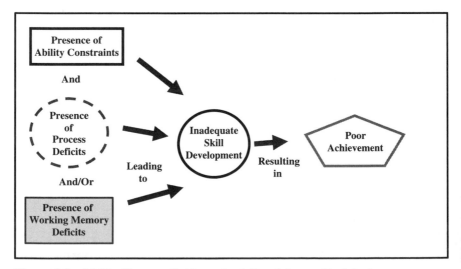

Figure 6.3. Ability-Process-Achievement Consistency Model of Learning Disability

3. The lack of basic, complex, and content domain skill development is reflected in poor performance on measures of achievement.

An example of this model for reading disability would involve poor reasoning and/or language abilities as reflected in low VCI scores or, more accurately, in low performance on the reasoning with verbal information and/or receptive language clusters mentioned in the first model above combined with low scores on measures of reading skill.

REPORTING WAIS-IV RESULTS IN AN INTEGRATED REPORT FORMAT

Examiners interested in organizing their reports to reflect a neuropsychologically oriented approach to interpretation can use the case study in Appendix C as a model for structuring the various sections. The report format used in the case study has some notable features that clinicians may find very helpful in communicating results clearly to clients of various backgrounds. These include:

1. Front-loading the summary sections of the report. This makes it easier for the clients to get the "big picture" quickly without having to wade through details that may or may not make sense to them.
2. When constructing reports for minors, provide a recommendations section that is broken down into three subsections:
   a. What the child can do for himself or herself
   b. What the parents can do for the child
   c. What school staff can do for the child
3. Address classification issues in a separate section appropriately labeled to reflect the fact that administrative classifications are not always consistent with the clinical information presented in your report; while administrative classifications and the specific professional addressing the client's needs may vary from state to state or by other geographical or administrative demarcations, your clinical impressions do not. For example, the reading problems that you identify in your report and what needs to be done to address those reading problems will not change from one state to another, although the school staff responsible for doing what needs to be done for the child might change from one state to another along with the classification label. It is essential that clinical findings remain independent from, but related to, the administrative issues of a case. This point applies to clinician's using the *Diagnostic and Statistical Manual* diagnostic categories as much as it does to professionals

in school systems, especially in today's health care environment where diagnoses often are required for reimbursement for services much more than for guiding the development of an intervention plan.

4. Provide interpretive details in an appendix to the report. The amount of detail offered can depend on the nature of the case.

5. Organize interpretation of the WAIS-IV and other cognitive testing by the cognitive capacities assessed rather than by the tests administered. This enables a coherent picture of findings to emerge across assessment methods and allows interpretation to be focused effectively at the cluster, subtest, item, and cognitive capacity levels consistent with the interpretive framework provided in this chapter.

≋ Rapid Reference 6.6

Operational Definitions for Understanding the Relationship between Cognition and Learning

"Cognitive capacities" can be operationally defined as the general class of patterns of neural activation within various regions of the neocortex that are involved in the production of perception, thought, action, and the cognitive dimension of emotion. Cognitive capacities can be differentiated into separate conceptual categories: basic processing, processing, processing speed, abilities, lexicons, skills, strategies, executive functions, memory capacities, learning, and achievement.

Basic Processes

• "Basic processes" are narrow-band cognitive capacities responsible for organization of input; they are responsible for the creation of basic mental representations.

• Basic processes enable and support learning and production.

• Basic process deficits obstruct learning and production but often can be bypassed or compensated for at least to some degree because of their narrow (i.e., relatively restricted) range of operation.

• In some instances, the effects of process deficits can be significantly reduced if the deficits are addressed during early developmental stages with a good intervention program (e.g., phonemic awareness training for young children). In these cases, the process deficit may have been due more to underutilization of intact neural networks than to the presence of damaged neural connections. In the case of underutilization, instruction increases the frequency and effectiveness of use of the process.

• It is possible that basic process deficits resulting from damage to neural networks can be remediated through early childhood intervention as well.

- Severe basic process deficits can result in learning disabilities involving slowed and/ or inconsistent learning and production.
- Basic processes include:
  - Auditory perception
  - Auditory discrimination
  - Auditory attention
  - Visual perception
  - Visual discrimination
  - Visual attention
  - Kinesthetic perception
  - Kinesthetic discrimination
  - Kinesthetic attention

Processing

"Processing" refers to neural activity involving the coordinated use of one or more basic processes often in conjunction with the accessing of lexicons (described below) under the direction of executive functions (described below).

Processing Speed

"Processing speed" is the speed with which one or more basic processes can be coordinated and applied, often in conjunction with the accessing of lexicons under the direction of executive functions.

Abilities

- "Abilities" are broad-band cognitive capacities that operate on mental representations initially formed through the use of basic processes.
- Abilities enable extended formulation and use of mental representations during learning and production.
- Ability deficits constrain learning and production; the degree of deficit places an upper limit on the quality (i.e., depth and complexity) of the learning and production; compensatory or bypass strategies typically are not very effective in countering ability deficits because of the broad range of influence of these more complex cognitive capacities.
- Severe ability deficits result in cognitive impairments that greatly constrain learning and production (e.g., severe language impairment, severe visuospatial impairment, mental retardation).
- Abilities include:
  - Reasoning abilities
  - Language abilities
  - Visual and visuospatial abilities

(continued)

Lexicons

"Lexicons" are stored knowledge bases from which information can be retrieved and used to inform learning or production. Lexicons can range from very basic, narrow forms of knowledge (e.g., the separate phonemes of the English language; how light strikes objects and creates shadows) to very complex forms of knowledge that vary greatly in depth and breadth (how to factor a polynomial; how to put a car engine [specific make and model] together; classical music influences on the early development of rock and roll).

Skills (Basic, Complex, Content specific)

- "Skills" are what are taught and learned through formal educational experiences. The term *skill* can be used in a temporal sense to represent what is being learned at the present time or to represent what was learned in the past or what will be learned in the future. Skills are a subclass of lexicons that specify the content of instructional lessons. Skills can be further delineated by content as basic, complex, or content domain.
- The term *basic skills* refers to the skills that form the foundation for all other skill areas. The four broad basic skill domains include:
  a. Oral communication
  b. Reading
  c. Writing
  d. Mathematics
- Each of these broad skill domains consists of many subdomains or subskills:
  - Basic reading skills include sight word recognition, phonological awareness, word decoding, and rapid word recognition.
  - Basic writing skills include graphomotor letter, number, and word formation and copying; word spelling; written sentence structure and written sentence formation; and rapid text production.
  - Basic mathematics skills include computation procedures, basic quantity problem solutions, and rapid application of computation procedures.
  - Basic oral communication skills include reflective listening, diction and projection of voice, prosody, and rapid speech production.
- Basic skills are the focus of instruction and learning in early elementary school. Basic skill learning represents the building of a set of general lexicons that will enable the application of oral communication, reading, writing, and mathematics to a wide range of subject content areas and to the learning of more complex skills. Skill building is an intermediate state between the immediate experiencing of new information and retrieval of information from an established lexicon; an established skill forms its own lexicon. "Automaticity" refers to the speed and ease with which basic skill lexicons can be accessed, retrieved and applied.
- Basic skill learning and use relies heavily on the use of basic processes under the direction of multiple executive functions. Basic skill learning and use, therefore, is most likely to be disrupted when process deficits are present.

- "Complex skills" are oral communication, reading, writing, and mathematics skills that enable a person to take the mental representations formed through the use of basic skills, add additional layers of representation, and manipulate all the information to produce relatively complex levels of meaning. The four complex skills include:
  a. Extended listening and/or speaking for meaning
  b. Reading comprehension
  c. Extended written text generation
  d. Applied mathematics problem solving

- Complex skills make use of the skill foundations built through basic skill learning and use. Complex skill development and use involves the application of one or more basic skills integrated with the use of one or more abilities and the accessing of one or more lexicons, all under the direction of multiple executive functions. For example, the skill of complex reading comprehension requires the application of the basic skills of word recognition and/or decoding and reading rate to form in the mind an accurate basic representation of the information that was on the page. The more complex the grammatic structure of the material that was read, the greater the need for involvement of specific language abilities to enable meaningful representation at a deeper level. If the material read relates to a specific topic, lexicons representing that person's knowledge of the topic will need to be accessed along with language ability to provide a context for what was read. If the ideas represented by the words are complex, reasoning abilities will need to be engaged to obtain the highest level of meaning possible from the material. The application of these skills, lexicons, and abilities requires extensive use of executive functions to coordinate the multitasking that must take place during such complex reading comprehension. In addition to the use of multiple basic skills, lexicons, and abilities, application of complex skills very often requires the direction and use of working memory capacities (described below).

- Complex skills are the focus of instruction and learning in the upper elementary grades. The development and use of complex skills can be disrupted by inadequate development and use of basic skills (resulting from the effects of process deficits or lack of direct instruction), by insufficient storage of information in lexicons, by constraints imposed by inadequate or underdeveloped abilities, by constraints imposed by inadequate or underutilized working memory capacity, and/or by constraints imposed by inadequate or underutilized executive functions.

- The term *content domain skills* refers to skills that are developed in specific subject domains and subdomains, such as the domain of science and the subdomains of biology, chemistry, and physics. Although basic and complex skills may be involved in learning in these content domains, the skills that are the focus of learning involve the building of lexicons related to the specific area of knowledge. The link between learning and lexicon building in these content areas is apparent in the language used to denote course and learning objectives. Educators speak of increasing a student's knowledge of biology rather than increasing or building a student's biology skills. Despite the emphasis on specific content knowledge storage, other lexicons that are acquired, such as how to use laboratory equipment, are more readily perceived as skills.

(continued)

Strategies

- "Strategies" are learned and stored or newly generated routines that can be applied to increase the efficiency of the use of abilities, processes, and/or skills.
- Strategies are ways to chain together in a specific order a combination of one or more executive function cues, basic processes, abilities, skills, and retrieval from lexicons to enhance learning and production.
- Strategy development, storage, and use are cued by executive functions or by an external mediating source, such as a teacher or parent.

Executive Functions

- "Executive functions" are a unique category of mental capacity delineated by their directive role. Executive functions cue and direct the use of other mental capacities and coordinate multitasking efforts.
- Executive functions can be used to guide all aspects of mental activity. They are not the processes, abilities, lexicons, skills, strategies, or memory states but rather orchestrate the use of all of these other mental capacities.

Memory Capacities or Memory States (Initial Registration, Manipulation, Retrieval)

- "Memory" represents a category of cognitive capacities that are distinct from processes, abilities, lexicons, skills, strategies, and executive functions.
- Memory represents a temporal state of mind; that is, memory is the essential mental manifestation of time and space; memory states provide the temporal and spatial contexts—a time signature—for all perception, emotion, cognition, and action.
- Memory capacities/states share some characteristics with abilities in that they are broad-band and constrain learning and production.
- Memory capacities/states share some characteristics with basic processes in that while weak states/poor capacity can obstruct learning and production, they often can be bypassed or compensated for at least to some degree.
- Memory capacities/states include:
  - Initial registration of information in the immediate moment; the experience of "now"
  - Retrieval from long-term storage; going back in time to recall previous "immediate" moments
  - Holding and manipulating information in mind; extending the immediate moment into the future, projecting possible immediate moments into the future, or creating scenarios for future immediate moments
- Lack of memory capacity can greatly obstruct learning.
- Poor initial registration constrains how much information can be represented in mind at one time.
- Poor retrieval capacity limits access to lexicons.

- Poor working memory capacity constrains how much information can be held in mind, how long that information can be held, and the extent to which the information being held in mind can be manipulated to enable extended states of learning, problem solving, and production.

Learning

"Learning" is the process of building new lexicons through the use of basic processes, basic and complex skills, and strategies along with the accessing of lexicons and the application of abilities. Learning can occur on a continuum from being mediated extensively by others to being self-mediated. The greater the self-mediation, the greater the demand for executive function involvement in the learning process.

Achievement

"Achievement" is the end result (the product) of the use of basic processes, basic and complex skills and strategies, accessing of lexicons, and application of abilities to a contextually meaningful task.

It is important to note that the boundaries of these categories are somewhat amorphous and changeable. At least theoretically, processes, abilities, and executive functions can be taught and learned, thereby becoming skills. Skills can be stored and retrieved and applied in the immediate moment, making them lexicons. The interrelated and overlapping nature of the category definitions, however, should not deter clinicians from making the important distinctions represented by each of these cognitive capacity categories.

🐟 TEST YOURSELF 🐟

....

1. **The focus of a neuropsychological approach to WAIS-IV interpretation is on**
   (a) *how* examinees perform the items of each WAIS-IV subtest, *rather than* the scores they earn on each of those subtests.
   (b) *how* examinees perform the items of each WAIS-IV subtest *in addition to* the scores they earn on each of those subtests.
   (c) the lowest scores in an examinee's profile.

2. **A neuropsychologically based WAIS-IV interpretation deemphasizes global scores and focuses mainly on the subtests, items, and cognitive capacities. TRUE or FALSE?**

3. **The interpretive validity and the reliability of the assessment process are increased by illuminating the unexplained sources of variability in performance that may be inferred from careful clinical observations of how examinees are using cognitive capacities. TRUE or FALSE?**

4. **VCI–PRI discrepancies in isolation are effective indexes of cerebral dysfunction. TRUE or FALSE?**

5. A child with a learning disability in the area of reading may have deficits in which of the following areas?

(a) phonology.

(b) orthography.

(c) oral-motor processes.

(d) executive function.

(e) any of the above.

Answers 1. b; 2. True; 3. True; 4. False; 5. E.

Seven

CLINICAL APPLICATIONS II: AGE AND INTELLIGENCE ACROSS THE ADULT LIFE SPAN

R esearch on the relationships between aging and intelligence had its inception nearly 100 years ago in comparisons between adults and children (Kirkpatrick, 1903), and the topic has captivated researchers in theoretical and clinical disciplines for over half a century (Willoughby, 1927). Whether intelligence declines with increasing age has long been the subject of research and debate by experts in the field (Baltes & Schaie, 1976; Horn & Donaldson, 1976). The nature of the complex relationship between aging and changes in intellectual functioning is of prime concern to clinicians who test clients across a wide age span, inasmuch as proper WAIS-IV interpretation demands understanding of normal, or expected, differential fluctuations in a person's ability spectrum from late adolescence and young adulthood to old age. Distinguishing between normal and pathological development is often the essence of competent diagnosis in clinical and neuropsychological assessment.

Probably the most comprehensive and cleverly conceived set of studies has been the life's work of K. Warner Schaie (1994) in collaboration with numerous colleagues (e.g., Hertzog & Schaie, 1988). His results have transformed the preconceptions of professionals throughout the world regarding the inevitability of declines in mental functioning along the path to old age. In particular, Schaie's clever sequential combination of cross-sectional and longitudinal research designs has shown the importance of considering cohort (generational) effects when conducting research on aging. Further, Schaie's research program suggests that when declines in intelligence do occur with age, they do so at far later ages than was formerly believed. But Schaie consistently used the group-administered, speeded Primary Ability Tests (PMA; Thurstone & Thurstone, 1949), normed only through age 18. As valuable as his findings are, they cannot replace research results based directly on the WAIS-IV, its predecessors, and other intelligence tests for adults in helping clinicians understand the kinds of changes to anticipate during clinical and neuropsychological evaluations. Consequently, we focus on individually administered clinical tests of intelligence in this chapter, including a recent study of the WAIS-IV (Kaufman, 2009).

Analyses of previous Wechsler adult scales focused on Horn's (1989) expansion of the Cattell-Horn-Carroll (CHC) *Gf-Gc* theory, a natural fit for Wechsler's Verbal-Performance dichotomy. More recent analyses of the WAIS-III and WAIS-IV are rooted in CHC theory, which fits nicely with the organization of the subtests into four factor indexes. The main questions of interest are whether intelligence is maintained through old age or whether it declines; or whether some abilities maintain, and even increase, as we age, while other abilities decline, perhaps precipitously, across the life span.

DO COGNITIVE ABILITIES DECLINE WITH ADVANCING AGE? A CROSS-SECTIONAL APPROACH

To answer the crucial questions that pertain to the relationship between adults' IQs and the aging process, we have integrated the results of both cross-sectional and longitudinal investigations. These different types of studies are treated in the sections that follow, with emphases on the pros and cons of each style and on an integration of the findings from both kinds of empirical investigation. Brief descriptions of different types of aging studies are shown in Rapid Reference 7.1.

Cross-Sectional Investigations of Wechsler's Adult Scales

The existence of large-scale standardization data on Wechsler's scales has provided clinicians and researchers with an impressive body of Census-representative data on the intelligence of adult samples at a wide cross-section of chronological ages. However, inferring developmental changes from cross-sectional data is a risky business. Groups that differ in chronological age necessarily differ on other variables that may confound apparent age-related differences. A child born in 1940 had different educational and cultural opportunities from one born in 1970. When tested in 2007 as part of the WAIS-IV standardization sample, the former child was in the 65- to 69-year-old sample, while the latter individual was a member of the 35- to 44-year-old group. Differences in their test performance may be partially a function of their chronological ages during the 2000s and partially a function of the generational or cohort differences that characterized their respective periods of growth from childhood to adulthood. Cohort differences, even seemingly obvious

≋ Rapid Reference 7.1

Types of Aging-IQ Studies

- **Cross-sectional.** Comparison of the test performance of different age groups at the same point in time (e.g., the adults tested during the standardization of an intelligence test, such as ages 20–24, 45–54, and 65–69).

- **Longitudinal.** Comparison of the test performance of the same groups of individuals at different points in time, for example, when they are 25, 40, and 70 years.

- **Longitudinal using independent samples.** Comparison of the test performance of different samples of adults at different points in time, where the samples are from the same cohort (year of birth). For example, comparing the test scores of adults born between 1971 and 1975 when the WAIS-III was standardized in 1995 (at ages 20–24) and when the WAIS-IV was standardized 12 years later (at ages 32–36) in 2007. The samples are independent, but they are comparable on important variables, such as gender and socioeconomic status, and they are from the same cohort.

- **Cross-sequential.** A blend of cross-sectional and longitudinal research popularized by Schaie (1983b) in his Seattle Longitudinal Study. Cross-sectional age groups are tested at a single point in time, and many of these adults are also followed up years later.

ones like the greater number of years of education enjoyed by adults born more recently, were mostly ignored by clinicians and researchers through the 1950s and even the 1960s. Wechsler (1958) himself inferred an early and rapid decline in intelligence by uncritically accepting changing mean scores across the adult age range as evidence of a developmental trend: "What is definitely established is . . . that the abilities by which intelligence is measured do in fact decline with age; and . . . that this decline is systematic and after age 30 more or less linear" (p. 142). Although such interpretations were prevalent a half century ago, researchers on aging are now thoroughly familiar with the impact of cultural change and cohort differences, including educational attainment, on apparent declines in intelligence with age, and have greatly revised the pessimism of Wechsler's conclusions.

Indeed, when examining mean IQ test performance for different age groups across the adult life span, the results can be sobering. Table 7.1 presents mean IQs for various adult age groups on the W-B I, WAIS, WAIS-R, and WAIS-III. Whereas mean IQs on Wechsler's scales are necessarily set at 100 for each age group, the data in Table 7.1 base the mean IQs on common yardsticks (see note to Table 7.1) to permit age-by-age comparisons. Overall, the striking apparent age-related changes in intelligence from the 20s through old age, especially in Performance IQ (P-IQ), are so overwhelming (and depressing, if taken at face value) that it is easy to understand why Wechsler and others concluded that the path to old age is paved by a steady, unrelenting loss of intellectual function. Also intriguing in Table 7.1 is the incredible similarity in the cross-sectional data for the four adult Wechsler batteries that were normed in 1937, 1953, 1978, and 1995. In particular, the mean P-IQs (relative to a common yardstick) for the WAIS, WAIS-R, and WAIS-III are uncannily similar for each age group between 20–24 and 65–69, never differing by more than 3 IQ points. Considering that each corresponding age group in the WAIS, WAIS-R, and WAIS-III samples was subject to huge generation or cohort effects, the similarities in the cross-sectional data seem quite remarkable. (Forty-year-olds in the WAIS sample, for example, were born just before World War I, while their age contemporaries in the WAIS-R sample were born just prior to World War II, and those in the WAIS-III sample were born just after the Korean War). Though the mean scores for adults over age 70 in the three standardization samples differ more substantially than the means for ages 20–69, the accumulated data over a 40-year span (1955–1995) indicate that adults who are in their 70s also earn mean Performance IQs in the 70s.

However, the data for separate age groups cannot be interpreted in isolation. Table 7.2 presents educational attainment data for the WAIS, WAIS-R, and WAIS-III standardization samples, showing the percent in each sample with 0–8 years of schooling and the percent with 13 or more years of schooling (at least 1 year of college). This table reveals the folly of interpreting changes in mean scores from age to age as evidence of developmental change. Good standardization samples match the U.S. Census proportions on key background variables, and some variables, such as educational attainment, differ widely from age group to age group. With each passing decade, an increasing proportion of adults stay longer in elementary and high school, and more and more people attend college. Consequently, the younger-adult age groups will tend to be relatively more educated than the older-adult age groups. Similarly, any age group tested in the early 1950s on the WAIS will be considerably less educated than that same age group tested in the late 1970s on the WAIS-R, which, in turn, will be less educated than its age mates in the mid-1990s WAIS-III sample (see Table 7.2).

When Tables 7.1 and 7.2 are viewed together, it is evident that the lower IQs earned by older adults, relative to younger adults mirror the older adults' lower level of education. For example, for the WAIS-R sample, 45% of adults ages 70–74 had less than 9 years of schooling, compared to only 5% of those ages 25–34; for the WAIS-III sample, the corresponding percentages were 16 and 4 (see

Table 7.1. Mean IQs across the Adult Life Span on the W-B I, WAIS, WAIS-R, and WAIS-III for Designated Cross-Sectional Age Groups

Age Group	Verbal IQ				Performance IQ				Full Scale IQ			
	W-B I	WAIS	WAIS-R	WAIS-III	W-B I	WAIS	WAIS-R	WAIS-III	W-B I	WAIS	WAIS-R	WAIS-III
20–24	100	98	96	97	105	102	101	99	103	100	97	98
25–34	100	100	98	100	100	100	99	99	103	100	97	100
35–44	98	99	94	102	93	95	93	97	95	98	94	100
45–54	95	97	95	104	86	89	89	92	91	93	92	99
55–64	93	95	93	99	83	84	84	86	88	90	88	94
65–69	—	91	91	98	—	80	79	81	—	86	84	90
70–74	—	85	90	97	—	72	76	79	—	78	82	89
75+	—	80	87	93	—	66	72	74	—	73	78	83

Note. W-B I data for ages 55–64 are based only on adults ages 55–59. All sums of scaled scores for all scales are based on scaled-score norms for ages 20–34. Mean IQs for the W-B I, WAIS, WAIS-R are based on the IQ conversion table for ages 25–34; mean IQs for the WAIS-III are based on the IQ conversion table for all ages. WAIS data for ages 65–69 through 75+ are for the stratified elderly sample tested by Doppelt and Wallace (1955). WAIS-R data for ages 20–74 are from Kaufman, Reynolds, and McLean (1989). WAIS-R data for ages 75+ are for the stratified elderly sample tested by Ryan, Paolo, and Brungardt (1990), and were kindly provided by Ryan (personal communication, March, 1998) for 115 individuals ages 75–89. WAIS-III data for all ages are from Kaufman (2001). Standardization data of the Wechsler Adult Intelligence Scale: Third Edition. Copyright © 1997 by The Psychological Corporation. Used by permission. All rights reserved.

Table 7.2. Percents of the Standardization Samples of the WAIS, WAIS-R, and WAIS-III with 0–8 and 13+ Years of Schooling, by Age Group

	0–8 Years of Schooling			13+ Years of Schooling		
Age Group	WAIS (1953)	WAIS-R (1978)	WAIS-III (1995)	WAIS (1953)	WAIS-R (1978)	WAIS-III (1995)
20–24	22	4	4	20	40	51
25–34	25	5	4	20	44	51
35–44	40	10	4	18	32	56
45–54	54	16	8	14	26	49
55–64	66	28	14	11	19	36
65–69	—	38	18	—	19	30
70–74	—	45	16	—	16	29
75–79	—	—	19	—	—	29
80–89	—	—	32	—	—	22

Note: Data are from the manuals for the WAIS (Wechsler, 1955), WAIS-R (Wechsler, 1981), and WAIS-III (Psychological Corporation, 1997).

Table 7.2). Maybe the entire "decline" in mean IQs across the adult life span is illusory, reflecting nothing more than the higher level of educational attainment for the younger age groups relative to the older ones. That possibility was explored with WAIS standardization data about 40 years ago in the United States (Birren & Morrison, 1961) and about 30 years ago in Puerto Rico (Green, 1969). Interestingly, these two cross-sectional studies gave different answers to the question. However, subsequent studies with the WAIS-R (Kaufman, Reynolds, & McLean, 1989), WAIS-III (Kaufman, 2000a, 2001), and other tests (e.g., Kaufman & Horn, 1996), have provided more definitive data for answering the aging-IQ questions via cross-sectional methodology.

CAUTION

Don't be fooled by declines in mean standard scores with increasing age in cross-sectional samples of adults. Remember that older samples tend to be less educated than younger samples. The declines in mean scores may be due to differences in *education* more so than *age*.

WAIS Studies

Birren and Morrison (1961) controlled education level statistically by parceling out years of education from the correlation of each WAIS subtest with chronological age, using standardization data for 933 Caucasian males and females aged 25–64. Scores on each of the 11 subtests initially correlated negatively with age, with all Performance subtests correlating more negatively ($-.28$ to $-.46$) than did the Verbal tasks ($-.02$ to $-.19$). After statistically removing the influence of educational attainment from the correlations, four of the six Verbal subtests produced *positive* correlations. On the Performance Scale, the removal of education level did not erase the negative correlations between IQ and age. Some of the partial correlations were strongly negative, even after the statistical removal of education, notably Digit Symbol ($-.38$) and Picture Arrangement ($-.27$). Birren and Morrison (1961) gave evidence that the decrease in verbal (but not nonverbal) abilities with age was an artifact of education level.

Green approached the problem differently in his analysis of the Puerto Rican standardization data for the Spanish WAIS. He added and subtracted subjects from each of four age groups (25–29, 35–39, 45–49, and 55–64) until they were balanced on educational attainment. Each sample comprised about 135 adults (total = 539), with mean years of education ranging from 7.6 to 7.8. Green's equated samples demonstrated an increase in Verbal sums of scaled scores and only a slight decrement in Performance scores. He concluded from his analyses that "[i]ntelligence as measured by the WAIS does not decline in the Puerto Rican population before about age 65. The same conclusion is almost certainly true for the United States" (Green, 1969, p. 626). Despite Birren and Morrison's (1961) contradictory finding with the WAIS Performance Scale, Green's assertions were accepted by writers such as Labouvie-Vief (1985), who praised his work as the "most careful study thus far of education-related effects on patterns of intellectual aging" (p. 515). However, Green's data had limited generalizability because his groups averaged fewer than 8 years of education, with 43% having between 0 and 5 years of formal education. It made no sense to generalize these findings to more educated samples of adults.

WAIS-R Studies

Kaufman et al. (1989) analyzed the WAIS-R standardization data for ages 20–74 years ($N = 1,480$), a sample that was carefully stratified on gender, race (Caucasian–non-Caucasian), geographic region, educational attainment, and occupation. The researchers used both ANOVA and multiple regression

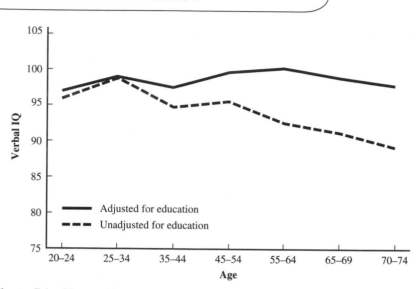

Figure 7.1. Change in WAIS-R Verbal IQ across the 20–74-Year Age Range, Both with and without a Control for Education; IQs were Based on Norms for Ages 25–34

Source: Data are from Kaufman et al. (1989).

methodology, controlled for educational attainment, and based norms for all adults on a reference group of 20-to 34-year-olds. The ANOVA results are depicted in Figures 7.1 and 7.2, which show the mean WAIS-R Verbal IQs (V-IQs) and P-IQs, respectively, for seven adult age groups, both with and without a control for education. After controlling for education, the decline in Verbal IQ disappeared, but the decline in P-IQ remained substantial. On the Verbal Scale, the peak IQ (99.8) occurred for ages 55–64 after equating for education level; even at ages 70–74, the weighted mean V-IQ was nearly 98. In contrast, education-controlled means in P-IQ dipped below 90 at ages 55–64 and below 80 for 70–74-year-olds.

The multiple regression analysis determined the percent of variance accounted for by age alone and by education alone differed substantially for WAIS-R V-IQ and P-IQ, as summarized in Rapid Reference 7.2. As shown, age alone accounted for 28 % of the variance in P-IQ but only 3% in V-IQ—and that 3% is dwarfed by the 45% value for education alone.

All of these results are consistent with Birren and Morrison's (1961) WAIS data but not Green's (1969). These WAIS-R findings give support to Botwinick's (1977) classic intellectual aging pattern, which posits maintenance of

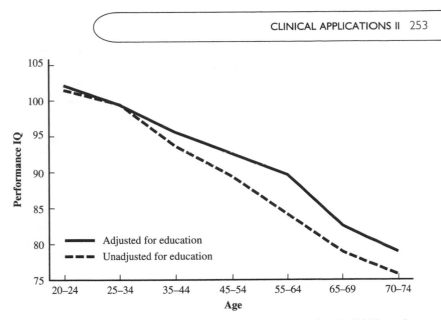

Figure 7.2. Change in WAIS-R Performance IQ across the 20–74-Year Age Range, Both with and without a Control for Education; IQs Were Based on Norms for Ages 25–34

Source: Data are from Kaufman et al. (1989).

performance on nontimed tasks versus decline on timed tasks. The results also support Horn's (1989) interpretation of the classic pattern from the *Gf-Gc* theory of intelligence and from the more contemporary CHC theory (McGrew, 2005): Crystallized abilities remain stable through old age ("maintained" abilities) while fluid abilities (and other abilities such as visualization and speed) decline steadily and rapidly, starting in young adulthood ("vulnerable" abilities).

≡ *Rapid Reference 7.2*
....

Relative Contributions of Age and Education to WAIS-R IQs for Ages 20–74

Percent of Variance

Accounted for by	Age Alone	Education Alone
Verbal IQ	3	45
Performance IQ	28	33

Source: Data are from Kaufman et al. (1989).

The distinction in the adult development literature of fluid versus crystallized abilities was first made by Horn and Cattell (1966, 1967) in the 1960s. Fluid intelligence (Gf), manifested by the ability to solve novel problems, is presumed to increase with neurological maturation during childhood and adolescence and to decline throughout adulthood concomitantly with neurological degeneration. In contrast, crystallized intelligence (Gc, knowledge and skills dependent on education and experience) is expected to continue to increase during one's life, reflecting cultural assimilation.

The results of these cross-sectional analyses also accord well with Baltes's (1997) two-component (mechanics–pragmatics) life span theory of intellectual development. The pragmatics component resembles crystallized ability and is believed by Baltes to be maintained across the adult life span. The array of abilities that make up P-IQ corresponds closely to the broad "mechanics" component of cognition in Baltes's theory. In contrast to the pragmatics component, the mechanics component is vulnerable to the effects of normal aging and subsumes reasoning, spatial orientation, memory, and perceptual speed (Baltes, Staudinger, & Lindenberger, 1999). This computer analogy refers to the mind's hardware (mechanics) and software (cognitive pragmatics).

WAIS-III Studies of IQs and Factor Indexes

Kaufman (2000a, 2001) analyzed data from the WAIS-III standardization sample of 2,450 individuals at ages 16–89 years (basing all IQs on a reference group ages 20–34). The increase in age range to almost 90 years made it clear that V-IQ is a maintained ability and remains robust well into the 70s, but it is decidedly *not* maintained through very old age (Kaufman, 2001). After age 79, Gc declined precipitously. In fact, V-IQ decreased just as much as P-IQ for people in their 80s, even with education controlled, as shown in Table 7.3 and depicted pictorially in Figure 7.3. P-IQ peaked in young adulthood, then declined steadily and dramatically across the age range (especially at ages 45 and above); education-adjusted mean P-IQs were below 80 for adults in their 80s.

The age-related patterns of mean V-IQ and P-IQ for the WAIS-III resemble closely the results for the WAIS and WAIS-R. Furthermore, similar patterns—including the decline in both Gc and Gf for the elderly—have been demonstrated for the Canadian WAIS-III (Lee, Gorsuch, Saklofske, & Patterson, 2008) and for a variety of batteries, such as the Kaufman tests (e.g., Kaufman & Horn, 1996; Kaufman, Johnson, & Liu, 2008) and the Woodcock-Johnson (McGrew, Woodcock, & Ford, 2006). And these differences are worldwide,

Table 7.3. Education Level and Mean WAIS-III IQs of Each Standardization Age Group (Mean IQs Adjusted for Educational Attainment Are in Parentheses)

Age Group	Percent High School Dropout	Percent College Graduate	Mean WAIS-III IQs		
			Verbal	Performance	Full Scale
20–24	15.0	11.0	97.1 (98.1)	99.4 (100.0)	98.5 (99.4)
25–29	14.0	23.5	99.4 (99.5)	99.9 (99.9)	99.9 (100.0)
30–34	14.0	23.0	101.0 (100.9)	98.4 (98.4)	99.9 (99.9)
35–44	9.5	29.0	102.4 (101.2)	97.3 (96.3)	100.1 (98.9)
45–54	17.5	25.0	103.8 (104.4)	91.8 (92.4)	99.0 (99.7)
55–64	26.5	18.0	98.9 (102.1)	86.3 (89.0)	93.8 (97.0)
65–69	32.0	14.0	98.2 (102.9)	80.9 (84.8)	90.2 (94.9)
70–74	31.5	14.0	97.1 (101.1)	78.8 (82.3)	88.7 (92.8)
75–79	34.0	13.5	96.0 (100.3)	76.2 (79.7)	86.8 (91.1)
80–84	49.3	11.3	91.4 (97.8)	72.9 (78.2)	81.0 (87.4)
85–89	50.0	12.0	89.8 (96.3)	69.9 (75.9)	78.6 (85.3)

Note: Percentages of high school dropouts and college graduates for the WAIS-III standardization sample are from The Psychological Corporation (1997, Table 2.6). Mean WAIS-III IQs for all ages are based on sums of scaled scores for ages 20–34. Education-adjusted IQs (values in parentheses) are adjusted to match the educational attainment of adults ages 25–34. Mean IQs and adjusted IQs are from Kaufman (2001). Standardization data of the Wechsler Adult Intelligence Scale: Third Edition. Copyright © 1997 by The Psychological Corporation. Used by permission. All rights reserved.

emerging in Germany (Baltes & Lindenberger, 1997; Melchers, Schürmann, & Scholten, 2006), the Netherlands (Mulder, Dekker, & Dekker, 2004), the United Kingdom (Rabbitt, 1993), and a diversity of other countries as well. These findings are entirely consistent with Horn's (1989) and Baltes's (1997) notions of maintained and vulnerable abilities during the adult aging process.

The familiar P-IQ decline is especially noteworthy in view of the exclusion from the standardization sample of many low-functioning adults. Eligibility requirements for the WAIS-III standardization samples were strict to ensure that the norms are truly based on "normal" people. For example, the sample excluded adults with sensory impairments (e.g., hearing loss) or coordination

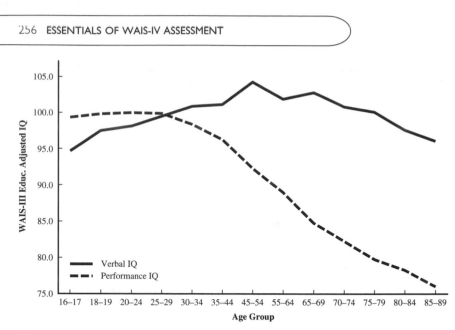

Figure 7.3. Mean "Reference Group" (Ages 20–34) WAIS-III Verbal and Performance IQs, by Age, for Adults Ages 16–17 to 85–89 Years, Adjusted for Educational Attainment (Values for Ages 16–19 are Unadjusted)

Source: Data are from Kaufman (2001).

problems; those who took antidepressants, or antianxiety medication, or had more than occasional drinks of alcohol; and those with known or possible neurological impairment (including people who went to a professional for memory problems) (Psychological Corporation, 1997). The liberal exclusion of adults with suspected or known thinking impairments has an upside for aging research: Any observed declines in cognitive function are likely to be "real" declines, not artifacts of the inclusion of many cognitively impaired adults in the older age groups.

The four WAIS-III Indexes display patterns of age-by-age education-adjusted means that are decidedly different from each other (see Figure 7.4), with each one corresponding to different CHC abilities: VCI = *Gc*, POI = *Gf/Gv*, WMI = (*Gsm*), PSI = *Gs* (Kaufman, 2000a). The four separate indexes foster better understanding of age changes in cognitive ability than is possible from the factorially complex V-IQ and P-IQ. As pictured, VCI (*Gc*) was maintained throughout most of the adult life span, whereas the other three Indexes were vulnerable to the effects of aging, consistent with predictions from theory (Horn & Hofer, 1992).

WMI (*Gsm*) was the least vulnerable of the three and PSI (*Gs*) was the most vulnerable, considerably more so than POI (now called PRI on the WAIS-IV).

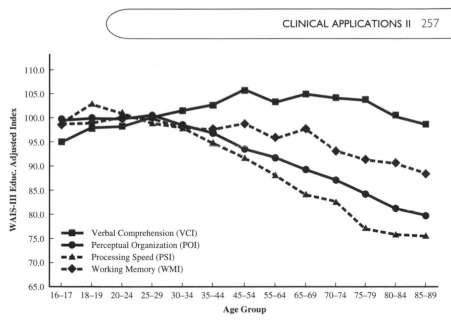

Figure 7.4. Mean "Reference Group" Indexes on the Four WAIS-III Factors for Adults Ages 16–17 to 85–89 Years, Adjusted for Educational Attainment (Values for Ages 16–19 Are Unadjusted)

Source: Data are from Kaufman (2001).

In Lee et al.'s (2008) study of the Canadian WAIS-III, the PSI was also considerably more vulnerable than the POI. Note in Figure 7.4 that the graphs for the U.S. sample converge prior to age 30 before following their distinct paths toward old age. Even at ages 45–54, when VCI peaks (mean = 105.9), the means for POI and PSI are already 12 to 14 points lower. In contrast, the V- and P-IQs are complex. WAIS-III IQs correspond to unitary constructs from CHC theory, with P-IQ basically composed of two major components, nonverbal and spatial problem solving (*Gf* and *Gv*) and speed of problem solving (*Gs*). Examination of the age-by-age changes on POI and PSI (Figure 7.4), in conjunction with age patterns on P-IQ (Figure 7.3), offers insight into the nature of the well-known dramatic decline on P-IQ during adulthood with increasing age. Interestingly, the age-by-age pattern of education-adjusted mean IQs on the WAIS-III P-IQ is closely similar to the pattern of Indexes on the POI during its period of early stability (ages 16–44), but they overlap with the pattern for PSI during the period of rapid decline with increasing age (especially ages 55–74). The rapid decline of P-IQ with increasing age, therefore, is likely more a function of the highly speeded nature of some of its subtests than of their *Gf* or *Gv* component.

Cautions Associated with Cross-Sectional Investigations

Despite the careful experimental designs of the cross-sectional investigations conducted on large standardization samples, this type of study, which uses educational attainment as the only control, has a few built-in problems that must be considered:

- *Equating on educational attainment.* Matarazzo (1972) wondered whether years of formal education is "a variable with identical meaning across generations" (p. 115), and his concern has merit (Kaufman, 2001). Equating groups that differ substantially in age on educational attainment is an inexact science and must be considered as approximate correction for a changing society's inequalities. For example, schooling beyond high school, commonplace now, was enjoyed primarily by the elite in the 1950s. The meaning of "attended college" or "graduated college," therefore, is not a constant across generations; analogously "high school dropout" has a far greater stigma for younger than for older adults in the 2000s than a half century earlier.
- *Cohort effects.* Regardless of consistencies across studies, instruments, and generations, inferences from cross-sectional studies about developmental (ontogenetic) changes in intelligence are speculative at best. When education level is controlled, one aspect of cohort differences is eliminated to some extent. However, numerous other variables associated with growing up at a given period of time are unknown, unmeasured, or unquantifiable. Yet such variables as motivation level, historical events, social customs and mores, the availability of television and personal computers, constant updates on current events, child-rearing techniques, nutrition, the quality and extent of prenatal care and knowledge, and the impact of mass media will affect apparent age-related changes in scores on mental tests.
- *Time-of-measurement effects.* In addition, time-of-measurement effects interact with performance on intelligence tests. Real changes either in mental ability or in test-taking ability could affect how every group of adults (regardless of cohort) performs on a given test. These sweeping cultural changes could affect individuals aging from 25 to 35 in much the same way that they affect others who age from 40 to 50 during the same time frame. For example, in the 1920s, tests were uncommon for everyone, and scores would likely be relatively low for a person of 20 or 40 or 60 tested on unfamiliar items like verbal or figure analogies; people of the same ages tested in the 1960s or 1970s would likely score relatively higher on these same tests because such tests had become a familiar part of U.S. culture. This type of control for cultural change was used by Owens (1966) in his

landmark longitudinal study (discussed in the next section). Not all cultural changes relate to test-taking ability, however, as Flynn (1987) made abundantly clear by showing that whole societies have increased in IQ at a steady rate and continue to do so (Flynn, 2007). Indeed, Flynn has probably come as close as anyone to quantifying these cultural or time-of-measurement effects by using cross-sectional data to show systematic IQ gains across generations. That these gains differ dramatically from country to country stresses their cultural-environmental origin. Because differences in IQs earned in different eras by individuals of the same age reflect both time-of-measurement and cohort effects, Kausler (1982, 1991) prefers to use the term *time lag* to denote these changes in intelligence scores.

• *Internal and external validity.* By controlling for education level in various cross-sectional studies, the investigators have conducted studies high in *internal validity*, permitting both the identification of causative factors and the generalization of these causative factors to other similar samples (Kausler, 1982, 1991). The downside of the high internal validity of the cross-sectional aging-IQ studies is low *external validity*, meaning poor generalization of the "adjusted" age differences to the population at large. In fact, in the real world, older individuals are less well educated than younger adults. Consequently, the actual, unadjusted values come closer to describing true differences in the mean scores of different age groups. With the WAIS-III, though, even the unadjusted values may not validly describe true differences in the population at large in view of the unusual number of exclusionary criteria applied to the selection of the standardization sample (criteria that were used for the WAIS-IV as well). However, unadjusted values cannot be used to infer causality of the differences, and they have limited value for implying developmental change. Because of the very nature of the limitations of cross-sectional research, it is essential that any conclusions about aging and IQ be buttressed by the results of longitudinal research.

DOES IQ DECLINE WITH ADVANCING AGE? A LONGITUDINAL APPROACH

Inferring developmental trends from cross-sectional data is risky, partly because of cohort effects and partly because of the failure to test the same individuals more than once. Longitudinal investigations of aging and intelligence solve both problems by holding constant cohort variance (each individual is, in effect, his or her own cohort control) and by observing developmental changes within the same person over time. In fact, longitudinal investigations of the Wechsler-Bellevue (Berkowitz & Green, 1963) and WAIS (Eisdorfer & Wilkie, 1973) have generally shown little age-related decline in ability, far less than has been revealed by cross-sectional analysis. Unfortunately, longitudinal studies of intelligence and aging are beset by problems different from the disadvantages of cross-sectional studies but nonetheless potentially debilitating.

In the next sections we discuss some of these pitfalls, especially in studies using Wechsler's adult tests. We then treat two of the best-designed and most influential longitudinal studies: Owens's (1953, 1966) Army Alpha investigation of adults tested originally in 1919 as Iowa State freshmen; and Schaie's (1983b) 21-year Seattle longitudinal study with the PMA that utilized sophisticated cohort-sequential methodology. We conclude this section with Kaufman's (1990, 2001, 2009) longitudinal investigations of Wechsler's scales (including the WAIS-IV) using independent samples.

Problems in Investigating Aging Longitudinally

Ideally, the alleged early and rapid decline in P-IQ—and other measures of Gf, Gv, and Gs—with increasing age could be verified or disproved by the continual retesting of the same individuals. Some excellent longitudinal investigations using the WAIS, or a portion of it, have been conducted (Schaie, 1983a), but the results have not answered the question. The main difficulty lies less with the research studies than with the WAIS itself.

Practice Effects and Progressive Error on Wechsler's Performance Scale

With all tests, the effects of using the same instrument repeatedly introduce unwanted error into the analysis, a confounding known as progressive error (Kausler, 1982, 1991). This type of error is important for any studies involving Wechsler's Performance Scale because of the nature of the items and the enormous practice effect associated with them. Adults who are retested on the WAIS or WAIS-R after about a month will gain only about 2 to 3 points on the Verbal Scale versus 8 to 9 points on the Performance Scale (Kaufman, 1994b). This profound practice effect on P-IQ extends for at least 4 months (Catron & Thompson, 1979). On the WAIS-III, the P-IQ practice effect was about 8 points for ages 16–54 years, 6 points for ages 55–74, and 4 points for 75–89 (Kaufman & Lichtenberger, 1999). For the WAIS-IV, practice effects for the PRI and PSI are about 4 to 5 points (Psychological Corporation, 2008, Table 4.5; see Rapid Reference 8.15).

Even if the practice effect dissipates after a year or two, this variable still looms large in longitudinal investigations. The practice effect may not impede the results of the first retest in a longitudinal study, but it surely will not disappear by the third, fourth, or fifth retest and may be quite large even for elderly individuals. In the first of two Duke longitudinal studies, comprising an initial sample of 267 adult volunteers between the ages of 59 and 94 from North Carolina, 42 "survivors" were tested up to 11 times on the WAIS between 1955 and 1976. The second Duke study involved a four-subtest WAIS short form administered to an initial sample of 502 adults, ages 46–70, from the same general area; the 331 survivors were given the short form four times between 1970 and 1976 (Siegler, 1983). The two Duke longitudinal investigations were exceptional studies, uncovering fascinating relationships among the cognitive, memory, personality, sensory, and motor variables administered repeatedly to the subjects. But it is impossible to make inferences about changes in P-IQ over time for samples that are so overexposed to the five Performance subtests.

These tasks are new the first time they are given, but the novelty wears off quickly. When people are retested after a few weeks or months, they seem to remember only a few specific nonverbal items; even if they recall many of the puzzles or pictures, no feedback for correctness is given either during or after the test. What people do tend to remember is the type of items they faced and the kinds of strategies and attack modes that seemed successful. When individuals are tested repeatedly on Wechsler's Performance tasks, they no longer measure the kind of intelligence that thrives on novel problem-solving tasks with visual-spatial stimuli, and it becomes questionable whether they are effective measures of intelligence the third or fourth time around.

Failure to account for the effects of practice when evaluating changes in intelligence with increasing age challenges the findings of a variety of longitudinal studies, such as the excellent Bonn longitudinal study that tested two cohorts of adults (ages 60–65 and 70–75) on the Hamburg-Wechsler (German WAIS) as many as six times between 1965 and 1980 (Schmitz-Scherzer & Thomae, 1983). The younger cohort performed fairly constantly on the Verbal Scale over the 12-year period, while the older cohort dropped significantly as they aged from the 70s to mid-80s. On the Performance Scale, both cohorts either maintained or improved their scores between the 1965 and 1972 testings (four administrations) before showing a sizable drop in 1976–1977. The Verbal changes are consistent with the results of other investigations. The Performance changes imply virtually no loss of function for the older cohort between the ages of about 72 to 79, and small gains in Performance scores for the younger cohort between ages 62 and 66. However, such interpretations of Performance abilities are fanciful, based on the problem of progressive error.

It should be noted, however, that not everyone interprets practice effects as an artifact. Flynn (1998) suggested that "decline after age 50 for fluid intelligence is less than we once believed; the elderly show a surprisingly robust gain from practice effects, which may not boost our estimate of their IQs but does show a lively ability to learn in old age" (p. 106).

Selective Attrition

A second major problem of longitudinal aging research is selective attrition of subjects. When using volunteer subjects, "at all ages in adulthood, those who do not volunteer initially and those who do not show up in retesting tend to be lower scorers on ability tests than those who do cooperate" (Horn & Donaldson, 1976, p. 717). The first Duke longitudinal study was especially valuable in generating research to help quantify this effect. Analysis of data from the first 10 years of the study (Eisdorfer & Wilkie, 1973) revealed "a substantial loss of _S_s, with the lowest IQ group sustaining a loss of 72 percent; the middle IQ group, a loss of 51.4 percent; and the high IQ group, a loss of only 36.8 percent" (p. 28). Even more dramatic evidence of the selective attrition factor came from Siegler and Botwinick's (1979) analysis of data from all 11 "waves" of the first Duke study. Individuals who continue to be retested over time are more intelligent than those who drop out early. Among 60- to 74-year-olds in the Duke study, the relationship is nearly linear between IQ at the initial assessment and the number of times the person returned to be tested, as depicted in Figure 7.5. Of the 179 individuals tested on the WAIS in the first wave, only 18 returned to be tested at all 10 subsequent assessments. Overall, the 60- to 74-year-olds who came once or twice earned mean sums of scaled scores on the Full Scale of 85 to 90, compared to means of close to 110 for those who came to be tested 10 or all 11 times. Obviously some of the elderly subjects died or were too ill to be tested, but many simply chose not to be retested for whatever reason; the selective attrition factor occurs as well for younger adults, although the effect seems to increase with age (Horn & Donaldson, 1976).

Hence, generalizations from longitudinal studies must be made quite cautiously because of the considerable selective attrition factor. At the very least, it is essential for researchers to partly compensate for this problem by following Eisdorfer and Wilkie's (1973) advice: "The appropriate analysis of longitudinal data should use data only from the same subjects across time, whether _S_s are lost secondary to death or drop out" (p. 28).

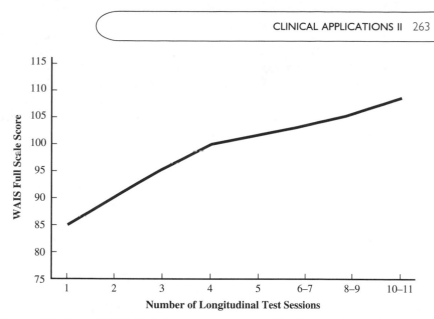

Figure 7.5. Mean WAIS Full Scale Scores earned by Adults (Aged 60–74 years) on the Initial Assessment, Shown as a Function of the Number of Longitudinal Test Sessions in Which the Subjects Participated

Source: Data are from Siegler & Botwinick (1979).

TWO GROUNDBREAKING LONGITUDINAL INVESTIGATIONS OF IQ AND AGING

We now turn to two of the most influential and well-designed investigations of IQ and aging: Owens's Iowa State Army Alpha Study and Schaie's 21-Year Seattle Cohort-Sequential Study.

Iowa State Army Alpha Study

Owens (1953) administered the Army Alpha test in 1950 to 127 men, age 50, who had previously been among 363 Iowa State University freshmen who had been administered the same test in 1919 at age 19. These initial results "were important in stimulating a critical reexamination of the inevitability of intellectual decline in adulthood" (Schaie, 1983c, pp. 13, 15); the study "ushered in an era of new ideas in research on adult development and intelligence" (Cunningham & Owens, 1983, p. 20). The study continued in 1961 when 96 of these men were tested once more, at age 61 (Owens, 1966); Owens also tested a random sample of 19-year-old Iowa State freshmen on the Army Alpha in 1961–1962 to permit a time-lag comparison, thereby estimating the impact of cultural change on the obtained test scores. The Army Alpha, one of Wechsler's primary sources for selecting

Verbal subtests, comprises eight tasks, including tests of Information, Practical Judgment (Comprehension), Arithmetical Problems, and Synonyms–Antonyms (Vocabulary).

Results of the Iowa State longitudinal investigation for the 96 men tested three times on the Army Alpha reveal improvement in Verbal and Total scores between ages 19 and 50, followed by a slight decline from age 50 to 61. Reasoning displayed small increments from one testing occasion to the next, while Numerical evidenced the opposite profile. The most noteworthy changes were the improvement in Verbal scores from age 19 to 50 and the sudden decrease in Numerical scores from age 50 to 61. Owens then corrected the data for cultural change, based on the better performance (especially in Reasoning) by the 19-year-olds tested in the early 1960s compared to the 19-year-olds tested in 1919. Following this time-lag correction, what had appeared to be slight increments in Reasoning were actually steady decrements in perform-ance. Despite the correction for cultural change, Verbal Factor scores contin-ued to show gains between ages 19 and 61; numerical scores showed a loss across this same age span, but a smaller loss than was observed for Reasoning.

Cunningham and Owens's (1983) overall conclusion from the Iowa State study: "The results suggest peak performance and the beginning of declines of overall intellectual functioning roughly in the decade of the 50s for this elite sample. The losses appear to be small and probably are not of much practical significance until at least age 60" (p. 34). The decline in Reasoning is especially noteworthy because the tasks that measured it included a heavy dose of *Gc*. Although Reasoning was interpreted by Owens (1996) as a measure of fluid ability, the scale was defined by *verbal* tests such as Analogies (e.g., *fear* is to *anticipation* as *regret* is to?).

Schaie's 21-Year Seattle Cohort-Sequential Study

Schaie's (1983b) sophisticated combination of cross-sectional and longitudinal designs was predicated on the contributions of three variables to the scores obtained by adults on intelligence tests: chronological age, cohort (year of birth), and time of measurement (the year the tests were administered). He conducted four independent cross-sectional studies with the group-administered PMA test in 1956 ($N = 500$, ages 25–67); in 1963 ($N = 996$, ages 25–74); in 1970 ($N = 705$, ages 25–81); and in 1977 ($N = 609$, ages 25–81). All samples comprised approximately equal numbers of men and women, with the groups tending to be relatively well educated for the 1960s and 1970s (about 50% with one or more years of college).

Coinciding with the last three cross-sectional studies were longitudinal investigations ranging from 7 to 21 years. Three 7-year studies included the retesting of as many subjects as possible from the 1956 ($N = 303$), 1963 ($N = 420$), and 1970 ($N = 340$) cross-sectional investigations. In addition, Schaie conducted two 14-year studies and one with a 21-year interval between testings. These rigorous cross-sequential, cohort-sequential, and longitudinal designs permitted Schaie and his colleagues to identify cohort and time-of-measurement variation in an attempt to understand "true" intelligence differences due to aging.

His 1968 investigation (Schaie & Strother, 1968) was widely publicized in popular texts at that time (Cronbach, 1970; Matarazzo, 1972) because it showed dramatic differences in the aging-IQ growth curve from cross-sectional data alone (his 1956 sample of 500) and the curve obtained from his first 7-year longitudinal study. The cross-sectional data for ages 20–70 revealed the same type of plunge in abilities with age that characterized the WAIS, WAIS-R, or WAIS-III Full Scale IQ prior to an adjustment for education (see Table 7.1); the mix of cross-sectional and longitudinal data for the smaller sample (a sequential analysis) demonstrated growth curves showing virtually no decline across the age range. These findings applied to the separate components of the PMA, whether measuring verbal ability or skills akin to Wechsler's Performance subtests, especially tasks like Block Design with a strong Gv component (Space, a measure of spatial orientation).

These data became the subject of controversy, with Horn and Donaldson (1976) and Botwinick (1977), for example, citing variables such as selective attrition to account for the apparent maintenance of both fluid and crystallized abilities through old age. Regardless of the arguments and counterarguments (Baltes & Schaie, 1976; Horn & Donaldson, 1977), the early Schaie data show both consistency and inconsistency with Wechsler cross-sectional results. In Schaie's findings, scores on the nonverbal, Gf/Gv tasks (Space and a measure of inductive reasoning) clearly began a decline much later in life than was found for Wechsler's Performance subtests. Yet, like the Wechsler findings, scores on Space and Reasoning peaked far earlier than the more crystallized PMA subtests (Verbal Meaning and Number).

Subsequent analyses (e.g., Schaie & Hertzog, 1983) revealed Schaie's responsiveness to the criticisms and the concomitant efforts by his research team to refine their methodologies and analyses. Schaie and Hertzog (1983) admitted that their original cross-sequential design was ill suited to evaluate age changes; further, the results of the two 14-year longitudinal studies they reported indicated earlier declines in intelligence (i.e., prior to age 60) than were previously observed in Schaie's laboratory. The best integration of the numerous analyses appears in Schaie's (1983b) thorough treatment of the 21-year Seattle project. Figure 7.6 depicts Schaie's results for Verbal Meaning (Gc), Space (Gv), and Reasoning (Gf).

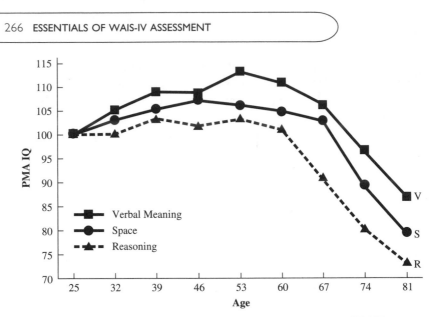

Figure 7.6. Performance on Three Primary Mental Abilities (PMA) Subtests at Ages 25–81 as a Proportion of Age 25 Performance (Set at 100), Corrected for Time of Measurement, Attrition, and Cohort Efforts

Source: From Schaie (Schaie, 1983b, Table 4.18), based on 7-year longitudinal data.

Gc increases steadily until age 53, with a notable decline occurring between ages 67 and 74. *Gv* peaks earlier than *Gc* (age 46) but has its first sizable decline between the same 67- to 74-year period. Nonetheless, its decline is more dramatic than that of the *Gc* test. *Gf* declines substantially after age 60, plunging to 73 by age 81.

These results are basically in agreement with the differential results for the measures of maintained abilities (*Gc, Gq*) versus vulnerable abilities (*Gf, Gv, Gs, Gsm*) described by Horn (1989) and observed on Wechsler's scales. Unlike the popular interpretations of the initial findings reported by Schaie and his colleagues, intelligence does indeed decline with chronological age, and that decline becomes precipitous in old age. However, the use of longitudinal data juxtaposed with cross-sectional results on the PMA suggest that the decrements may not begin until relatively late in life.

LONGITUDINAL INVESTIGATIONS OF WECHSLER'S SCALES USING INDEPENDENT SAMPLES

The key question that remains unanswered from cross-sectional investigations of Wechsler's series of scales is whether the rapid decline on Wechsler's *Gf, Gv, Gs,* and working memory scales, even after control for years of formal education, is an artifact of other unknown cohort variables. Another important question is whether the substantial decline in *Gf* in old age is an artifact of uncontrolled cohort variables. While writing the aging chapter in the first edition of this book, Kaufman (1990, chapter 7) was troubled by the lack of an answer to the important question about P-IQ decline and conducted a study that was inspired by the methodologies of Owens (1966), Schaie (1983b), and Parker (1986), and by Kausler's (1982) detailed discussions of the pros and cons of diverse methodologies. Parker (1986) had the clever idea of examining the comparative performance of year-of-birth cohorts by equating the standardization samples of the Wechsler-Bellevue I, WAIS, and WAIS-R. However, he focused solely on the Full Scale IQ, when it was the separate V-IQs and P-IQs that were of the greatest theoretical interest for analyses of aging. But Parker's article made Kaufman (1990) realize the analogy between the WAIS and WAIS-R standardization samples and Schaie's repeated cross-sectional analyses between 1956 and 1977.

For example, people born in 1905 would have been 48 years old in 1953, when the WAIS was standardized, and 73 years old when the WAIS-R was standardized 25 years later in 1978. By comparing the performance of people born in the same year (i.e., from the same cohort) at two points in time, it was suddenly possible to easily conduct a longitudinal study of aging and IQ with cohort effects controlled.

The use of independent samples, or "cohort substitution" (Kausler, 1982), if they are truly comparable and random, makes it "possible to compute age-change estimates that are controlled for the effects of testing and experimental mortality" (Schaie, 1983b, p. 106). Kaufman (1990) used the cohort substitution method with the WAIS and WAIS-R normative samples serving as the data source, primarily to determine whether longitudinal data would replicate the cross-sectional finding of rapidly declining P-IQ across most of the life span. He then used the same method with the WAIS-R and WAIS-III standardization samples (Kaufman, 2001), and recently did it again with the WAIS-III and WAIS-IV samples (Kaufman, 2009) thanks to the kindness of Pearson Assessments for making the pertinent WAIS-IV data available. In the WAIS-IV study, it was possible to compare age changes on the four Indexes between 1995, when the WAIS-III was standardized, and 2007, when the WAIS-IV was normed.

Longitudinal Studies of WAIS, WAIS-R, and WAIS-III Verbal and Performance IQs

The WAIS and WAIS-R standardization samples are quite similar to each other, each matching relevant Census data on numerous key variables. They differ in that the data were collected 25 years apart, in approximately 1953 and 1978. Thus, several cohorts in the WAIS sample are also represented in the WAIS-R sample. For example, adults born in the 1909–1913 cohort were tested at ages 40–44 in 1953 (on the WAIS) and again at ages 65–69 in 1978 (on the WAIS-R). To the degree that the two samples are comparable, a comparison of the test performance of 40- to 44-year-olds on the WAIS with that of the 65- to 69-year-olds 25 years later on the WAIS-R represents a longitudinal comparison of adults from the same cohort.

There are four adult cohorts represented within both the WAIS and WAIS-R standardization samples, as shown in Table 7.4. In essence, Kaufman (1990) followed each of four cohorts longitudinally from 1953 to 1978 to see if individuals born in the same era gained or lost IQ points over the course of a generation. Before making the comparisons, he had to perform some essential empirical steps:

- Verify that the independent samples were extremely well matched and comparable within each of the four cohorts on the important variables of gender, ethnicity, geographic region, and educational attainment.
- Convert sums of scaled scores on the WAIS and WAIS-R to a common yardstick to permit age-by-age comparisons. (Kaufman chose to the norms for ages 25–34.)
- Control for the fact that different tests (WAIS versus WAIS-R) were administered at the two points in time. He added 6 to 6½ points to each WAIS-R IQ (the median IQ differences from 20 studies totaling over 1,300 subjects) (Kaufman, 1990, Table 3.13) to convert these IQs to WAIS IQs. These "corrections" to the WAIS-R IQs helped answer the crucial question: How many IQ points higher would adults have scored had they been administered the WAIS instead of the WAIS-R?

Table 7.4. The Four Adult Age Cohorts Represented in the WAIS and WAIS-R Standardization Samples

Cohort (Year of Birth)	Age in 1953 (WAIS Standardization)	Age in 1978 (WAIS-R Standardization)
1924–1933	20–29	45–54
1914–1923	30–39	55–64
1909–1913	40–44	65–69
1904–1908	45–49	70–74

Source: Data are from Kaufman (1990, 2001).

- Apply a time-lag correction to control for cultural change during the 25-year span, just as Owens (1966) did in his Iowa State study. Adjustment for cultural change requires a comparison of the IQs earned by each cohort in 1953 with the IQs earned by adults of the *same age* in 1978. The 1909–1913 cohort, for example, was 40–44 years old in 1953. This group was compared to adults aged 40–44 in 1978 to determine how cultural changes have affected test scores for this age group. Similar time-lag comparisons were conducted for each of the other three cohorts who, in 1953, were ages 20–29, 30–39, and 45–49. The analyses showed that cultural change affected each of the four cohorts about equally, producing about a 3-point IQ gain on the Verbal and Scale and about a 5-point gain on the Performance Scale, presumably due to some type of culture-related change between 1953 and 1978 that affected all adults who were between the ages of 20 and 49 in 1953. Kaufman (1990) adjusted the estimated WAIS IQs earned by each cohort in 1978 for these time-lag effects to remove the influence of cultural change.

Kaufman (2001) repeated this same procedure a decade later, using data from the WAIS-R and WAIS-III standardization samples. The methodology was virtually identical with only slight variations—for example, the reference group was based on ages 20–34 instead of 25–34. In this study, Kaufman examined changes on the V-IQ and P-IQ for seven cohorts over the 17-year span from 1978 to 1995. These cohorts, summarized in Table 7.5, range from individuals born between 1954 and 1958 (tested at age 22 and again at 39) to adults born between 1904 and 1908, who were 72 during the WAIS-R standardization and 89 when the WAIS-III was normed.

Table 7.5 presents the four age cohorts from the first study (WAIS/WAIS-R) alongside the seven cohorts from the second study. As shown, the four cohorts from the initial study were also in the follow-up study, so in actuality these four cohorts were tested at three different points in time, spanning a total of 42 years. For example, individuals born between 1909 and 1913 were tested on the WAIS at ages 40–44, on the WAIS-R at ages 65–69, and on the WAIS-III at ages 82–86.

The results of both longitudinal studies are summarized in Table 7.6 (changes in V-IQ over time) and Table 7.7 (changes in P-IQ over time). The changes in IQ shown in the tables have been adjusted for instrument (whether WAIS versus WAIS-R or WAIS-R versus WAIS-III) and time lag. The tables show the median age of each cohort at each point in time (1953, 1978, and 1995) and the number of IQ points that each cohort either increased or decreased as they got older. For

Table 7.5. Age Cohorts (Independent Samples) Tested on the WAIS in 1953, on the WAIS-R in 1978, and on the WAIS-III in 1995

Cohort (Year of Birth)	Age in1953 (WAIS)	Age in 1978 (WAIS-R)	Age in 1995 (WAIS-III)
1954–1958	—	**22** (20–24)	**39** (37–41)
1944–1953	—	**29.5** (25–34)	**46.5** (42–51)
1934–1943	—	**39.5** (35–44)	**56.5** (52–61)
1924–1933	**24.5** (20–29)	**49.5** (45–54)	**66.5** (62–71)
1914–1923	**34.5** (30–39)	**59.5** (55–64)	**76.5** (72–81)
1909–1913	**42** (40–44)	**67** (65–69)	**84** (82–86)
1904–1908	**47** (45–49)	**72** (70–74)	**89** (87–91)

Source: Data are from Kaufman (1990, 2001). Standardization data of the *Wechsler Adult Intelligence Scale: Third Edition* Copyright © 1997 by The Psychological Corporation. Used by permission. All rights reserved. "Wechsler Adult Intelligence Scale" and "WAIS" are trademarks, in the United States and/or other countries, of Pearson Education, Inc. or its affiliate(s).

Table 7.6. Adjusted Age Changes in Wechsler's Verbal IQ for Adult Cohorts (Independent Samples) Tested Two or Three Times between 1953 and 1995

Cohort (Year of Birth)	Median Age			Adjusted Verbal IQ Change		
	WAIS 1953	WAIS-R 1978	WAIS-III 1995	1953–1978 (25-yr interval)	1978–1995 (17-yr interval)	1953–1995 (42-yr interval)
1954–1958	—	22	39	—	+6.3	—
1944–1953	—	29.5	46.5	—	+3.2	—
1934–1943	—	39.5	56.5	—	−1.0	—
1924–1933	24.5	49.5	66.5	−1.5	−5.6	−7.1
1914–1923	34.5	59.5	76.5	−3.3	−2.9	−6.2
1909–1913	42	67	84	−3.9	−7.4	−11.3
1904–1908	47	72	89	−5.5	−8.3	−13.8

Note: Changes in Wechsler's Verbal IQ are adjusted for instrument and time lag.

Source: Data are from Kaufman (1990, 2001). Standardization data of the *Wechsler Adult Intelligence Scale: Third Edition* Copyright © 1997 by The Psychological Corporation. Used by permission. All rights reserved. "Wechsler Adult Intelligence Scale" and "WAIS" are trademarks, in the United States and/or other countries, of Pearson Education, Inc. or its affiliate(s).

example, consider again the 1909–1913 cohort. As shown in Table 7.7, their mean Verbal IQs decreased by 3.9 points between ages 42 and 67 and decreased by 7.4 points between ages 67 and 84. Overall, the decrease over the 42-year span was 11.3 points.

Consider first the results of the 1990 study. The most striking finding in the data is the difference between the Verbal and Performance Scales. The mean Verbal IQs for the four cohorts (see Table 7.6) decreased by a few points over the 25-year span between 1953 and 1978—ranging from 1.5 points for the 1924–1933 cohort to 5.5 points for the oldest cohort (1904–1908). In contrast, the decreases in mean Performance IQs for same four cohorts (see Table 7.7) are huge, ranging from 11.6 to 13.5 IQ points (an average decrease of 12.6 points, or .84 standard deviations [SDs]). Substantial decreases in P-IQ occurred for each cohort, whether they advanced in age from 24.5 to 49.5 (on the average) or from 47 to 72.

The results of the WAIS-R/WAIS-III longitudinal study, also summarized in Tables 7.6 and 7.7, reinforce the findings from the first study and expand those findings by including more cohorts. The two youngest cohorts had higher mean

Table 7.7. Adjusted Age Changes in Wechsler's Performance IQ for Adult Cohorts (Independent Samples) Tested Two or Three Times between 1953 and 1995

Cohort (Year of Birth)	Median Age			Adjusted Performance IQ Change		
	WAIS 1953	WAIS-R 1978	WAIS-III 1995	1953–1978 (25-yr interval)	1978–1995 (17-yr interval)	1953–1995 (42-yr interval)
1954–1958	—	22	39	—	−2.1	—
1944–1953	—	29.5	46.5	—	−5.8	—
1934–1943	—	39.5	56.5	—	−9.3	—
1924–1933	24.5	49.5	66.5	−11.6	−10.9	−22.5
1914–1923	34.5	59.5	76.5	−12.5	−10.1	−22.6
1909–1913	42	67	84	−12.9	−9.2	−22.1
1904–1908	47	72	89	−13.5	−10.1	−23.6

Note: Changes in Wechsler's Performance IQ are adjusted for instrument and time lag.

Source: Data are from Kaufman (1990, 2001). Standardization data of the *Wechsler Adult Intelligence Scale: Third Edition* Copyright © 1997 by The Psychological Corporation. Used by permission. All rights reserved. "Wechsler Adult Intelligence Scale" and "WAIS" are trademarks, in the United States and/or other countries, of Pearson Education, Inc. or its affiliate(s).

V-IQs in their 40s than in their 20s. Otherwise, each cohort lost IQ points on each scale. The decreases in mean Verbal IQ are small in magnitude, except for the two oldest cohorts. By contrast, the Performance IQ decreases were substantial in magnitude, and similar in value, for the five oldest cohorts. Over the 17-year period, adults born before 1944 lost 10 points (±1) of Performance IQ, or about two-thirds of a SD, whether they were about 60, 70, 80, or 90 years of age in 1995.

When the changes in Performance IQ are examined for the four cohorts that were tested at all three points in time, spanning 42 years, the results are remarkable in their consistency from cohort to cohort (Table 7.7). Each cohort lost 22 to 23 points (mean = 22.7), or 1.5 SDs over that interval, whether they aged from about 25 to 65 or from about 45 to 85. The changes in 42 years on Verbal IQ are substantial for the two oldest cohorts, averaging 12.6 points (.84 SD). Taken together, the results of the two longitudinal investigations of independent samples support the maintenance of Verbal IQ, except for a loss of verbal skills for adults in their 80s, and the vulnerability of Performance IQ across the life span. These findings are entirely consistent with the cross-sectional analyses of Wechsler's scales, with or without a control for education.

LONGITUDINAL STUDY OF WAIS-III AND WAIS-IV FACTOR INDEXES

As soon as the WAIS-IV was published, Pearson Assessments kindly agreed to make the pertinent data available to permit Kaufman (2009) to continue his series of longitudinal investigations of independent samples. This analysis focused on the four indexes that had appeared on the WAIS-III alongside V-IQ and P-IQ, and that replaced those IQs on the WAIS-IV. Once again, Kaufman (2009) applied his familiar methodology to the 11 cohorts who were administered the WAIS-III and WAIS-IV during their respective standardizations (see Table 7.8). This time the interval was 12 years between the 1995–1996 standardization of the WAIS-III and the 2007–2008 standardization of the WAIS-IV. (The first WAIS-IV standardization case was received in March 2007, and the last case was received in April 2008; D. L. Coalson, personal communication, October 6, 2008.)

Two of the indexes comprised identical subtests on the WAIS-III and WAIS-IV (VCI and PSI) and two were modified. For WMI, Kaufman used the two-subtest WAIS-IV scale (Digit Span-Arithmetic) rather than the three-subtest WAIS-III scale, because Letter-Number Sequencing was not administered above age 69. The WAIS-III POI, renamed PRI on the WAIS-IV, overlapped on two subtests (Block Design and Matrix Reasoning). The third

Table 7.8.   11 Age Cohorts Tested on the WAIS-III in 1995 and on the WAIS-IV in 2007

Cohort (Year of birth)	Age in 1995 (WAIS-III)	Age in 2007 (WAIS-IV)
1978–1979	16–17	28–29
1976–1977	18–19	30–31
1971–1975	20–24	32–36
1966–1970	25–29	37–41
1961–1965	30–34	42–46
1951–1960	35–44	47–56
1941–1950	45–54	57–66
1931–1940	55–64	67–76
1926–1930	65–69	77–81
1921–1925	70–74	82–86
1916–1920	75–79	87–90

Source: Data are from Kaufman (2009). Analysis results from the *Wechsler Adult Intelligence Scale— Fourth Edition* (WAIS-IV). Copyright © 2008 by NCS Pearson, Inc. Reproduced with permission. All rights reserved. "Wechsler Adult Intelligence Scale" and "WAIS" are trademarks, in the United States and/or other countries, of Pearson Education, Inc. or its affiliate(s).

POI subtest was Picture Completion, which is supplemental on the WAIS-IV. Kaufman (2009) recomputed WAIS-IV PRI with Picture Completion instead of Visual Puzzles to ensure that the cohort changes in mean scores from the WAIS-III to WAIS-IV were based on the identical set of subtests. He then adjusted the cohort changes on the four indexes for instrument effects, using the mean differences obtained in the counterbalanced WAIS-III/WAIS-IV study of 240 adults reported in the *WAIS-IV Manual* (Psychological Corporation, 2008, Table 5.5). And, again, he adjusted the changes for time lag to determine age changes over time on the four indexes.

The results of this study, summarized in Table 7.9, are remarkably similar to the results of Kaufman's previous longitudinal studies, especially the WAIS-R/ WAIS-III comparisons. VCI and WMI displayed the same curvilinear pattern of increases in mean scores for the younger cohorts and decreases for the older cohorts that characterized V-IQ (Table 7.6). PRI and PSI dropped substantially for most cohorts, particularly for adults born between 1916 and 1960. Decreases

Table 7.9. 12-Year Changes in WAIS-III/WAIS-IV Factor Indexes for 11 Age Cohorts

Cohort (Year of Birth)	Median Age 1995	Median Age 2007	12-Year Change in Standard Score Point			
			VCI	PRI (POI)	WMI	PSI
1978–1979	16 ¹/₂	28 ¹/₂	+7.0	−1.2	+4.3	+2.2
1976–1977	18 ¹/₂	30 ¹/₂	+3.4	−1.4	+0.6	+2.7
1971–1975	22	34	+1.6	2.0	+0.4	−5.0
1966–1970	27	39	+1.0	−4.0	+1.2	−1.1
1961–1965	32	44	+1.5	−3.4	−1.9	−4.5
1951–1960	39 ¹/₂	51 ¹/₂	+2.4	−4.6	−3.0	−4.8
1941–1950	49 ¹/₂	61 ¹/₂	−0.8	−5.4	−3.4	−6.2
1931–1940	59 ¹/₂	71 ¹/₂	−3.2	−6.3	−3.5	−7.0
1926–1930	67	79	−5.0	−9.6	−4.8	−10.5
1921–1925	72	84	−6.4	−7.2	−7.2	−8.6
1916–1920	77	89	−8.8	−8.4	−8.3	−7.3

Source: Data are from Kaufman (2009). Analysis results from the *Wechsler Adult Intelligence Scale— Fourth Edition* (WAIS-IV). Copyright © 2008 by NCS Pearson, Inc. Reproduced with permission. All rights reserved. "Wechsler Adult Intelligence Scale" and "WAIS" are trademarks, in the United States and/or other countries, of Pearson Education, Inc. or its affiliate(s).

Note: All scaled scores are based on the norms for ages 20–34 years. All Indexes are based on WAIS-III norms for both WAIS-III and WAIS-IV (exception—WMI is based on WAIS-IV norms for both instruments because 2-subtest norms are not available for the WAIS-III). Twelve-year standard-score change is adjusted for Instrument Effects (WAIS-III versus WAIS-IV) and for Time Lag Effects (cultural change). VCI = Verbal Comprehension Index; PRI = Perceptual Reasoning Index; POI = Perceptual Organization Index (includes Picture Completion instead of Visual Puzzles); WMI = Working Memory Index; PSI = Processing Speed Index. PRI is composed of Block Design, Matrix Analogies, and Picture Completion to be comparable to WAIS-III POI.

in function were especially large for the four cohorts who were at least 70 years of age in 2007, with mean decrements in index scores averaging 8.0 for PRI and 8.4 points for PSI. Loss of cognitive function was also substantial on the VCI and WMI for the two cohorts who were at least 80 years of age (mean decreases of 7.6 and 7.8 points, respectively).

Technically, it is methodologically incorrect to construct age gradients from a combination of longitudinal and cross-sectional data: "the use of cross-sequential results to evaluate age changes [is] ill considered" (Schaie & Hertzog, 1983, p. 532). Nonetheless, we believe that the best way to show differences across the life span on the abilities that are measured by the four WAIS-IV Indexes is to do just that. In Figure 7.7 we present smoothed trend lines based on polynomial regression to represent the age gradients for each of the four Indexes. Data points are the two standard scores on each index for each cohort (i.e., the WAIS-III Index earned in 1995 and the WAIS-IV Index, adjusted for instrument effects). Hence, Figure 7.7 shows the polynomial curve of best fit for the 22 data points for each Index.

VCI (Gc) is a maintained ability for most of the adult life span, increasing into the 50s before declining substantially in old age. Both PRI (Gf/Gv) and PSI (Gs) are vulnerable across the entire age span, with Gs the most vulnerable ability of

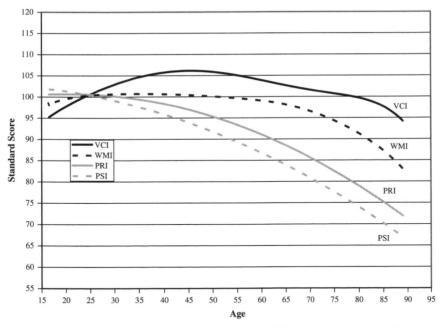

Figure 7.7. Age Gradients for the Four WAIS-IV Indexes Based on Mean Scores Earned by the 11 Cohorts when Tested in 1995 on the WAIS-III and in 2007 on the WAIS-IV

all. WMI (*Gs*) too is vulnerable to the aging process, but it is maintained longer than *Gs*, *Gv*, or *Gf* and is clearly less vulnerable than PRI and PSI. The age gradients for the four Indexes are extremely similar to the gradients of these same Indexes in the cross-sectional investigation of the WAIS-III (see Figure 7.4), and the aging curves for VCI and PRI mirror the cross-sectional age gradients for V-IQ and P-IQ, respectively (see Figure 7.3).

OVERVIEW OF THE WECHSLER LONGITUDINAL INVESTIGATIONS WITH INDEPENDENT SAMPLES

The three Wechsler cohort-substitution studies provide results that agree remarkably well with the cross-sectional data for Wechsler's adult scales and for other adult scales, such as the Kaufman Adolescent and Adult Intelligence Test (KAIT; Kaufman & Kaufman, 1993). Combining cross-sectional and longitudinal data suggests a loss of about 0.5 points per year in Performance IQ, or 5 points per decade, which is precisely Horn's (1985; Horn, Donaldson, & Engstrom, 1981) best estimate of the adult decline in fluid intelligence based on his reviews and results of numerous studies.

Taken together, the three cohort-substitution studies offer broad support to the developmental reality of a loss in nonverbal intellectual function (*Gf*, *Gv*, *Gs*) across virtually the entire adult life span; a loss in *Gsm*, especially working memory, as adults enter old age, and even a considerable loss in verbal function (primarily *Gc*) during the decade of the 80s. These meaningful declines on the WAIS-III and WAIS-IV, in particular, are dramatic in view of the systematic exclusion of so many potentially low-functioning adults from their normative samples. On the WAIS-IV, adults were excluded from the sample for many different reasons—for example, being diagnosed with a learning disorder or ADHD, currently taking medication that might impact test performance (e.g., some antidepressants), or previously diagnosed with substance dependence (Psychological Corporation, 2008, Table 3.1).

The consistency in the P-IQ, PRI, PSI, and WMI decrease with increasing age for U.S. men and women born during the first 80 years of the 20th century—from cross-sectional and longitudinal data on the WAIS, WAIS-R, WAIS-III, and WAIS-IV—is simply phenomenal.

INTERPRETATION OF COGNITIVE DECLINE: SPEED OR PROBLEM SOLVING

The accumulated cross-sectional and longitudinal data obtained on several versions of Wechsler's adult scales, including cross-sectional data on the Canadian

WAIS-III (Lee et al., 2008) and Kaufman tests (e.g., Kaufman & Horn, 1996; Kaufman et al., 2008) and longitudinal data on the Woodcock-Johnson (McArdle, Ferrer-Caja, Hamagami, & Woodcock, 2002), provide a compelling picture of aging and cognition. This picture extends worldwide, as similar findings have occurred in the United Kingdom (Rabbitt, Donlan, Watson, McInnes, & Bent 1995), Germany (Baltes & Lindenberger, 1997; Melchers et al., 2006; Zimprich & Martin, 2002), and the Netherlands (Mulder, Dekker, & Dekker 2004). Adults' performance on tests of crystallized ability (Horn) or pragmatics (Baltes) is maintained during much of the life span and does not decline appreciably until the mid-70s or 80s; in contrast, their performance on tests of fluid–visualization–speed abilities (Horn) or mechanics (Baltes) declines early in the life span and continues the steady descent throughout middle and old age. This pattern of maintenance and decline applies to academic skills. Adults maintained their ability to read words from their early 20s to late 80s, with no decline evident even in old age, but they declined substantially with age on academic skills that are dependent on reasoning ability: reading comprehension, math, and written expression (Kaufman et al., 2008).

On the WAIS-IV, this dichotomy is depicted by the maintenance of V-IQ and VCI and the vulnerability of P-IQ, PRI, and PSI. The Horn and Baltes theoretical explanations of the "classic aging pattern" stand in opposition to Botwinick's (1977) speeded-unspeeded rationale for the tasks that decline with normal aging versus those that are maintained throughout most of the adult life span. In this section we examine the evidence for these competing hypotheses, especially to evaluate whether the age-related decline on PRI and PSI are primarily a function of diminished cognitive capacity or of diminished speed.

Numerous investigators have interpreted the classical pattern from Botwinick's perspective: for example, Jarvik and Bank (1983) in their longitudinal analysis of aging among elderly twins. Indeed, the decline in speed with advancing age is a fact. This slowing "is not only an acknowledged laboratory result but also of considerable practical importance. Age-related slowness is evident in tasks of daily living such as zipping a garment, dialing a telephone, picking up coins, unwrapping a band-aid, cutting with a knife, and even putting on a shirt" (Salthouse, 1985, p. 400). It is also evident from the WAIS-III cross-sectional data and the WAIS-IV longitudinal data that the tests that depend the most on visual-motor speed—the ones that comprise the PSI—show declines with aging that are steeper than the declines for vulnerable subtests that are less speed-dependent (Figures 7.4 and 7.7).

There is no doubt that the decline in speed is crucial and accounts for a portion of the variance in the decline in *Gf* and *Gv*, and in working memory as well. Botwinick (1977) argued that decreased processing speed with age was *the* cause of decreasing performance ability. Salthouse (1985) has also emphasized that the decline in *Gf* is partly a function of the well-known age-related decrease in virtually all tasks that require speed of performance. Probably the best integration of the wealth of accumulated data suggests that processing speed plays a moderate to substantial role in accounting for the decline in *Gf* across the adult life span (Berg, 2000). In general, the results of cross-sectional studies often suggest that processing speed accounts for much of the age-related decline on *Gf* (Verhaeghen & Salthouse, 1997), whereas longitudinal data suggest a more modest role for processing speed and age-related decline (Sliwinski & Buschke, 1999; Zimprich & Martin, 2002). Nonetheless, Salthouse (2004) maintains that a decline in processing speed is the main culprit to account for most of the age-related declines in cognitive function, regardless of the specific abilities measured by the tasks. Hartley (2006) believes that the main cause of cognitive decline is not the processing speed per se but the greatly reduced ability to process the *symbols* used in the various tests of processing speed (which, more broadly, may reflect multidimensional physiological decline).

Even though processing speed, or the processing of symbols, may underlie cognitive decline in all aspects of functioning, evidence does show that problem-solving ability suffers even when speed of performance is not a factor in determining test scores. Some of this evidence is summarized briefly here.

- Doppelt and Wallace (1955) administered WAIS Arithmetic and all Performance subtests to an "old age" sample aged 60 and above under standard conditions and also under "irregular" conditions, when elderly adults were allowed to solve each item with unlimited time. (Bonus points were not considered in their analysis.) The subjects improved their scores only trivially on all tasks except Block Design. Storandt (1977), in a similar investigation with 40 young and 40 elderly adults matched on verbal ability, supported Doppelt and Wallace's results. The elderly group improved their raw scores significantly on only one of the five WAIS subtests, this time Picture Arrangement, while the younger subjects (ages 20–30) failed to improve their scores significantly on any of the tasks. The 20-second time limit for Picture Completion items was adequate in both studies because none of the groups of subjects improved its Picture Completion raw scores significantly with unlimited time. In fact, trivial gains of less than $1/2$ point were observed for all subsamples in the two studies.
- The aging pattern for the untimed WAIS-III Matrix Reasoning subtest is virtually identical to highly speeded subtests such as Block Design and Object Assembly (Kaufman, 2000a). Similarly, the nonspeeded Kaufman tests of Matrices and Gestalt Closure subtests display the same vulnerability

as tests that place a premium on response speed (Kaufman et al., 2008; Kaufman, Kaufman, Chen, & Kaufman, 1996; Wang & Kaufman, 1993).

- Visual-motor speed, rather than mental processing speed per se, seems to be the most vulnerable to normal aging. In fact, when vocal answers are required rather than motor responses, the relationship between speed and aging no longer holds (Salthouse, 1985). This consistent research finding was supported by the age trends for the WAIS-R and WAIS-III Arithmetic (Kaufman, 2000a; McLean, Kaufman, & Reynolds, 1988). On the WAIS-R, when education was controlled, each adult age group between 20–24 and 70–74 earned a mean scaled score of about 10 (range of 9.9 to 10.4). Yet all WAIS-R Arithmetic items are timed (the first nine items allow only 15–30 seconds apiece) and the last five items award 1 bonus point apiece for quick, perfect performance. On the WAIS-III, mean values ranged from 9.9 to 10.8 at ages 20–24 to 70–74; not until ages 85–89 did the education-adjusted mean Arithmetic scaled score dip below 9.6. And processing speed is rewarded even more on WAIS-III than WAIS-R Arithmetic, as the final two WAIS-III items award 2 possible bonus points for rapid solutions. (WAIS-IV Arithmetic allots no bonus points for any Arithmetic items.) Clearly, the speeded component of Arithmetic did not impair the performance of elderly adults on this Wechsler subtest.

- Zimprich (1998) used a statistical technique called *latent growth curve methodology* to investigate the contention that the loss of speed during aging leads directly to decrements in fluid ability. Using data from the Bonn Longitudinal Study of aging ($N = 127$; mean age $= 67$) at four measurement points, Zimprich analyzed data on two markers of mental speed (WAIS Digit Symbol and a simple psychomotor task) and two measures of *Gf* (WAIS Object Assembly and Block Design, both of which actually measure *Gf* and *Gv*). After analyzing separate and combined Latent Growth Curve Models for speed and *Gf*, Zimprich concluded that the results were not supportive of the speed hypothesis as changes in *Gf* within each individual did not relate to change in mental speed.

- On Wechsler's adult scales, the PSI produces the most dramatic age declines. However, cognitive research suggests that poor Digit Symbol—Coding performance is not just a function of speed of responding. Storandt (1976) examined the speed and cognitive components of this Performance subtest. First, Storandt tested the pure motor speed of young and elderly adults by simply having them copy symbols as rapidly as possible without the matched pairs. Younger adults far outstripped the elderly in this task. However, when these groups were also given the standard WAIS Digit Symbol subtest, a clear-cut cognitive differential was evident as well; the superior performance by the younger subjects could not be explained by the speed differential alone. In fact, the cognitive and speed components contributed about equally to the differential. And as Hartley (2006) suggests, the processing of symbols may underlie all cognitive decline.

• Creative contributions of men and women provide indirect support for the early decline in fluid ability. Matarazzo (1972, Table 7.4) presented the average ages when people in diverse fields (e.g., math, medicine, physics, chemistry, botany) made their greatest innovations. Virtually all creative works in these fields—the products primarily of fluid intelligence—were contributed by men and women in their 20s and 30s. The only field in which the most creative works were developed by people in their 40s was literature (when authors wrote their "best" books), which seems to relate to Gc more so than writing poetry, coming up with practical inventions, or making discoveries in science and mathematics.

• Rabbitt et al.'s (2007) cranial magnetic resonance imaging (MRI) study with 40 men and 25 women ages 64 to 85 years found that increases in "white matter lesion prevalence" accounted for all of the age-related variance on tests of speed but none of the age-related variance on tests of Gf. Ultimately, however, declines in processing speed, processing symbols, and fluid reasoning are only three of many variables that contribute to lower scores by older than younger adults on cognitive tests. Volumes have been written about the roles of other possible variables that play a considerable role in cognitive decline and that indoubtedly interact with Gf and Gs—for example, *sensory acuity* (Baltes & Lindenberger, 1997), *working memory* (Salthouse, 1992), *executive functions and frontal lobe functioning* (Raz, 2000), and *physical health* (Backman, Small, Wahlin, & Larsson, 2000).

CAN COGNITIVE DECLINE BE SLOWED OR PREDICTED IN ADVANCE?

Data from a 5-year longitudinal study that compared the intelligence and memory of 69 eminent academics (aged 70 and older) with 30 elderly blue-collar workers led the researchers to reach two sobering conclusions: (1) slower rates of decline are *not* associated with high ability, and (2) cognitive deterioration on nonverbal IQ tests is *universal* (Christensen, Henderson, Griffiths, & Levings, 1997). Although the authors of another study of eminent adults, Berkeley professors, included the optimistic phrase "evidence for successful aging" in their title (Shimamura, Berry, Mangels, Rusting, & Jurica, 1995), their results belie their optimism. Their oldest sample of professors, who averaged only 64.7 years of age, performed about equally to middle-aged and young professors in their ability to recall factual passages that were read to them (*Gc*). On all other tasks in the study, however, the elderly professors scored significantly and substantially lower than the other professors.

If elderly professors in these two studies show basically characteristic patterns of age-related decline on measures of *Gf*, speed, and memory, are these losses in cognitive functioning inevitable, or can they be slowed down?

Engagement in Cognitive Activities and Maintenance of Intelligence

Evidence does exist that lifestyle is related to decline in intellectual functioning. Much of the research on participation in diverse activities and cognitive performance has been cross-sectional; hence, one cannot attribute causality to these relationships because they tend to be reciprocal. How can one distinguish whether engagement in the activities helped maintain intelligence or whether the more intelligent people sought out the stimulating activities? Nonetheless, in summarizing the findings from many cross-sectional investigations, Hultsch, Hertzog, Small, and Dixon (1999) concluded that, generally, "these studies have reported that greater participation in physical, social, and intellectual activities is associated with higher levels of cognitive performance on a wide range of cognitive tasks" (p. 246). In addition, cross-sectional data from Hultsch, Hammer, and Small (1993) suggest that the relationship between engagement and cognitive performance may become stronger in old age.

Longitudinal data from the Seattle Longitudinal Study (Schaie, 1984, 1994) suggest that people who pursue much environmental stimulation and who continue their formal and informal educations throughout their life spans tend to display strong mental functioning in later years (Gribbin, Schaie, & Parham, 1980). Being involved in a stimulating early work experience has also been associated with IQ maintenance (Willis, 1985), as has coming from high socioeconomic status and remaining fully engaged with the environment (Schaie, 1984). In contrast, the largest declines tend to be shown by older adults (most notably by intelligent females) who have faced family dissolution or personal disengagement (Willis, 1985); widowed women who were never in the workforce and who were disengaged were particularly vulnerable to cognitive decline (Schaie, 1984). Additionally, longitudinal data obtained on World War II veterans tested twice (40-year interval) revealed significant relationships between participation in cognitive activities (and health, and education) and maintenance of intelligence (Arbuckle, Gold, Andres, Schwartzman, & Chaikelson, 1992).

However, as Hultsch et al. (1999) pointed out, both the Schaie and Arbuckle data used lifestyle criteria that are confounded with numerous factors, such as socioeconomic status and education, raising the possibility that differences in initial ability level were largely responsible for producing the apparent maintenance of intellectual ability in old age. Consequently, many of the longitudinal findings, like the cross-sectional findings, prevent a clear understanding of cause versus effect. Probably the best data for addressing the causality issue are provided by the Victoria Longitudinal Study of 250 middle-aged and older adults tested three times in six years (the initial sample at time 1 comprised 487 adults ages 55–86) (Hultsch et al., 1999). The investigators administered a battery of tests that measured nine hypothesized latent variables, three of which involved crystallized intelligence (vocabulary, story recall, reading comprehension) with the rest emphasizing memory or processing speed. In a very well-designed and well-controlled study, they assessed activity lifestyle in a variety of areas such as physical fitness, social activities, and novel information processing activities (e.g., playing bridge, learning a language) while also measuring the self-reported health and personality of the subjects.

They identified a significant relationship between intellectually related activities (but not social and physical activities) and change in cognitive functioning, but overall their hypotheses involving health, personality, and lifestyle were not supported. Furthermore, the results of Hultsch et al.'s (1999) structural equation modeling were just as supportive of the hypothesis that intelligent people lead intellectually stimulating lives as vice versa. In addition, their failure to include *Gf* tasks in their design prevented a possible understanding of differences in the maintenance of *Gf* versus *Gc*. Overall, the data are inconclusive.

Prediction of Declining Cognitive Ability

It might, however, be possible to predict which elderly adults will decline most in their cognitive ability (Gregory, Nettelbeck, Howard, & Wilson, 2008). Gregory et al. (2008) administered a computerized measure of *inspection time* (IT) to a sample of 124 adults (79 women, 45 men; mean age = 77 years) from an Australian study of aging. The IT task required the adults to respond rapidly, using a keyboard, to stimuli presented on the screen for a brief time. The stimuli were two vertical lines (one about twice the length of the other) connected at the top by a vertical line. Many stimuli were presented, one after the other, separated by a warning sign (a small cross). The task was to indicate, using a keyboard, whether the shorter of the two vertical lines was on the right or left. This measure of IT was administered to the sample of elderly adults on three occasions (Time 1 in 2003, Time 2 six months later in 2004, and Time 3 one year after that in 2005). People with slow ITs in 2003 performed relatively poorly in 2005 on measures of *Gf*, *Gs*, and working memory but not on measures of *Gc*. Elderly adults whose IT slowed down after 2003 (the ones who became slower at processing information as they aged) performed relatively poorly in 2005 on *Gf* and *Gs*. However, changes in IT were *not* directly associated with analogous changes in *Gf*, *Gs*, or other cognitive abilities. "Thus, there is evidence that IT level is associated with cognitive decline but no evidence that declines in IT are accompanied by concurrent changes in cognitive abilities" (Gregory et al., 2008, p. 669).

☚ TEST YOURSELF ☚

1. **Which of the following abilities is considered a maintained ability?**
   (a) Crystallized ability (*Gc*)
   (b) Fluid reasoning (*Gf*)
   (c) Processing speed (*Gs*)
   (d) Visual processing (*Gv*)
   (e) Short-term memory (*Gsm*)

2. **What major variable, if left uncontrolled, tends to confound the results of cross-sectional analyses of aging and intelligence (and, therefore, has been controlled in most studies)?**
   (a) Educational attainment
   (b) Physical health
   (c) Home environment
   (d) Emotional intelligence
   (e) Gender

3. **Schaie and his colleagues believe that their research supports the notion that intelligence is basically maintained through old age or, at most, declines late in the adult life span. TRUE or FALSE?**

4. **What kind of abilities are fluid reasoning (*Gf*) and processing speed (*Gs*) concerning changes in cognitive ability across the life span?**
   (a) Maintained
   (b) Responsive to intervention
   (c) Vulnerable
   (d) Static
   (e) Unreliable

5. The biggest threats to the conclusions that can be drawn from longitudinal studies of aging and intelligence are progressive error (the effects of practice) and

   (a) boredom.

   (b) verbal expression.

   (c) short-term memory.

   (d) selective attrition.

   (e) all of the above.

6. Most researchers on aging and intelligence have documented empirically that speed is responsible for all of the decline that Horn and others have attributed to diminished fluid intelligence. TRUE or FALSE?

7. Kaufman's longitudinal studies of aging and intelligence on Wechsler's scales, using independent samples, yielded results that contradicted the results of previous cross-sectional investigations of Verbal IQ and Performance IQ. TRUE or FALSE?

8. Which Wechsler scale shows the greatest declines between young adulthood in both cross-sectional and longitudinal studies of aging and intelligence?

   (a) Perceptual Reasoning Index (PRI)

   (b) Processing Speed Index (PSI)

   (c) Working Memory Index (WMI)

   (d) Verbal Comprehension Index (VCI)

   (e) Verbal IQ

9. Research studies on elderly samples have consistently shown that if time limits are removed on Wechsler's Performance subtests, then elderly adults improve their scores significantly on virtually all subtests. TRUE or FALSE?

10. What activity in old age has been *most* associated with maintenance of intelligence in old age?

    (a) Engaging in intellectual activities (e.g., playing Scrabble)

    (b) Engaging in social activities (e.g., hosting parties)

    (c) Engaging in physical activities (e.g., jogging)

    (d) Engaging in restful activities (e.g., getting 8 hours of sleep each night)

    (e) All of the above

Answers: 1. a; 2. a; 3. True; 4. c; 5. d; 6. False; 7. False; 8. b; 9. False; 10. a.

Eight

CLINICAL APPLICATIONS III: WAIS-IV USE WITH SPECIAL GROUPS AND PRACTICE EFFECTS IN NORMAL SAMPLES

In this chapter, we focus on the application of the WAIS-IV with special clinical groups. The *WAIS-IV Technical and Interpretive Manual* (Psychological Corporation, 2008) provided data on relatively small samples of individuals in these clinical groups: intellectually gifted, major depressive disorder, autistic and Asperger's disorder, Attention-Deficit/Hyperactivity Disorder (ADHD), mild cognitive impairment, reading and mathematics disorders, traumatic brain injury, probable Alzheimer's dementia, borderline intellectual functioning, and mild and moderate intellectual disability. No other clinical studies were published when this book went to press, so this chapter is limited to the clinical validity data presented in the *Manual*. In addition to the extended discussion of the WAIS-IV test profiles of clinical populations, this chapter includes an analysis of the practice effects observed for normal samples on FSIQ, Indexes, and scaled scores. The data on practice effects provide a baseline reference for evaluating the gains observed for clinical patients who are tested more than once on the WAIS-IV.

As the *WAIS-IV Technical and Interpretive Manual* (Psychological Corporation, 2008) aptly points out, these data should be interpreted with caution for a number of reasons. The studies' samples were not randomly selected and typically were based on small numbers (mean sample size = 38, ranging from as few as 16 to as many as 73 subjects). In most cases, data are included from a number of independent clinical settings that did not guarantee that the same criteria and procedures were used for diagnosis. In a number of cases, the groups consisted of participants with a heterogeneous set of diagnoses and treatments. For example, the individuals with ADHD and major depression consisted of some who were taking medication for the treatment of symptoms and some who were not. The group of individuals with traumatic brain injuries did not differentiate patients with open versus closed head injuries, and included different causes and severities of brain injury (although all were recent injuries, occurring in the past 6–18 months). Due to the time frame in which the data were collected, the individuals with "probable Alzheimer's-type dementia" were not diagnosed with the scientific and technological advancements in imaging that the most recent studies employ (Dubois et al., 2007).

Although these group data are useful for beginning to develop a preliminary understanding of how certain clinical populations perform on the WAIS-IV, these data should not be used to make differential diagnoses. In addition to the variables just mentioned, which limit generalizability, it is important to note that these clinical groups are not necessarily representative of a whole diagnostic class and do not reflect the individual differences within a diagnostic class. For each individual within a diagnostic group, many variables interact and affect performance on a test battery such as the WAIS-IV. These individual variables, including academic, developmental, medical, and family history; behavioral observations; and other test data must be integrated to properly interpret the results of any individual assessment battery. Thus, use caution when applying the results of these group data to the interpretation of any individual test results. A summary of these group data for the clinical samples is provided in Rapid Reference 8.1.

≡ Rapid Reference 8.1

Mean Indexes and Full Scale IQs for Clinical Samples

	N	VCI	PRI	WMI	PSI	FSIQ
Intellectually Gifted	34	127.2	119.6	123.3	**112.4**	126.5
Major Depressive Disorder	41	101.8	97.8	99.5	**95.8**	98.6
Asperger's Disorder	40	104.5	100.0	96.0	**88.4**	97.5
ADHD	44	100.9	98.6	94.7	**94.0**	96.9
Mild Cognitive Impairment	53	99.0	**93.9**	96.6	94.9	94.8
Reading Disorder	34	89.5	91.1	**88.9**	94.5	88.7
Mathematics Disorder	41	91.2	86.8	**84.1**	93.2	86.2
Traumatic Brain Injury	22	92.1	86.1	85.3	**80.5**	83.9
Probable Alzheimer's Dementia—Mild	44	86.2	85.8	84.3	**76.6**	81.2
Autistic Disorder	16	80.9	89.7	85.7	**75.1**	79.8
Borderline Intellectual Functioning	27	77.3	75.8	**74.2**	80.9	72.7
Intellectual Disability—Mild	73	65.9	65.4	**61.5**	63.8	58.5
Intellectual Disability—Moderate	31	56.8	55.0	**53.1**	53.8	48.2

Source: Data are from The Psychological Corporation (2008), Tables 5.21 to 5.32.

Note: Clinical samples are ordered by their mean FSIQ. The lowest index for each sample is in **bold**.

INDIVIDUALS WITH AUTISTIC DISORDER AND ASPERGER'S DISORDER

Rapid Reference 8.2 details the highest and lowest mean WAIS-IV subtest scaled scores for individuals with autistic disorder and Asperger's disorder. Given that individuals with Asperger's disorder are unlike individuals with autistic disorder because they do not show clinically significant delays in language, it not surprising that two of three of their highest scores are on tasks dependent on language (i.e., Information and Vocabulary). In contrast, for individuals with autistic disorder, whose difficulties include language disorders, one of their three lowest scores was on a language-based task (e.g., Comprehension), and their three highest scores were on nonverbal tasks. Like many of the special groups, the lowest performances for both groups were on subtests that make up the PSI, which likely reflects the sensitivity of these measures to generalized cognitive impairment.

≡ Rapid Reference 8.2

Highest and Lowest Mean WAIS-IV Scaled Scores of Adults with Autistic Disorder or Asperger's Disorder

Autistic Disorder (N=16) (Ages 16–28, M=20.3 yrs) (FSIQ=79.8; 93.7% Male)		Asperger's Disorder (N=40) (Ages 16–40, M=22.5 yrs) (FSIQ=97.5; 77.5% Male)	
Highest Subtests	**Scaled Score**	**Highest Subtests**	**Scaled Score**
Matrix Reasoning	8.6	Information	11.6
Visual Puzzles	8.3	Vocabulary	10.9
Block Design	7.9	Block Design	10.2
Lowest Subtests	**Scaled Score**	**Lowest Subtests**	**Scaled Score**
Comprehension	5.7	Symbol Search	8.4
Symbol Search	5.6	Cancellation	7.7
Coding	5.1	Coding	7.3

Sources: WAIS-IV data are from The Psychological Corporation (2008), Tables 5.19, 5.28, and 5.29 WISC-IV data are from The Psychological Corporation (2003) and Flanagan & Kaufman (2009).

Note: Both of these clinical samples performed remarkably similar to comparable samples tested on the WISC-IV. The three lowest subtests on the WISC-IV and WAIS-IV for children with autistic disorder were identical and ranked in the same order (e.g., Coding was the most difficult). This exact finding held true for the sample of children with Asperger's disorder as well. Strengths for both samples were similar (not identical) for the WISC-IV and WAIS-IV. On the WISC-IV, the children with autistic disorder did best on Block Design and Matrix Reasoning; the children with Asperger's disorder did best on Similarities and Information.

Individuals with autistic disorder and Asperger's disorder often obtain lower FSIQs than GAIs (Flanagan & Kaufman, 2009). According the *WAIS-IV Technical and Interpretive Manual* (Psychological Corporation, 2008), more than 55% of the individuals in the WAIS-IV special group studies with diagnoses of Asperger's disorder and 38% of the individuals with diagnoses of autism showed GAIs 5 or more points greater than their FSIQs. This finding suggests that their WMIs or PSIs (or both) negatively influenced the expression of their general intellectual abilities measured by their VCIs and PRIs. The general pattern of lower PSI and WMI scores paired with higher VCI and PRI scores has also been reported on the WISC-IV (Mayes & Calhoun, 2008), which provides validation for these findings on the WAIS-IV.

INDIVIDUALS WHO ARE INTELLECTUALLY GIFTED

Rapid Reference 8.3 indicates that the sample of 34 intellectually gifted adults performed best on tasks involving crystallized knowledge and short-term memory,

≡ *Rapid Reference 8.3*

Highest and Lowest Mean WAIS-IV Scaled Scores of Individuals Who Are Intellectually Gifted

Intellectually Gifted (N = 34)
(Ages 17–64, M = 34.4 yrs)
(FSIQ = 126.5; 38.2% Male)

Highest Subtests	Scaled Score
Vocabulary	15.2
Digit Span	14.7
Information	14.6
Lowest Subtests	**Scaled Score**
Picture Completion	12.5
Symbol Search	11.9
Cancellation	11.6

Sources: WAIS-IV data are from The Psychological Corporation (2008), Tables 5.19 and 5.20. WISC-IV data are from The Psychological Corporation (2003) and Flanagan & Kaufman (2009).

Note: On the WISC-IV, intellectually gifted children scored highest on Vocabulary and lowest on Cancellation, but otherwise the WISC-IV and WAIS-IV strengths and weaknesses did not correspond to each other. In fact, Digit Span—a strength on the WAIS-IV—was a relative weakness on the WISC-IV.

but, consistent with previous research, showed relatively weaker performance on tasks dependent on speeded processing. This finding is particularly important because clinicians are sometimes tempted to infer the presence of acquired deficits in bright individuals who do not show Above Average or better performances across all subtest scores. With Average-level performance on speeded tasks, individuals with intellectual giftedness may show Superior conceptual ability or skills with acquired knowledge. This pattern of performance in individuals who are intellectually gifted reveals a response set reflecting that they are more interested in optimal performance that may entail reflective processing and accuracy than speed.

INDIVIDUALS WITH INTELLECTUAL DISABILITY OR BORDERLINE INTELLECTUAL FUNCTIONING

Data from individuals with intellectual disabilities (mental retardation) are often difficult to interpret because this group combines multiple etiologies. Intellectual disability may result from acquired brain damage as well as a variety of genetic and congenital conditions, each potentially affecting the brain and the development of intelligence in a different way. Rapid Reference 8.4 presents the highlights of the subtest profiles for 73 adolescents and adults with mild disability and 31 individuals with moderate disability. In two samples from the *WAIS-IV Technical and Interpretative Manual* (Psychological Corporation, 2008), the pattern weaknesses for individuals with mild or moderate intellectual disability consistently include poorest performances on those tasks that rely heavily on processing speed. However, the pattern of strengths differs for individuals with mild versus moderate intellectual disability. For individuals with mild intellectual disability, Matrix Reasoning, Visual Puzzles, and Block Design were among the highest subtest scores. For individuals with moderate intellectual disability, Information, Vocabulary, and Block Design were among the highest subtest scores. Thus, Block Design was the only subtest that was among the highest for each of the groups with intellectual impairment.

Contrary to results on the WISC-IV (Flanagan & Kaufman, 2009), both groups of individuals with intellectual disability more often showed a higher WAIS-IV GAI than FSIQ because they appeared to do better on the more complex tasks emphasizing reasoning and acquired knowledge that compose the VCI and PRI than on the on the speed- and memory-based tasks that make up the PSI and WMI. Analysis of the FSIQ and GAI discrepancy for individuals with intellectual disability shows that 53% of individuals with mild intellectual disability and 39% of individuals with moderate intellectual disability obtained GAI scores that were 5 or more points greater than their FSIQ scores.

≡ Rapid Reference 8.4

Mild Intellectual Disability (N=73) (Ages 16–63, M=32.0 yrs) (FSIQ=58.5; 45.2% Male)		Moderate Intellectual Disability (N=31) (Ages 16–63, M=30.5 yrs) (FSIQ=48.2; 61.3% Male)	
Highest Subtests	**Scaled Score**	**Highest Subtests**	**Scaled Score**
Matrix Reasoning	8.6	Information	11.6
Visual Puzzles	8.3	Vocabulary	10.9
Block Design	7.9	Block Design	10.2
Lowest Subtests	**Scaled Score**	**Lowest Subtests**	**Scaled Score**
Comprehension	5.7	Symbol Search	8.4
Symbol Search	5.6	Cancellation	7.7
Coding	5.1	Coding	7.3

Sources: WAIS-IV data are from The Psychological Corporation (2008), Tables 5.19, 5.21, and 5.22. WISC-IV data are from The Psychological Corporation (2003) and Flanagan & Kaufman (2009).

Note: Individuals with mild and moderate intellectual disability displayed entirely different patterns of subtest strengths and weaknesses on the WISC-IV and WAIS-IV. Matrix Reasoning, a strength on the WAIS-IV for individuals with mild lintellectual disability, was a weakness for that clinical sample on the WISC-IV. Similarly, for individuals with moderate intellectual disability, Cancellation was a strength on the WISC-IV but is a weakness on the WAIS-IV.

Rapid Reference 8.5 shows the highest and lowest scores for a sample of 27 adolescents and adults with borderline intellectual disability. Individuals with borderline intellectual functioning (with an average FSIQ of 72.2) showed a different pattern of performance than those with mild intellectual disabilities (with an average FSIQ of 58.9). For example, in the group with borderline intellectual functioning, Symbol Search was among one of the highest subtest scores, while it was among the lowest for those with mild intellectual disabilities. Also, three of the PRI subtests were among the lowest for the borderline intellectual functioning group, but these were not among the lowest for those who were in the Mildly Impaired range.

INDIVIDUALS WITH ATTENTION-DEFICIT/ HYPERACTIVITY DISORDER

Rapid Reference 8.5 summarizes the profiles of a sample of 44 young adults diagnosed with ADHD. Individuals with ADHD would be expected to show strengths in verbal and perceptual reasoning areas (as long as their attentional

≡ Rapid Reference 8.5

Highest and Lowest Mean WAIS-IV Scaled Scores of Individuals with Borderline Intellectual Functioning or Attention-Deficit/Hyperactivity Disorder

Borderline Intellectual Functioning (N=27) (Ages 16–65, M=30.1 yrs) (FSIQ=72.7; 37.0% Male)		ADHD (N=44) (Ages 18–31, M=23.1 yrs) (FSIQ=96.9; 63.6% Male)	
Highest Subtests	**Scaled Score**	**Highest Subtests**	**Scaled Score**
Symbol Search	6.7	Picture Completion	10.4
Cancellation	6.7	Vocabulary	10.4
Picture Completion	6.7	Information	10.3
		Comprehension	10.3
Lowest Subtests	**Scaled Score**	**Lowest Subtests**	**Scaled Score**
Vocabulary	5.6	Matrix Reasoning	9.3
Matrix Reasoning	5.6	Arithmetic	8.6
Block Design	5.6	Coding	8.4
Figure Weights	5.4		
Arithmetic	5.1		

Sources: WAIS-IV data are from The Psychological Corporation (2008), Tables 5.19, 5.23, and 5.26. WISC-IV data are from The Psychological Corporation (2003) and Flanagan & Kaufman (2009).

Note: On the WISC-IV and WAIS-IV, individuals with ADHD displayed similar subtest profiles. As on the WAIS-IV, children with ADHD were strong in WISC-IV Picture Completion and weak on both Arithmetic and Coding.

problems are not so great as to interfere with test taking itself). Poor performance on WMI and PSI tasks would likely be related to the premium these tasks place on attention, concentration, and speed—all critical areas of concern in this population. Somewhat supportive of this pattern were the facts that among the lowest subtests for this ADHD sample were one PSI task (Coding), one WMI task (Arithmetic), and one PRI task (Matrix Reasoning). The highest performances for the ADHD sample were on Picture Completion and Vocabulary. Flanagan and Kaufman (2009) reported a similar pattern in the WISC-IV data for individuals with ADHD.

Individuals with ADHD tend to have difficulties with working memory and processing speed, which may result in lower FSIQ scores. The data presented in the *WAIS-IV Technical and Interpretive Manual* (Psychological Corporation, 2008) indicate that more than 30% of individuals with ADHD obtained GAIs 5 or more points greater than their FSIQs. Individuals with ADHD tend to perform relatively poorly on the subtests comprising the WMI and PSI, accounting for their lower FSIQs than GAIs (Mayes & Calhoun, 2007).

INDIVIDUALS WITH LEARNING DISABILITIES IN READING OR MATHEMATICS

Rapid Reference 8.6 presents the highest and lowest subtest scores for 34 individuals with learning disabilities in reading (mean age = 18.1) and 41 individuals with learning disabilities in mathematics (mean age = 17.8). These groups show similar patterns of strengths but different patterns of weaknesses. Both groups of individuals with learning disabilities had their strongest performance on tasks

≡ Rapid Reference 8.6

Highest and Lowest Mean WAIS-IV Scaled Scores of Individuals with Learning Disabilities in Reading or Math

Reading Disorder (N=34) (Ages 16–24, M=18.1 yrs) (FSIQ=88.7; 50.0% Male)		Math Disorder (N=41) (Ages 16–24, M=17.8 yrs) (FSIQ=86.2; 46.3% Male)	
Highest Subtests	**Scaled Score**	**Highest Subtests**	**Scaled Score**
Symbol Search	9.9	Symbol Search	9.5
Picture Completion	9.2	Picture Completion	9.4
Figure Weights	8.8	Similarities	8.7
		Comprehension	8.7
Lowest Subtests	**Scaled Score**	**Lowest Subtests**	**Scaled Score**
Coding	8.2	Visual Puzzles	7.5
Comprehension	8.2	Figure Weights	7.3
Arithmetic	7.5	Arithmetic	6.6
Vocabulary	7.5		

Sources: WAIS-IV data are from The Psychological Corporation (2008), Tables 5.19, 5.24, and 5.25. WISC-IV data are from The Psychological Corporation (2003) and Flanagan & Kaufman (2009).

Note: On the WISC-IV, children with reading disorders scored high on Symbol Search and low on Arithmetic, but their other strengths and weaknesses did not correspond to their high and low scaled scores on the WAIS-IV. Children with math disorders scored lowest on WISC-IV Arithmetic (consistent with their specific learning disability), but otherwise their WISC-IV and WAIS-IV subtest profiles were inconsistent.

that required processing speed (Symbol Search) or that required simple verbal responses (Picture Completion). Not surprisingly, individuals who have mathematics disorders struggled more with Figure Weights, likely because of the quantitative reasoning skill that is required to solve the problems. The Arithmetic subtest is among the lowest scores for the individuals with both types of learning disorder as well, suggesting that this subtest measures a wider range of processes than arithmetic ability alone.

INDIVIDUALS WITH TRAUMATIC BRAIN INJURY

Rapid Reference 8.7 contains the highest and lowest subtest scores for 22 adults ages 20–44 with traumatic brain injury (TBI). This TBI group is heterogeneous with respect to the localization and severity of their brain damage. The highest subtest scores are in verbal areas known to be fairly well preserved in TBI, while

≣ *Rapid Reference 8.7*

Highest and Lowest Mean WAIS-IV Scaled Scores of Adults with Traumatic Brain Injury or Major Depression

TBI (N=22)
(Ages 20–44, M=29.0 yrs)
(FSIQ=83.9; 72.7% Male)

Major Depression (N=41)
(Ages 50–86, M=62.8 yrs)
(FSIQ=98.6; 26.8% Male)

Highest Subtests	Scaled Score	Highest Subtests	Scaled Score
Vocabulary	8.9	Vocabulary	10.6
Information	8.8	Matrix Reasoning	10.4
Picture Completion	8.5	Information	10.4
Lowest Subtests	**Scaled Score**	**Lowest Subtests**	**Scaled Score**
Cancellation	7.1	Visual Puzzles	9.2
Matrix Reasoning	7.1	Figure Weights	9.2
Symbol Search	6.1	Coding	9.0

Sources: WAIS-IV data are from The Psychological Corporation (2008), Tables 5.19, 5.27, and 5.30. WISC-IV data are from The Psychological Corporation (2003) and Flanagan & Kaufman (2009).

Note: On the WISC-IV, the clinical sample with closed head injuries displayed similar subtest profiles to the ones displayed by the TBI clinical sample on the WAIS-IV. Like the TBI sample, the group with closed head injuries had strengths in Picture Completion and Information and weaknesses in Cancellation and Symbol Search. The WISC-IV clinical sample with open head injuries had a weakness in Symbol Search but otherwise had a different pattern of high and low scores than the WAIS-IV TBI clinical sample.

the lowest would be consistent with the conventional wisdom that traumatic brain injuries impact speed of processing (Lezak, Howieson, & Loring, 2004). However, expected pattern of low performance on all the WMI subtests was not present. This pattern likely reflects the diffuse cortical and subcortical pathology in many traumatic brain injuries rather than focal or localized damage (Hebben, 2009). As expected, a large effect size was noted for individuals with TBI when compared to matched control groups on a speeded paper-and-pencil task (Symbol Search) and on a mental math test (Arithmetic). However, several perceptual reasoning tasks also showed relatively large effect sizes when compared to matched controls: Matrix Reasoning, Visual Puzzles, and Figure Weights. Examination of the Digit Span process scores is informative for this TBI population. The group with TBI showed a larger effect size compared to matched controls for Digit Span Sequencing than Digit Span Backward. The TBI group's average scores were 7.1 for Digit Span Sequencing versus 8.6 on Digit Span Backward. According to the test publisher, the Digit Span Sequencing task "appears to increase the sensitivity of Digit Span to TBI" (Psychological Corporation, 2008, p. 112).

INDIVIDUALS WITH MAJOR DEPRESSION

Rapid Reference 8.7 presents strengths and weaknesses for a clinical sample of 41 older adults ages 50–86 diagnosed with major depressive disorder. It is important to evaluate the WAIS-IV results in light of the fact that a significant number (78%) were taking medication for their depression symptoms at the time of the testing. Due to this fact, it is likely that fewer depressive symptoms, and an atypical cognitive profile for depression, may have characterized this sample. There was a relatively small effect size for the PSI compared to a matched control group and for two of the three Processing Speed subtests. Overall, the lowest subtest scaled scores were on Coding and two Perceptual Reasoning subtests (Visual Puzzles and Figure Weights). Although there was little variability overall in the profile of individuals with depression (the lowest scaled score was 9.0 and the highest was 10.6), there were some consistencies with previous findings on cognitive tests for individuals with major depression—namely, individuals with major depressive disorder consistently show lower performance on processing speed tasks compared to other cognitive tasks (Gorlyn et al., 2006). Likewise, some studies (e.g., Naismith et al., 2003) have shown that compared to normal controls, individuals with major depression show poorer performance on timed tests. (Visual Puzzles and Figure Weights have time limits.)

INDIVIDUALS WITH PROBABLE ALZHEIMER'S-TYPE DEMENTIA AND MILD COGNITIVE IMPAIRMENT

Rapid Reference 8.8 shows the highest and lowest mean WAIS-IV scaled scores of 44 elderly adults with probable Alzheimer's dementia (mean age = 77.2) and 53 elderly adults with mild cognitive impairment (mean age = 73.7). By definition, individuals in the WAIS-IV clinical sample who met the criteria for probable dementia of the Alzheimer's type showed "deficits in two or more areas of cognition, and progressive decline in memory and other cognitive functions" (Psychological Corporation, 2008, p. 120). For this clinical sample, the lowest subtest scaled scores were obtained for Symbol Search, Coding, and Information, and this trio of subtests also showed the largest effect sizes, when comparing the clinical group to matched controls. The Digit Span process scores for this clinical group also revealed that the lowest score was on Digit Span Sequencing. Digit ordering tasks have been shown to be sensitive to the

---

≡ *Rapid Reference 8.8*

Highest and Lowest Mean WAIS-IV Scaled Scores of Elderly Adults with Probable Alzheimer's Dementia—Mild or Mild Cognitive Impairment

Probable Alzheimer's Dementia—Mild (N=44) (Ages 58–90, M=77.2 yrs) (FSIQ=81.2; 25.0% Male)		Mild Cognitive Impairment (N=53) (Ages 59–90, M=73.7 yrs) (FSIQ=94.8; 52.8% Male)	
Highest Subtests	**Scaled Score**	**Highest Subtests**	**Scaled Score**
Vocabulary	8.4	Vocabulary	10.1
Comprehension	7.8	Similarities	9.9
Block Design	7.8	Information	9.8
Lowest Subtests	**Scaled Score**	**Lowest Subtests**	**Scaled Score**
Information	6.5	Block Design	8.9
Coding	6.1	Visual Puzzles	8.6
Symbol Search	5.3	Picture Completion	8.5

Source: Data are from The Psychological Corporation (2008), Tables 5.19, 5.31, and 5.32.

Note: The elderly adults with mild cognitive impairment earned among their lowest scaled scores on Cancellation (7.9), Letter-Number Sequencing (8.0), and Figure Weights (8.9), but these subtests—which are not administered to adults above age 69—were given to only N = 14.

cognitive declines noted in individuals with probable dementia of the Alzheimer's type (MacDonald, Almor, Henderson, Kempler, & Andersen, 2001). In contrast to these areas of weaker performance, the highest subtests for this group were Vocabulary, Comprehension, and Block Design. These relatively stronger scores on two of the VCI subtests may indicate more preserved functioning in the cognitive domains that require crystallized abilities or acquired knowledge.

In contrast to individuals with probable dementia of the Alzheimer's type, one of the criteria for the clinical group with mild cognitive impairment (MCI) was that they could not meet the diagnostic criteria for dementia. The diagnostic criteria for the MCI group yielded a heterogeneous group of individuals who exhibited memory impairment or impairment in another cognitive domain, along with preserved basic daily living functioning. This MCI sample was also unique because it contained a higher number of college-educated individuals than is typically seen in a normal population. The lowest subtests for the MCI group were the PRI subtests of Picture Completion, Visual Puzzles, and Block Design. In contrast, the verbal tasks appeared relatively preserved. The highest subtest scaled scores were noted for Vocabulary, Similarities, and Information. Because of the heterogeneity of this MCI sample and the relatively small sample size, additional research is needed to determine if this pattern of strong verbal and weak perceptual is replicable and generalizable in other samples.

COMPARISON OF THE VERBAL COMPREHENSION INDEX AND THE PERCEPTUAL REASONING INDEX FOR THE CLINICAL SAMPLES

Historically, many researchers have examined the Wechsler verbal-performance profiles of clinical samples to determine if patterns existed for certain groups (Kaufman & Lichtenberger, 2006). With the removal of the VIQ and PIQ from the WAIS-IV, the focus of interpretation has now shifted from the verbal-performance dichotomy to the patterns among the four Factor Indexes. However, clinicians and researchers alike will may still be interested in studying patterns between the verbal (VCI) and nonverbal (PRI) indexes of the WAIS-IV or patterns within these separate WAIS-IV index subtests. Those interested in a thorough review of research on verbal-performance patterns on earlier editions of Wechsler's adult scales are directed to Kaufman and Lichtenberger (2006). Our interpretive approach for the WAIS-IV, presented in chapter 5, suggests examining patterns among the indexes, and the *WAIS-IV Technical and Interpretive*

Manual (Psychological Corporation, 2008) also suggests beginning basic profile analysis with an evaluation of discrepancies among the indexes, to "help the practitioner identify potentially meaningful patterns of strengths and weaknesses" (pp. 126). Rapid Reference 8.9 lists the differences between the VCI and PRI composite scores for the special study groups. Although group data cannot be evaluated by the same criteria as those employed in individual profile analysis, it is useful to note that a significant VCI-PRI discrepancy at the .05 level is 8.82 points. Just over half of the clinical groups displayed a VCI-PRI difference of 4 or more points, with the largest difference of 8.8 points for the individuals with Autism (PRI > VCI) and the second largest (7.6 points in favor of VCI) for the intellectually gifted sample. Except for the reading disorder group and the autism group, all groups displayed a VCI > PRI pattern, although only the samples of gifted, TBI, and MCI had discrepancies of 5 or more points. Note that such small differences between Indexes do not reflect functional or clinically significant differences in individuals.

≡ *Rapid Reference 8.9*

Differences between the VCI and PRI for the Clinical Groups

Clinical Group	VCI	PRI	VCI–PRI Discrepancy
Intellectually Gifted	127.2	119.6	7.6
Traumatic Brain Injury	92.1	86.1	6.0
Mild Cognitive Impairment	99.0	93.9	5.1
Asperger's Disorder	104.5	100.0	4.5
Mathematics Disorder	91.2	86.8	4.4
Major Depressive Disorder	101.8	97.8	4.0
ADHD	100.9	98.6	2.3
Intellectual Disability—Moderate	56.8	55.0	1.8
Borderline Intellectual Functioning	77.3	75.8	1.5
Intellectual Disability—Mild	65.9	65.4	0.5
Probable Alzheimer's Dementia—Mild	86.2	85.8	0.4
Reading Disorder	89.5	91.1	−1.6
Autistic Disorder	80.9	89.7	−8.8

Source: Data are from The Psychological Corporation (2008), Tables 5.21 to 5.32.

Note: Data are sorted from highest to lowest VCI > PRI discrepancy.

COMPARISONS INVOLVING THE FSIQ, GAI, AND CPI FOR THE CLINICAL SAMPLES

The GAI, first introduced for the WISC-III (Prifitera, Weiss, & Saklofske, 1998) and utilized in our WAIS-IV interpretive system presented in chapter 5 of this book, eliminates the contribution of the subtests comprising measures of working memory and processing speed that are included in the FSIQ. The GAI may be particularly useful for individuals in those special groups for whom there are frequently significant and abnormally large discrepancies between the scales that reflect verbal comprehension, crystallized knowledge, fluid reasoning, and visual processing (VCI/PRI) and the scales that measure attentional abilities and processing speed (WMI/PSI). There are multiple special populations for whom this is true, including individuals with intellectual giftedness (VCI and PRI > WMI and PSI), individuals with intellectual disability (WMI and PSI > VCI and PRI), and individuals sustaining head injuries (lower PSI than other indexes) (Strauss, Sherman, & Spreen, 2006).

If deficiencies in working memory and processing speed have lowered the FSIQ, Saklofske, Weiss, Raiford, and Prifitera (2006) suggest examining the difference between the FSIQ and GAI to determine "the impact of reducing the emphasis on working memory and processing speed on the estimate of general cognitive ability for individuals with difficulty in those areas due to traumatic brain injury or other neuropsychological difficulties" (p. 116). Thus, use of the GAI may be clinically informative in ways that the FSIQ is not. The *WAIS-IV Technical and Interpretive Manual* (Psychological Corporation, 2008, pp. 165–179) provides a table summarizing the distribution of the FSIQ-GAI discrepancies for the special groups included in the *Manual*. Use of this table allows examiners to compare the magnitude of an individual's discrepancy with the percentage of adults who obtained similar or greater levels of discrepancies (for both the standardization sample and special clinical samples).

In addition to the GAI, our interpretive system in chapter 5 incorporates the Cognitive Proficiency Index (CPI), a combination of WMI and PSI. The tasks that comprise this new composite represent an individual's ability to proficiently process certain types of cognitive information using visual speed and mental control (Dumont & Willis, 2001; Weiss, Saklofske, Prifitera, & Holdnack, 2006). In our interpretive system, we suggest interpreting the CPI only when it is psychometrically sound, meaning that there are not uncommonly large differences between the WMI and the PSI. It is especially important to consider the differences between clinical groups on these Indexes because interpretation of the CPI has been proposed as being valuable for such clinical groups (Hebben, 2009).

Rapid Reference 8.10 provides the mean FSIQ, GAI, and CPI obtained by the clinical samples. Mean FSIQs are provided in the *Manual* (Psychological Corporation, 2008). We calculated the mean GAI and CPI by summing each clinical sample's mean score on the pertinent WAIS-IV subtests and entering that sum into the appropriate conversion table. Upon examination of these data and the data presented in the *Manual*'s basc rate tables, on average, most of the clinical groups showed a pattern of FSIQ < GAI performance. However, the magnitude of these differences is consistently small (4 points or less) and of little or no

≣ *Rapid Reference 8.10*

Mean Standard Scores on GAI, CPI, and FSIQ for the Clinical Groups

Group	FSIQ	GAI	CPI	GAI-CPI Discrepancy	FSIQ-GAI Discrepancy
Asperger's Disorder	98	102	91	11	—4
Traumatic Brain Injury	84	88	80	8	—4
Intellectual Disability—Moderate	48	52	45	7	—4
Intellectual Disability—Mild	59	63	57	6	—4
ADHD	98	100	94	6	—2
Autistic Disorder	80	83	78	5	—3
Probable Alzheimer's Dementia—Mild	81	83	78	5	—2
Intellectually Gifted	127	126	121	5	1
Major Depressive Disorder	99	100	98	2	—1
Mathematics Disorder	86	88	87	1	—2
Mild Cognitive Impairment	97	97	96	1	0
Borderline Intellectual Functioning	73	74	75	—1	—1
Reading Disorder	89	89	91	—2	0

Source: Data are from The Psychological Corporation (2008), Tables 5.21 to 5.32.

Note: GAI and CPI were calculated by obtaining the average subtest scaled score for each clinical group, then calculating the rounded sums of scaled scores for the appropriate subtests that comprise each Index. These sums of scaled scores were finally converted to a standard score by using the appropriate conversion table in the *Manual* or this book. Data are sorted from highest to lowest GAI-CPI discrepancy.

clinical significance. The FSIQ-GAI discrepancy should not be used to establish a diagnosis or distinguish among the individuals in these special groups, but analysis of the discrepancy and its direction can provide evidence of whether an individual is similar to others in the diagnostic group under consideration and of strengths and weaknesses to target in a treatment program.

The differences for clinical samples were much more dramatic for GAI versus CPI. Most groups displayed a GAI > CPI profile with differences for eight of the samples ranging from 5 to 11 points. The huge 11-point difference emerged for the sample of individuals diagnosed with Asperger's disorder, and the difference for the sample with TBI (8 points) also exceeded ½ SD. The remaining samples with a substantial GAI > CPI difference (5–7 points) included people diagnosed with ADHD and those at the extremes of the FSIQ distribution: individuals identified as intellectually disabled (mild and moderate), as having probable Alzheimer's Disorder, and as intellectually gifted. For the sample of intellectually gifted individuals, the pattern of GAI > CPI is consistent with the g loadings of the tasks (GAI subtests tend to be "high g" and CPI subtests tend to be "low g"). Gifted individuals, of course, perform better on tasks that are strong measures of general intelligence. For the other clinical samples with a notable GAI > CPI profile, it is likely that the disorder (e.g., Asperger's, Alzheimer's, TBI) directly affected the adults' working memory and processing speed. For all of these samples, including the gifted, the GAI probably reflects a better estimate of their global intelligence than does the FSIQ (because the latter composite includes all of the CPI subtests).

The group data for these clinical samples indicate that in many cases, it may be psychometrically justified to combine the WMI and PSI into a single CPI index, and the GAI > CPI profile is surely meaningful in a clinical, practical sense. But that does not mean that either the CPI or discrepancies involving the CPI are meaningful from a *neuropsychological* perspective. As Hebben (2009) explains:

> There is a great deal of evidence linking various aspects of working memory to different parts of the frontal cortex (i.e., prefrontal, dorsomedial, and dorsolateral all seem to make some contribution). This is not the case for processing speed, which involves a wider array of cortical and subcortical areas; though it is possible the frontal cortex has some role in modulating processing speed. Other brain structures that might contribute to processing speed include the entire cortex itself, the basal ganglia, the various brainstem nuclei that factor into arousal, and the cerebellum. Even if both domains were impaired or limited in a single individual, there is no scientific basis to conclude this was caused by a compromise within the same area of the brain, even though this might be the case. (p. 220)

COMPARISON OF THE WORKING MEMORY INDEX AND THE PROCESSING SPEED INDEX FOR THE CLINICAL SAMPLES

In examining the differences between the WMI and the PSI in the clinical samples from the *WAIS-IV Manual*, some trends are apparent. Notably, all of the clinical samples showed a pattern of WMI > PSI. In the overall WAIS-IV standardization sample, a pattern of WMI > PSI was equally as common as a PSI > WMI pattern. The three clinical groups with the largest WMI > PSI patterns were the intellectually gifted sample (10.9-point difference), the autistic disorder sample (10.6-point difference), and the mathematics disorder sample (9.1-point difference). Conversely, the groups with the smallest WMI-PSI discrepancies were the intellectual disability–moderate group (.7 point), the ADHD group (.7 point), and the mild cognitive impairment group (1.7 points). Rapid Reference 8.11 lists the WMI-PSI discrepancies for each of the clinical samples.

≡ Rapid Reference 8.11

Discrepancies between the WMI and PSI for Clinical Groups

Clinical Group	WMI	PSI	WMI-PSI Discrepancy
Intellectual Disability—Moderate	**53.1**	53.8	0.7
ADHD	94.7	**94.0**	0.7
Mild Cognitive Impairment	96.6	94.9	1.7
Intellectual Disability—Mild	**61.5**	63.8	2.3
Major Depressive Disorder	99.5	**95.8**	3.7
Traumatic Brain Injury	85.3	**80.5**	4.8
Reading Disorder	**88.9**	94.5	5.6
Borderline Intellectual Functioning	**74.2**	80.9	6.7
Asperger's Disorder	96.0	**88.4**	7.6
Probable Alzheimer's Dementia—Mild	84.3	**76.6**	7.7
Mathematics Disorder	**84.1**	93.2	9.1
Autistic Disorder	85.7	**75.1**	10.6
Intellectually Gifted	123.3	**112.4**	10.9

Source: Data are from The Psychological Corporation (2008), Tables 5.21 to 5.32.

Note: Data are sorted from lowest to highest WMI > PSI discrepancy.

CLINICAL SAMPLES WITH RELATIVELY LOW SCORES ON THE PROCESSING SPEED INDEX

Rapid Reference 8.12 compares the PSI composite scores relative to the combined mean of the VCI, PRI, and WMI composite scores for the special study groups. In interpreting individual WAIS-IV profiles, a significant discrepancy between the PSI and the mean of all indexes is a difference of 7.5 standard score points between the two scores. (However, as mentioned, group data cannot be evaluated by the same criteria as those employed in individual profile analysis.) It is important to notice that all groups except for three displayed a *deficit* on the PSI relative to the mean index on the VCI, PRI, and WMI. Thus, a pattern of lower performance on the PSI does not provide adequate evidence for differential diagnosis. The individuals with mathematics disorders, reading disorders, and

=== *Rapid Reference 8.12*

Key Role of the Processing Speed Index: Clinical Samples that Scored Lowest or Highest on the PSI

	Mean of the Other 3 Indexes	PSI	Difference
PSI Is the LOWEST Index			
Asperger's Disorder	100.2	88.4	+11.8
Intellectually Gifted	123.4	112.4	+11.0
Autistic Disorder	85.4	75.1	+10.3
Probable Alzheimer's Dementia—Mild	85.4	76.6	+8.8
Traumatic Brain Injury	87.8	80.5	+7.3
ADHD	98.1	94.0	+4.1
Major Depressive Disorder	99.7	95.8	+3.9
PSI Is the HIGHEST Index			
Mathematics Disorder	87.4	93.2	−5.8
Borderline Intellectual Functioning	75.8	80.9	−5.1
Reading Disorder	89.8	94.5	−4.7

Source: Data are from The Psychological Corporation (2008), Tables 5.21 to 5.32.

Note: Difference equals the mean of the "other" three indexes (VCI, PRI, WMI) minus the PSI. Clinical samples are ordered by the magnitude of the difference.

borderline intellectual functioning had a PSI that was higher than the mean of their other three Indexes. (All were about 5–6 points higher.) This finding of higher PSI scores in groups with learning disabilities is in contrast to results reported on the WISC-IV (Flanagan & Kaufman, 2004, 2009), which show a more typical pattern of weaker performance on the PSI in such samples. In contrast, groups of individuals with Asperger's and autistic disorder or those who were intellectually gifted showed WAIS-IV PSIs that were lower (by 10–11 points) than the mean of their other three indexes. These data may provide evidence that those who are intellectually gifted will not necessarily also have superior processing speed. Likewise, individuals who have autistic or Asperger's disorder may show deficits in their processing speed relative to their other intellectual abilities.

UTILITY OF THE PROCESS APPROACH

The *WAIS-IV Technical and Interpretive Manual* (Psychological Corporation, 2008) advises the clinician that "the final step in a profile analysis is the qualitative analysis of individual responses" (p. 131). Similarly, we suggest that using a process analysis such as that described in chapter 6 of this volume may provide useful interpretive information. The focus of the *process approach* (Kaplan, 1988) is on the various processes an individual uses to solve a problem correctly and the processes that might lead to the failure to solve a problem (Hebben & Milberg, 2002).

Hebben (2009) points out some of the weaknesses of the process approach:

Though the process approach is intellectually and intuitively appealing, with its emphasis on breaking performance down into elements with potential relevance to rehabilitation and education, its empirical basis is not sufficiently well developed to allow for scientifically supportable clinical predictions by all clinicians. Without precise norms and a clearly spelled-out blueprint of how and when these procedures should be used, there is likely to be tremendous variation in the skill and accuracy with which this approach is applied. (p. 237)

Process scores in the *WAIS-IV Administration and Scoring Manual* (Wechsler, 2008) for the Block Design, Digit Span, and Letter-Number Sequencing tasks provide a quantitative picture of some of the processes that may be involved in the performance of these subtests. However, as with other data derived from the clinical samples, these analyses cannot be used routinely for differential diagnosis.

CLINICAL SAMPLES WITH NOTABLE DIFFERENCES BETWEEN SCALED SCORES ON DIGITS FORWARD AND DIGITS BACKWARD

The scaled score differences between Digits Forward and Digits Backward shown in Rapid Reference 8.13 range from 0.6 to 1.4. The small differences obtained by most of the clinical groups are not likely to be clinically significant and may not even be specific to the clinical samples. Table C.2 in the *WAIS-IV Administration and Scoring Manual* (Wechsler, 2008) indicates that individuals must show a greater than 3.65 scaled score difference between Digits Forward and Digits Backward for the difference to be statistically significant at the .05 level. Digit Span Backward is more difficult than Digit Span Forward, so it is not surprising that Digits Forward is better than Digits Backward for the groups with Alzheimer's dementia, major depressive disorder, and mild cognitive impairment.

It is difficult to explain why some groups paradoxically seemed to have more difficulty with Digits Forward than Digits Backward; however, these data are derived from a single small sample of individuals and may not be generalizable to other patients with similar diagnostic labels. As suggested in chapter 6, one

≋ *Rapid Reference 8.13*

WAIS-IV Process Scores: Clinical Samples with Notable Differences between Scaled Scores on Digits Forward and Digits Backward that Scored Lowest or Highest on the PSI

	Mean Digits Forward	Mean Digits Backward	Difference
Forward > Backward			
Probable Alzheimer's Dementia—Mild	8.8	7.8	+1.0
Major Depressive Disorder	10.8	10.0	+0.8
Mild Cognitive Impairment	10.2	9.5	+0.7
Backward > Forward			
Intellectually Gifted	13.3	14.7	−1.4
Reading Disorder	7.8	8.9	−1.1
Autistic Disorder	7.9	8.7	−0.8
Asperger's Disorder	9.0	9.7	−0.7
Traumatic Brain Injury	8.0	8.6	−0.6

Source: Data are from The Psychological Corporation (2008), Tables 5.21 to 5.32.

Note: Difference equals Mean Digits Forward minus Mean Digits Backward. Clinical samples are ordered by the magnitude of the difference.

explanation for this finding is that it is possible that the requirement to actively manipulate numbers in the backward condition may have engaged these individuals more than passively reciting them in the forward condition, but a hypothesis such as this requires testing before it can be applied to clinical practice.

INTERESTING FACTS ABOUT THE WAIS-IV PROFILES OF SELECT CLINICAL SAMPLES

Rapid Reference 8.14 summarizes a number of notable characteristics of the performances of the special study groups on the WAIS-IV. Some cautions should be observed, however, before using these data clinically. The findings reported

≡ Rapid Reference 8.14

Interesting Facts about the Strengths and Weaknesses of Clinical Samples on the WAIS-IV

- Vocabulary was among the three highest scaled scores for 8 of the 13 samples and was the very highest for 5 samples. It was a weakness for only two groups, individuals with reading disorders or borderline intellectual functioning. This finding reinforces Vocabulary's niche as an ability that is maintained in the face of aging or brain damage and that is commonly used as an estimate of premorbid mental functioning. Information, likewise, was a strength for 8 clinical samples; it was a weakness only for elderly individuals with probable Alzheimer's-type dementia.

- In contrast, Coding was a weakness for 8 of the 13 samples and a strength for none, reinforcing a wealth of research and clinical findings that show it to be vulnerable to aging and brain damage to both hemispheres and susceptible to distractibility, depression, and poor attention span. Symbol Search, however, was a strength as often as it was a weakness (three times).

- Eleven of the 13 samples had a low score on one or more processing speed subtests (all except individuals with major depression or borderline intellectual functioning).

- The samples of individuals with mild and moderate intellectual disability had virtually identical high and low scaled scores. Both clinical samples scored highest on Visual Puzzles and did relatively well on Information; and both had the identical three weaknesses—Letter-Number Sequencing, Digit Span, and Coding. Yet the subtest profile for individuals with borderline intellectual functioning was entirely different from the profiles of the clinical samples with intellectual disability.

- The samples of individuals with autistic disorder and Asperger's disorder had entirely different strengths. The former sample scored highest on perceptual reasoning subtests and the latter on measures of verbal comprehension. However, both samples had nearly identical weaknesses: low scores on the Processing Speed subtests of Coding and Symbol Search.

- Digit Span was the second-highest scaled score earned by intellectually gifted individuals. Otherwise, no working memory subtest was among the top three scaled scores for any clinical sample.

from the clinical samples need to be replicated before being considered a reliable feature of these disorders. In addition, findings from the profile analysis of group data cannot be meaningfully applied consistently to individual cases.

INTERPRETATION OF GAIN SCORES FOR NORMAL SAMPLES

Wechsler's scales for children and adults have long been known to produce substantial gains from test to retest, with this practice effect especially large for nonverbal tasks, such as those on the Performance IQ or Perceptual Reasoning and Processing Speed Indexes. On earlier editions of Wechsler's adult test, gain scores over an interval of several weeks or months have averaged about 2–3 points for V-IQ, 9 to 10 points for P-IQ, and 6 to 7 points for FSIQ (Kaufman, 1990, 1994b; Matarazzo & Herman, 1984). The larger gains on the Performance Scale probably reflect the fact these tasks are novel only the first time they are administered. On subsequent administrations, the tasks are more familiar, and many examinees undoubtedly remember the strategies they used to solve the items (such as arranging the Block Design cubes to match the target stimuli) even if they do not recall specific items.

The impact of this practice effect on interpretation is to anticipate higher IQs on a retest simply due to the effects of practice and not to real gains in intellectual functioning. Or, at least, an individual's gains should be substantially higher than "normal" or "baseline" gains before inferring improved intelligence. Another by-product of the gains concerns the differential practice effects for verbal versus nonverbal tasks (i.e., VCI and WMI versus PRI and PSI). Because the PRI and PSI usually will improve much more than the VCI on a retest, examiners can easily be misled by the magnitude of a person's VCI-PRI discrepancy on a retest. On the WAIS-R, for example, adults improved by about $8 \frac{1}{2}$ points on P-IQ and 3 points on V-IQ (Wechsler, 1981), for a net P > V gain of 5 to 6 points. On the WAIS-III, adults improved by 7 points on the P-IQ and about 2 points on the V-IQ. Examination of the WAIS-III indexes showed a similar pattern for the verbal versus nonverbal tasks with median test-retest gains of 2.3 and 2.6 points for the VCI and WMI, respectively, in contrast to the 5.6- and 4.2-point gains for the PRI and PSI, respectively (Psychological Corporation, 1997). On the WISC-IV, the differential is similar. PRI improved by 5.2 points and PSI improved by 7.1 points, compared to just 2.1 points for VCI and 2.6 points for WMI (*WISC-IV Technical and Interpretive Manual*, Psychological Corporation, 2003). Clinically, WISC-IV examiners might see a nonsignificant 7-point PRI > VCI profile on the first test jump to a significantly different 12 points on the second test, or jump from an 18-point PRI > VCI discrepancy to an uncommonly large 23-point discrepancy. Conversely, a significant VCI > PRI profile of 12 points on Test 1 might diminish to a trivial 3 points on Test 2. In both instances, the changes in the

VCI-PRI discrepancy on the retest is totally misleading and does not accurately portray the person's true difference between verbal and nonverbal abilities.

For the WAIS-IV, 298 retest subjects were obtained (interval averaging about 5 weeks; see Psychological Corporation, 2008, pp. 47–52), with four age groups represented (16–29, 30–54, 55–69, and 70–90). Rapid Reference Box 8.15

≡ Rapid Reference 8.15

WAIS-IV Test-Retest Gains across the Age Range

Subtest/Scale	Point Gain from First to Second Testing				
	Ages 16–29	Ages 30–54	Ages 55–69	Ages 70–90	Total
Picture Completion	2.4	2.2	1.7	1.2	1.8
Visual Puzzles	1.2	1.1	0.4	1.1	0.9
Symbol Search	1.1	1.0	1.1	0.2	0.9
Block Design	1.2	1.0	0.6	0.5	0.8
Figure Weights	0.9	1.0	0.4	—	0.8
Information	0.7	0.8	0.8	0.6	0.7
Coding	0.5	1.0	0.6	0.7	0.7
Cancellation	1.0	0.5	0.2	—	0.6
Digit Span	0.6	0.5	0.8	0.7	0.6
Similarities	0.4	0.7	0.8	0.5	0.5
Arithmetic	0.5	0.3	0.9	0.4	0.5
Letter-Number Sequencing	0.7	0.5	0.1	—	0.4
Matrix Reasoning	0.2	0.1	0.8	0.3	0.4
Comprehension	0.0	0.2	0.0	0.4	0.2
Vocabulary	0.2	0.1	0.2	0.0	0.1
VCI	2.2	3.0	3.4	2.1	2.6
PRI	5.0	4.4	3.9	3.8	4.2
WMI	2.7	2.0	4.6	3.4	3.3
PSI	4.6	5.6	5.4	3.2	4.6
FSIQ	4.6	4.4	5.0	3.9	4.5

Source: Data are from The Psychological Corporation (2008), Table 4.5. The gain scores are based on the Standard Difference column reported in Table 4.5 of the WAIS-IV Technical Manual.

Note: Subtests are ordered by the size off the practice effect for the total sample. The Standard Difference is the difference of the two test means divided by the square root of the pooled variance, computed using Cohen's (1996) Formula 10.4. This method yields slightly different values than a simple subtraction of Test 1 from Test 2 mean, but it provides a more accurate indication of the exact practice effect for each scale and subtest.

summarizes the gain scores for the 15 subtests, FSIQ, and four factor indexes. The inclusion of a substantial sample of retest cases across the entire WAIS-IV age range permitted an analysis of gain scores by age. The two youngest age groups did not differ notably in their gain scores, mirroring the results of the two similarly aged retest samples for the WAIS-R and WAIS-III. However, there are interesting differences between the 30–54 group and the 55–69 group. Specifically, the overall gains in FSIQ, VCI, and WMI continued to increase from one age group to another, but there was a decrease in gain scores on the PRI. The PSI gain remained steady between ages 30–54 and 55–69. When data for the two oldest WAIS-IV retest groups (ages 55–69 and 70–90) are analyzed alongside each other, other age trends are apparent. After age 69, the gain scores drop steadily for every index except PRI (which already showed a precipitous drop at age 55). The most notable decrease in gain scores was on the PSI in the 70–90 age group, which decreased from a gain of 5.4 to a gain of only 3.2. As discussed in chapter 7 of this book, tasks that depend the most on visual-motor speed—the ones that comprise the PSI—show declines with aging that are steeper than the declines for vulnerable subtests that are less speed-dependent. Whatever the reason, the increase in FSIQs from the first to second testing shows this age-related pattern on both the WAIS-III and the WAIS-IV:

GAIN SCORE ON FSIQ

Age Group	WAIS-III	WAIS-IV
16–29	5.7 points	4.6 points
30–54	5.1 points	4.4 points
55–69*	3.9 points	5.0 points
70–90*	3.2 points	3.9 points

*Note that the last two age groups for the WAIS-III and WAIS-IV are slightly different. The WAIS-IV age groups are reported in the table, but the last two WAIS-III age groups were 55–74 and 75–89.

Furthermore, the notable nonverbal > verbal gain that has been axiomatic for Wechsler retests applies only to individuals ages 16–54 on the WAIS-IV. At those ages, expect a nonverbal > verbal (i.e., when nonverbal is PRI+PSI and verbal is VCI+WMI) gain of about 5 points. For ages 55–90, the nonverbal > verbal gain is about 1.5 points. These age-related differences need to be internalized by WAIS-IV examiners. When retesting elderly individuals (ages 70+) especially, do not expect the substantial gains that have long been associated with Wechsler's scales. Expect increases of only about 2 to 4 points on the individual Factor

Indexes. However, gains of 7 or 8 points (about $\frac{1}{2}$ SD) in FSIQ on a retest are noteworthy for an adult of any age because they are substantially higher than the average gain of 4 to 4.5 points for most adults. In contrast, gains of 4 or fewer points (less than $\frac{1}{3}$ SD) on the Full Scale are probably nothing more than a reflection of the practice effect.

Typically, decreases in IQs on a retest are considered a cause for some concern, because such losses have been shown to be rare within the normal population (Kaufman, 1990; Matarazzo & Herman, 1984). That axiom requires modification in view of the WAIS-IV data. When a person age 70 or older scores lower on FSIQ or any Index on a retest, such a decrease may reflect normal variability around the relatively small average gain scores found for these individuals. As a rule of thumb for examiners, losses in IQs or Index scores on a retest for adults ages 70–90 years should be at least $\frac{1}{2}$ SD (7 or 8 points) below the initial value before inferring loss of function. For adults below age 70, decreases of about 5 points on a retest are likely to denote loss of function, a generalization that is consistent with the data for the WAIS-III (Kaufman & Lichtenberger, 1999).

Rapid Reference 8.15 lists the subtests in order of their average gain score across the age span. Largest gains were found for the Picture Completion subtest (1.8 scaled-score points). Four subtests had average gains of 0.8–0.9: Visual Puzzles, Symbol Search, Block Design, and Figure Weights. For the total retest sample, the smallest gains (0.1–0.2 point) were for two Verbal subtests (Vocabulary and Comprehension). In addition to these small gains, the untimed Matrix Reasoning subtest had a small 0.4-point gain, as did Letter-Number Sequencing. As on the WAIS-III, the very small gains on WAIS-IV's Matrix Reasoning are undoubtedly partially responsible for the smaller PRI gains, in general, for the WAIS-IV relative to the older WAIS, WAIS-R, and other Wechsler scales that did not include this subtest on the nonverbal scales.

One final point is worth noting. Although practice effects are present on the WAIS-IV, these gain scores are relatively small (typically $\frac{1}{7}$ to $\frac{1}{3}$ of an SD). Thus, these practice effects do not detract from the fact that the WAIS-IV is quite a stable test battery. Test-retest reliability coefficients for all ages combined were excellent: FSIQ = .96, VCI = .96, PRI = .87. WMI = .88, and PRI = .87 (Psychological Corporation, 2008, Table 4.5).

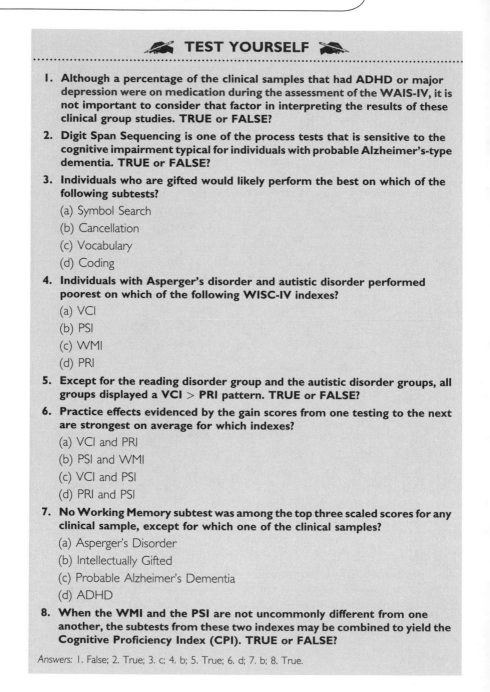

TEST YOURSELF

1. Although a percentage of the clinical samples that had **ADHD** or major depression were on medication during the assessment of the **WAIS-IV**, it is not important to consider that factor in interpreting the results of these clinical group studies. **TRUE or FALSE?**

2. Digit Span Sequencing is one of the process tests that is sensitive to the cognitive impairment typical for individuals with probable Alzheimer's-type dementia. **TRUE or FALSE?**

3. Individuals who are gifted would likely perform the best on which of the following subtests?

   (a) Symbol Search

   (b) Cancellation

   (c) Vocabulary

   (d) Coding

4. Individuals with Asperger's disorder and autistic disorder performed poorest on which of the following WISC-IV indexes?

   (a) VCI

   (b) PSI

   (c) WMI

   (d) PRI

5. Except for the reading disorder group and the autistic disorder groups, all groups displayed a **VCI > PRI** pattern. **TRUE or FALSE?**

6. Practice effects evidenced by the gain scores from one testing to the next are strongest on average for which indexes?

   (a) VCI and PRI

   (b) PSI and WMI

   (c) VCI and PSI

   (d) PRI and PSI

7. No Working Memory subtest was among the top three scaled scores for any clinical sample, except for which one of the clinical samples?

   (a) Asperger's Disorder

   (b) Intellectually Gifted

   (c) Probable Alzheimer's Dementia

   (d) ADHD

8. When the WMI and the PSI are not uncommonly different from one another, the subtests from these two indexes may be combined to yield the Cognitive Proficiency Index (CPI). **TRUE or FALSE?**

Answers: 1. False; 2. True; 3. c; 4. b; 5. True; 6. d; 7. b; 8. True.

Nine

STRENGTHS AND WEAKNESSES OF THE WAIS-IV

Ron Dumont and
John O. Willis

T he authors of this chapter believe that, on balance, the WAIS-IV is a very good instrument. We think enough of it and of other Wechsler scales to use them in our own practices, to teach them to our captive audiences of graduate students, and to write this chapter. Both of us have had extensive experience with many other cognitive assessment instruments long before the WAIS-IV was published. Because the test has been released only recently, there is little published information regarding how it has been accepted by practitioners. These authors have used the WAIS-IV many times in real assessment cases and have developed opinions, both positive and negative, about it. Although we find the test to be overall a vast improvement over the prior edition and have welcomed many of the changes in the update, we still find several aspects of the test annoying or problematic. Admittedly, we are easily annoyed.

The WAIS-IV provides an efficient, thorough, reasonable, and statistically reliable and valid assessment of cognitive abilities. It is designed with features that enhance useful interpretation.

STRENGTHS OF THE WAIS-IV

This chapter first presents the strengths of the WAIS-IV followed by a section on the test's weaknesses. Within these two dichotomous sections, we have organized the test's pros and cons in these categories: test development, administration and scoring, reliability and validity, standardization, and interpretation. This list of assets and detriments is by no means finite, but it does reflect what we view as the key positive and negative aspects. A summary of these points is provided at the end of this chapter.

Test Development

In the process of developing the WAIS-IV, many positive changes were made to Wechsler's adult test. The key assets that we describe include updating of the theoretical foundations; adding new strong measures of fluid reasoning, working memory, and visual processing; and adding normed process scores. The test materials were also improved during the process of test development.

Update of Theoretical Foundations

One of the revision goals for the WAIS-IV was to "update theoretical foundations" (Psychological Corporation, 2008, p. 17). As we note, the important goal of enhancing measurement of fluid reasoning was at least partially met by the valuable addition of the Figure Weights subtest, although we would have liked to have normative scores for fluid reasoning included in the test norms. The issue is complicated by the fact that almost all theorists and researchers would agree that Figure Weights and Matrix Reasoning measure fluid reasoning; there would be differing opinions about the Similarities subtest.

Also as will be noted, assessment of working memory has been considerably increased. Finally, the increased measurement of processing speed is also in line with current theory and research. All three areas are especially critical for assessment of cognitive changes over the adult life span.

As will be discussed at length, the lack of explicit adherence to Cattell-Horn-Carroll (CHC) categories disappoints those of us who lean on that particular taxonomy, but the WAIS-IV was never intended to conform to the CHC ability structure. The explicit goals of updating theoretical foundations, increasing developmental appropriateness, increasing user-friendliness, enhancing clinical utility, and improving psychometric properties were, in our opinion, all met, despite our quibbles.

Addition of Figure Weights: Adds Another Strong Gf Measure

When the WAIS-III was released in 1997, we were especially excited about the inclusion of the then-new Matrix Reasoning subtest because the Wechsler scales had, since their creation, lacked any clear measure of fluid reasoning. Our excitement was short-lived when we realized that the Matrix Reasoning subtest was not sufficient by itself for examiners to feel confident in explaining a person's fluid reasoning abilities. Usually at least two subtests of the same broad area (in this case fluid reasoning, or Gf)[1] are necessary to compute an area score. With the current addition of the Figure Weights subtest, a fluid reasoning subtest that appears to be measuring the narrow ability of Quantitative Reasoning, examiners can interpret a person's fluid reasoning skills and do so with more confidence.

Addition of Digit Sequencing: A Measure of WM to Accompany DB and LNS
Like our concern about the WAIS-III's limitation for interpreting the Fluid Reasoning abilities of an examinee, we believed that the WAIS-III had similar problems with the interpretability of Short-term Memory (*Gsm*) ability. On the WAIS-III, short-term memory, called "Working Memory," was composed of two subtests (Digit Span and Arithmetic). While both subtests might be considered measures of *Gsm*, in our opinion, Digit Span, with both a digit-forward and a digit-backward task, was a mixture of memory span (*Gsm*-MS) and working memory (*Gsm*-MW) (see, e.g., Hale, Hoeppner, & Fiorello, 2002), while Arithmetic was a measure of both working memory (*Gsm*-MW) and quantitative ability (*Gq*). This combination of different narrow abilities often made the interpretation of the Working Memory Index problematic.

With the addition of the new Digit Sequencing task to the Digit Span subtest, a stronger measure of working memory has been added to the test. The Digit Span subtest now includes three tasks: Forward, Backward, and Sequencing. Comparing a person's results from the Digits Forward task (Memory Span) to those of the Digits Backward task, Digit Sequencing task, and Letter-Number Sequencing subtest (all measures of Working Memory) with the aid of the interpretive tables in Appendixes B and C of the *Administration and Scoring Manual* (Wechsler, 2008, pp. 229–253) may allow for a clearer interpretation of the different short-term memory abilities measured by the WAIS-IV.

Addition of Visual Puzzles: Enhances Measures of Gv
The addition of the new Visual Puzzles subtest to the WAIS-IV has increased the interpretability of Visual Spatial (*Gv*) abilities. When Visual Puzzles is combined with Block Design, there are two strong measures of *Gv*, with one, Visual Puzzles, measuring the narrow ability of visualization (VZ), and Block Design measuring spatial relations (SR).

---

1. We are using names and notations for Cattell-Horn-Carroll (CHC) Broad and Narrow abilities taken from Carroll (1997); Flanagan & McGrew (1997); Flanagan, Ortiz, & Alfonso (2007); Flanagan, Ortiz, Alfonso, & Mascolo (2006); and Horn & Blankson (2005).

Block Design: Process Score for No Time Bonus (BDN)
Like the WISC-IV (Wechsler, 2003), the WAIS-IV provides norms for pass-fail scoring of Block Design. Time limits still apply, but time-bonus points are not used. Although the BDN may not be substituted for the regular Block Design score, the additional Process Score still provides useful information for examinees who have slow motor responses, slow decision speed, poor motor coordination, or a tendency toward high levels of uncertainty. Appendix C in Wechsler (2008, pp. 242–248) provides scaled scores for BDN as well as critical values and base rates for differences between Block Design and Block Design No Time Bonus.

Update of Materials, Artwork, and Record Form
The materials for the WAIS-IV have been updated to include new artwork, a revised Record Form, and enlarged Symbol Search and Coding subtest materials. We are especially happy with the revised Record Form, as there is now much more room for recording an examinee's responses. For just one example, the section of the form for recording the responses to the Digit Span subtest has been enlarged so that the examiner can now record verbatim the numbers given as a response. On the WAIS-III, there was very little room in the space provided to fit the actual responses.

Administration and Scoring

There are several positive aspects to the WAIS-IV's administration and scoring procedures. The key points that we elaborate on include the generally easy procedures for administration and scoring, streamlining of starting and stopping points, and improving scoring for Vocabulary.

Fairly Easy Administration
The WAIS-IV is not effortless to administer, but it is not unduly or unnecessarily difficult. With the elimination of both the Object Assembly and Picture Arrangement subtests, the WAIS-IV has become less cumbersome with its manipulatives. Only Block Design requires anything other than the Stimulus Booklets for administration. No more fumbling for Object Assembly boxes and pieces, no more shield to hide the placement of the puzzle parts, and no more Picture Arrangement cards to shuffle, deal, and drop on the floor. Examiners do need to use both the *Administration Manual* and the Record Form along with a Stimulus Booklet and a stopwatch for some subtests, especially Block Design, but this divided-attention task is not difficult to master.

Generally Easy Scoring

Difficult judgments and subjectivity in scoring rules cause interexaminer variation and errors in scores. Some mistakes are frequent, and some result in serious errors in subtest and total test scores (e.g., Alfonso & Pratt, 1997; Belk, LoBello, Ray, & Zachar, 2002; Willis, 2001). With the exception of three Verbal subtests (Similarities, Vocabulary, and Comprehension), on which items can be scored as 2, 1, or 0, the scoring rules for all other subtest items (with some minor exceptions noted below) strike us as generally clear and unequivocal.

Streamlining of Discontinue Rules, Entry Points

The administration of the WAIS-IV seems to flow a bit more efficiently, and one reason for this may be the revised discontinue rules, which have been shortened for the most part. Many subtest discontinuations have been reduced by at least one item (e.g., from four consecutive failures to three) while two subtests (Vocabulary and Information) have been reduced from six to three consecutive failures. Entry points and other essential information generally have been made clear and user-friendly on the Record Form.

Scoring of Vocabulary

Unlike some vocabulary tests, the WAIS-IV Vocabulary instructions (Wechsler, 2008) state: "All word meanings recognized by standard dictionaries are acceptable and are scored according to the quality of the definition" (p. 101). Although "regionalisms or slang" are not acceptable, the examiner is instructed to query such responses and other responses when the examiner is "unsure about the acceptability of a response." Subjectively, there do not appear to be enough difficult words for examinees with college or postgraduate education, but scaled scores of 19 are available at all ages, although they do require perfect raw scores at ages 35:0 to 84:11.

Start Points

All subtests except for Digit Span, Symbol Search, Coding, Letter-Number Sequencing, and Cancellation have starting points (after any sample items) higher than Item 1. There are clear rules for dropping back from the starting item when necessary, and examinees who are believed to have intellectual disabilities "should always begin with Item 1." These rules should minimize both boredom and frustration.

Reliability and Validity

With the state-of-the-art procedures for test development and standardization, it is no surprise that the psychometric qualities of the WAIS-IV are strong. We detail the assets of the test's reliability and validity next.

Reliability

The WAIS-IV Composite, Indexes, and subtests generally have strong reliability. This topic is discussed at length in chapter 4 of the *Technical and Interpretive Manual* (Psychological Corporation, 2008). Test scores cannot be trusted unless the tests are internally consistent and likely to yield very similar scores for the same person under similar circumstances, so reliability is an essential foundation for any responsible use of test scores. It is a necessary, but not sufficient, basis for application of test scores. A test can be reliable but still not valid for a particular purpose; without reliability, however, it cannot be valid for any purpose.

It is still too early to be able to measure long-term stability of WAIS-IV scores, and long-term stability statistics are depressed by genuine changes in the abilities of the persons being retested. Short-term stability coefficients for all subtests (including process scores) at all tested ages (Psychological Corporation, 2008, p. 48), ranged from .71 (adequate) to .90 (reliable). For the core subtests, short-term stability coefficients were .74 to .90, with a median of .82.

Evidence of Validity

Validity data for the WAIS-IV are discussed in chapter 1 of this book and in the WAIS-IV *Technical and Interpretive Manual* (Psychological Corporation, 2008, pp. 57–122). Validity evidence from comparisons with tests of cognitive abilities and tests of academic achievement supports the use of the WAIS-IV for cognitive assessment and prediction of achievement.

Evidence of Validity with Special Groups

While the WAIS-IV is not normed on individuals with severe disabilities or disabilities likely to invalidate test scores, studies were done with 13 special groups (Psychological Corporation, 2008, pp. 98–122). When assessing individuals with special characteristics, that information in the *Manual* is extremely helpful. Additional analyses of these data were discussed by Lichtenberger and Kaufman in chapter 8 of this book.

The *Administration and Scoring Manual* (Wechsler, 2008, pp. 10–19) provides some brief, helpful considerations for testing individuals with special needs and detailed recommendations for testing examinees who are deaf or hard of hearing; additional information is available in the *Technical and Interpretive Manual* (Psychological Corporation, 2008, Appendix D, pp. 185–187) adapted from Hardy (1993) and Hardy-Braz (2003).

Standardization

Normative samples are important for tests, just as for opinion polls. If the normative sample does not resemble the population to whom examinees will be compared, scores will be misleading. The normative sample of the WAIS-IV is described in chapter 3 of the *Technical and Interpretive Manual* (Psychological Corporation, 2008). We consider it to meet or exceed good current practice and to provide a trustworthy basis for an individual's scores.

Examinee candidates for the normative sample were screened extensively for potentially confounding issues that presumably might impair the validity of test performance. A complete list of the exclusionary criteria for the normative sample is presented in Table 3.1 (p. 31) of the *Technical and Interpretive Manual* (Psychological Corporation, 2008). Special consideration was given to acknowledging that there is a trend for increased prescription medication use in older adults. Procedures were established to evaluate individuals' medication use, particularly those medications that could potentially affect cognitive test performance.

Interpretation

The newest version of the WAIS has made interpretation easier, and the test publishers have provided additional interpretive information for clinicians in the test kit. We describe these assets and additional strengths related to the topic of interpretation next.

Easier Interpretation

The WAIS-III (Wechsler, 1997) subtest scores were shuffled into confusing combinations. Three subtests contributed to the Verbal Comprehension Index (VCI), Verbal IQ (VIQ), and Full Scale IQ (FSIQ). A fourth Verbal subtest contributed to the VIQ and FSIQ but not to the VCI or any other index score. Two other Verbal subtests contributed to the VIQ and FSIQ but to the Working Memory Index (WMI) rather than to the VCI. The remaining Verbal subtest was included in the WMI but not in the VIQ and PIQ.

Three Performance subtests were included in the WAIS-III: Performance IQ (PIQ), FSIQ, and Perceptual Organization Index (POI). One was included in the PIQ and FSIQ, but in the Processing Speed Index (PSI) rather than in the POI. Another Performance subtest was included in the PIQ and FSIQ scores, but in none of the Index scores. Yet another was part of the PSI score but not of the PIQ or FSIQ. Finally, one Performance subtest (Object Assembly) was not included in any index or IQ scores.

Coherent explanations of the composition of the various WAIS-III IQ and Index scores were elusive for both evaluators and readers of our reports. The composition of the WAIS-IV components is much easier to understand, as

Table 9.1. Comparison of WISC-IV, WAIS-III, and WAIS-IV Index and Full Scale IQ Composition

Subtest	WISC-IV	WAIS-III*	WAIS-IV
Information	*supplemental*	VCI + FSIQ	VCI + FSIQ
Comprehension	VCI + FSIQ	FSIQ	*supplemental*
Similarities	VCI + FSIQ	VCI + FSIQ	VCI + FSIQ
Vocabulary	VCI + FSIQ	VCI + FSIQ	VCI + FSIQ
Word Reasoning	*supplemental*	—	—
Picture Completion	*supplemental*	POI + FSIQ	*supplemental*
Block Design	PRI + FSIQ	POI + FSIQ	PRI + FSIQ
Matrix Reasoning	PRI + FSIQ	POI + FSIQ	PRI + FSIQ
Picture Concepts	PRI + FSIQ	—	—
Visual Puzzles	—	—	PRI + FSIQ
Figure Weights	—	—	*supplemental*
Picture Arrangement	—	FSIQ	—
Object Assembly	—	*supplemental*	—
Arithmetic	*supplemental*	WMI + FSIQ	WMI + FSIQ
Digit Span	WMI + FSIQ	WMI + FSIQ	WMI + FSIQ
Letter—Number Sequencing	WMI + FSIQ	WMI	*supplemental*
Coding	PSI + FSIQ	PSI + FSIQ	PSI + FSIQ
Symbol Search	PSI + FSIQ	PSI	PSI + FSIQ
Cancellation	*supplemental*	—	*supplemental*

*WAIS-III FSIQ subtests are also included in the Verbal IQ (VIQ) or Performance IQ (PIQ). VCI = Verbal Comprehension Index, PRI = Perceptual Reasoning Index, WMI = Working memory Index, PSI = Processing Speed Index, FSIQ = Full Scale IQ.

shown in Table 9.1. Each subtest either contributes to both an Index Scale and the FSIQ or else serves as a supplementary subtest.

Additional Interpretive Information

As with the WISC-IV (Wechsler, 2003), the WAIS-IV provides valuable "Critical Value and Base Rates Tables for Discrepancy Comparisons" (Wechsler, 2008, pp. 229–240) and "Process Analysis Tables" (pp. 241–253) for the Block Design with no time-bonus points and for the various Digit Span tasks. Critical values are given for .15 and .05 but not .10 significance levels. Tables for comparing WAIS-IV and Wechsler Individual Achievement Test (2nd Ed.; WIAT-II) scores are provided in the WAIS-IV *Technical and Interpretive Manual* (Psychological Corporation, 2008, Appendix B, pp. 151–163). These WIAT-II comparisons appear to be based on correlational data from 93 high school students, which suggests cautious interpretation. Tables B.4 and B.8 (Psychological Corporation, 2008, pp. 158, 161), include the limitation "for Ages 16:0–19:11." Examiners who wish to use the WIAT-II college norms with the WAIS-IV need to exercise caution.

Aligning the Indexes to Be Compatible with WISC-IV

As the Wechsler Scales have developed over the years, they have each gradually shifted from the original Wechsler Verbal/Performance dichotomy to the current utilization of a Full Scale IQ and four index scores. We are happy to find that the WAIS-IV has totally replaced the Verbal-Performance IQ designations with terminology and labels that are much more in alignment with the *Wechsler Intelligence Scale for Children, Fourth Edition* (Wechsler, 2003; WISC-IV). However, we are not entirely comfortable with the assertion "*The terms VCI and PRI should be substituted for the terms VIQ and PIQ in clinical decision-making and other situations where VIQ and PIQ were previously used*" (Wechsler, 2008, p. 5, emphasis in the original). The old VIQ included both VCI and WMI subtests, and the old PIQ contained both PRI and PSI subtests. Table 9.1 shows the subtest composition for the Full Scale IQ and the four indexes of the WISC-IV, the WAIS-III, and the WAIS-IV. As can be seen, the tests derive their respective FSIQs and indexes from different combinations of subtests, with only the Processing Speed Index having a direct subtest match between the WISC-IV and WAIS-IV. Although specific differences still remain between the two tests, and some of those differences may be developmentally appropriate, the alignment of the WAIS-IV into the four indexes will, we hope, lead to easier understanding and interpretation across the two tests, particularly for those individuals who have been administered the WISC-IV and then, later, administered the WAIS-IV.

WEAKNESSES OF THE WAIS-IV

Although our overall impression of the WAIS-IV is a positive one, we did find some negative aspects that we discuss next in categories that parallel those discussed in the section on the test's strengths.

Test Development

The goals of the test publisher's development team led them to develop a stronger test when they revised the WAIS-III. Thus, only one detriment to the WAIS-IV's test development is described.

Loss of Object Assembly and Picture Arrangement

Although, as noted, removal of Object Assembly and Picture Arrangement has greatly simplified administration and clarified interpretation of the WAIS-IV and has removed two subtests of questionable reliability and validity, a few old practitioners will miss those venerable subtests, which were for many decades integral parts of the Wechsler scales. We are left with only one hands-on constructional subtest, Block Design. Some examiners believed we gained useful information by being able to watch the examinee work on the items of those subtests. The vast majority of examiners, most of whom did not administer those subtests on the WAIS-III and never saw the WAIS-R, WAIS, or Wechsler-Bellevue, will not agree with this opinion.

Administration and Scoring

The administration and scoring procedures of the WAIS-IV have a few little quirks that we viewed as detriments. We elaborate on these issues: problems related to substitutions and prorating, poor instructions for certain tests, and questionable scoring rules for certain subtests.

Substitutions and Prorating

Although we agree that it is better to allow subtest substitutions and prorating than to invalidate an entire test, be unable to compute a FSIQ score, or have to report results that are obviously biased against an examinee's disability, we do have concerns about the potential for IQ roulette when substitutions are allowed. The *Administration and Scoring Manual* (Wechsler, 2008, pp. 29–30, 51–54) discusses substitutions and prorating and limits substitutions to no more than one per index scale and two for the entire test. Those rules still allow a tremendous number of different versions of the WAIS-IV composed of different subtests with varying reliabilities and different correlations with their index scales and the FSIQ. We would have preferred to see even stronger cautions about substitutions and prorating.

Poor Instructions for Scoring Certain Tasks

Although the instructions provided in the *Administration and Scoring Manual* (Wechsler, 2008) are typically clear and unambiguous, there remain, in our opinion, several aspects of administration and scoring that need clarification. (Some of these concerns apply to other Wechsler tests as well.)

Picture Completion—20-Second Rule

For the Picture Completion subtest, there is an explicit 20-second time limit for each item and, additionally, the *Manual* states: "If an examinee does not respond to an item within 20 seconds or if the examinee responds incorrectly in less than 20 seconds, proceed to the next appropriate item if the discontinuation criterion has not been met" (Wechsler, 2008, p. 199). Although this may seem straightforward, how does one define "respond"? Does it refer to the onset of the examinee's utterance (e.g., the "Well" in "Well . . . um . . . I think . . . maybe. . . it could be . . . uh . . . I guess . . . maybe . . . missing . . . that thing over there . . . where it comes together like the other one.") or the words that specify the missing part ("that thing") or the end of the examinee's comment ("other one")? For example, what is an examiner to do if the person being tested starts to respond to an item at the 18-second mark but correctly completes the response at 25 seconds? Is this scored as a 0 because the response was not given "within 20 seconds," or do we score it as a passed item because the person began his or her response within the 20 seconds? Or what of the case where a person responds incorrectly within the 20 seconds and then spontaneously self-corrects his or her answer, but the corrected response runs over the 20-second time limit? How strict are we to be with the 20-second rule? Unfortunately, there is no clear guidance in the *Manual* or from the test company.

Figure Weights—Time Pressure

The older coauthor of this chapter had no difficulty with any of the Figure Weights items but was unable to solve some of the problems within the 20- and 40-second time limits. The constant interruption with the examiner's "Do you have an answer?" on every item 10 seconds before the time limit elapsed was not only a severe annoyance but a significant distraction. After the first few items, anticipation of the inevitable interruption developed into a distraction in its own right, making the subtest an unnecessarily unpleasant experience.

Block Design—Rotations

Block Design (Wechsler, 2008, pp. 66–68) still counts as an error any rotation of 30 degrees or more of the design. Many evaluators would consider this rule proper and a strength of the test. We have come to prefer the approach taken by Elliott (2007) on the Differential Ability Scales of simply not penalizing rotations. Precisely distinguishing between 29 and 30 degrees can be challenging, and there seem to be many reasons for rotating designs, including an effort to turn them so the examiner can see them correctly. Even if such a benign error is not repeated after a single correction, as prescribed in the *Manual*, the examinee has still lost 2 or, more likely, 4 points.

Comprehension—What Is a Response?

Similar to our concerns regarding what constitutes a response on the Picture Completion subtest, we also have problems with the Comprehension subtest. Several items are flagged (§) as a reminder to the examiner that, for maximum points, the item requires distinct answers from at least two separate categories designated in the *Manual*. It is noted that if the "first response" to an item is clearly incorrect, the examiner does not query at all for a second response. However, the instructions also note that if the examinee's answer contains information from only one general concept, the examiner is to query using the specific wording provided in the *Manual* to obtain an additional response. If the additional response refers to the same general category, the examiner does not ask for an additional response. Confusion comes from just what constitutes a "response." What if the person's first answer (response) contains two parts, both descriptions from one general concept? Is that answer considered to be one response or two? For example, for item 5, a person responds with "To kill germs so you don't get sick." In the *Manual*, the responses "To kill germs" and "So you don't get sick" are both correct acceptable responses from one general concept. Is that specific response therefore referring to only one general concept, or is this actually two responses, both from the same general concept? If the person had simply said "To kill germs," that would clearly be one response from one general category, and we would query the response. If after the query the person says "So you don't get sick," we would have two clear responses, the second from the same general concept, and therefore would not ask for any additional response to the item. But if, as in our example, we consider that the answer as a whole was one response, we would then be required to query for a second response.

Information—Questionable Scoring Rules

We noticed only two items on the Information subtest that may cause scoring difficulty for the examiner. Although we cannot put the specific test item questions or the responses from the *Manual* in this book, we do note that the examples given in the *Administration and Scoring Manual* (Wechsler, 2008) call for queries (Q) to some, but not other, responses for reasons that we simply cannot fathom. These seemingly minor quibbles about queries are very perplexing to student examiners and lead to interscorer unreliability among even experienced evaluators.

Although these issues in scoring responses may seem minor, with the reduction in consecutive items scored as zero needed for discontinuation, ambiguity in scoring may affect the overall scaled score. What if one of the items just given as examples were the last in the short discontinuation series? Scoring the item as a failure would end the subtest while scoring it as a passed item would allow the examiner to continue and potentially increase the examinee's chances of passing more items, thus possibly increasing the scaled score for the subtest.

Cancellation

The WISC-IV (Wechsler, 2003) Cancellation subtest includes two tasks requiring speeded marking of animal pictures among various other pictures. The examinee is free to work in any direction(s) she or he might wish. The two tasks differ only in the arrangement of the pictures—aligned in straight rows or scattered randomly about the page—and examiners are encouraged to observe the examinee's approach to the task. In contrast, the WAIS-IV Cancellation subtest has two tasks that appear to be very similar to each other, and a left-to-right progression with no going back is strictly enforced. The rationale for these changes eludes us.

Interpretation

The interpretation process has been helped by some changes on the WAIS-IV but was hindered by others. Next we discuss some of the challenges: the paucity of interpretive materials, not enough information about including supplementary subtests in interpretation, missing data for Cognitive Proficiency Index (CPI) calculations, and a lack of adequate CHC structure and taxonomy.

Paucity of Interpretive Materials: New Tests and New Procedures but an Apparent Lack of Any Interpretive Information to Aid Examiners Unfamiliar with the Tasks

Although the Wechsler scales have been prominent in cognitive assessments for years and have extensive research backing, the inclusion on the WAIS-IV of new subtests (Visual Puzzles, Figure Weights, and Cancellation) has left examiners with new interpretive possibilities. Unfortunately, the *WAIS-IV Interpretive Manual* lacks explanations or examples of just how an examiner might interpret WAIS-IV results. For example, what would be the correct interpretation for or implications of a significant difference between the Block Design and Visual Puzzles subtests or differences between the three aspects of the Digit Span subtest (DSF, DSB, and DSS)? Appendixes B and C of the *Administration and Scoring Manual* (Wechsler, 2008, pp. 229–253) provide useful normative data but no information about the implications of those data.

The Pearson Assessment web site Support and Resources Home Sample Reports page (2009a) offers eight sample reports based on the WISC-IV, but none we could find for the WAIS-IV. Similarly, we found eight Technical Reports on the WISC-IV and one on the WAIS-III at the Pearson Assessment web site Technical Reports (2009b), but none on the WAIS-IV.

Determining S and W Based on Only the Core Subtests

The *Administration and Scoring Manual* (Wechsler, 2008, p. 239, Table B.5) provides examiners with critical values that can be used to determine if a subtest differs significantly from the overall mean of 10 subtests or the mean of 3 Verbal Comprehension or of 3 Perceptual Reasoning subtests. Unfortunately, this information, typically used to determine strengths and weaknesses, is incomplete. If an examiner administers the supplemental subtests (e.g., administering all 15 subtests) to gain additional information about the person, the *Manual* provides no way of determining if those additional subtests differ significantly from the person's mean subtest score. This information could easily have been provided, as was done for the WISC-IV by Sattler and Dumont (2004, Table A-4, pp. 291–302).

GAI but No CPI

The WAIS-IV *Technical and Interpretative Manual* (Psychological Corporation, 2008 pp. 165–183) provides examiners with information regarding the use of the General Ability Index (GAI). The GAI is derived from the three subtests that enter the VCI and the three subtests that enter the PRI. (The table of significant differences between FSIQ and GAI [Psychological Corporation, 2008, p. 170] has been corrected by Pearson Assessment [2009c, 2009d].) No information is provided about how examiners might calculate a CPI, which would be derived from the two subtests that comprise the WMI and the two subtests that comprise the PSI. Weiss, Saklofske, Prifitera and Holdnack (2006) and Weiss and Gabel (2008) have provided guidelines for their CPI for the WISC-IV (Wechsler, 2003). These four subtests (i.e., Digit Span, Arithmetic, Symbol Search, and Coding) are not as highly correlated with verbal and nonverbal intelligence as are the six other Verbal and Perceptual subtests and load on independent factors in the four-factor solution of the WAIS-IV.

If an examiner did choose to calculate the GAI, tables for calculating the CPI and then for the examination of significant differences between the two indexes would have been very useful. (However, note that Lichtenberger and Kaufman did provide such information for the calculation and interpretation of the CPI in chapter 5 of this book.) Estimates of overall abilities calculated in this way should always be clearly identified as GAI and CPI scores in both text and tables of reports. These scores must not be confused with the Full Scale IQ, although they may be more useful estimates of intellectual ability in some cases, for example, for some gifted children and for some children with relative weaknesses in working memory and/or processing speed. For the latter group, the GAI and CPI may help avoid Dumont and Willis's Mark Penalty (Willis & Dumont, 2002, pp. 131–132), the depression of a measure of intelligence by a low score on a measure of a student's specific weakness. Other children may score significantly higher on the WMI and PSI indices than on the VCI and PSI indices, which may mask important difficulties with conceptual thinking if the FSIQ is used without the GAI and CPI.

Lack of Adequate Cattell-Horn-Carroll Structure and Taxonomy

Cattell-Horn-Carroll theory has become a common language—a periodic table of cognitive ability elements—for evaluators (e.g., Carroll, 1997; Horn & Blankson, 2005). CHC theory allows evaluators to compare and contrast different measures of cognitive ability and achievement for research and for the McGrew, Flanagan, and Ortiz Integrated Cross-Battery Assessment (e.g., Flanagan & McGrew, 1997; Flanagan, Ortiz, & Alfonso, 2007; Flanagan, Ortiz, Alfonso, & Mascolo, 2006).

Like most recently published tests of cognitive abilities, the WAIS-IV can be organized by CHC broad and narrow abilities. However, despite that fact that the test acknowledges the historical changes in the conception of intelligence and the contributions made by the CHC taxonomy, the test does not explicitly utilize the CHC categories. It instead uses labels and groupings that, while based on current theoretical models and research results in cognition and neuroscience (see, e.g., Psychological Corporation, 2008, pp. 1–5, 17–20, 57–122), do not facilitate interpretation within the CHC Cross-Battery model (e.g., Flanagan, & McGrew, 1997; Flanagan et al., 2006, 2007). This problem—for examiners who wish to use the CHC structure—is particularly evident with the Perceptual Reasoning Index. Although the technical *Manual* makes it clear that certain subtests were added to the new WAIS in order to enhance the measurement of specific domains (e.g., Visual Puzzles to enhance Visual Spatial abilities and Figure Weights to enhance Fluid Reasoning), the Perceptual Reasoning Index remains, within the CHC taxonomy, a mixed measure of both Visual Spatial Reasoning (Gv) (Block Design and Visual Puzzles) and Fluid Reasoning (Gf) (Matrix Reasoning). Figure Weights remains a supplemental subtest that may, unfortunately, not be administered, leaving the examiner with only one measure of CHC Gf and a loss of potentially valuable information. We wish that the test had made Figure Weights a core subtest and then clearly divided the Perceptual Reasoning Index into two indices, Visual Spatial Thinking and Fluid Reasoning. This would have, in our opinion, increased the overall interpretability of the WAIS-IV within the CHC framework and avoided the need to estimate the individual domains of *Gv* and *Gf.* (In chapter 5 of this book, Lichtenberger and Kaufman provide an alternate model by which to interpret the WAIS-IV data that allows for a separate calculation of *Gv* and *Gf* factors.)

Similar issues are evident with the Working Memory Index. When the index is interpreted, care must be taken to analyze whether the two abilities being measured are different from each other, thus reducing the overall interpretability of the index. The availability on the Record Form of "Process" scaled scores for Digit Span Forward, Digit Span Backward, and Digit Span Sequencing; critical values and base rates for differences among those scaled scores; and base rates for the greatest number of digits recalled in each condition and the differences among those spans would all allow the examiner to take some of that necessary care. The *Administration and Scoring Manual* (Wechsler, 2008, Table B.3, p. 237) also provides critical values for differences among scaled scores for Digit Span, Arithmetic, and Letter-Number Sequencing and (Table B.4, p. 238) base rates for differences between Digit Span and Arithmetic.

FINAL COMMENT

Although we have identified some concerns with the new WAIS-IV, we definitely consider it a significant improvement over the WAIS-III and, on balance, find it to be a valuable instrument with significant strengths. Rapid Reference 9.1 provides a summary of the WAIS-IV's strengths and weaknesses.

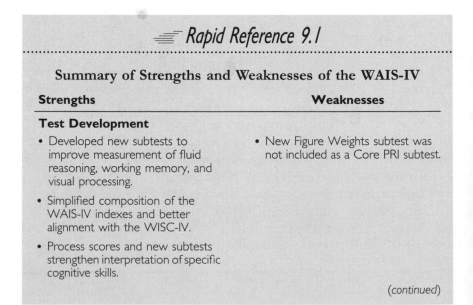

≡ Rapid Reference 9.1

Summary of Strengths and Weaknesses of the WAIS-IV

Strengths	Weaknesses
Test Development	
• Developed new subtests to improve measurement of fluid reasoning, working memory, and visual processing.	• New Figure Weights subtest was not included as a Core PRI subtest.
• Simplified composition of the WAIS-IV indexes and better alignment with the WISC-IV.	
• Process scores and new subtests strengthen interpretation of specific cognitive skills.	

(continued)

Strengths	Weaknesses
Administration and Scoring	
• Easier to administer because of fewer manipulatives.	• Ambiguity regarding some scoring criteria.
• Much more user-friendly Record Form.	• Annoying instructions on one subtest.
• Improvement in artwork and response forms.	• Some questionable scoring rules.
• Scoring rules generally clear and unequivocal.	
• Streamlined discontinuation rules.	
Reliability and Validity	
• Generally strong reliability.	• WIAT-II predicted achievement scores based on 93 high school students.
• Generally strong validity evidence for cognitive assessment and prediction of achievement.	
• Validity demonstrated for 13 special groups.	
Standardization	
• Normative sample meets or exceeds current psychometric practice.	
• Normative sample provides a trustworthy basis for an individual's scores.	
• Special consideration for increased prescription medication use in older adults and other confounding issues.	
Interpretation	
• Subtests and indices based on both theory and research in cognitive abilities.	• Paucity of interpretive materials.
• Alignment of the WAIS-IV into the four indexes.	• Substitution and prorating flexibility.
	• Determination of Strengths and Weaknesses based on only the core subtests.
• Composition of the WAIS-IV components much easier to understand.	• No information provided for calculation of a Cognitive Processing Index.
• Useful information on testing examinees who are deaf or hard of hearing.	• Lack of complete Cattell-Horn-Carroll structure and taxonomy for examiners who prefer that structure.

🦅 TEST YOURSELF 🦅

1. One of the weaknesses of the WAIS-IV is that the new battery barely resembles the WISC-IV in content or structure. TRUE or FALSE?

2. One notable strength of the WAIS-IV is its improved measurement of visual processing, working memory, and

   (a) verbal comprehension.

   (b) creativity.

   (c) fluid reasoning.

   (d) verbal expression.

   (e) arithmetic skills.

3. A strength of the WAIS-IV is inclusion in the test manual of numerous validity studies with clinical samples. TRUE or FALSE?

4. An advantage of the WAIS-IV over previous Wechsler adult scales is easier administration because of fewer concrete materials to manipulate. TRUE or FALSE?

5. Strengths of the WAIS-IV include

   (a) generally strong reliability.

   (b) a much more user-friendly Record Form.

   (c) a high-quality standardization sample.

   (d) subtests and indices guided by theory and research in cognitive abilities.

   (e) all of the above.

6. One weakness of the WAIS-IV is the paucity of interpretive materials provided in the manual. TRUE or FALSE?

Answers: 1. False; 2. c; 3. True; 4. True; 5. e; 6. True.

Ten

ILLUSTRATIVE CASE REPORTS

This chapter includes the case studies of one adolescent and one adult who were referred for neuropsychological and psychological evaluation. The WAIS-IV profile of Laura O. was presented in chapter 5 to exemplify how to progress through the steps of interpretation; here the culmination of her case is presented in the first case report. The second case report examines the profile of a 64-year-old male, Jim W., who was referred for the evaluation of possible dementia.

Chapters 1 through 9 of this book have reviewed the key features of the WAIS-IV and how to administer, score, and interpret the instrument. The goal of this chapter is to bring all of these other facets of the book together and illustrate how the WAIS-IV may be utilized as part of a comprehensive test battery. Specifically, the case reports demonstrate how hypotheses are cross-validated with behavioral observations, background information, and supplemental tests. Throughout the first case report, Rapid Reference boxes provide information on

DON'T FORGET
....
Outline of Report

1. Identifying Information
2. Reason for Referral
3. Background Information
4. Appearance and Behavioral Observations
5. Tests Administered
6. Test Results and Interpretations
7. Summary (or Summary and Conclusions; Summary and Diagnostic Impression)
8. Recommendations
9. Signature
10. Psychometric Summary of Scores

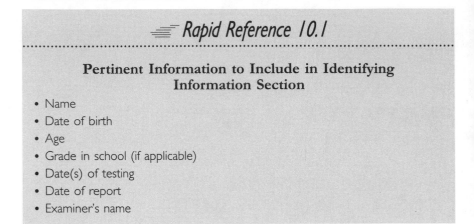

≡ *Rapid Reference 10.1*

Pertinent Information to Include in Identifying Information Section

• Name
• Date of birth
• Age
• Grade in school (if applicable)
• Date(s) of testing
• Date of report
• Examiner's name

what data should be included in each section of the report; the Don't Forget box details the basic outline for the reports we present. Final portions of the reports demonstrate how to translate results of the tests into effective recommendations.

For all cases presented in this book, the names and other pertinent identifying information have been changed to protect confidentiality of clients.

CASE REPORT: LAURA O., AGE 17, IMPAIRED SOCIAL SKILLS, POOR MOTIVATION, AND WEAK ATTENTION ABILITIES

Reason for Evaluation

Laura O. is a 17-year-old young woman who lives with her parents and her sisters, ages 15 and 13. Laura attends the 12th grade at her local high school. Her parents are both physicians. This evaluation was initiated by her mother, Dr. O., due to concerns regarding Laura's impaired social skills, her lack of motivation in all areas, poor attention abilities, and her "sluggishness." The aim of this neuropsychological assessment is to assess Laura's neurocognitive and psychological functioning to determine whether any deficits in this regard are impairing her performance. Furthermore, appropriate academic modifications will be recommended, along with other necessary treatment recommendations.

Background Information

Developmental History and Health

Laura was raised in a small town in the southern United States. According to Dr. O., Laura is the product of a normal, full-term pregnancy. However, at

≡ Rapid Reference 10.2

Pertinent Information to Include in Reason for Referral Section of Report

A. Who referred the client:
  1. Name and position of referral source.
  2. Questions of referral source.
B. Specific symptoms and concerns:
  1. Summarize current behaviors and relevant past behaviors.
  2. List any separate concerns that the client has him-/herself.

35 weeks' gestation, Dr. O. was involved in a severe car accident and was very seriously injured. Laura did not apparently sustain any damage during this accident. She was delivered 11 days after her due date via a normal labor and delivery. Laura weighed 7 lbs. 7 oz. at birth, and no health problems were reported. She was described as an easygoing baby who ate and slept well. All developmental milestones were reached within appropriate limits.

≡ Rapid Reference 10.3

Pertinent Information to Include in Background Information

Present in paragraph form the information you have obtained from all sources, including referral source, client, family members, social worker, teachers, medical records, and so on. State pertinent information only, not needless details.

This information may be included:

• Current family situation (spouse, children, siblings, etc.). NO gossip.
• Other symptoms.
• Medical history (including emotional disorders).
• Developmental history.
• Educational history.
• Employment history.
• Previous treatment (educational or psychological).
• New or recent developments. Include Stressors.
• Review of collateral documents (past evaluations).

Dr. O. described Laura as having no sensory sensitivities but noted that Laura has a "strange gait when walking." Laura tends to be a healthy young woman who does not have many somatic complaints and sleeps well at night. No surgeries or hospitalizations were reported, and Laura has not had any head injuries, although she did suffer an abrasion on her head when a dresser fell on top of her as a toddler. Laura wears corrective lenses for a visual acuity deficit. No hearing problems were reported. She takes allergy medications and uses an inhaler as needed for mild reactive airway disease.

According to Dr. O., there is no reported paternal family history of any psychological or neurocognitive problems. A maternal uncle committed suicide and a maternal cousin is described as evidencing Asperger-like traits. No other notable maternal family history was reported.

Academic History

Laura attended a mother's day out program twice a week from age 18 months, and she was cared for at home by her parents and nanny during the remainder of the week. When she transitioned to a half-day kindergarten program, no problems were noted. School records indicated that Laura never excelled academically but obtained a B average throughout elementary school, and generally she was able to complete her homework without any difficulty. During these years, Laura's teachers did not note any significant concerns about her academic or social functioning.

During her middle school years, her mother reported that Laura's sluggishness, her tendency to do as little as possible to get by, and her obstinacy were more evident. These problems continued throughout high school. Her mother indicated that Laura also began to demonstrate some notable struggles with math and science, and she failed a state standardized math test three times. Tutoring through Kumon Math center was ineffective, according to Laura and her parents. Although Laura had no problems learning to read, her comprehension has always been poor, and she has struggled to grasp more abstract concepts when reading. She is reluctant to read for pleasure. She does not have good note-taking skills and will sit patiently rewriting the text from a page rather than summarizing major points. However, Laura tends to be a good speller. Laura's school counselor indicated that "Laura has always wanted to be a high-achieving student and has tried very hard to achieve her goals . . . unfortunately, many times her expectations do not match the outcome and when this happens she becomes depressed and loses concentration in her academics and has feelings of not being worthy. . . . She had the same types of experiences in extracurricular activities."

Despite her difficulties, Laura independently completed and submitted applications to four colleges. However, her parents have some concerns about Laura's abilities to live away from home, and Laura may take classes through a local community college after graduating high school.

Emotional and Social Development

Laura's parents described her as a young woman who is "reliant" and has a strong musical ability. In addition, they said, "she is not easily beaten down by life, despite encountering frequent rejection." Her counselor described Laura as "a very polite young lady" who is very personable. However, Dr. O. indicated that Laura has many difficulties, and she appears to her mother to be somewhat depressed. Laura's apparent "laziness and her reluctance to exert effort in any area" is of concern to her parents. Laura loves singing and is a talented piano player. However, her parents stated that she is inconsistent in terms of the effort she exerts in this regard and cannot motivate herself to practice her piano exercises. Her parents said that they are concerned because "she tends to lie about completing her homework and will do the bare minimum in order to get by." Laura also indicated to the examiner that she does tend to be lazy and that she often lies but "is working on this."

According to her parents, Laura tends to be socially awkward, and she has some notable difficulty maintaining friendships. She is often mistreated and teased by her peers, and she is not included in many social activities. She has an odd sense of humor and is a very concrete, literal thinker. Laura tends to be short-tempered with her sisters, who are described as high-achieving young women. Laura had a boyfriend for a period of time, but she terminated this relationship due to her discomfort with his public displays of affection. Her parents have set limits on the Internet access available to Laura after noting that she had made some inappropriate choices in this regard.

Her mother noted that Laura does not demonstrate good personal hygiene. She would rather lose privileges, such as her allowance or cell phone, rather than complete her chores (i.e., clean her room and bathroom). Her mother indicated further concern that Laura does not appear to learn from the consequences of her actions and "demonstrates a lack of realism in some regard."

Behavioral Observations

Laura presented as a polite and pleasant young woman. She appeared comfortable interacting with the examiner, and rapport was easily established. Laura was extremely verbal throughout the testing; however, at times she appeared to be

≡ Rapid Reference 10.4

Pertinent Information to Include in Appearance and Behavioral Characteristics

- Talk about significant patterns or themes you see going on during testing.
- Sequence information in order of importance rather than in order of occurrence. (Do not just do a chronological list.)
- Describe the behavioral referents to your hypotheses. (Use specific examples.)
- Describe what makes this client unique. (Paint a picture for the reader.)

Suggested areas to review: (Note only significant behavior.)

Appearance

- Size: height and weight
- Facial characteristics
- Grooming and cleanliness
- Posture
- Clothing style
- Maturity: Does the person look his or her age?

Behavior

- Speech articulation, language patterns
- Activity level (foot wiggling, excessive talking, nail biting, tension, etc.)
- Attention span/distractibility
- Cooperativeness or resistance
- Interest in doing well
- How does the individual go about solving problems?
  - Trial and error? Quickly or reflectively? Check answers?
- Reactions to failure or challenge:
  - Does client continue to work until time is up?
  - Does client ask for direction or help?
  - Did failure reduce interest in the task or working on other tasks?
  - When frustrated, is the client aggressive or dependent?
- Attitude toward self:
  - Regards self with confidence? Superior attitude? Inadequate? Defeated?
  - How did client strive to get approval? Response to your praise of effort?

Validity of Test Results

- For example, state: "On the basis of John's above behaviors, the results of this assessment are considered a valid indication of his current level of cognitive and academic ability."
- Or if not, state why.

verbally uninhibited and notably impulsive. Laura was never inappropriate in her behavior, but she clearly did not always pick up on social cues. Her mood and affect were normal. Laura did not appear reactive or notably sensitive to the nature of the tasks or the levels of difficulty of the tasks.

Laura was not noted to be distractible or inattentive. She did not seem to have difficulty with restlessness during the testing, although some impulsivity was evident. No problems with initiation and persistence were observed. Both Laura's receptive language and her expressive language appeared intact. However, she did not always focus on the essential factors in a situation, and when giving a verbal answer to a question, she tended to overgeneralize or focus on less relevant details. As a result, her responses were often long-winded, somewhat confusing, and less meaningful than a more concise and integrated response might be. During informal discussion, Laura seemed to be reciting "the correct response" but did not demonstrate the associated affective import that would be expected.

Laura worked diligently throughout the testing and persevered with all tasks. On the basis of these behavior observations, this assessment appears to be a valid measure of Laura's functioning at this time.

Assessment Procedures

- Clinical interview with Laura and her parents
- Wechsler Adult Intelligence Scale—Fourth Edition (WAIS-IV)
- Wechsler Individual Achievement Test—Second Edition (WIAT-II)
- IVA+Plus Continuous Performance Test (IVA+Plus)
- The Beery-Buktenica Developmental Test of Visual-Motor Integration (Beery VMI)
- California Verbal Learning Test—Second Edition (CVLT-II)
- Delis-Kaplan Executive Function System (D-KEFS): Selected Subtests
- Wisconsin Card Sort Test-64 Computer Version 2 (WCST-64)
- Beck Youth Inventory—Second Edition (BYI)
- Millon Adolescent Clinical Inventory (MACI)
- Thematic Apperception Test (TAT): Selected Cards
- Gilliam Asperger's Disorder Scale (GADS)
- Clinical Assessment of Interpersonal Relationships (CAIR)
- Adaptive Behavior Assessment System—Second Edition (ABAS-II)
- Achenbach Youth Self Report (YSR)
- Conners Comprehensive Behavior Rating Scales—Parent & Teacher Forms
- Conners Third Edition: Self Report & Parent Short Forms

≣ Rapid Reference 10.5

Pertinent Information to Include in Test Results and Interpretation

- Use paragraph form.
- Put numbers in this section, including IQs and index scores with confidence intervals and percentile ranks. When discussing performance on subtests, use *percentile ranks*. (Most people are not familiar with a mean of 10 and standard deviation of 3); do *not* include Raw Scores.
- *Tie in behaviors* with results to serve as logical explanations or reminders wherever appropriate.
- With more than one test, *find similarities* in performances and differences (discrepancies) and try to hypothesize if you have enough information to do so.
- Support hypotheses with *multiple sources* of data, including observed behaviors.
- Do not contradict yourself.
- Be sure that you are *describing the subtests*, not just naming them. Remember, the reader has no idea what "Picture Completion" means.
- Describe the underlying abilities that the task is tapping.
- Talk about the *person's abilities*, not the test.
- Be *straightforward* in your writing, not too literary; do not use metaphors.

Test Results

Intellectual Abilities

In order to assess Laura's intellectual ability, she was administered the *Wechsler Adult Intelligence Scale—Fourth Edition* (WAIS-IV), which is an individually administered test of an individual's intellectual ability and cognitive strengths and weaknesses. This test yields five composite scores: Verbal Comprehension Index, Perceptual Reasoning Index, Working Memory Index, Processing Speed Index, and Full Scale IQ. In addition, this test also yields a General Ability Index, which is less sensitive to the influence of working memory and processing speed. Laura's general cognitive ability is in the Average Range/Within Normal Limits, as indicated by both her Full Scale IQ (FSIQ standard score of 89; 78–88 with 90% confidence; 13th percentile) and her General Ability Index (GAI standard score of 86; 82–93 with 90% confidence; 18th percentile). However, there are notable strengths and weaknesses in her cognitive profile, so it is informative to understand these specific abilities in addition to her global measures of functioning.

Laura's verbal reasoning abilities as measured by the Verbal Comprehension Index are in the Average range and above those of approximately 39% of her

Table 10.1. Psychometric Summary of WAIS–IV Profile for Laura O.

Index/IQ Subtest	Score	90% Confidence Interval	Percentile Rank	Descriptive Category
Verbal Comprehension	96	91–101	39	Average Range/Within Normal Limits
Similarities	9		37	
Vocabulary	11		63	
Information	8		25	
(Comprehension)	10		50	*Does not contribute to Index or IQ*
Perceptual Reasoning	79	74–84	8	Below Average/ Normative Weakness
Block Design	5		5	
Matrix Reasoning	7		16	
Visual Puzzles	7		16	
(Figure Weights)	4		2	*Does not contribute to Index or IQ*
(Picture Completion)	6		9	*Does not contribute to Index or IQ*
Working Memory	95	90–100	37	Average Range/Within Normal Limits
Digit Span	11		63	
Arithmetic	7		16	
(Letter-Number Sequencing)	4		2	*Does not contribute to Index or IQ*
Processing Speed	97	92–102	42	Average Range/Within Normal Limits
Symbol Search	10		50	
Coding	9		37	
(Cancellation)	9		37	*Does not contribute to Index or IQ*

(continued)

Table 10.1. (continued)

Index/IQ Subtest	Score	90% Confidence Interval	Percentile Rank	Descriptive Category
Full Scale IQ	83	78–88	13	Below Average/ Normative Weakness
GAI	86	82–93	18	Average Range/Within Normal Limits
CPI	96	90–102	39	Average Range/Within Normal Limits
Clinical Cluster				
Verbal Fluid Reasoning	97	42	91–104	Average Range/Within Normal Limits
Lexical Knowledge	100	50	95–105	Average Range/Within Normal Limits
General Information	94	34	89–100	Average Range/Within Normal Limits
Long-Term Memory	97	42	92–102	Average Range/Within Normal Limits
Short-Term Memory	86	18	81–93	Average Range/Within Normal Limits
Fluid Reasoning	75	5	71–83	Below Average/ Normative Weakness
Visual Processing	78	7	73–86	Below Average/ Normative Weakness

peers (VCI = 96). The Verbal Comprehension Index is designed to measure verbal reasoning and concept formation. When examining clinical clusters of scores within the Verbal Comprehension scale, Laura's consistent abilities in this domain are evident. For example, her facility with words and her knowledge of factual information are equally well developed and both in the Average Range/ Within Normal Limits. These similar skills were evident from her Lexical Knowledge Cluster (50th percentile) and her General Information Cluster (34th percentile). Additionally, her ability to reason with verbal information was comparable to her long-term memory of verbally encoded information. Her skills in these domains were also in the Average range (both the Verbal Fluid Reasoning Cluster and Long-Term Memory Cluster were in the 42nd percentile).

Similar to her Average skills noted on the Verbal Comprehension scale of the WAIS-IV, Laura's expressive language ability was intact on a separate measure of verbal fluency. Both her semantic and phonemic fluency were Average to High Average (63rd and 75th percentiles respectively). However, Laura's basic word retrieval was mildly impaired on a measure of dysnomia.

In contrast to her Average Range abilities in the areas of verbal reasoning, lexical knowledge, general information, and verbal fluency, Laura's nonverbal reasoning abilities are in the Below Average Range. This weaker area of ability was evident from her score on the Perceptual Reasoning Index that was above those of only 8% of her peers (PRI standard score of 79). Compared to her other abilities, her equally impaired visual processing and nonverbal fluid reasoning skills are personal weaknesses and are also Normative Weaknesses when compared with others her age. These deficits were noted from her Fluid Reasoning Cluster (5th percentile) and her Visual Processing Cluster (7th percentile), which were both Below Average and considered Normative Weaknesses. Her ability to reason *verbally* is notably stronger than her ability to reason with *visual* material. In fact, the difference between her Verbal Fluid Reasoning Cluster (42nd percentile) and her Fluid Reasoning Cluster (5th percentile) is uncommonly large and occurs less than 10% of the time in the normative population.

Laura's impaired nonverbal problem-solving and spatial planning abilities were further supported by her Below Average performance on a challenging executive-function task requiring her to build a designated tower in the fewest number of moves possible by moving disks of varying size (9th percentile). Also consistent with her areas of personal weakness on the WAIS-IV Perceptual Reasoning scale was her visual-motor integration ability. When required to copy a series of geometric figures with paper and pencil, Laura's skills were in the Below Average range (10th percentile on the Developmental Test of Visual Motor Integration). Overall, Laura's notable personal and normative weaknesses in the areas of visual processing and nonverbal fluid reasoning indicate that she has a disorder in these basic psychological processes, which is a finding that should play an essential role in developing specialized interventions.

Despite her deficits in visual processing and nonverbal fluid reasoning, Laura demonstrated Average ability to quickly process simple or routine visual material without making errors (Processing Speed Index = 97; 42nd percentile). Laura's difficulties with visual stimuli may be mitigated when the stimuli are less spatially complex or when a lower level of cognitive processing is demanded, such as on the WAIS-IV Processing Speed tasks.

Laura also demonstrated Average Range abilities in her short-term memory. This Within Normal Limits performance was evident from her Working Memory Index standard score of 95 (37th percentile). Although Laura scored in the Average range on a measure of digit span recall, reversal, and sequencing (63rd percentile) and on a measure of her ability to mentally solve a series of arithmetic problems (16th percentile), she struggled on a supplementary task that required her to sequence a string of letters and numbers (2nd percentile). A higher level of attention and cognitive shifting are needed on the letter-number sequencing task, which may have caused the inconsistency in her performance on these memory tasks.

Laura's memory skills were further assessed with the *California Verbal Learning Test—Second Edition* (CVLT-II) and the *Wechsler Memory Scale—Third Edition* (WMS-III). She demonstrated intact performance on a demanding task of verbal list-learning memory. Her overall immediate recall was generally Average, and her short delay and long delay free and cued recall was within the normal range. Her number of repetition errors and intrusion errors was within normal limits. Laura's performance was intact on recognition testing. Similarly, her performance was intact on a measure assessing memory for organized verbal material (63rd percentile on both immediate and delayed recall trials). Consistent with her verbal memory skills, on a simple measure of visual recall, Laura demonstrated Average performance both on immediate and on delayed recall trials (50th and 63rd percentiles respectively).

Attention and Executive Functioning

Sustained Visual and Auditory Attention. Laura's performance on WAIS-IV and WMS-III tests of memory required sustained attention and concentration for successful completion. Her sustained attention was further assessed by means of the IVA+Plus Continuous Performance Test (IVA+Plus). This task is intended to be mildly boring and demanding of sustained attention over a 13-minute period of time. On this task Laura was required to respond to target stimuli (the number "1" presented in either an auditory or visual format on the computer) and refrain from responding to nontarget stimuli (the number "2" presented in the same formats). A diagnosis of Attention-Deficit/Hyperactivity Disorder, Predominantly Hyperactive-Impulsive Type was supported by the IVA+Plus test data. Laura was mildly impaired in her ability to inhibit responses to nontarget auditory stimuli; she exhibited some problems with auditory response control. In addition, Laura's Visual Prudence was extremely impaired. That is, Laura clicked impulsively numerous times to the nontarget visual stimuli. This weakness in response control suggests that Laura is likely to be overreactive and easily distracted in her daily life by any changes in her visual environment. Problems were noted in impulse control, particularly under high-demand conditions. Laura was intact in her ability to be consistent in her responses to both visual and auditory stimuli. Her stamina was strong, and her response time to auditory stimuli became faster over the course of the test. She was also able to maintain her mental processing speed in the visual domain during the test.

Laura did not show any problems with her general auditory and visual attentional functioning under low-demand or high-demand conditions. However, her Auditory Focus fell in the moderately to severely impaired range. At times Laura showed difficulty due to delays in her response to auditory test stimuli. Her pattern of responding indicated that her attention frequently "drifted off." Similarly, Laura's Visual Focus fell in the slightly impaired range. Most of the time she was able to process and stay focused on visual stimuli. Occasionally, momentary lapses in visual response times were found. These lapses in visual processing may be due to slight fatigue or to her preoccupation with distracting thoughts.

Laura did not show any problems with her overall auditory or visual processing speed. Her recognition reaction time falls within the Average range. Similarly, she demonstrated no relative difference between her visual and auditory mental processing speeds. Thus, she has a balanced ability to process information in these two different sensory modalities. Laura's recognition response time to stimuli under low-demand conditions was much quicker than it was under high-demand conditions. In other words, her response times are clearly slower when she is required to make rapid, repeated responses.

In addition to the IVA, Laura and her parents completed various rating scales to give more information about Laura's attentional functioning. Laura's parents indicated some concerns regarding her attentional functioning, and she was rated as demonstrating mild to moderate deficits with inattention, hyperactivity, and impulsivity. In contrast, Laura described herself as functioning within the normal range on measures of attention and hyperactivity/impulsivity.

Cognitive Flexibility. Laura was administered the Trails, Verbal Fluency, Design Fluency, and Color-Word subtests from the D-KEFS in order to assess her cognitive flexibility. Notable variability in her performances was observed. Laura struggled on the Trails measure requiring her to shift between connecting numbers and letters in sequence (0.1 percentile). This indicates a deficit in cognitive flexibility on nonverbal tasks, although some definite problems with inhibition did impair Laura's performance on this task (i.e., she was distracted by two letters or two numbers close together). In contrast, Laura did not evidence this deficit on the Design Fluency task, and her nonverbal cognitive flexibility was intact on this measure (63rd percentile). Similarly, Laura's verbal fluency was also intact (37th–50th percentile). However, mild impairment in Laura's inhibition and cognitive flexibility were evident on the Color-Word task (16th–25th percentile).

Concept Formation. Laura's verbal-semantic and visual-perceptual concept formation skills were assessed by means of the D-KEFS Sorting Test. Her overall scores were in the Average range (50th percentile) on measures of free sorting, indicating an intact ability to perceive and form conceptual relationships and to express these relationships in abstract terms. However, Laura struggled on the component of this subtest requiring her to recognize those sorts made by the examiner (16th percentile). Frequently, people who demonstrate this deficit are especially vulnerable to distraction and become mentally derailed by the sorts generated by the examiner.

Laura demonstrated intact performance on a computerized assessment of her concept formation skills (WCST-64; 47th percentile), reflecting intact conceptual reasoning.

Academic Skills

In addition to her cognitive and neuropsychological abilities, Laura's academic skills were measured with the *Wechsler Individual Achievement Test—Second Edition* (WIAT-II). Laura's overall academic skills were in the Average range.

Reading. Laura presented consistent skills on different aspects of reading. Her strongest performance was on tasks that assessed her capability to correctly apply phonetic decoding rules when reading a series of nonsense words (79th percentile). Similarly, Laura scored in the High Average range on tasks that assessed her capability to read sentences and paragraphs and answer questions about what was read (77th percentile). Her reading speed was normal. She had Average performance on tasks that required her to correctly read a series of printed words (61st percentile).

Mathematics. Laura's skills in mathematics varied slightly. She performed in the Average range on tasks that evaluated her ability to add, subtract, multiply, and divide one- to three-digit numbers, fractions, and decimals; and solve simple linear equations (53rd percentile). In contrast, Laura's performance was Low Average on tasks that required her to understand number, consumer math concepts, geometric measurement, basic graphs, and solve single-step and multistep word problems (18th percentile). When considering the 90% confidence interval, her Mathematical Reasoning abilities fall between the Below Average and Average range. The relative difficulty that Laura had on the WIAT-II Mathematical Reasoning is consistent with her academic history (which includes failing math tests) as well as her cognitive profile (which showed she has a disorder in these basic psychological processes of fluid reasoning). Taken together, these results indicate that she has a learning disorder in the area of mathematics reasoning.

Written Language. On tasks that required her to correctly spell verbally presented words, Laura performed in the Average range. Her skills in this area exceed those of approximately 73% of students her age. Laura also demonstrated Average performance on tasks that required her to generate words within a category, generate sentences to describe visual cues, combine sentences, and compose an organized, persuasive essay on a named topic (45th percentile).

Emotional Functioning

On various rating scales, Laura's parents rated Laura as demonstrating notable emotional distress and very significant social problems. On the GADS, Laura was rated by her parents as being borderline for a diagnosis of Asperger's disorder. In contrast, Laura did not rate herself as having difficulties in any area.

Laura's parents indicated some concerns regarding her adaptive functioning. Adaptive skills are practical everyday skills required to function and meet environmental demands, including effectively taking care of oneself and interacting with other people. The categories of adaptive behaviors assessed by the ABAS-II include Conceptual (communication and academic skills), Social (interpersonal and social competence skills), and Practical (independent living and daily living skills). Laura's parents rated her as demonstrating Below Average adaptive functioning overall. Laura's Conceptual Skills were rated as Below Average and her Social Skills were rated as Extremely Low. Her Practical Skills were rated as Average. Laura was rated by her parents as demonstrating relative weaknesses in the "Social" and "Self-Care" skill areas. She was rated as demonstrating a strength in "Community Use" and "Health and Safety."

Family and Peer Relationships. When asked to draw a picture of herself with her family doing something together, Laura drew her family in the swimming pool. She drew herself as significantly smaller than her siblings, almost in an infantile manner, and she was inserted close to her mother in the picture. Laura described herself as a "mama's girl" and indicated that "I have to be close to my mother, I love my mom so much, she is my best friend, she has done so much for me." On other tests, Laura indicated a desire to spend more time alone with her mother and not to share her as much with her siblings. However, on the TAT, Laura told a story about a young woman who had different aspirations from her family, and the mother in the story asked, "Why isn't my daughter like me or the family?" Therefore, it is likely that although Laura is clearly seeking intense closeness with her mother, she continues to see herself as dissimilar from the other family members.

On the CAIR, Laura rated her relationship with her mother as a strength and rated her relationship with her father as Average. Laura further noted close relationships with her sisters along with close friendships with peers. She rated her relationships with her female peers and her teachers as Average. However, she rated her relationships with male peers as a weakness.

≡ Rapid Reference 10.6

Pertinent Information to Include in Summary and Diagnostic Impressions

- Summary information should already be stated earlier in the body of the report.
- Include summary of referral, key background, or behavioral observation points.
- Summarize the most important interpretations of global scores and strengths and weaknesses.
- Defend your diagnosis if one is made.

Personality Profile. Laura identified "schoolwork" as the problem that is troubling her the most. A tendency toward avoiding self-disclosure is evident in her response style. There is the likelihood of deficits in introspectiveness and psychological-mindedness. What is most noticeable about Laura is her anxious conformity to the expectations of others, particularly family and authority, her overcontrol of emerging impulses, and her defensiveness about admitting psychological problems. Beneath her controlled facade and pseudopoise are marked feelings of personal insecurity that are evident in a tendency to downgrade herself and to keep a comfortable emotional distance from others and an anticipation of rejection should she act inappropriately. Her major defense against such events is an excessive conformity and the inhibition of any affect that might evoke ridicule or contempt from others. Notable also is her focus on minor irrelevancies that serves to distract her attention from growing sexual feelings. Her facade of conformity may also hide repressed resentments felt toward those who may have humiliated her in the past. However, surges of anger will only rarely break through the surface restraint.

Laura's self-doubts and low self-esteem may have led her to seek the quiet conformity of a supportive institution such as her church or other social or school organizations. In this way, she hopes to gain a measure of security and may be able to identify with others, especially those in authority, whose actions cannot possibly be met with disfavor. A consistent and rigid behavioral pattern is maintained in which all signs of autonomy are restrained and conformity to the rules of others is emphasized.

Summary

Laura is a 17-year-old girl who was referred for a neuropsychological evaluation due to difficulties with motivation, attention, and social skills. Her behavior during the testing revealed a tendency to be verbally uninhibited and impulsive as well as somewhat insensitive to social cues. Laura's general cognitive ability was in the

Average range (WAIS-IV FSIQ of 89). However, there were notable areas of weakness in addition to her many cognitive abilities that were Within Normal Limits. Laura's cognitive abilities that were intact and in the Average range included: verbal reasoning, lexical knowledge, general information, verbal fluency, short-term memory (verbal and visual), and processing speed. In contrast, Laura had personal and normative weaknesses in visual processing and nonverbal fluid reasoning, which indicate that she has a disorder in these basic psychological processes (evident from her WAIS-IV Perceptual Reasoning Index—8th percentile; VMI—10th percentile; and Tower Test—9th percentile).

On academic testing, Laura demonstrated a relative weakness in her math reasoning skills (WIAT-II Mathematical Reasoning score of 86). This difficulty with math reasoning is consistent with her educational history as well as her disorder in the basic psychological process of fluid reasoning. In contrast, her other academic abilities were in the Average range. As a whole, these academic and cognitive test results, paired with her academic history, indicate that she has a learning disorder in the area of mathematics reasoning.

Laura demonstrated variable performances on measures of attention and executive functioning. On a continuous performance test, Laura's response control was poor and was consistent with impaired inhibition noted on other measures. Her performance was indicative of a diagnosis of ADHD, Predominately Hyperactive-Impulsive Type. Parent rating scales further confirmed problems in this regard. Although Laura did not rate herself as demonstrating problems with response control, she did indicate on numerous occasions during informal conversation that she fails to think before she acts and speaks, and she tends to be highly impulsive. Laura demonstrated very impaired cognitive flexibility on one measure of higher-level cognitive functioning. In addition, her spatial planning and problem solving was mildly impaired on another measure.

Laura's neuropsychological profile is consistent with a nonverbal learning disability. This is a disorder in which the core deficit resides in the capacity to process nonlinguistic perceptual information and is primarily a right-hemisphere disorder. The Personal Weakness and Normative Weakness on her WAIS-IV Perceptual Reasoning Index is suggestive of this diagnosis when coupled with other factors. Specifically, Laura's difficulties with visual-spatial organization, her variable nonverbal problem solving, attentional problems, and variable executive functions, along with her history of social-emotional difficulties, are consistent with a nonverbal learning disability.

From a psychological perspective, it is apparent that Laura is functioning below age expectancy. She appears to be struggling to separate from her mother and has a wish to be in the infantile stage, bound closely with her mother. Laura fears criticism and derogation and is inclined toward self-blame and self-punishment. There is a hesitation about expressing emotions, particularly hostility or sexuality. Laura demonstrates excessive conformity and the inhibition of any affect that might evoke rejection. Strong defensiveness along with guilt and self-condemnation appear to be prominent.

Diagnostic Impressions

314.01 Attention-Deficit/Hyperactivity Disorder, Predominantly Hyperactive-Impulsive Type
315.9 Learning Disability Not Otherwise Specified (i.e., Nonverbal Learning Disability)
315.1 Mathematics Disorder
V313.82 Identity Problem

Recommendations

Due to Laura's diagnosis of ADHD, nonverbal learning disability, and a mathematics disorder, she would benefit from some interventions in a college setting. It is strongly recommended that Laura seek out services through the learning center at any college she should attend and request these modifications:

- Laura will benefit from extended time on all written tests.
- *Preferential seating* in all classes is strongly recommended. Whenever possible, minimize distractions in Laura's study area.
- *Reduce the amount of note taking required.* It is likely that Laura will benefit from having *instructor handouts* and *lecture outlines* available prior to the lecture for her to review. She would benefit from a *note taker*.
- *A private room for testing* should be available upon request.
- *A certified educational consultant* might be helpful in terms of assisting Laura in making appropriate choices regarding college choices. I am happy to provide a referral in this regard.

Stimulant medication to address symptoms of ADHD should be considered. In addition, Laura would clearly benefit from *psychotherapy* in order to help foster her emotional growth. I am happy to make an appropriate recommendation upon request.

Books on nonverbal-learning-disabled youth and appropriate interventions might be helpful for Laura and her parents to read, as well as those that provide academic support or tutoring. For example, *Nonverbal Learning Disabilities: A Clinical Perspective* by Joseph Palombo and *Syndrome of Nonverbal Learning Disabilities: Neurodevelopmental Manifestations* by Byron P. Rourke.

Michelle Lurie, PsyD
Clinical Neuropsychologist

Table 10.2.
Psychometric Summary of Additional Tests for Laura O.

Wechsler Memory Scale—Third Edition-Abbreviated (WMS-III-Abbreviated)

Subtest	Scaled Score	Percentile Rank
Logical Memory I	11	63
Logical Memory II	11	63
Family Pictures I	10	50
Family Pictures II	11	63

Beery-Buktenica Developmental Test of Visual-Motor Integration (VMI)

Standard Scores	Percentile
81	10

Delis-Kaplan Executive Function System (D-KEFS)

Trail Making Test	Primary Measure: Completion Times	Scaled Score	Percentile Rank
	Visual Scanning	7	16
	Number Sequencing	11	63
	Letter Sequencing	8	25
	Number-Letter Switching	1	0.1
Verbal Fluency	Primary Measure	Scaled Score	Percentile Rank
	Letter Fluency	12	75
	Category Fluency	11	63
	Category Switching: Responses	9	37
	Category Switching: Accuracy	10	50
Design Fluency	Primary Measure	Scaled Score	Percentile Rank
	Filled Dots: Total Correct	11	63

(continued)

Design Fluency	Primary Measure	Scaled Score	Percentile Rank
	Empty Dots Only: Correct	10	50
	Switching: Total	11	63
Color-Word Interference Test	**Primary Measures: Completion Times**	**Scaled Score**	**Percentile Rank**
	Color Naming	10	50
	Word Reading	11	63
	Inhibition	8	25
	Inhibition/Switching	7	16
Sorting Test	**Primary Measures: Completion Times**	**Scaled Score**	**Percentile Rank**
	Confirmed Correct Sorts	10	50
	Free Sorting Description Score	10	50
	Sort Recognition Description Score	7	16
Tower Test	**Primary Measures**	**Scaled Score**	**Percentile Rank**
	Total Achievement Score	6	9

Gilliam Asperger's Disorder Scale (GADS)

Subscale	Scaled Score	Probability of Asperger's Disorder
Social Interaction	4	
Restricted Patterns of Behavior	6	
Cognitive Patterns	6	
Pragmatic Skills	10	
Asperger's Disorder Quotient	77	**Borderline**

Adaptive Behavior Assessment System—Second Edition (ABAS-II)

Composite	Composite Score	Percentile Rank	Qualitative Range
GAC	82	12	Below Average

Composite	Composite Score	Percentile Rank	Qualitative Range
Conceptual	85	16	Below Average
Social	68	2	Extremely Low
Practical	90	25	Average

Wisconsin Card Sort Test-64 Computer Version 2

WCST Scores	Standard Scores	Percentile
Perseverative Errors	99	47

CASE REPORT: JIM W., AGE 64, POSSIBLE DEMENTIA

Reason for Referral

Mr. W. has a history of memory problems that began 37 years ago following a motorcycle accident resulting in a severe coma. He also reported increased depression and irritability within the last year following an accident at work. He was referred for neuropsychological evaluation in order to evaluate his current

CAUTION

Common Errors to Avoid in Report Writing

- Inappropriate detail
- Unnecessary jargon or technical terms
- Vague language
- Abstract statements
- Not supporting hypotheses with adequate data
- Gross generalizations from isolated information
- Inserting value judgments
- Discussing the test itself rather than the person's abilities
- Poor grammar
- Presenting behaviors or test scores without interpreting them
- Failure to adequately address reasons for referral
- Failure to provide confidence intervals or otherwise denote that all obtained test scores include a band of error
- Giving test results prematurely (e.g., in the section on "Appearance and Behavioral Characteristics")

level of cognitive and personality functioning, to assist in making a diagnosis, and to make recommendations regarding his treatment needs. Specifically, assessing for the presence of dementia is of concern.

Background Information

Mr. W. is a married, Caucasian male. He completed eight years of education and later earned his high school diploma. He is currently employed as a janitor and lives with his wife of 40 years, and has two adult children. English is his primary language and he is right-hand dominant.

Mr. W. was born and raised in an intact family on the East Coast. To his knowledge, there were no complications with his mother's pregnancy, labor, or delivery. He denied any history of developmental, emotional, or behavioral problems while growing up. Both his parents had a sixth-grade education. His father worked as a carpenter and died from a stroke. His mother worked as a waitress and died from throat cancer. He has three siblings who live out of state. He denied that his siblings have any significant health issues.

In his educational history, Mr. W. identified math as his best subject and reading and spelling as his worst. He noted that he had difficulty learning to read, that he had to repeat the third grade, and that he was placed in a special program to help him learn to read in ninth grade. He dropped out of high school and enlisted in the Marine Corps at the age of 16. However, he indicated that later he attended an adult education program through the Veteran's Association and received his high school diploma.

In a review of his employment history, Mr. W. stated that he served over 10 years in the Marine Corps. However, following his accident, he was no longer able to perform his duties effectively and was honorably discharged due to his disability. He then worked as a forklift operator for 28 years and has worked part time as a janitor for the last 2 years.

Medical History

According to Mr. W., he was involved in a motorcycle accident 37 years ago in which he apparently drove off the road and may have then hit his head on a rock. He stated that he does not remember the incident but that he has been told that someone found him the next morning and he was then taken to the hospital. Ms. W. confirmed that her husband was comatose for 2 weeks, following which he was "semiconscious" for a period of time. She noted that he continued to be "not coherent and confused" for approximately 6 months and that he remained in the hospital for 1 year. Mr. W. stated that he was subsequently diagnosed with "organic brain syndrome secondary to trauma" but that he has never undergone a neuropsychological evaluation.

More recently, Mr. W. reported being involved in an accident at work last summer that caused serious injury to his back along with his right knee and foot. His injury required surgery to place a steel rod in his back, and he has had two surgeries on his right foot. Mr. W. noted that he is taking Hydrocodone 5/500 mg and Percocet 5 mg for back pain as well as vitamin supplements. He reported that since the injury, he has been increasingly depressed and irritable, indicating that he can become very angry and explosive. Ms. W. also noted that her husband experiences "stress from the injury on the job." Other than these injuries and medical issues in his adult history, Mr. W. reported that he had measles as a child and that he has had pneumonia.

A thorough review of neuropsychological symptoms was conducted with Mr. W. during his interview:

Sensory-Perceptual. Mr. W. reported that he wears glasses for both reading and distance. He also reported experiencing a change in his sense of taste and being overly sensitive to noise since his head injury. As a result of his injury last year, he indicated that he experiences pain in his back, knee, and foot, along with numbness, loss of feeling, and the feeling of pins and needles in his foot. He also noted that he experienced problems with loss of vision, blurred and double vision, and seeing unusual things following the first accident. He denied experiencing these problems more recently. He reported having "infrequent" headaches but denied having any other sensory-perceptual difficulties or pain-related problems.

Cognition-Thinking. Mr. W. and his wife reported that he experiences numerous cognitive difficulties. These difficulties include trouble with common sense, problem solving, judgment, mathematics, and thinking quickly. Also identified were difficulties concentrating, being easily distracted, inconsistent performance on tasks, disorganization, and experiencing periods where he loses time. Mr. W. also reported being inflexible, getting stuck on a problem, and having a hard time doing more than one thing at a time while also finding it hard to stay on task.

Communication. Mr. W. reported experiencing a number of problems related to written and verbal communication. He indicated that he had difficulties with spelling, writing, and reading. He also reported having trouble understanding others and following the story in a movie or television show as well as having difficulty remembering words and naming common objects. Fluctuations in talkativeness are also reported, noting both times of talking too much as well as talking too little.

Memory. The patient reported having numerous problems with his memory, including both short- and long-term memory. These problems include forgetting what he is doing, where he is, people's names and faces, and recent events. He also noted difficulty learning new things, being told that he repeats himself, memory loss around the time of his accident, and forgetting things from long ago. He commented, "My memory's been shot for a long time."

Motor Functioning. Mr. W. reported that he has difficulties with balance and coordination, muscle weakness, and trouble walking due to his accident and the resulting injuries from last year. He denied experiencing any such difficulties prior to his accident or experiencing any other problems with motor functioning.

Social. Mr. W. and his wife reported that he experiences difficulties in most interpersonal relationships, including with his wife, children, friends, coworkers, and employer. They also reported that he lacks tact and can be insensitive and aggressive. He reported a tendency to isolate himself at times. Mrs. W. stated that her husband became "a jerk and hotheaded" following the accident. She reported that he has frequent problems with anger and irritability, noting that there was frequent yelling in their relationship and that more recently her husband was unable to keep a job due to his argumentativeness and yelling.

Psychological. Mr. W. reported having symptoms of depression and anxiety. He also admitted experiencing mood swings, irritability, restlessness and agitation, anger outbursts, paranoia, intrusive thoughts, and difficulty handling stress. He noted that he can be impatient and impulsive but also experiences a lack of energy and passivity at times. Changes in sleep, appetite, weight, and sex drive were also reported.

Adaptive Behavior. Currently, Mr. W. is employed as a janitor. He reported that his wife does most of the work around the house (e.g., preparing meals, cleaning, yard work, and paying bills), but that he takes out the trash and also collects cans and bottles for recycling as a hobby. He reported watching approximately three hours of television per day. He visits with friends and family and has people over to visit. However, his wife indicated that Mr. W. has a general lack of planning and engagement in leisure activities, particularly those of a social nature. She also noted that he has a "lack of social awareness of others' needs and appropriate social reciprocity." Conversely, Mr. W. denied any problems with self-care and is able to drive. However, he indicated that he needs clear and detailed instructions on how to reach the desired location or he will become lost.

Psychiatric History

Mr. W. denied experiencing any mental health symptoms outside of those identified previously in relation to his accidents: primarily depression, irritability, anxiety, lability, and impulsivity. His wife reported that they had been in marriage counseling previously and that they have again recently begun marriage counseling. Mr. W. denied having ever been diagnosed with a psychiatric illness besides organic brain syndrome. He reported taking lorazepam 1 mg for anxiety. The family psychiatric history is unremarkable.

Behavioral Observations

Mr. W. arrived on time for his appointments, having driven himself. He was a well-groomed man of average height and weight who was casually and appropriately dressed. He has a tattoo on his left upper arm of the Marine Corps bulldog. His posture and gait were unremarkable. He was initially irritable during his second appointment, noting confusion and frustration with having to come to the appointment by himself. However, he was cooperative and made good eye contact. His behavior and level of activity were initially appropriate. As the evaluation progressed, Mr. W. became increasingly tired and his impulse control diminished: He became playful, joking, and expansive in his behavior. There was no evidence of any tics or tremor.

During the administration of the various testing procedures, Mr. W. demonstrated adequate frustration tolerance and persistence on tasks that he found difficult. His response style was initially normal but became increasingly impulsive as he tired. He appeared to try his best on tasks presented to him. His work pace was slow, and he evidenced difficulties focusing his attention. He engaged in self-talk that was helpful to him in completing tasks.

Mr. W.'s speech was fluent and of normal rate, volume, and prosody. There was no evidence of any paraphasias or errors of articulation. He initiated conversation spontaneously and appropriately. He had somewhat limited comprehension and required frequent clarification of questions and directions. Associations were typically logical and goal-directed, although he occasionally became tangential in his thinking.

When asked to describe his usual mood during the past month, Mr. W. stated: "Irritable. I get upset over nothing." He also reported having feelings of depression and low self-esteem and stated: "I have no future, no friends, no brain power." He also described himself as "restless" and "always in fifth gear." He said he is quick to become irritable and angry, during which times he becomes explosive and yells. He appeared depressed with labile affect during the interview.

Thought content was negative for hallucinations, delusions, paranoid ideation, obsessions, compulsions, phobias, and suicidal or homicidal ideation. He denied any history of suicidal thoughts or behaviors.

Level of Effort and Validity of Performance. During his interview, Mr. W. reported his symptoms and history in a consistent manner. There was no indication that he attempted to either minimize or exaggerate his reported symptoms. He put forth adequate effort on the tasks presented to him. What follows is judged to be an accurate assessment of both Mr. W.'s current cognitive and personality functioning.

Means of Assessment

Clinical interview with Mr. and Ms. W.
Mental Status Examination
Wechsler Adult Intelligence Scale—Fourth Edition (WAIS-IV)
Wechsler Test of Adult Reading (WTAR)
Wechsler Memory Scale—Third Edition (WMS-III)
Minnesota Multiphasic Personality Inventory-2-Restructured Form (MMPI-2-RF)

Test Results and Interpretation

Mr. W. was administered the *Wechsler Adult Intelligence Scale—Fourth Edition* (WAIS-IV), which is an individually administered test of intellectual functioning and cognitive abilities. The WAIS-IV is comprised of 15 separate subtests, which can be grouped into five global areas or factors[1]: Crystallized Intelligence, which measures the depth of knowledge acquired from one's culture; Fluid Reasoning, which involves solving problems nonverbally; Visual Processing, which requires perceiving, storing, and manipulating visual patterns; Short-Term Memory, which involves taking in and holding information to use within seconds; and Processing Speed, which measures cognitive processing efficiency. On the WAIS-IV, Mr. W. earned a Full Scale IQ (FSIQ) of 83, which indicates that his general intellectual ability is in the Below Average Range when compared to other adults his age. This overall level of performance ranked him at the 13th percentile, indicating that he scored higher than 13% of other adults of the same age in the standardized sample. The chances are good (90%) that Mr. W.'s true FSIQ is somewhere within the range of 78–88. Mr. W.'s general ability is considered a normative weakness as compared to others his age in the normal population.

---

1. Note that these five global areas are a different reorganization of the WAIS-IV subtests from the traditional Wechsler indexes: the Verbal Comprehension Index, Perceptual Reasoning Index, Working Memory Index, and Processing Speed Index. The scores for these four Wechsler indexes are reported in the Psychometric Summary, but the interpretation of the client's WAIS-IV profile is based on the five global factors just described.

Table 10.3. Psychometric Summary of WAIS-IV Profile for Mr. W.

Index/IQ Subtest	Score	90% Confidence Interval	Percentile Rank	Descriptive Category
Verbal Comprehension	**85**	**80–90**	**16**	**Average Range/Within Normal Limits**
Similarities	9		37	
Vocabulary	8		25	[Contributes to Keith *Gc* Factor]
Information	5		5	[Contributes to Keith *Gc* Factor]
(Comprehension)	4		2	
Perceptual Reasoning	**90**	**85–95**	**25**	**Average Range/Within Normal Limits**
Block Design	9		37	[Contributes to Keith *Gv* Factor]
Matrix Reasoning	5		5	[Contributes to Keith *Gf* Factor]
Visual Puzzles	11		63	[Contributes to Keith *Gv* Factor]
(Figure Weights)	6		9	[Contributes to Keith *Gf* Factor]
(Picture Completion)	8		25	
Working Memory	**92**	**87–97**	**30**	**Average Range/Within Normal Limits**
Digit Span	8		25	[Contributes to Keith *Gsm* Factor]
Arithmetic	9		37	
(Letter-Number Sequencing)	8		25	[Contributes to Keith *Gsm* Factor]
Processing Speed	**79**	**74–84**	**8**	**Below Average/Normative Weakness**
Symbol Search	6		9	[Contributes to Keith *Gs* Factor]

(continued)

Table 10.3. (continued)

Index/IQ Subtest	Score	90% Confidence Interval	Percentile Rank	Descriptive Category
Processing Speed	79	74–84	8	Below Average/Normative Weakness
Coding	6		9	[Contributes to Keith *Gs* Factor]
(Cancellation)	5		5	
Full Scale IQ	83	78–88	13	Below Average/Normative Weakness
GAI	86	82–93	18	Average Range/Within Normal Limits
CPI	82	77–89	12	Below Average/Normative Weakness
Keith Factor				
Crystallized Intelligence (*Gc*)	81	77–86	10	Below Average/Normative Weakness
Short–Term Memory (*Gsm*)	89	84–95	23	Average Range/Within Normal Limits
Fluid Reasoning (*Gf*)	75	71–83	5	Below Average/Normative Weakness
Visual Processing (*Gv*)	100	94–106	50	Average Range/Within Normal Limits
Processing Speed (*Gs*)	79	74–88	8	Below Average/Normative Weakness

Mr. W.'s cognitive profile showed both areas of relative strength and weakness. For example, within the nonverbal realm, his abilities ranged from the Average range to the Below Average range. Specifically, on tasks that demanded visual-spatial processing, Mr. W. scored in the Average range, earning a standard score of 100 (50th percentile) on the Visual Processing Factor. Mr. W.'s ability to process visual information is a significant relative strength compared to his abilities in other areas. In contrast, his ability to reason with visual information was significantly weaker. This weaker ability was evident from his standard score of 75 (5th percentile) on the Fluid Reasoning Factor. His performance on these problem-solving tasks was

Below Average/Normative Weakness compared to others his age, and the underlying abilities are considered a personal weakness for him. The discrepancy between his stronger visual processing skills and his weaker visual reasoning skills is uncommonly large (occurring in less than 10% of the time in the normal population). Due to this difference, Mr. W. may be able to see specific details in visual information but may have difficulty integrating visual information to solve problems. He is challenged when tasks require a dynamic, flexible approach to problem solving and involve the capacity to discern the most salient aspects of a problem-solving situation, respond, and monitor the effectiveness of the response and change strategies as needed. Mr. W. has difficulty using the feedback provided to him and systematically testing possible solutions when problem solving.

Another related cognitive domain that was challenging for Mr. W. was processing speed. Like his personal weakness with processing visual information, when he was required to quickly respond to visual stimuli and use fine motor coordination to deliver a response, he had difficulty relative to others his age. Mr. W. demonstrated Below Average abilities on the Processing Speed Factor with his standard score of 79 (8th percentile). Thus, his ability to fluently and automatically perform cognitive tasks, especially when under pressure to maintain focused attention and concentration, is a Normative Weakness. His difficulties in both the domains of visual processing and speed of processing are consistent with his self-reported difficulties with motor functioning and vision since his motorcycle accident.

Mr. W.'s ability to focus and sustain his concentration was not only required for processing speed tasks but was also required on specific tasks designed to measure his memory skill. Short-term memory is the ability to hold information in immediate awareness and then use it within a few seconds. Mr. W.'s short-term memory skills were variable, ranging from the Average range to the Below Average range, compared to others his age. On the Short-Term Memory Factor of the WAIS-IV, his abilities were Within Normal Limits, as he earned a standard score of 89 (23rd percentile) on that factor.

However, when examining separate areas of his memory functioning on the *Wechsler Memory Scale—Third Edition* (WMS-III), some areas of weakness are also evident. On measures of immediate memory from the WMS-III, Mr. W. demonstrated mild to moderate impairment overall (4th percentile). However, this overall score does not reflect the significantly discrepant scores on measures of auditory and visual immediate memory. He performed in the Average range on visual tasks involving the recall of faces and family pictures (34th percentile) while demonstrating a moderate degree of impairment on auditory tasks involving the recall of stories and word pairs (1st percentile). On another measure of immediate verbal memory in which Mr. W. was asked to recall a list of unrelated words he has learned over several trials following a distracter task, he again demonstrated moderate to severely impaired range performance (below 1st percentile). On a measure of visual immediate memory in which he was asked to recall a complex abstract figure he had copied 3 minutes earlier, he scored in the mild range of impairment (10th percentile).

In contrast to short-term memory, long-term memory is the ability to store and fluently retrieve new or previously acquired information. Mr. W.'s ability to retrieve remote information from long-term memory lies within the mild to moderately impaired range (5th percentile). His general memory ability as measured on the WMS-III also lies in the mild to moderately impaired range (2nd percentile). The 23-point difference between his actual and predicted score on this measure is significant and unusual, as less than 4% of the standardization sample demonstrates a discrepancy of this magnitude. His retrieval fluency lies in the average range (47th percentile).

In regard to overall *verbal memory* ability, Mr. W. demonstrated moderately impaired range performance overall (2nd percentile). When asked to recall a list of unrelated words he had previously learned following a half-hour delay, he scored in the moderate to severely impaired range (below 1st percentile). On other measures of auditory long-term memory involving meaningful stimuli from the WMS-III, he performed in the mild to moderately impaired range (3rd percentile). He also demonstrated mild to moderate impairment on a measure involving the recall of stories as well as on a measure involving the recall of word pairs (both 5th percentile). The 22-point discrepancy between his actual and predicted score on measures of auditory long-term memory is significant and unusual, as less than 4% of the standardization sample demonstrates a discrepancy of this magnitude. He performed in the moderately impaired range when presented with auditory information in a recognition format (1st percentile). The 29-point discrepancy between his actual and predicted score is significant and unusual, as less than 2% of the standardization sample demonstrates a discrepancy of this magnitude.

On overall *visual memory* ability, Mr. W. demonstrated Average-range performance (19th percentile). When asked to recall a complex abstract drawing he had copied following a half-hour delay, he scored in the mild to moderately impaired range (6th percentile). His performance was in the mildly impaired range when presented with this information in a recognition format (13th percentile). On measures of visual long-term memory from the WMS-III, he performed within the Below Average range (14th percentile). There is not a significant difference between his actual and predicted scores on these measures. He performs in the mildly impaired range on a measure of facial recognition (9th percentile). However, he performed within the Average range on a measure involving the recall of information from several different pictures of a family (37th percentile).

Like the variability noted in both his nonverbal skills and memory skills, Mr. W.'s abilities in the verbal domain also showed relative strengths and weaknesses. On verbal tasks that required Mr. W. to demonstrate the breadth and depth of his knowledge acquired from his culture, his abilities were in the Below Average range. These abilities were evident from his standard score of 81 (10th percentile) on the Crystallized Intelligence Factor of the WAIS-IV. However, when specific clinical clusters of scores were examined on the WAIS-IV verbal tasks, discrepancies in his abilities were noted. For example, his lexical knowledge (or word knowledge) was significantly stronger than his knowledge of factual information. In fact, the WAIS-IV revealed that his Lexical Knowledge Cluster standard score of 91 (27th percentile) was uncommonly larger than his General Information Cluster standard score of 71 (3rd percentile). Discrepancies as large as Mr. W.'s occur less than 10% of the time in the normal population. This pattern of performance indicates that Mr. W. has facility with words and can reason with words (Average Range abilities) but may have difficulty applying his knowledge in specific situations due to his lack of background knowledge (Below Average range). His eighth-grade education (and later GED) likely contribute to his Below Average range of factual information.

On measures of academic functioning related to language, Mr. W. scored in the Below Average on a measure of his ability to read a list of words (2nd percentile). There is a 24-point discrepancy between his actual score and his predicted score based on his overall level of intellectual functioning. This difference is both significant and unusual, as only 2% of the standardization sample demonstrates a discrepancy of this magnitude. He also demonstrated moderately impaired range performance on a measure of his ability to spell to dictation (1st percentile). The 27-point discrepancy between his actual and predicted score is both significant and unusual, as less than 1% of the standardization sample demonstrates a discrepancy of this magnitude. His level of academic performance is consistent with the level of formal education that he acquired and with his areas of deficit in his cognitive profile on the WAIS-IV.

Personality Functioning

Mr. W. was administered a measure of general personality functioning, the MMPI-2RF. Mr. W. reported a number of clinical concerns on this measure. He reported that he is experiencing poor health and feels weak and tired. He is likely to complain of sleep disturbance, fatigue, low energy, and sexual dysfunction as well as multiple other somatic complaints. His responses indicate that he is also experiencing significant and pervasive emotional distress. He reported feeling sad, unhappy, hopeless, and depressed. He also reported being dissatisfied with his current life circumstances and is likely to feel overwhelmed, stressed, and worried. He lacks confidence, feels useless, and is prone to ruminate, be self-doubting, and feel insecure and inferior. He indicates that there is a lack of positive emotional experiences in his life and that he is generally pessimistic about life. He also reported being anger-prone and is likely to have problems with anger, irritability, and low frustration tolerance and to hold grudges, have temper tantrums, and be argumentative and abusive toward others. He reported having cynical beliefs, a hostile worldview, and being distrustful of others. He is likely to feel alienated and to have negative interpersonal experiences due to his cynicism.

Diagnostic Impression

Axis I: Dementia Due to Head Trauma (294.1)
   Major Depressive Disorder, moderate, recurrent (296.23)
   Reading Disorder (315.00)
Axis II: No diagnosis (V71.09)
Axis III: Head injury and chronic pain per client report
Axis IV: Inadequate social support
Axis V: Current GAF—53 (symptoms of moderate severity that
   interfere with social and adaptive functioning)

Summary and Conclusions

Mr. W. is a 64-year-old man who was referred for an evaluation of his cognitive functioning to assist in making a diagnosis and to assess for the presence of dementia. He has a history of memory problems that arose following a motor-cycle accident and subsequent severe coma. Mr. W.'s overall level of intellectual ability is in the Below Average range (FSIQ of 83; 13th percentile). This level of overall functioning is generally consistent with what would be expected, given premorbid indicators of functioning. However, specific areas of impairment and strength were evident upon examination of his results on individual measures of cognitive and neuropsychological functioning.

Mr. W. generally demonstrates Average range functioning in the areas of visual processing, lexical knowledge, and certain parts of short-term memory. In contrast, he has Below Average abilities in these global areas: fluid reasoning, processing speed, and general information as well as parts of his short- and long-term memory. He also evidences moderate impairment on academic measures of reading and spelling. Mr. W.'s performance on measures of memory is significantly varied. He evidences visual short-term memory within the Average range; however, his performance declines to the mildly impaired range when asked to remember an abstract design. Visual long-term memory is in the low average to mildly impaired range, while verbal short- and long-term memory lie in the moderately impaired range. This varied pattern of scores on the various memory tasks would suggest that Mr. W.'s memory deficits are the result of specific injury, as opposed to being due to a more global dementia, such as Alzheimer's disease. However, his longstanding memory impairment may be particularly troublesome to him at this time because of his recent injury and the resulting stress and chronic pain, which he indicates is generally in the mild to moderate range.

In regard to personality functioning, Mr. W. reported feeling tired, overwhelmed, and stressed. He indicates that he is sad and unhappy and feels hopeless and useless, which he likely ruminates about a great deal. He also reported feeling overly frustrated, irritable, and angry, which may result in explosive behavior. Mr. W. also reported symptoms that are typical of posttraumatic stress disorder; however, a number of these symptoms appear to be related more to brain injury and cognitive impairment. Once immediate concerns regarding his level of stress and current functioning are addressed, trauma history and possible symptoms may be addressed more specifically.

In general, most of Mr. W.'s current problems appear related more to his depressive disorder, which is complicated by pain, and to the cognitive dysfunction related to his brain injury from 37 years ago. There is no evidence of dementia of a more recent onset. His current cognitive functioning is worsened by his mood disorder and pain symptoms. Improvement in these areas should also result in improved cognitive functioning.

Recommendations

1. Mr. W. could benefit from individual therapy to address his depression, help him develop techniques to assist with memory deficits, and increase resiliency. It will be important to address stress and anger management as well as feelings of hopelessness and despair, and feelings of cynicism and distrust. Continued participation in couples therapy is also indicated to help his wife understand his deficits as well as to improve the patient's interpersonal functioning.

2. The patient is also likely to benefit from participation in a brain injury group, such as the one at Mesa College, to provide further assistance with cognitive impairments and life functioning.

3. Mr. W. should undergo a psychiatric reevaluation to determine if changes in his psychiatric medications are warranted in light of the current evaluation.

4. Mr. W. should be referred to a pain management specialist for an evaluation of his current medication regime and to provide psychological interventions.

5. In working with Mr. W., it will be important to be cognizant of his deficits in memory (particularly verbal memory), slower processing speed, and limited reading ability. For example, whenever possible, he should be given information in writing to decrease reliance on verbal memory; however, the material must be written at an appropriate level and may need to use diagrams as well.

6. It will also be important to revisit topics and issues in subsequent sessions, given Mr. W.'s limited memory and slower processing speed. He will need more time to learn new material and will be slower in gaining new skills.

7. He will likely have difficulty understanding and following new instructions and should be assisted with clarifications, visual cues, and written reminders.

8. Given his varied attention, it will also be important to actively engage him and take steps to verify his attentiveness (e.g., asking him to summarize what has been said in his own words). Learning and utilizing other memory aids will also be important.

9. In situations where there are high demands of his concentration, he may have more problems functioning and have difficulty thinking things through before doing them; therefore, minimizing these demands will be important to decreasing impulsive and inappropriate behaviors.

10. Mr. W. also tires quickly, which contributes to impulsive and inappropriate behavior, and he should be encouraged to take breaks from demanding tasks and naps to help him revitalize. Helping him recognize when these breaks are needed will also be important.

Clark R. Clipson, PhD
Licensed Psychologist

🪶 TEST YOURSELF 🪶

1. In the referral section of the report, you should be sure to include all of the following **EXCEPT**

   (a) name and position of the person who referred the client for testing.

   (b) specific referral question.

   (c) previous test scores.

   (d) a summary of current behaviors/problems relevant to the referral concern.

2. It is especially important to include the details that you have heard from gossip in the Background section of the report. **TRUE or FALSE?**

3. The information in the **Appearance and Behavioral Characteristics** section of the report should be sequenced in

   (a) the order of occurrence of the behaviors.

   (b) order of importance.

   (c) alphabetical order.

   (d) reverse chronological order.

4. In addition to describing important features of the subject's appearance and pertinent behaviors, the **Appearance and Behavioral Characteristics** section of the report should include

   (a) test results.

   (b) a statement about the validity of the test results.

   (c) brief recommendations.

   (d) summary of the referral question.

5. It is good practice to mention any of these types of scores in the **Test Results and Interpretation** section of the report **EXCEPT**

   (a) percentile ranks.

   (b) confidence intervals.

   (c) raw scores.

   (d) standard scores.

6. It is often a good idea to include in the **Summary and Diagnostic Impressions** section of the report test results that were not mentioned previously in the report. **TRUE or FALSE?**

7. List four common errors that examiners typically make in report writing:

   (a) _____

   (b) _____

   (c) _____

   (d) _____

Answers: 1. c; 2. False; 3. b; 4. b; 5. c; 6. False; 7. See Caution box on page 349.

References

Alfonso, V. C., LaRocca, R., Oakland, T., & Spanakos, A. (2000, March). The course on individual cognitive assessment. *School Psychology Review, 29*(1), 52–64.

Alfonso, V. C., & Pratt, S. I. (1997). Issues and suggestions for training professionals in assessing intelligence. In D. P. Flanagan, J. L. Genshaft, & P. L. Harrison (Eds.), *Contemporary intellectual assessment: Theories, tests, and issues* (pp. 326–344). New York: Guilford Press.

American Psychiatric Association (1994). *Diagnostic and statistical manual of mental disorders: DSM-IV* (4th ed.). Washington, DC: Author.

American Psychiatric Association (2000). *Diagnostic and statistical manual of mental Disorders, Fourth Edition, Text Revision: DSM-IV-TR.* Washington, D. C.: Author.

Anastasi, A., & Urbina, S. (1997). *Psychological testing* (7th ed.). Upper Saddle River, NJ: Prentice-Hall.

Arbuckle, T. Y., Gold, D., Andres, D., Schwartzman, A. E., & Chaikelson, J. (1992). The role of psychosocial context, age, and intelligence in memory performance of older men. *Psychology and Aging, 7*, 25–36.

Archer, R. P., Buffington-Vollum, J. K., Stredny, R. V., & Handel, R. W. (2006). A survey of test use patterns among forensic psychologists. *Journal of Personality Assessment, 87*, 64–94.

Archer, R. P., & Newsom, C. R. (2000). Psychological test usage with adolescent clients: Survey update. *Assessment, 7*, 227–236.

Atkinson, L. (1992). Mental retardation and WAIS-R scatter analysis. *Journal of Intellectual Disability Research, 36*, 443–448.

Atkinson, L., & Cyr, J. J. (1988). Low IQ samples and WAIS-R factor structure. *American Journal on Mental Retardation, 93*, 278–282.

Backman, L., Small, B. J., Wahlin, A., & Larsson, M. (2000). Cognitive functioning in very old age. In F. I. M. Craik & T. A. Salthouse (Eds.), *The handbook of aging and cognition* (2nd ed., pp. 499–558). Mahwah, NJ: Lawrence Erlbaum.

Baltes, P. B. (1997). On the incomplete architecture of human ontogeny: Selection, optimization, and compensation as foundation of developmental theory. *American Psychologist, 52*, 366–380.

Baltes, P. B., & Lindenberger, U. (1997). Emergence of a powerful connection between sensory and cognitive functions across the adult life span: A new window to the study of cognitive aging? *Psychology & Aging, 12*, 12–21.

Baltes, P. B., & Schaie, K. W. (1976). On the plasticity of adult and gerontological intelligence: Where Horn and Donaldson fail. *American Psychologist, 31*, 720–725.

Baltes, P. B., Staudinger, U. M., & Lindenberger, U. (1999). Lifespan psychology: Theory and application to intellectual functioning. *Annual Review of Psychology, 50*, 471–507.

Bannatyne, A. (1974). Diagnosis: A note on recategorization of the WISC scaled scores. *Journal of Learning Disabilities, 7*, 272–274.

Barkley, R. A. (1996, January). *ADHD in children, adolescents, and adults.* Symposium presented at University of California, Northridge, CA.

Barkley, R. A. (1997). Behavioral inhibition, sustained attention, and executive functions: Constructing a unifying theory of ADHD. *Psychological Bulletin, 121*, 65–94.

Barron, J. H., & Russell, E. W. (1992). Fluidity theory and neuropsychological impairment in alcoholism. *Archives of Clinical Neuropsychology, 7*, 175–188.

Belk, M. S., LoBello, S. G., Ray, G. E., & Zachar, P. (2002). WISC-III administration, clerical, and scoring errors make by student examiners. *Journal of Psychoeducational Assessment, 20*(3), 290–300.

Belter, R. W., & Piotrowski, C. (2001). Current status of doctoral-level training in psychological testing. *Journal of Clinical Psychology, 57,* 717–726.

Benton, A. L., Eslinger, P. J., & Demasio, A. R. (1981). Normative observations on neuropsychological test performances in old age. *Journal of Clinical Neuropsychology, 3,* 33–42.

Berg, C. A. (2000). Intellectual development in adulthood. In R. J. Sternberg (Ed.), *Handbook of intelligence* (pp. 117–137). New York: Cambridge University Press.

Berkowitz, B., & Green, R. F. (1963). Changes in intellect with age: I. Longitudinal study of Wechsler-Bellevue scores. *Journal of Genetic Psychology, 103,* 3–21.

Beuhner, M., Krumm, S., Ziegler, M., & Pluecken, T. (2006). Cognitive abilities and their interplay: Reasoning, crystallized intelligence, working memory components, and sustained attention. *Journal of Individual Differences, 27*(2), 57–72.

Binet, A. (1890a). Recherches sur les mouvements de quelques jeunes enfants. *La Revue Philosophique, 29,* 297–309.

Binet, A. (1890b). Perceptions d'enfants. *La Revue Philosophique, 30,* 582–611.

Binet, A. (1911). Nouvelle recherches sur la mesure du niveau intellectual chez les enfants d'école. *L'Année Psychologique, 17,* 145–210.

Binet, A., & Henri, V. (1895). La psychologie individuelle. *L'Année Psychologique, 2,* 411–465.

Binet, A., & Simon, T. (1905). Méthodes nouvelles pour le diagnostic du niveau intéllectuel des anormaux. *L'Année Psychologique, 11,* 191–244.

Binet, A., & Simon, T. (1908). Le développement de l'intelligence chez les enfants. *L'Année Psychologique, 14,* 1–94.

Birren, J. E., & Morrison, D. F. (1961). Analysis of the WAIS subtests in relation to age and education. *Journal of Gerontology, 16,* 363–369.

Bornstein, R. A. 1983. Verbal IQ–Performance IQ discrepancies on the Wechsler Adult Intelligence Scale—Revised in patients with unilateral or bilateral cerebral dysfunction. *Journal of Consulting and Clinical Psychology, 51,* 779–780.

Botwinick, J. (1977). Intellectual abilities. In J. E. Birren & K. W. Schaie (Eds.), *Handbook of the psychology of aging* (pp. 580–605). New York: Van Nnostrand Reinhold.

Brinkman, S. D., & Braun, P. (1984). Classification of dementia patients by a WAIS profile related to central cholinergic deficiencies. *Journal of Clinical Neuropsychology, 6,* 393–400.

Camara, W. J., Nathan, J. S., & Puente, A. E. (2000). Psychological test usage: Implications in professional psychology. *Professional Psychology: Research and Practice, 31,* 141–154.

Carroll, J. B. (1993). *Human cognitive abilities: A survey of factor analytic studies.* New York: Cambridge University Press.

Carroll, J. B. (1997). The three-stratum theory of cognitive abilities. In D. P. Flanagan, J. L. Genshaft, & P. L. Harrison (Eds.), *Contemporary intellectual assessment: Theories, tests, and issues* (pp. 122–130). New York: Guilford Press.

Carroll, J. B. (1998). Foreword. In McGrew, K. S., & Flanagan, D. P., *The intelligence test desk reference (ITDR): Gf-Gc cross-battery assessment* (pp. xi–xii). Boston: Allyn & Bacon.

Catron, D. W., & Thompson, C. C. (1979). Test-retest gains in WAIS scores after four retest intervals. *Journal of Clinical Psychology, 35,* 352–357.

Cattell, R. B. (1943). The measurement of adult intelligence. *Psychological Bulletin, 40*(3), 153–193.

Cattell, R. B. (1963). Theory of fluid and crystallized intelligence: A critical experiment. *Journal of Educational Psychology, 54,* 1–22.

Cattell, R. B., & Horn, J. L. (1978). A check on the theory of fluid and crystallized intelligence with description of new subtest designs. *Journal of Educational Measurement, 15,* 139–164.

Christensen, H., Henderson, A. S., Griffiths, K., & Levings, C. (1997). Does aging inevitably lead to declines in cognitive performance? A longitudinal study of elite academics. *Personality & Individual Differences, 23*, 67–78.

Cicchetti, D. V. (1994). Guidelines, criteria, and rules of thumb for evaluating normed and standardized assessment instruments in psychology. *Psychological Assessment, 6*, 284–290.

Cohen, B. H. (1996). *Explaining psychological statistics*. Pacific Grove, CA: Brooks & Cole.

Cohen, J. (1952). A factor-analytically based rationale for the Wechsler-Bellevue. *Journal of Consulting Psychology, 16*, 272–277.

Cohen, J. (1983). The cost of dichotomization. *Applied Psychological Measurement, 7*, 249–253.

Cornell, E. L., & Coxe, W.W. (1934). *A performance ability scale: Examination manual*. New York: World Book.

Costa, L. D. (1975). The relation of visuospatial dysfunction to digit span performance in patients with cerebral lesions. *Cortex, 11*, 31–36.

Cronbach, L. J. (1970). *Essentials of psychological testing* (3rd ed.) New York: Harper & Row.

Cunningham, W. R., & Owens, W. A. (1983). The Iowa State study of the adult development of intellectual abilities. In K. W. Schaie (Ed.), *Longitudinal studies of adult psychological development* (pp. 20–39). New York: Guilford Press.

Daniel, M. H. (1997). Intelligence testing: Status and trends. *American Psychologist, 52*, 1038–1045.

Diller, L., Ben-Yishay, Y., Gerstman, L. J., Goodkin, R., Gordon, W., & Weinberg, J. (1974). *Studies in cognitive and rehabilitation in hemiplegia*, Rehabilitation Monograph No. 50. New York: New York University Medical Center Institute of Rehabilitation Medicine.

Doppelt, J. E., & Wallace, W. L. (1955). Standardization of the Wechsler Adult Intelligence Scale for older persons. *Journal of Abnormal and Social Psychology, 51*, 312–330.

Dubois, B., Feldman, H. H., Jacova, C., DeKosky, S. T., Barberger-Gateau, P., Cummings, J.,et al. (2007). Research criteria for the diagnosis of Alzheimer's disease: Revising the NINCDS-ADRA criteria. *Lancet Neurology, 6*, 734–746.

Dubois, P. H. (1970). *A history of psychological testing*. Boston: Allyn & Bacon.

Dumont, R., & Willis, J. (2001). Use of the Tellegen & Briggs formula to determine the Dumont-Willis Indexes (DWI-1 & DWI-2) for the WISC-IV. Retrieved May 14, 2009 from Fairleigh Dickinson University Web site: http://alpha.fdu.edu/psychology/ WISCIV_DWI.htm.

Eisdorfer, C., & Wilkie, F. (1973). Intellectual changes with advancing age. In L. E. Jarvik, C. Eisdorfer, & J. E. Blum (Eds.), *Intellectual functioning in adults*. New York: Springer.

Elliott, C. D. (2007). *Differential Ability Scales (DAS-II) 2nd ed., Administration and scoring manual*. San Antonio, TX: The Psychological Corporation.

Evans, J. J., Floyd, R. G., McGrew, K. S., & Leforgee, M. H. (2002). The relations between measures of Cattell-Horn-Carroll (CHC) cognitive abilities and reading achievement during childhood and adolescence. *School Psychology Review, 31*(2), 246–262.

Feagans, L. V., & McKinney, J. D. (1991). Subtypes of learning disabilities: A review. In L. V. Feagans, E. J. Short, & L. J. Meltzer (Eds.), *Subtypes of learning disabilities* (pp. 3–31). Hillsdale, NJ: Lawrence Erlbaum.

Finkel, D., Reynolds, C. A., McArdle, J. J., & Pederson, N. L. (2007). Age changes in processing speed as a leading indicator of cognitive aging. *Psychology and Aging, 22*(3), 558–568.

Flanagan, D. P. (2000). Wechsler-based CHC cross-battery assessment and reading achievement: Strengthening the validity of interpretations drawn from Wechsler test scores. *School Psychology Quarterly, 15*, 295–229.

Flanagan, D. P., Genshaft, J. L., & Harrison, P. L. (Eds.). (2005). *Contemporary intellectual assessment: Theories, tests, and issues* (2nd ed.). New York: Guilford Press.

Flanagan, D. P., & Kaufman, A. S. (2004). *Essentials of WISC-IV assessment.* Hoboken, NJ: John Wiley & Sons.

Flanagan, D. P., & Kaufman, A. S. (2009). *Essentials of WISC-IV assessment* (2nd ed.). Hoboken, NJ: John Wiley & Sons.

Flanagan, D. P., Kaufman, A. S., Kaufman, N. L. & Lichtenberger, E.O. (2008). *Agora: The marketplace of ideas. Best practices: Applying response to intervention (RTI) and comprehensive assessment for the identification of learning disabilities* [Motion picture]. United States: Pearson.

Flanagan, D. P., & McGrew, K. S. (1997). A cross-battery approach to assessing and interpreting cognitive abilities: Narrowing the gap between practice and cognitive science. In D. P. Flanagan, J. L. Genshaft, & P. L. Harrison (Eds.), *Contemporary intellectual assessment* (pp. 314–325). New York: Guilford Press.

Flanagan, D. P., McGrew, K. S. & Ortiz, S. O. (2000). *The Wechsler intelligence scales and Gf-Gc theory: A contemporary approach to interpretation.* Boston: Allyn & Bacon.

Flanagan, D. P., & Ortiz, S. O. (2001). *Essentials of cross-battery assessment.* Hoboken, NJ: John Wiley & Sons.

Flanagan, D. P., Ortiz, S. O., & Alfonso, V. C. (2007). *Essentials of cross-battery assessment* (2nd ed.). Hoboken, NJ: John Wiley & Sons. See also the official site of the CHC Cross-Battery Approach by Dawn P. Flanagan and Samuel O. Ortiz at http://facpub.stjohns.edu/~ortizs/cross-battery, retrieved February 29, 2008.

Flanagan, D. P., Ortiz, S. O., Alfonso, V. C., & Dynda, A. (2008). Best practices in cognitive assessment. In A. Thomas & J. Grimes (Eds.), *Best practices in school psychology* (5th ed.) (pp. 633–659). Washington, DC: National Association of School Psychologists.

Flanagan, D. P., Ortiz, S. O., Alfonso, V. C., & Mascolo, J. (2002). *The achievement test desk reference (ATDR): Comprehensive assessment and learning disabilities.* Boston: Allyn & Bacon.

Flanagan, D. P., Ortiz, S. O., Alfonso, V. & Mascolo, J. T. (2006). *Achievement test desk reference (ATDR-II): A guide to learning disability identification* (2nd ed.). Hoboken, NJ: John Wiley & Sons.

Fletcher, J. M., Lyon, G. R., Fuchs, L. S., & Barnes, M. A. (2007). *Learning disabilities: From identification to intervention.* New York: Guilford Press.

Floyd, R. G., Evans, J. J., & McGrew, K. S. (2003). Relations between measures of Cattell-Horn-Carroll (CHC) cognitive abilities and mathematics achievement across the school-age years. *Psychology in the Schools, 40*(2), 155–171.

Flynn, J. R. (1987). Massive IQ gains in 14 nations: What IQ tests really measure. *Psychological Bulletin, 101,* 171–191.

Flynn, J. R. (1998). Rising IQ scores: Implications for the elderly. *Australian Journal on Ageing, 17,* 106–107.

Flynn, J. R. (2007). *What is intelligence?* New York: Cambridge University Press.

Flynn, J. R., & Weiss, L. (2007). American IQ Gains from 1932 to 2002: The WISC Subtests and Educational Progress. *International Journal of Testing, 7*(2), 209–224.

Frauenheim, J. G., & Heckerl, J. R. (1983). A longitudinal study of psychological and achievement test performance in severe dyslexic adults. *Journal of Learning Disabilities, 16,* 339–347.

Fry, A. F., & Hale, S. (1996). Processing speed, working memory, and fluid intelligence: Evidence for a developmental cascade. *Psychological Science, 7,* 237–241.

Fuld, P. A. (1984). Test profile of cholinergic dysfunction and of Alzheimer-type dementia. *Journal of Clinical Neuropsychology, 6,* 380–392.

Gallagher, R. W., Somwaru, D. P., & Ben-Porath, Y. S. (1999). Current usage of psychological tests in state correctional settings. *Corrections Compendium, 24*(7), 1–20.

Galton, F. (1869). *Hereditary genius: An inquiry into its laws and consequences.* London: Macmillan.

Galton, F. (1883). *Inquiries into human faculty and its development.* London: Macmillan.

Gittleman, R., Mannuzza, S., Shenker, R., & Bongura, N. (1985). Hyperactive boys almost grown up. *Archives of General Psychiatry*, *42*, 937–947.

Glasser, A. J., & Zimmerman, I. L. (1967). *Clinical interpretation of the WISC.* New York: Grune & Stratton.

Glutting, J. J., & Oakland, T. (1993). *The guide to the assessment of test session behavior.* San Antonio, TX: The Psychological Corporation.

Goddard, H. H. (1911). A revision of the Binet scale. *Training School*, *8*, 56–62.

Gold, J. M., Carpenter, C., Randolph, C., Goldberg, T. E., & Weinberger, D. R. (1997). Auditory working memory and Wisconsin Card Sorting test performance in schizophrenia. *Archives of General Psychiatry*, *54*, 159–165.

Goldstein, K. (1948). *Language and language disturbances.* New York: Grune & Stratton.

Gorlyn, M., Keilp, J. G., Oquendo, M. A., Burke, A. K., Sackeim, H. A., & Mann, J. J. (2006). The WAIS-III and major depression: Absence of VIQ/PIQ differences. *Journal of Clinical and Experimental Neuropsychology*, *28*, 1145–1157.

Green, R. F. (1969). Age-intelligence relationship between ages sixteen and sixty-four: A rising trend. *Developmental Psychology*, *1*, 618–627.

Gregg, N., Hoy, C., & Gay, A. F. (1996). *Adults with learning disabilities: Theoretical and practical perspectives.* New York: Guilford Press.

Gregory, R. J. (1987). *Adult intellectual assessment.* Boston: Allyn & Bacon.

Gregory, T., Nettelbeck, T., Howard, S., & Wilson, C. (2008). Inspection time: A biomarker for cognitive decline. *Intelligence*, *36*, 664–671.

Gribbin, K., Schaie, K. W., & Parham, I. (1980). Complexity of life style and maintenance of intellectual abilities. *Journal of Social Issues*, *36*, 47–61.

Groth-Marnat, G. (2009). *Handbook of psychological assessment* (5th ed.). Hoboken, NJ: John Wiley & Sons.

Guilford, J. P. (1967). *The nature of human intelligence.* New York: McGraw-Hill.

Guilford, J. P., & Fruchter, B. (1978). *Fundamental statistics in psychology and education* (6th ed.). New York: McGraw-Hill.

Hale, J. B., & Fiorello, C. A. (2004). *School neuropsychology: A practitioner's handbook.* New York: Guilford Press.

Hale, J. B., Hoeppner, J. B., & Fiorello, C. A. (2002). Analyzing Digit Span components to assessment of attention processes. *Journal of Psychoeducational Assessment*, *20*(2), 128–143.

Hardy, S. T. (1993). *Proper and effective use of sign language interpreters by school psychologists.* Workshop presented at the meeting of the National Association of School Psychologists, Washington, DC.

Hardy-Braz, S. T. (2003). *Enhancing school-based psychological services: Assessments and interventions with students who are deaf or hard of hearing.* Workshop presented at the meeting of the National Association of School Psychologists, Toronto, Canada.

Harrison, P. L., Kaufman, A. S., Hickman, J. A., & Kaufman, N. L. (1988). A survey of tests used for adult assessment. *Journal of Psychoeducational Assessment*, *6*, 188–198.

Hartley, A. (2006). Changing roles of the speed of processing construct in the cognitive psychology of human aging. In J. E. Birren & K. W. Schaie (Eds.), *Handbook of the psychology of aging* (6th ed., pp. 183–208). San Diego: Academic Press.

Heaton, R. K., Nelson, L. M., Thompson, D. S., Burks, J. S., & Franklin, G. M. (1985). Neuropsychological findings in relapsing-remitting and chronic-progressive multiple sclerosis. *Journal of Consulting and Clinical Psychology*, *53*, 103–110.

Hebben, N. (2009). Review of special group studies and utility of the process approach with the WISC-IV. In D. P. Flanagan & A. S. Kaufman, *Essentials of WISC-IV Assessment* (2nd ed., pp. 216–242). Hoboken, NJ: John Wiley & Sons.

Hebben, N., & Milberg, W. (2002). *Essentials of neuropsychological assessment.* New York: John Wiley & Sons.

Helms, J. E. (1997). The triple quandary of race, culture, and social class in standardized cognitive ability testing. In D. P. Flanagan, J. L. Genshaft, & P. L. Harrison (Eds.). *Contemporary intellectual assessment: Theories, tests, and issues* (pp. 517–532). New York: Guilford Press.

Herring, J. P. (1922). *Herring revision of the Binet-Simon tests: Examination manual—Form A.* London: World Book.

Hertzog, C., & Schaie, K. W. (1988). Stability and change in adult intelligence: Simultaneous analysis of longitudinal means and covariance structures. *Psychology and Aging, 3,* 122–130.

Horn, J. L. (1985). Remodeling old model in intelligence. In B. B. Wolman (Ed.), *Handbook of intelligence: Theories, measurements, and applications* (pp. 267–300). New York: John Wiley & Sons.

Horn, J. L. (1989). Cognitive diversity: A framework of learning. In P. L. Ackerman, R. J. Sternberg, & R. Glaser (Eds.), *Learning and individual differences* (pp. 61–116). New York: Freeman.

Horn, J. L. (1991). Measurement of intellectual capabilities: A review of theory. In K. S. McGrew, J. K. Werder, & R. W. Woodcock (Eds.), *Woodcock-Johnson Technical manual: A reference on theory and current research* (pp. 197–246). Allen, TX: DLM Teaching Resources.

Horn, J. L., & Blankson, B. (2005). Foundations for better understanding of cognitive abilities. In D. P. Flanagan & P. L. Harrison (Eds.), *Contemporary intellectual assessment* (2nd ed., pp. 41–68). New York: Guilford Press.

Horn, J. L., & Cattell, R. B. (1966). Refinement and test of theory of fluid and crystallized intelligence. *Journal of Educational Psychology, 57,* 253–270.

Horn, J. L., & Cattell, R. B. (1967). Age differences in fluid and crystallized intelligence. *Acta Psychologica, 26,* 107–129.

Horn, J. L., & Donaldson, G. (1976). On the myth of intellectual decline in adulthood. *American Psychologist, 31,* 701–719.

Horn, J. L., & Donaldson, G. (1977). Faith is not enough: A response to the Baltes-Schaie claim that intelligence will not wane. *American Psychologist, 32,* 369–373.

Horn, J. L., Donaldson, G., & Engstrom, R. (1981). Apprehension, memory, and fluid intelligence decline in adulthood. *Research on Aging, 3,* 33–84.

Horn, J. L., & Hofer, S. M. (1992). Major abilities and development in the adult period. In R. J. Sternberg & C. A. Berg (Eds.), *Intellectual development* (pp. 44–99). Boston: Cambridge University Press.

Hultsch, D. F., Hammer, M., & Small, B. (1993). Age differences in cognitive performance in later life: Relationships to self-reported health and activity life style. *Journal of Gerontology: Psychological Sciences, 48,* 1–11.

Hultsch, D. F., Hertzog, C., Small, B. J., & Dixon, R. A. (1999). Use it or lose it: Engaged lifestyle as a buffer of cognitive decline in aging? *Psychology and Aging, 14,* 245–263.

Individuals with Disabilities Education Improvement Act of 2004, 20 U.S.C. §§1401 *et seq.* (2004).

Jarvik, L. F., & Bank, L. (1983). Aging twins: Longitudinal psychometric data. In K. W. Schaie (Ed.), *Longitudinal studies of adult psychological development* (pp. 40–63). New York: Guilford Press.

Jensen, A. R. (1998). *The g factor: The science of mental ability.* Westport, CT: Praeger.

Jensen, A. R., & Figueroa, R. A. (1975). Forward and backward digit-span interaction with race and IQ. *Journal of Educational Psychology, 67,* 882–893.

Kail, R. (2000). Speed of information processing: Developmental changes and links to intelligence. *Journal of School Psychology, 38,* 51–61.

Kail, R., & Hall, L. K. (1994). Processing speed, naming speed, and reading. *Developmental Psychology, 30,* 949–954.

Kail, R., & Salthouse, T. A. (1994). Processing speed, naming speed, and reading. *Developmental Psychology, 30*, 949–954.

Kamphaus, R. W. (1993). *Clinical assessment of children's intelligence*. Boston: Allyn & Bacon.

Kamphaus, R. W., Petosky, M. D., & Morgan, A. W. (1997). A history of intelligence test interpretation. In D. P., Flanagan, J. L., Genshaft, & P. L. Harrison (Eds.), *Contemporary intellectual assessment: Theories, tests, and issues* (pp. 32–47). New York: Guilford Press.

Kamphaus, R. W., & Reynolds, C. R. (1987). *Clinical and research applications of the K-ABC*. Circle Pines, MN: American Guidance Service.

Kaplan, E. (1988). A process approach to neuropsychological assessment. In T. Boll and B. K. Bryant (Eds.), *Clinical neuropsychology and brain function: Research, measurement, and practice* (pp. 125–167). Washington, DC: American Psychological Association.

Kaplan, E., Fein, D., Morris, R., Kramer, J. H., & Delis, D. C. (1999). *The WISC-III as a processing instrument*. San Antonio: The Psychological Corporation.

Kaufman, A. S. (1979a). *Intelligent testing with the WISC-R*. New York: John Wiley & Sons.

Kaufman, A. S. (1979b). Role of speed on WISC-R performance across the age range. *Journal of Consulting and Clinical Psychology, 47*, 595–597.

Kaufman, A. S. (1983). Intelligence: Old concepts-new perspectives. In G. W. Hynd (Ed.), *The school psychologist: An introduction* (pp. 95–117). Syracuse, NY: Syracuse University Press.

Kaufman, A. S. (1985). Review of Wechsler Adult Intelligence Scale—Revised. In J. V. Mitchell (Ed.), *The ninth mental measurements yearbook* (pp. 1699–1703). Lincoln: University of Nebraska Press.

Kaufman, A. S. (1990). *Assessing adolescent and adult intelligence*. Boston: Allyn & Bacon.

Kaufman, A. S. (1994a). *Intelligent testing with the WISC-III*. New York: John Wiley & Sons.

Kaufman, A. S. (1994b). Practice effects. In R. J. Sternberg (Ed.), *Encyclopedia of intelligence: Vol. 2* (pp. 828–833). New York: Macmillan.

Kaufman, A. S. (1998, August). *What happens to our WAIS-III scores as we age from 16 to 89 years and what do these changes mean for theory and clinical practice?* Invited Division 16 award address presented at the meeting of the American Psychological Association, San Francisco.

Kaufman, A. S. (2000a). Seven questions about the WAIS-III regarding differences in abilities across the 16 to 89 year life span. *School Psychology Quarterly, 15*, 3–29.

Kaufman, A. S. (2000b). Tests of intelligence. In R. J. Sternberg (Ed.), *Handbook of intelligence* (pp. 445–476). New York: Cambridge University Press.

Kaufman, A. S. (2001). WAIS-III IQs, Horn's theory, and generational changes from young adulthood to old age. *Intelligence, 29*, 131–167.

Kaufman, A. S. (2009). Age and intelligence on the WAIS-IV: Cross-sectional and longitudinal methodologies. Manuscript in preparation.

Kaufman, A. S., & Horn, J. L. (1996). Age changes on tests of fluid and crystallized intelligence for females and males on the Kaufman Adolescent and Adult Intelligence Test (KAIT) at ages 17 to 94 years. *Archives of Clinical Neuropsychology, 11*, 97–121.

Kaufman, A. S., Johnson, C. K., & Liu, X. (2008). A CHC theory-based analysis of age differences on cognitive abilities and academic skills at ages 22 to 90 years. *Journal of Psychoeducational Assessment. 26*, 350–381.

Kaufman, A. S., Kaufman, J. C., Chen, T., & Kaufman, N. L. (1996). Differences on six Horn abilities for fourteen age groups between 15–16 and 75–94 years. *Psychological Assessment, 8*, 161–171.

Kaufman, A. S., & Kaufman, N. L. (1977). *Clinical evaluation of young children with the McCarthy Scales*. New York: Grune & Stratton.

Kaufman, A. S., & Kaufman, N. L. (1990). *Administration and scoring manual for Kaufman Brief Intelligence Test (K-BIT)*. Circle Pines, MN: American Guidance Service.

Kaufman, A. S., & Kaufman, N. L. (1993). *Manual for Kaufman Adolescent & Adult Intelligence Test (KAIT)*. Circle Pines, MN: American Guidance Service, Inc.

Kaufman, A. S., & Kaufman, N. L. (1994). *Kaufman Functional Academic Skills Test*. Circle Pines, MN: American Guidance Service.

Kaufman, A. S., & Kaufman, N. L. (2004). *Kaufman Assessment Battery for Children* (2nd ed.) *(KABC-II)*. Circle Pines, MN: American Guidance Service.

Kaufman, A. S., & Lichtenberger, E. O. (1998). Intellectual assessment. In A. S. Bellack & M. Hersen (Series Eds.) & C. R. Reynolds (Vol. Ed.), *Comprehensive clinical psychology: Vol. 4. Assessment* (pp. 187–238). New York: Pergamon Press.

Kaufman, A. S., & Lichtenberger, E. O. (1999). *Essentials of WAIS-III assessment*. New York: John Wiley & Sons.

Kaufman, A. S., & Lichtenberger, E. O. (2000). *Essentials of WISC-III and WPPSI-R assessment*. New York: John Wiley & Sons.

Kaufman, A. S., & Lichtenberger, E. O. (2002). *Assessing adolescent and adult intelligence* (2nd ed.). Boston: Allyn & Bacon.

Kaufman, A. S., & Lichtenberger, E. O. (2006). *Assessing adolescent and adult intelligence* (3rd ed.) Hoboken, NJ: John Wiley & Sons.

Kaufman, A. S., Lichtenberger, E. O., Fletcher-Janzen, E., & Kaufman, N. L. (2005). *Essentials of KABC-II assessment*. New York: John Wiley & Sons.

Kaufman, A. S., Reynolds, C. R., & McLean, J. E. (1989). Age and WAIS-R intelligence in a national sample of adults in the 20- to 74-year age range: A cross-sectional analysis with educational level controlled. *Intelligence, 13*, 235–253.

Kausler, D. H. (1982). *Experimental psychology and human aging*. New York: John Wiley & Sons.

Kausler, D. H. (1991). *Experimental psychology, cognition, and human aging*. New York: Springer-Verlag.

Keith, T. Z., Cool, V. A., Novak, C. G., White, L. J., & Pottebaum, S. M. (1988). Confirmatory factor analysis of the Stanford-Binet fourth edition: Testing the theory-test match. *Journal of School Psychology, 26*, 253–274.

Kemp, S. L., Kirk, U., & Korkman, M. (2001). *Essentials of NEPSY assessment*. New York: Wiley.

Kirkpatrick, E. A. (1903). *Fundamentals of child study: A discussion of instincts and other factors in human development with practical applications*. New York: Macmillan.

Kite, E. S. (1916). *Translation of A. Binet & T. Simon, The development of intelligence in children*. Baltimore, MD: Williams & Wilkins.

Kohs, S. C. (1923). *Intelligence measurement*. New York: Macmillan.

Korkman, M., Kirk, U., & Kemp, S. L. (2007). *The NEPSY Second Edition (NEPSY-II)*. San Antonio: The Psychological Corporation.

Labouvie-Vief, G. (1985). Intelligence and cognition. In J. E. Birren & K. W. Schaie (Eds.), *Handbook of the psychology of aging* (2nd ed., pp. 500–530). New York: Van Nostrand Reinhold.

Leckliter, I. N., Matarazzo, J. D., & Silverstein, A. B. (1986). A literature review of factor analytic studies of the WAIS-R. *Journal of Clinical Psychology, 42*, 332–342.

Lee, H. F., Gorsuch, R. L., Saklofske, D. H., & Patterson, C. A. (2008). Cognitive differences for ages 16 to 89 (Canadian WAIS-III): Curvilinear with Flynn and processing speed corrections. *Journal of Psychoeducational Assessment, 26*, 382–394.

Lezak, M. D. (1995). *Neuropsychological assessment* (3rd ed.) New York: Oxford University Press.

Lezak, M. D., Howieson, D. B., & Loring, D. W. (Eds.). (2004). *Neuropsychological assessment* (4th ed.). New York: Oxford University Press.

Lichtenberger, E. O., & Kaufman, A. S. (2004). *Essentials of WPPSI-III assessment*. New York: John Wiley & Sons.

Lichtenberger, E. O., Mather, N., Kaufman, N. L., & Kaufman, A. S. (2004). *Essentials of assessment report writing*. New York: John Wiley & Sons.

Lipsitz, J. D., Dworkin, R. H., & Erlenmeyer-Kimling, L. (1993). Wechsler Comprehension and Picture Arrangement subtests and social adjustment. *Psychological Assessment, 5*, 430–473.

Longman, R. S. (2004). Values for comparison of WAIS-III index scores with overall means. *Psychological Assessment, 16,* 323–325.

Loro, B., & Woodward, J. A. (1976). Verbal and Performance IQ for discrimination among psychiatric diagnostic groups. *Journal of Clinical Psychology, 32,* 107–114.

Luria, A. R. (1966). *Human brain: An introduction to neuropsychology.* New York: Basic Books.

Luria, A. R. (1970). The functional organization of the brain. *Scientific American, 222,* 66–78.

Luria, A. R. (1973). *The working brain: An introduction to neuropsychology.* New York: Basic Books.

Luria, A. R. (1980). *Higher cortical functions in man* (2nd ed.). New York: Basic Books.

MacDonald, M. C., Almor, A., Henderson, V. W., Kempler, D., & Andersen, E. S. (2001). Assessing working memory and language comprehension in Alzheimer's disease. *Brain and Language, 78,* 17–42.

Mandes, E., Massimino, C., & Mantis, C. (1991). A comparison of borderline and mild mental retardates assessed on the Memory for Designs and the WAIS-R. *Journal of Clinical Psychology, 47,* 562–567.

Matarazzo, J. D. (1972). *Wechsler's measurement and appraisal of adult intelligence* (5th ed.). New York: Oxford University Press.

Matarazzo, J. D. (1985). Review of Wechsler Adult Intelligence Scale-Revised. In J. V. Mitchell (Ed.), *The ninth mental measurements yearbook* (pp. 1703–1705). Lincoln, NE: Buros Institute of Mental Measurements, University of Nebraska.

Matarazzo, J. D., & Herman, D. O. (1984). Base rate data for the WAIS-R: Test-retest stability and VIQ-PIQ differences. *Journal of Clinical Neuropsychology, 6,* 351–366.

Mayes, S. D., & Calhoun, S. L. (2007). Wechsler Intelligence Scale for Children-Third and -Fourth Edition predictors of academic achievement in children with Attention-Deficit/Hyperactivity Disorder. *School Psychology Quarterly, 22,* 234–249.

Mayes, S. D., & Calhoun, S. L. (2008). WISC-IV and WIAT-II profiles in children with high-functioning autism. *Journal of Autism and Developmental Disorders, 38*(3), 428–439.

Mayman, M., Schafer, R., & Rappaport, D. (1951). Interpretation of the WAIS in personality appraisal. In H. H. Anderson & G. L. Anderson (Eds.), *An introduction to projective techniques* (pp. 541–580). New York: Prentice-Hall.

McArdle, J. J., Ferrer-Caja, E., Hamagami, F., & Woodcock, R. W. (2002). Comparative longitudinal structural analyses of the growth and decline of multiple intellectual abilities over the life span. *Developmental Psychology, 38,* 113–142.

McCloskey, G. (2009). The WISC-IV Integrated. In D. P. Flanagan & A. S. Kaufman, *Essentials of WISC-IV Assessment* (2nd ed., pp. 310–467). Hoboken, NJ: John Wiley & Sons.

McCloskey, G., & Maerlender, A. (2005). The WISC-IV Integrated. In A. Prifitera, D. H. Saklofske, & L. G. Weiss (Eds.), *WISC-IV clinical use and interpretation: Scientist-practitioner perspectives* (pp. 101–149). Burlington, MA: Elsevier.

McDermott, P. A., Fantuzzo, J. W., Glutting, J. J., Watkins, M. W., & Baggaley, A. R. (1992). Illusions of meaning in the ipsative assessment of children's ability. *Journal of Special Education, 25,* 504–526.

McGrew, K. S. (2005). The Cattell-Horn-Carroll theory of cognitive abilities: Past, present, and future. In D. P. Flanagan & P. L. Harrison (Eds), *Contemporary intellectual assessment: Theories, tests, and issues* (2nd ed., pp. 136–181). New York: Guilford Press.

McGrew, K. S., & Flanagan, D. P. (1998). *The intelligence test desk reference.* Boston: Allyn & Bacon.

McGrew, K. S., Flanagan, D. P., Keith, T. Z., & Vanderwood, M. (1997). Beyond g: The impact of Gf-Gc specific cognitive abilities research on the future use and interpretation of intelligence tests in the schools. *School Psychology Review, 26,* 177–189.

McGrew, K. S., & Knopik, S. N. (1996). The relationship between intra-cognitive scatter on the Woodcock-Johnson Psycho-Educational Battery-Revised and school achievement. *Journal of School Psychology, 34*(4), 351–364.

McGrew, K. S., Werder, J. K., & Woodcock, R. W. (1991). *WJ-R technical manual*. Chicago: Riverside Press.

McGrew, K. S., Woodcock, R., & Ford, L. (2006). The Woodcock-Johnson Battery, Third Edition. In A. S. Kaufman & E. O. Lichtenberger, *Assessing adolescent and adult intelligence* (3rd ed., pp. 561–628). New York: John Wiley & Sons.

McLean, J. E., Kaufman, A. S., & Reynolds, C. R. (1988, November). What role does formal education play in the IQ–age relationships across the adult life-span? *Mid-South Educational Researcher, 17*(1), 6–8, 13–18.

Melchers, P., Schürmann, S., & Scholten, S. (2006). *Kaufman Test zur Intelligenzmessung für Jugendliche und Erwachsene handbuch* [Kaufman test for intelligence measurement for young people and adults manual]. Leiden, the Netherlands: PITS.

Meyer, G. J., Finn, S. E., Eyde, L. D., Kay, G. G., Moreland, K. L., Dies, R. R., et al. (2001). Psychological testing and psychological assessment: A review of evidence and issues. *American Psychologist, 56*(2), 128–165.

Miller, G. A. (1956). The magical number seven, plus or minus two: Some limits on our capacity for processing information. *Psychological Review, 63*, 81–97.

Miller, L. S., & Rohling, M. L. (2001). A statistical interpretive method for neuropsychological test data. *Neuropsychology Review, 11*, 143–169.

Moran, J. L., & Mefford, R. B. Jr. (1959). Repetitive psychometric measures. *Psychological Reports, 5*, 269–275.

Morgan, A. W., Sullivan, S. A., Darden, C. A., & Gregg, N. (1994, March). *Measuring intelligence of college students with learning disabilities: A comparison of results obtained on the Wechsler Adult Intelligence Scale—Revised (WAIS-R) and the Kaufman Adolescent and Adult Intelligence Test (KAIT)*. Paper presented at the annual meeting of the National Association of School Psychologists, Seattle, WA.

Morris, R. D., et al. (1998). Subtypes of reading disability: Variability around a phonological core. *Journal of Educational Psychology, 90*(3), 347–373.

Mulder, J. L., Dekker, R., & Dekker, P. H. (2004). *Kaufman Intelligentietest voor Adolescenten en Volwassenen* [Kaufman intelligence test for adolescents and adults]. Leiden, The Netherlands: PITS.

Murphy, G. (1968). Psychological views of personality and contributions to its study. In E. Norbeck, D. Price-Williams, & W. M. McCord (Eds.), *The study of personality* (pp. 15–40). New York: Holt, Rinehart and Winston.

Murray, M. E., Waites, L., Veldman, D. J., & Heatly, M. D. (1973). Differences between WISC and WAIS scores in delinquent boys. *Journal of Experimental Education, 42*, 68–72.

Naglieri, J. A., & Das, J. P. (1997). *Cognitive Assessment System*. Chicago: Riverside.

Naglieri, J. A., & Goldstein, S. (Eds.) (2009). *A practitioner's guide to assessment of intelligence and achievement*. Hoboken, NJ: John Wiley & Sons.

Naglieri, J. A., Lichtenberger, E. O., & Kaufman, A. S. (2009). *Ipsative comparisons of WAIS-IV Factors*. Manuscript submitted for publication.

Nair, N. P. V., Muller, H. F., Gutbrodt, E., Buffet, L., & Schwartz G. (1979). Neurotropic activity of lithium: Relationship to lithium levels in plasma and red blood cells. *Research Communications in Psychology, Psychiatry, and Behavior, 4*, 169–180.

Naismith, S. L., Hickie, I. B., Turner, K., Little, C. L., Winter, V., Ward, P. B., et al. (2003). Neuropsychological performance in patients with depression is associated with clinical, etiological, and genetic risk factors. *Journal of Clinical and Experimental Neuropsychology, 25*(6), 866–877.

Nixon, S. J. (1996). Alzheimer's disease. In R. L. Adams, O. A. Parsons, J. L. Culbertson, & S. J. Nixon (Eds.), *Neuropsychology for clinical practice: Etiology, assessment and treatment of common neurological disorders* (pp. 65–105). Washington, DC: American Psychological Association.

Oakland, T., & Zimmerman, S. (1986). The course on individual mental assessment: A national survey of course instructors. *Professional School Psychology, 1,* 51–59.

Oh, H., Glutting, J. J., Watkins, M. W., Youngstrom, E. A., & McDermott, P. A. (2004). Correct interpretation of latent versus observed abilities: Implications from structural equation modeling applied to the WISC-III and WIAT linking sample. *Journal of Special Education, 38*(3), 159–173.

Owens, W. A. (1953). Age and mental abilities: A longitudinal study. *Genetic Psychology Monographs, 48,* 3–54.

Owens, W. A. (1959). Is age kinder to the initially more able? *Journal of Gerontology, 14,* 334–337.

Owens, W. A. (1966). Age and mental ability: A second adult follow-up. *Journal of Educational Psychology, 57,* 311–325.

Parker, K. C. H. (1986). Changes with age, year-of-birth cohort, age by year-of-birth interaction, and standardization of the Wechsler adult intelligence tests. *Human Development, 29,* 209–222.

Parsons, O. A. (1996). Alcohol abuse and alcoholism. In R. L. Adams, O. A. Parsons, J. L. Culbertson, & S. J. Nixon (Eds.), *Neuropsychology for clinical practice: Etiology, assessment and treatment of common neurological disorders* (pp. 175–201). Washington, DC: American Psychological Association.

Pearson Assessments. (2009a). Support and resources home sample reports. Retrieved January 26, 2009, from http://pearsonassess.com/haiweb/Cultures/en-US/Site/SupportAndResources/ResourceLibrary/Reports/SampleReports/reslist.htm.

Pearson Assessments. (2009b). Support and resources home technical reports. Retrieved January 26, 2009, from http://pearsonassess.com/haiweb/Cultures/en-US/Site/SupportAndResources/ResourceLibrary/Reports/TechnicalReports/reslist.htm.

Pearson Assessments. (2009c). WAIS-IV corrected table. Retrieved January 26, 2009, from http://pearsonassess.com/NR/rdonlyres/76496E27–0B90–478B-B7D5-CF05983EBCD8/0/WAISIVTechManual_TableC2.pdf.

Pearson Assessments. (2009d). WAIS-IV correction letter. Retrieved January 26, 2009, from http://pearsonassess.com/NR/rdonlyres/9663B2CF-529C-4B61-A289–9472728BF7E3/0/WAISIVTechManual_Letter.pdf.

Pernicano, K. M. (1986). Score differences in WAIS-R scatter for schizophrenics, depressives and personality disorders: A preliminary analysis. *Psychological Reports, 59,* 539–543.

Pintner, R., & Paterson, D. D. (1925). *A scale of performance tests.* New York: Appleton & Co.

Prifitera, A., Saklofske, D. H., Weiss, L. G., & Rolfhus, E. (Eds.). (2005). *WISC-IV clinical use and interpretation: Scientist-practitioner perspectives.* San Diego: Academic Press.

Prifitera, A., Weiss, L. G., & Saklofske, D. H. (1998). The WISC-III in context. In A. Prifitera & D. H. Saklofske (Eds.), *WISC-III clinical use and interpretation* (pp. 1–39). San Diego: Academic Press.

Psychological Corporation, The. (1997). *WAIS-III and WMS-III technical manual.* San Antonio, TX: Author.

Psychological Corporation, The. (2003). *WISC-IV technical and interpretive manual.* San Antonio, TX: Author.

Psychological Corporation, The. (2008). *WAIS-IV Technical and interpretive manual.* San Antonio, TX: Author.

Rabbitt, P. (1993). Baseline changes in cognitive performance with age. In R. Levy & R. Howard (Eds.), *Treatment and care in old age psychiatry* (pp. 11–30). Petersfield, England: Wrightson Biomedical Publishing.

Rabbitt, P., Donlan, C., Watson, P., McInnes, L., & Bent, N. (1995). Unique and interactive effects of depression, age, socioeconomic advantage, and gender on cognitive performance of normal healthy older people. *Psychology and Aging, 10,* 307–313.

Rabbitt, P., Scott, M., Lunn, M., Thacker, N., Lowe, C., Pendleton, N., et al. (2007). White matter lesions account for all age-related declines in speed but not in intelligence. *Neuropsychology, 21,* 363–370.

Rabin, L. A., Barr, W. B., & Burton, L. A. (2005). Assessment practices of clinical neuropsychologists in the United States and Canada: A survey of INS, NAN, and APA division 40 members. *Archives of Clinical Psychology, 20,* 33–65.

Raiford, S. E., Rolfhus, E., Weiss, L. G. T., & Coalson, D. (2005). *General Ability Index* (WISC IV Technical Report #4). Retrieved January 17, 2005, from http://harcourtassessment.com/hai/Images/pdf/wisciv/WISCIVTechReport4.pdf.

Raven, J. C. (1938). *Progressive matrices.* London: Lewis.

Raz, N. (2000). Aging of the brain and its impact on cognitive performance: Integration of structural and functional findings. In F. I. M. Craik & T. A. Salthouse (Eds.), *The handbook of aging and cognition* (2nd ed., pp. 1–90). Mahwah, NJ: Lawrence Erlbaum.

Reitan, R. M. (1988). Integration of neuropsychological theory, assessment, and application. *The Clinical Neuropsychologist, 2,* 331–349.

Reitan, R. M., & Wolfson, D. (1992). *Neuropsychological evaluation of older children.* South Tucson, AZ: Neuropsychology Press.

Reschly, D. J., & Grimes, J. P. (1995). Best practices in intellectual assessment. In A. Thomas & J. P. Grimes (Eds.), *Best practices in school psychology III* (pp. 763–773). Washington, DC: National Association of School Psychologists.

Reynolds, C. R., Chastain, R. L., Kaufman, A. S., & McLean, J. E. (1987). Demographic characteristics and IQ among adults: Analysis of the WAIS-R standardization sample as a function of the stratification variables. *Journal of School Psychology, 25,* 323–342.

Reynolds, C. R., & Fletcher-Janzen, E. (1989). *Handbook of clinical child neuropsychology.* New York: Plenum.

Roid, G. (2003). *Stanford-Binet Intelligence Scales, Fifth Edition.* Itasca, IL: Riverside.

Roszkowski, M. J. (2001). Review of the Revised Minnesota Paper Form Board Test (2nd ed.). In J. C. Impara & B. S. Plake (Eds.), *Buros' fourteenth mental measurements yearbook* (pp. 1012–1015). Lincoln: Buros Institute, University of Nebraska.

Saklofske, D. H., Weiss, L. G., Raiford, S. E., & Prifitera, A. (2006). Advanced interpretive issues with the WISC-IV full-scale IQ and general ability index scores. In L. G. Weiss, D. H. Saklofske, A. Prifitera, & J. Holdnack (Eds.), *WISC-IV advanced clinical interpretation* (pp. 99–138). New York: Elsevier.

Salthouse, T. A. (1985). Speed of behavior and its implications for cognition. In J. E. Birren & K. W. Schaie (Eds.), *Handbook of the psychology of aging* (2nd ed., pp. 400–426). New York: Van Nostrand Reinhold.

Salthouse, T. A. (1992). *Mechanisms of age–cognition relations in adulthood.* Hillsdale, NJ: Lawrence Erlbaum.

Salthouse, T. A. (2004). Localizing age-related individual differences in a hierarchical structure. *Intelligence, 32,* 541–561.

Sandoval, J., Sassenrath, J., & Penzloza, M. (1988). Similarity of WISC-R and WAIS-R scores at age 16. *Psychology in the Schools, 25,* 373–379.

Sattler, J. M. (1982). *Assessment of children* (2nd ed.). La Mesa, CA: Author.

Sattler, J. M. (1988). *Assessment of children* (3rd ed.) San Diego: Author.

Sattler, J. M. (1992). *Assessment of children: WISC-III and WPPSI-R supplement.* San Diego: Author.

Sattler, J. M. (1998). *WAIS-III supplement.* San Diego: Author.

Sattler, J. M. (2001). *Assessment of children: Cognitive applications* (4th ed.). La Mesa, CA: Author.

Sattler, J. M. (2008). *Assessment of children: Cognitive foundations* (5th ed.). San Diego: Author.

Sattler, J. M., & Dumont, R. (2004). *Assessment of children: WISC-IV and WPPSI-III supplement.* San Diego: Author.

Sattler, J. M., & Ryan, J. (in press). *Assessment with the WAIS-IV.* San Diego: Author.

Schaie, K. W. (1958). Rigidity-flexibility and intelligence: A cross-sectional study of the adult life-span from 20 to 70. *Psychological Monographs, 72* (9, Whole No. 462).

Schaie, K. W. (Ed.). (1983a). *Longitudinal studies of adult psychological development.* New York: Guilford Press.

Schaie, K. W. (1983b). The Seattle Longitudinal Study: A 21-year exploration of psychometric intelligence in adulthood. In K. W. Schaie (Ed.), *Longitudinal studies of adult psychological development* (pp. 64–135). New York: Guilford Press.

Schaie, K. W. (1983c). What can we learn from the longitudinal study of adult psychological development? In K. W. Schaie (Ed.), *Longitudinal studies of adult psychological development* (pp. 1–19). New York: Guilford Press.

Schaie, K. W. (1984). Midlife influences upon intellectual functioning in old age. *International Journal of Behavior Development, 7,* 463–478.

Schaie, K. W. (1994). The course of adult intellectual development. *American Psychologist, 49,* 304–313.

Schaie, K. W., & Hertzog, C. (1983). Fourteen-year cohort sequential analyses of adult intellectual development. *Developmental Psychology, 19,* 531–543.

Schaie, K. W., & Strother, C. R. (1968). The cross-sequential study of age changes in cognitive behavior. *Psychological Bulletin, 70,* 671–680.

Schmitz-Sherzer, R., & Thomae, H. (1983). Constancy and change of behavior in old age: Findings from the Bonn Longitudinal Study on Aging. In K. W. Schaie (Ed.), *Longitudinal studies of adult psychological development* (pp. 191–221). New York: Guilford Press.

Schwean, V. L., & Saklofske, D. H. (1998). WISC-III assessment of children with Attention-Deficit/Hyperactivity Disorder. In A. Prifiteria & D. H. Saklofske (Eds.), *WISC-III clinical use and interpretation* (pp. 91–118). San Diego: Academic Press.

Sharp, S. E. (1898–99). Individual psychology: A study in psychological method. *American Journal of Psychology, 10,* 329–391.

Shiffrin, R. M., & Schneider, W. (1977). Controlled and automatic human information processing: II. Perceptual learning, automatic attending, and a general theory. *Psychological Review, 84*(2), 127–190.

Shimamura, A. P., Berry, J. M., Mangels, J. A., Rusting, C. L., & Jurica, P. J. (1995). Memory and cognitive abilities in university professors: Evidence for successful aging. *Psychological Science, 6,* 271–277.

Shouksmith, G. (1970). *Intelligence, creativity and cognitive style.* New York: John Wiley & Sons.

Siegel, L. S. (1990). IQ and learning disabilities: RIP. In H. L. Swanson & B. Keogh (Eds.), *Learning disabilities: Theoretical and research issues* (pp. 111–128). Hillsdale, NJ: Lawrence Erlbaum.

Siegler, I. (1983). Psychological aspects of the Duke Longitudinal studies. In K. W. Schaie (Ed.), *Longitudinal studies of adult psychological development* (pp. 136–190). New York: Guilford Press.

Siegler, I., & Botwinick, J. (1979). A long-term longitudinal study of intellectual ability of older adults: The matter of selective subject attrition. *Journal of Gerontology, 34,* 242–245.

Silver, L. B. (Ed.). (1993). *Child and Adolescent Psychiatric Clinics of North America, 2,* 181–353.

Singet, J. M., Barlaug, D. G., & Torjussen, T. M. (2004). The end of the Flynn effect? A study of secular trends in mean intelligence test scores of Norwegian conscripts during half a century. *Intelligence, 32,* 349–362.

Sliwinski, M., & Buschke, H. (1999). Cross-sectional and longitudinal relationships among age, cognition, and processing speed. *Psychology and Aging, 14,* 18–33.

Sparrow, S. S., Balla, D. A., & Cicchetti, D. V. (1984). *Vineland Adaptive Behavior Scales.* Circle Pines, MN: American Guidance Service.

Spearman, C. E. (1904). "General Intelligence," objectively determined and measured. *American Journal of Psychiatry, 15,* 201–293.

Spearman, C. E. (1927). *The abilities of man.* New York: Macmillan.

Sperry, R. W. (1968). Hemisphere deconnection and unity in conscious awareness. *American Psychologist, 23,* 723–733.

Spruill, J. S. (1984). Wechsler Adult Intelligence Scale-Revised. In D. J. Keyser & R. C. Sweetland (Eds.), *Test critiques* (Vol. 1, pp. 728–739). Kansas City, MO: Test Corporation of America.

Sternberg, R. J. (1985). *Beyond IQ: A triarchic theory of human intelligence.* New York: Cambridge University Press.

Sternberg, R. J. (1995). *In search of the human mind.* Fort Worth, TX: Harcourt Brace College.

Sternberg, R. J. (2000). *Handbook of intelligence.* New York: Cambridge University Press.

Sternberg, R. J., Kaufman, J. C., & Grigorenko, E. L. (2008). *Applied intelligence.* New York: Cambridge University Press.

Sternberg, S. (1966). High-speed scanning in human memory. *Science, 153,* 652–654.

Storandt, M. (1976). Speed and coding effects in relation to age and ability level. *Developmental Psychology, 12,* 177–178.

Storandt, M. (1977). Age, ability level, and method of administering and scoring the WAIS. *Journal of Gerontology, 32,* 175–178.

Strauss, E., Sherman, E. M. S., & Spreen, O. (2006). *A compendium of neuropsychological tests: Administration, norms, and commentary* (3rd ed.). New York: Oxford University Press.

Talland, G. A., & Schwab, R. S. (1964). Performance with multiple sets in Parkinson's disease. *Neuropsychologia, 2,* 45–57.

Teasdale, T. W., & Owen, D. R. (2005). A long-term rise and recent decline in intelligence test performance: The Flynn Effect in reverse. *Personality & Individual Differences, 39,* 837–843.

Teasdale, T. W., & Owen, D. R. (2008). Secular declines in cognitive test scores: A reversal of the Flynn Effect. *Intelligence, 36,* 121–126.

Tellegen, A., & Briggs, P. F. (1967). Old wine in new skins: Grouping Wechsler subtests into new scales. *Journal of Consulting Psychology, 31,* 499–506.

Terman, L. M. (1916). *The measurement of intelligence.* Boston: Houghton-Mifflin.

Terman, L. M., & Childs, H. G. (1912). A tentative revision and extension of the Binet-Simon measuring scale of intelligence. *Journal of Educational Psychology, 3,* 61–74, 133–143, 198–208, 277–289.

Terman, L. M., & Merrill, M. A. (1937). *Measuring intelligence.* Boston: Houghton-Mifflin.

Terman, L. M., & Merrill, M. A. (1960). *Stanford-Binet Intelligence Scale.* Boston: Houghton-Mifflin.

Terman, L. M., & Merrill, M. A. (1973). *Stanford-Binet Intelligence Scale: 1972 Norms editions.* Boston: Houghton Mifflin.

Thorndike, R. L., Hagen, E. P., & Sattler, J.M. (1986). *Stanford-Binet Intelligence Scale* (4th ed.). Chicago: Riverside Press.

Thurstone, L. L., & Thurstone, T. G. (1949). *Examiner's manual for the SRA Primary Mental Abilities Test.* Chicago: Science Research Associates.

Tulsky, D. S., Saklofske, D. H., Wilkins, C., and Weiss, L. G. (2001). Development of a General Ability Index for the Wechsler Adult Intelligence Scale—Third Edition. *Psychological Assessment, 13,* 566–571.

Unsworth, N., & Engle, R. W. (2007). On the division of short-term and working memory: An examination of simple and complex span and their relation to higher order abilities. *Psychological Bulletin, 133*(6), 1038–1066.

Vanderwood, M. L., McGrew, K. S., Flanagan, D. P., & Keith, T. Z. (2002). The contribution of general and specific cognitive abilities to reading achievement. *Learning and Individual Differences, 13*, 159–188.

Vane, J. R., & Motta, R.W. (1984). Group intelligence tests. In G. Goldstein & M. Hersen (Eds.), *Handbook of psychological assessment* (pp. 100–116). New York: Pergamon Press.

Verhaeghen, P., & Salthouse, T. A. (1997). Meta-analyses of age-cognition relations in adulthood: Estimates of linear and nonlinear age effects and structural models. *Psychological Bulletin, 122*, 231–249.

Wang, J., & Kaufman, A. S. (1993). Changes in fluid and crystallized intelligence across the 20- to 90-year age range on the K-BIT. *Journal of Psychoeducational Assessment, 11*, 29–37.

Watkins, M., & Canivez, G. (2004). Temporal stability of WISC-III subtest composite strengths and weaknesses. *Psychological Assessment, 16*, 133–138.

Wechsler, D. (1939). *Measurement of adult intelligence*. Baltimore, MD: Williams & Wilkins.

Wechsler, D. (1944). *The measurement of adult intelligence* (3rd ed.) Baltimore, MD: Williams & Wilkins.

Wechsler, D. (1946). *The Wechsler-Bellevue Intelligence Scale, Form II*. New York: The Psychological Corporation.

Wechsler, D. (1949). *Manual for the Wechsler Intelligence Scale for Children*. New York: The Psychological Corporation.

Wechsler, D. (1955). *Manual for the Wechsler Adult Intelligence Scale (WAIS)*. San Antonio, TX: The Psychological Corporation.

Wechsler, D. (1958). *Measurement and appraisal of adult intelligence* (4th ed.). Baltimore, MD: Williams & Wilkins.

Wechsler, D. (1974). *Manual for the Wechsler Intelligence Scale for Children-Revised (WISC-R)*. San Antonio: The Psychological Corporation.

Wechsler, D. (1981). *Manual for the Wechsler Adult Intelligence Scale-Revised (WAIS-R)*. San Antonio, TX: The Psychological Corporation.

Wechsler, D. (1991). *Manual for the Wechsler Intelligence Scale for Children—Third Edition (WISC-III)*. San Antonio: The Psychological Corporation.

Wechsler, D. (1997). *Wechsler Adult Intelligence Scale—Third Edition (WAIS-III) administration and scoring manual*. San Antonio: The Psychological Corporation.

Wechsler, D. (2003). *Wechsler Intelligence Scale for Children (WISC-IV)* (4th ed.). San Antonio, TX: The Psychological Corporation.

Wechsler, D. (2008). *WAIS-IV administration and scoring manual*. San Antonio, TX: The Psychological Corporation.

Wechsler, D., & Naglieri, J. A. (2006). *Wechsler Nonverbal Scale of Ability*. San Antonio, TX: Harcourt Assessment.

Weiss, L. G., & Gabel, A. D. (2008). *Using the Cognitive Proficiency Index in psychoeducational assessment. Wechsler Intelligence Scale for Children, 4th ed. Technical Report #6*. San Antonio: Pearson Education. Retrieved January 26, 2009, from http://pearsonassess.com/NR/rdonlyres/E15367FE-D287-46B4-989A-609160D94DA8/0/WISCIVTechReport6.pdf.

Weiss, L. G., Prifitera, A., Holdnack, J. A., Saklofske, D. H., Rolfhus, E., & Coalson, D. (2006). The essentials and beyond. In L. G. Weiss, D. H. Saklofske, & J. Holdnack (Eds.), *WISC-IV advanced clinical interpretation* (pp. 59–97). Burlington, MA: Academic Press.

Weiss, L. G., Saklofske, D. H., Coalson, D., & Raiford, S. E. (Eds.) (in press). *WAIS-IV clinical use and interpretation: Scientist-practitioner perspectives*. San Diego: Academic Press.

Weiss, L. G., Saklofske, D. H., Schwartz, D. M., Prifitera, A., & Courville, T. (2006). Advanced clinical interpretation of WISC-IV index scores. In L. G. Weiss, D. H. Saklofske, A. Prifitera, & J. Holdnack (Eds.), *WISC-IV advanced clinical interpretation* (pp. 99–138). San Diego: Elsevier, Inc.

Weiss, L. G., Saklofske, D., Prifitera, A., & Holdnack, J. (2006). *WISC-IV advanced clinical interpretation.* San Diego: Academic Press.

Wesman, A. G. (1968). Intelligent testing. *American Psychologist, 23,* 267–274.

Whitworth, R. H., & Gibbons, R. T. (1986), Cross-racial comparison of the WAIS and WAIS-R. *Educational and Psychological Measurement, 46,* 1041–1049.

Willis, J. O. (2001). Scoring errors necessitate double-checking protocols. *Today's School Psychologist, 4*(5), 7.

Willis, J. O., & Dumont, R. P. (2002). *Guide to identification of learning disabilities* (3rd ed.) Peterborough, NH: Author.

Willis, S. L. (1985). Towards an educational psychology of the older adult learner: Intellectual and cognitive bases. In J. E. Birren and K. W. Schaie (Eds.), *Handbook of the psychology of aging* (2nd ed., pp. 818–847). New York: Van Nostrand Reinhold.

Willoughby, R. R. (1927). Family similarities in mental-test abilities. *Genetic Psychology Monographs, 2,* 239–277.

Wissler, C. (1901). The correlation of mental and physical tests. *Psychological Review, 3* (Monograph Supplement 16).

Woodcock, R. W. (1990). Theoretical foundations of the WJ-R measures of cognitive ability. *Journal of Psychoeducational Assessment, 8,* 231–258.

Yerkes, R. M. (1917). The Binet versus the point scale method of measuring intelligence. *Journal of Applied Psychology, 1,* 111–122.

Yoakum, C. S., & Yerkes, R. M. (1920). *Army mental tests.* New York: Henry Holt.

Zhou, X., & Zhu, J. (2007, August). *Peeking inside the "blackbox" of Flynn effect: Evidence from three Wechsler instruments.* Paper presented at 115th annual convention of American Psychological, San Francisco, CA.

Zimmerman, I. L., & Woo-Sam, J. M. (1973). *Clinical interpretation of the Wechsler Adult Intelligence Scale.* New York: Grune & Stratton.

Zimmerman, I. L., & Woo-Sam, J. M. (1985). Clinical applications. In B. B. Wolman (Ed.), *Handbook of Intelligence* (pp. 873–898). New York: John Wiley & Sons.

Zimprich, D. (1998). Geschwindigkeit der Informationsverarbeitung und fluide Intelligenz im hoeheren Erwachsenenalter: Eine Sekundaeranalyse des Datenmaterials der Bonner Laengsschnittstudie des Alterns anhand von "Latent Growth Curve Models." [Speed of information processing and fluid intelligence in the elderly.] *Zeitschrift Fuer Gerontologie und Geriatrie, 31,* 89–96.

Zimprich, D., & Martin, M. (2002). Can longitudinal changes in processing speed explain longitudinal age changes in fluid intelligence? *Psychology and Aging, 17,* 690–695.

Annotated Bibliography

Flanagan, D. P., Ortiz, S. O., & Alfonso, V. C. (2007). *Essentials of cross-battery assessment* (2nd ed.). Hoboken, NJ: John Wiley & Sons.

This second edition provides a comprehensive set of guidelines and procedures for organizing assessments based on contemporary CHC theory and research, integrating test results from different batteries in a psychometrically defensible way, and interpreting test results within the context of research on the relations between cognitive and academic abilities and processes. It also includes guidelines for assessing culturally and linguistically diverse populations and individuals suspected of having a specific learning disability. This book includes a CD-ROM containing three software programs for assisting in data management and interpretation, making decisions regarding specific learning disability, and discerning difference from disability in individuals whose cultural and linguistic backgrounds differ from the mainstream.

Flanagan, D. P., & Kaufman, A. S. (2009). *Essentials of WISC-IV assessment* (2nd ed.). Hoboken, NJ: John Wiley & Sons.

This text provides details on administration, scoring, and interpretation of the WISC-IV. It details a theory-based approach to interpretation and includes step-by-step guidelines for applying this interpretive approach. The book also includes a CD-ROM containing software that automates the interpretive system for the WISC-IV. In addition, it provides information on many clinical populations and on the WISC-IV Integrated, as well as sample case reports.

Groth-Marnat, G. (2009). *Handbook of psychological assessment* (5th ed.). Hoboken, NJ: John Wiley & Sons.

This revision of this resource on psychological assessment features thorough coverage of the principles of assessment, evaluation, referral, treatment planning, and report writing. Material is presented in a practical, skills-based manner (e.g., how to integrate test data into treatment plans and writing psychological reports) and offers coverage of the most widely used assessment instruments (including the newly revised WAIS-IV and Wechsler Memory Scales-IV, as well as the WISC-IV, Rorschach, Thematic Apperception Test, Neuropsychological screening, Behavioral, CPI, MCMI-III, and MMPI-2/MMPI-A). This reference provides clinical psychologists, therapists, school psychologists, and counselors with step-by-step, expert guidance on how to conduct a comprehensive psychological evaluation.

Kaufman, A. S., & Lichtenberger, E. O. (2006). *Assessing adolescent and adult intelligence* (3rd ed.). Hoboken, NJ: John Wiley & Sons.

This book on the WAIS-III provides in-depth discussion of topics that pertain to adult assessment in general. The review of research studies conducted on the W-B, WAIS, WAIS-R, and WAIS-III is especially relevant to the WAIS-IV. Topics include relationship of IQ to background variables (occupation, race/ethnicity, education, gender) as well as studies of patients with unilateral brain damage, Alzheimer's disease, Huntington's chorea, dyslexia, alcoholism, mental retardation, multiple sclerosis, learning disabilities, and other disorders. The book presents a discussion of the scales from a theoretical perspective, along with numerous hypothesized explanations for patterns of typical performance on the Wechsler scales. The philosophy of the intelligent testing approach is woven throughout the text and is exemplified in several case studies. The history of the Wechsler scales is also presented.

Psychological Corporation. (2008). *WAIS-IV technical and interpretive manual.* San Antonio, TX: NCS Pearson.

This manual comes as part of the WAIS-IV kit and provides introductory information on the WAIS-IV. The text details development of the norms and the standardization procedures. Reliability and validity studies are presented. The WAIS-IV is compared to other measures of cognitive ability, memory functioning, language functioning, and motor speed. Studies on groups with neurological disorders such as Alzheimer's disease, Huntington's disease, Parkinson's disease, Traumatic Brain Injury, Multiple Sclerosis, and Temporal Lobe epilepsy are reviewed. In addition, studies of mental retardation, Attention-Deficit/Hyperactivity Disorder, learning disabilities, and other disorders are addressed. Global information on interpretation is provided, along with a plethora of statistical tables for clinicians and researchers.

Wechsler, D. (2008). *WAIS-IV administration and scoring manual.* San Antonio, TX: Psychological Corporation.

This manual comes as part of the WAIS-IV kit. It provides a basic description of the WAIS-IV scales and subtests. Revisions from the WAIS-III to the fourth edition are reviewed subtest by subtest. WAIS-IV examiners can gather important information about administration from this manual. For each WAIS-IV subtest, the starting, discontinue, and timing rules are articulated. Examiners are provided a basic script and detailed directions for how to administer each subtest in a standardized manner. Subtest norms tables are provided in the back of the Manual along with supplementary tables for determining the size of differences needed for significance.

About the Authors

Elizabeth O. Lichtenberger, PhD is a licensed clinical psychologist in California and an author whose works have focused on psychological assessment. In addition to her current professional roles, she has worked as an Adjunct Faculty member at Alliant International University in San Diego and a researcher at the Laboratory for Cognitive Neuroscience at the Salk Institute for Biological Studies in La Jolla, CA. Her work at the Salk Institute focused on the cognitive and neuropsychological patterns in children with genetic developmental disorders. Because of her expertise in psychological, psychoeducational, and neuropsychological assessment, Liz also serves as a psychoeducational test/measurement consultant and trainer for organizations and provides consultation to individual psychologists.

Liz is a published author of numerous books, book chapters, and articles on assessment and assessment instruments, including *Assessing Adolescent and Adult Intelligence* (3rd ed.), *Essentials of Assessment Report Writing, Essentials of KABC-II Assessment, Essentials of WIAT-II*® *and KTEA-II Assessment, Essentials of Cognitive Assessment with KAIT and Other Kaufman Measures, Essentials of WAIS-III Assessment, Essentials of WMS-III Assessment, Essentials of WPPSI-III Assessment,* and *Essentials of WISC-III and WPPSI-R Assessment.* In addition, Liz has served in an editorial capacity for books and journals. For example, she served as a consulting editor of the second edition of the *Encyclopedia of Special Education: A Reference for the Education of the Handicapped and Other Exceptional Children and Adults* and is currently on the editorial board of the journal *Psychology in the Schools.*

Alan S. Kaufman, PhD, a leading expert on intelligence testing, is Clinical Professor of Psychology at the Child Study Center at the Yale University School of Medicine. His books, tests, and *intelligent testing* approach have had worldwide impact on clinical assessment. Mentored by David Wechsler and Robert Thorndike, Dr. Kaufman's tests with his wife Nadeen (e.g., KABC-II and KTEA-II) and his approach to test interpretation reflect an integration of psychometric, theoretical, and clinical perspectives. Alan and Nadeen are the Series Editors of Wiley's *Essentials of Psychological Assessment* series.

Index

About the CD-ROM

INTRODUCTION

This appendix provides you with information on the contents of the CD that accompanies this book. For the latest information, please refer to the ReadMe file located at the root of the CD.

System Requirements

- A computer with a processor running at 120 Mhz or faster
  At least 32 MB of total RAM installed on your computer; for best performance, we recommend at least 64 MB
  A CD-ROM drive

NOTE: Many popular spreadsheet programs are capable of reading Microsoft Excel files. However, users should be aware that formatting might be lost when using a program other than Microsoft Excel.

Using the CD with Windows

To install the items from the CD to your hard drive, follow these steps:

1. Insert the CD into your computer's CD-ROM drive.
   The CD-ROM interface will appear. The interface provides a simple point-and-click way to explore the contents of the CD.

If the opening screen of the CD-ROM does not appear automatically, follow these steps to access the CD:

1. Click the Start button on the left end of the taskbar and then choose Run from the menu that pops up.
   In the dialog box that appears, type *d*:\start.exe. (If your CD-ROM drive is not drive d, fill in the appropriate letter in place of *d*.) This brings up the CD Interface described in the preceding set of steps.

WHAT'S ON THE CD

The following sections provide a summary of the software and other materials you'll find on the CD.

Content

The accompanying CD-ROM contains worksheet files written and programmed in Microsoft Excel that allow readers to enter WAIS-IV data along with other specific test data and have it analyzed following the steps outlined in chapter 5 of this book. The Excel program called *WAIS-IV Data Management and Interpretive Assistant* (WAIS-IV DMIA) v1.0 was programmed by Elizabeth Lichtenberger. Note that the WAIS-IV steps from chapter 5 may be completed by hand, following the WAIS-IV Interpretive Worksheet included in Appendix A.1 (found in the "Contents" folder), or may be performed automatically using the WAIS-IV DMIA v1.0.

Examples of the Excel worksheets on the CD are presented as figures in the book. These automated worksheets are provided on the CD for your convenience in using, applying, and understanding the interpretive method described in this book. The WAIS-IV DMIA v1.0 is meant to expedite analysis and interpretation of WAIS-IV data.

It is important to note that the WAIS-IV DMIA does not convert WAIS-IV *raw scores* to any metric. Users of this program are responsible for following the test publisher's administration and scoring guidelines. That is, all WAIS-IV scores entered into this program must be derived from the norms and procedures provided by the test publisher. Note that the WAIS-IV clinical clusters created by Elizabeth Lichtenberger and Alan Kaufman are automatically computed by the WAIS-IV DMIA v1.0 based on actual norms provided to them by the test publisher. See chapter 5 for details.

Also included on the CD-ROM are all the appendices mentioned throughout the book. These appendices may be found in a folder marked "Appendices." The following appendices are included:

Appendix A.1   WAIS-IV Interpretive Worksheet
Appendix A.2   CPI Equivalents of Sums of Scaled Scores
Appendix A.3   Crystallized Intelligence (*Gc*) Factor Equivalents of Sums of Scaled Scores
Appendix A.4   Short-Term Memory (*Gsm*) Factor Equivalents of Sums of Scaled Scores

Applications

The following applications are on the CD:

Adobe Reader

Adobe Reader is a freeware application for viewing files in the Adobe Portable Document format.

OpenOffice.org

OpenOffice.org is a free multi-platform office productivity suite. It is similar to Microsoft Office or Lotus SmartSuite, but OpenOffice.org is absolutely free. It includes word processing, spreadsheet, presentation, and drawing applications that enable you to create professional documents, newsletters, reports, and presentations. It supports most file formats of other office software. You should be able to edit and view any files created with other office solutions.

Shareware programs are fully functional, trial versions of copyrighted programs. If you like particular programs, register with their authors for a nominal fee and receive licenses, enhanced versions, and technical support.

Freeware programs are copyrighted games, applications, and utilities that are free for personal use. Unlike shareware, these programs do not require a fee or provide technical support.

GNU software is governed by its own license, which is included inside the folder of the GNU product. See the GNU license for more details.

Trial, demo, or evaluation versions are usually limited either by time or functionality (such as being unable to save projects). Some trial versions are very sensitive to system date changes. If you alter your computer's date, the programs will "time out" and no longer be functional.

CUSTOMER CARE

If you have trouble with the CD-ROM, please call the Wiley Product Technical Support phone number at (800) 762-2974. Outside the United States, call 1(317) 572–3994. You can also contact Wiley Product Technical Support at **http://support.wiley.com**. John Wiley & Sons will provide technical support only for installation and other general quality control items. For technical support on the applications themselves, consult the program's vendor or author.

To place additional orders or to request information about other Wiley products, please call (877) 762-2974.